"*In Pursuit of Prosperity* articulates a compelling case for more clearly and closely linking natural resource scarcity and environmental trends to U.S. national security policy. Thoroughly researched and well-documented, this is an important and timely book for policy makers and national security practitioners."

—General Carter Ham, U.S. Army (Retired),
Former Commander, U.S. Africa Command

"The combined effects of natural resource scarcity and climate change pose both immediate and longer-term challenges to the business practices and supply chains of every global company. As this compelling book makes clear, ignoring these twin threats comes only at great peril."

—Neville Isdell, Chairman, WWF-US Board of Directors,
and Former Chairman of the Board of Directors
and CEO, The Coca-Cola Company

"A much-needed hard look at the risks associated with growing resource scarcity in our increasingly complex and interdependent global system—not just sounding an alarm our leaders should heed, but offering substantive, thoughtful direction for U.S. leadership going forward."

—David Rothkopf, CEO and Editor of Foreign Policy *magazine*

IN PURSUIT OF PROSPERITY

In Pursuit of Prosperity provides a much-needed exploration of the evolution of environmental sustainability in U.S. foreign policy.

Through expert analysis of nine countries and regions of strategic importance, David Reed and his stellar team of experts in foreign policy and environmental affairs identify emerging threats to the prosperity and national security of the United States. They assert that U.S. foreign policy must shift away from its 100-year-old focus on obtaining energy and mineral inputs for the industrial economy. In the new millennium, U.S. foreign policy must be geared toward ensuring the prosperity of the country's trading and political partners around the globe. To the degree that our partners' economies and social stability are threatened by the natural resource scarcities and environmental change unfolding within their borders and in neighboring countries, threats to U.S. prosperity and national security increase proportionately.

Directed toward U.S. foreign policy makers, the intelligence and security communities, and influential think tanks and research organizations, the book proposes specific recommendations the U.S. government should embrace to respond to the disruption of global supply chains, social instability in partner countries, disruptive impacts on regional relations, and expansion of illegal trade and criminal networks. This unique focus establishes *In Pursuit of Prosperity* as a seminal work in understanding the challenges facing the United States in this period of global environmental change.

David Reed is Senior Vice President for Policy at WWF-US. He holds a PhD and other graduate degrees from the University of Geneva, Switzerland. He has worked for 25 years in social and economic development programs in Latin America, Africa, and Asia at both the grassroots and managerial levels. His areas of expertise include environmental impacts of macroeconomic reforms, poverty-environment nexus, international architecture for climate finance, and environmental dimensions of U.S. foreign policy.

IN PURSUIT OF PROSPERITY

U.S. Foreign Policy in an Era of Natural Resource Scarcity

Edited by David Reed

Routledge
Taylor & Francis Group
NEW YORK AND LONDON

First published 2015
by Routledge
711 Third Avenue, New York, NY 10017

and by Routledge
2 Park Square, Milton Park, Abingdon, Oxon OX14 4RN

Routledge is an imprint of the Taylor & Francis Group, an informa business

Library of Congress Cataloging-in-Publication Data
A catalog record for this book has been requested

Library of Congress Control Number: 2014949125

ISBN: 978-1-138-79189-3 (hbk)
ISBN: 978-1-138-79190-9 (pbk)
ISBN: 978-1-315-75137-5 (ebk)

Typeset in Bembo
by Apex CoVantage, LLC

Printed and bound in the United States of America by Publishers Graphics, LLC on sustainably sourced paper.

To the memory of Robert Goodland

Trusted friend, valued colleague, uncompromising environmentalist

CONTENTS

TABLES

FIGURES

ACRONYMS

A5	the 5 maritime nations of the Arctic: Russia, Canada, Denmark (Greenland), Norway, and U.S.
A8	the 8 Arctic countries: Russia, Canada, U.S., Denmark (Greenland), Norway, Sweden, Finland, and Iceland
ACORE	American Council on Renewable Energy
ADB	Asian Development Bank
AfDB	African Development Bank
AMEC	Arctic Military Environmental Cooperation Program
ANFAVEA	National Association of Automobile Manufacturers
APEC	Asia-Pacific Economic Cooperation
AQSIS	General Administration of Quality Supervision, Inspection, and Quarantine
ASEAN	Association of Southeast Asian Nations
AZRF	Arctic Zone of the Russian Federation
BECC	Border Environment Cooperation Commission
BEIF	Border Environment Infrastructure Fund
BIC	Brazil, India, and China
BIMSTEC	Bay of Bengal Initiative for Multi-Sectoral Technical and Economic Cooperation
BIT	Bilateral Investment Treaty
BNDES	Brazilian Development Bank
BRICS	Brazil, Russia, India, China, and South Africa
BTS	Bureau of Transportation Statistics
CAE	Chinese Academy of Engineering
CAP	Center for American Progress
CBFP	Congo Basin Forest Partnership
CEC	Commission for Environmental Cooperation

CERC	Clean Energy Research Center
CFR	Council on Foreign Relations
CIA	Central Intelligence Agency
CILA	Comisión Internacional de Límites y Aguas
CINDES	Centro de Estudos de Integração e Desenvolvimento
CITES	Convention on International Trade in Endangered Species
CO_2	Carbon Dioxide
COMIFAC	Central African Forests Commission
COP	Conference of Parties [to the United Nations Framework Convention on Climate Change]
CREIA	Chinese Renewable Energy Industries Association
CSF	Coalition Support Fund
CSIS	Center for Strategic and International Studies
DOE	Department of Energy
DRC	Democratic Republic of the Congo
EADB	East African Development Bank
ECO	Economic Cooperation Organization
EDF	Environmental Defense Fund
EEZ	Exclusive Economic Zone
EIA	Energy Information Administration
EMBRAPA	Empresa Brasileira de Pesquisa Agropecuária (Brazilian Agricultural Research Corporation)
ENS	Environmental News Service
EPA	Environmental Protection Agency
ESAS	East Siberian Arctic Shelf
EXIM	Export-Import Bank
FAO	Food and Agriculture Organization
FATA	Federally Administered Tribal Areas
FDI	Foreign Direct Investment
FIESP	Federation of Industries of the State of São Paulo
FLEGT	Forest Law Enforcement, Governance, and Trade
FTA	Free Trade Agreement
FTF	Feed the Future
G-8	Group of Eight
G-20	Group of Twenty
G-77	Group of Seventy-Seven
GCRP	Global Change Research Program
GDP	Gross Domestic Product
GEF	Global Environment Facility
GHG	greenhouse gas
GNEB	Good Neighbor Environmental Board
GNI	Gross National Income
GSP	Generalized System of Preferences
HIV/AIDS	Human Immunodeficiency Virus Infection/Acquired Immuno-Deficiency Syndrome

IBRD	International Bank for Reconstruction and Development
IBWC	International Boundary and Water Commission
ICBC	Industrial and Commercial Bank of China
ICONE	Institute for International Trade Negotiations
IDSA	Institute for Defence Studies and Analyses
IEA	International Energy Agency
IFPRI	International Food Policy Research Institute
IIE	Institute of International Education
IISD	International Institute for Sustainable Development
IMF	International Monetary Fund
INPE	National Institute of Space Technology
IP	Intellectual Property
IPCC	Intergovernmental Panel on Climate Change
IRIN	Integrated Regional Information Networks
JCERDC	Joint Clean Energy Research and Development Center
MCC	Millennium Challenge Corporation
MEA	Millennium Ecosystem Assessment
MEP	Ministry of Environmental Protection
MIT	Massachusetts Institute of Technology
MNRE	Russian Ministry of Natural Resources and Ecology
MoFA	Ministry of Foreign Affairs
MOFCOM	Ministry of Commerce
MP	Member of Parliament
MRAG	Marine Resources Assessment Group
MRC	Mekong River Commission
MWR	Ministry of Water Resources
NADB	North American Development Bank
NAFTA	North American Free Trade Agreement
NARCC	National Assessment Report on Climate Change
NATO	North Atlantic Treaty Organization
NBS	National Bureau of Statistics
NDRC	National Development and Reform Commission
NEA	National Energy Administration
NEC	National Energy Commission
NEP	National Environment Policy
NGO	Non-Governmental Organization
NIC	National Intelligence Council
NOAA	National Oceanic and Atmospheric Administration
NSPD-66	National Security Presidential Directive 66
NSS	National Security Strategy
ODNI	Office of the Director of National Intelligence
OECD	Organisation for Economic Co-operation and Development
OPEC	Organization of the Petroleum Exporting Countries
OPIC	Overseas Private Investment Corporation
OSTP	Office of Science and Technology Policy

PAC	Growth Acceleration Program
PACE	Partnership to Advance Clean Energy
PAISS	Joint Plan for Supporting Industrial Technological Innovation in the Sugar-Based Energy and Chemical Sectors
PEPFAR	President's Emergency Plan for AIDS Relief
$PM_{2.5}$	extremely small particulates
PM_{10}	small particulates
PML-N	Pakistan Muslim League-Nawaz
POP	Persistent Organic Pollutant
PRC	People's Republic of China
PRI	Institutional Revolutionary Party
PRODES	Surveillance of the Brazilian Amazonian Forest by Satellite
PSDP	Public Sector Development Programme
PV	photovoltaic
QDDR	Quadrennial Diplomacy and Development Review
QDR	Quadrennial Defense Review
QHSR	Quadrennial Homeland Security Review
REE	Rare Earth Elements
RFBS	Russian Federal Border Service
RITEGs	Radioisotope Thermoelectric Generators
RMB	renminbi
S&ED	Strategic and Economic Dialogues
S/P	Bureau of Policy Planning
SAARC	South Asian Association for Regional Cooperation
SAR	Search and Rescue
SARI	South Asia Regional Initiative
SARI/Energy	South Asia Regional Initiative for Energy
SBP	State Bank of Pakistan
SCO	Shanghai Cooperation Organization
SCS	South China Sea
SED	Strategic Energy Dialogue
SEIA	Solar Energy Industries Association
SEMARNAT	Secretariat of Environment and Natural Resources
SEPA	State Environmental Protection Administration
SLCFs	Short-Lived Climate Forcers
SMPCSRA	State Marine Pollution Control, Salvage, and Rescue Administration
START	Strategic Arms Reduction Treaty
TFCA	Tropical Forest Conservation Act of 1998
TOE	Tons Oil Equivalent
TPP	Trans-Pacific Partnership
UN	United Nations
UNCED	United Nations Conference on Environment and Development
UNCHR	United Nations Commission on Human Rights
UNCLOS	United Nations Convention on the Law of the Sea

UNCTAD	United Nations Conference on Trade and Development
UNDESA	United Nations Department of Economic and Social Affairs
UNDP	United Nations Development Programme
UNEP	United Nations Environment Programme
UN-REDD	United Nations Collaborative Programme on Reducing Emissions from Deforestation and Forest Degradation in Developing Countries
U.S. AFRICOM	United States Africa Command
USAID	U.S. Agency for International Development
USCG	U.S. Coast Guard
USGCRP	U.S. Global Change Research Program
USSR	Union of Soviet Socialist Republics
USTR	U.S. Trade Representative
WFP	World Food Programme
WHO	World Health Organization
WRI	World Resources Institute
WTO	World Trade Organization
WWC	Woodrow Wilson Center
WWF	World Wildlife Fund

FOREWORD

The exceptional work contained in this volume constitutes what we in the military would call a "red flare"—a bright warning, fired to alert all of us to an acute and pressing danger that requires urgent attention and mitigating action.

The threatened future of the world's natural resources is just such a danger. Once apparently unlimited and immune to harm from human activities, this diverse resource base is now being undermined before our eyes. It is possible there will be no greater challenge to the United States and the world in the century that lies before us than in developing a shared framework for husbanding, sustaining, and cultivating these resources. Meeting these challenges will require thriving, but mindful, economies and good governance, combined with wisdom and courage in national and global leadership that is currently absent.

In very immediate ways, resource scarcity is already acting as a risk multiplier in parts of Africa, the Middle East, and other regions. And, as a national security practitioner, I can hardly count the times I have had to participate directly or indirectly in responding to natural disasters, which seemed to strike with an accelerating tempo: from the tsunami off Indonesia in 2004, to flooding in Pakistan, to the combined earthquake and tsunami off the coast of Japan in 2010. Hurricane Sandy and Typhoon Haiyan, which struck the Philippines with such devastating impact in 2013, are more recent examples. Although the precise effect of a demonstrably changing climate on any of these specific events is a matter of debate—and it is not for me to enter that debate—the pressures of accelerating human activity on our habitat are not open to question. This volume helps define those pressures more precisely.

As a leader in the U.S. military over the past decade, I have repeatedly stressed the organic link between security and economic prosperity. These two principles stand like two pillars supporting a future that should provide improved well-being generation after generation. But the solidity of both pillars depends in large part on sustaining our natural resources. They are crucial to providing for the livelihood of a human population that will reach 9.5 billion by 2050.

As urban centers develop into megacities and as population densities increase along waterways and seacoasts, we must grasp how the changes are impacting our renewable natural resources, such as freshwater and saltwater, forests, fisheries, and arable land, as well as nonrenewables, such as increasingly diverse types of oil or natural gas. Only if they are equipped with the type of objective, evidence-based picture provided in the chapters in this book can decision makers begin to make strategic choices that adequately balance current and future needs. The fact-based analysis lays out an imperative for immediate and aggressive action on behalf of our own citizens and the citizens of the world to properly harness, harvest, distribute, and renew the awe-inspiring resources with which our planet has been endowed.

Here in the United States, that action must include a fundamental shift in mind-set. At home, we must cease to regard these issues in such dramatically partisan terms. Whether we describe ourselves as red or blue, we are all affected—for all of us breathe the air and drink the water and all of us eat of the fruits of this earth, enjoy its habitats, and warm ourselves by its energy. Politicizing these issues as we do paralyzes all progress.

As we look abroad, natural resource sustainability and protection must move to the center of our foreign policy agenda. The world has arrived at a seminal point in history. We cannot afford to get this wrong. Whether it is water in Pakistan or Yemen, temporary oil abundance (not independence) in America, food shortfalls in Africa, disappearing rainforests in Brazil or the Democratic Republic of the Congo, devastated fisheries in the South China Sea or the Arabian Sea, rapid change in resource consumption in China, or the shrinking Arctic ice pack, we are globally linked as never before in history. These linkages cannot be a bondage from which we are unable to escape but must rather be an inspiration to collective action.

It may not be readily apparent that sustained shortfalls of the kinds discussed will result directly in instability and conflict, but as someone who has watched the impact of conflicts in resource-poor regions and has seen the societal dislocation and political disruption caused by natural disasters—as well as the dangerously growing gap between the haves and have-nots—I strongly believe that conflict will follow if these conditions persist and worsen. Without thoughtful, aggressive American leadership, it is likely that other international actors may drag their feet, while at home we continue to strip our margins and resilience to the bone, thereby matching too many areas of the world that already operate too close to the bone as it is.

This book brings a laser focus on the ways in which these issues play out in specific contexts. The facts laid out indicate that we are nearly moving beyond our ability to sustain and renew a number of vital natural resources. If ever there was a red flare, this is one. Passing a point of no return equates to a sentence on future humanity that we cannot in conscience allow to be handed down. The alternative is to incorporate these issues into the very being of U.S. national and foreign policy decision making, now and henceforth.

This book is designed to help us get beyond the political rhetoric and move the United States into the premier leadership position globally on sustaining our natural resources and a way of life respectful of them such as to inspire other world leaders to do the same. We simply cannot continue on the current path, for it is a path leading to instability, conflict, global decay, and crisis, which will not support the peoples of the world.

Is this the most important national security issue of our time? If not, you will have to prove it to me based on the facts.

Admiral Mike Mullen

PREFACE

For more than 50 years, the World Wildlife Fund (WWF) has been dedicated to protecting wildlife and conserving nature around the world. Despite extraordinary accomplishments during this time, we have also witnessed accelerated loss in the planet's biodiversity, widespread deforestation, overfishing, and exhaustion of fish stocks—along with an increased frequency and intensity of weather phenomena such as droughts, floods, and hurricanes. The impacts on the planet's environmental fabric and communities have been severe and enduring.

One of the lessons we have learned from our years of dedicated work is that local environmental issues are woven deeply into a far broader chain of social and economic dynamics with consequences that often reach around the world. We depend on forests to stabilize climates and secure watersheds. We depend on rivers as vital sources of freshwater. We depend on marine systems to meet the needs of people and protect vulnerable species and habitats. And, of course, we depend on a stable climate for secure crop production, an adequate freshwater supply, species health, and so much more.

And now, more recently, the explosion in wildlife crime reveals that these senseless crimes—committed locally—are often part of global criminal networks involved in drug smuggling, human trafficking, and even terrorism. Such activities bear consequences strong enough to spur the U.S. government to recognize them as national security threats, leading President Obama to issue an unprecedented response and order a National Strategy on Wildlife Trafficking involving key government agencies and partners.

In Pursuit of Prosperity sets forth a compelling case as to why natural resource scarcities and climate change affecting our trading and political partners around the world have direct consequences for America's prosperity and national security. Increased drought and flooding in Pakistan's Swat Valley, water scarcity along the

U.S.-Mexico border, and growing competition over fish stocks in the South China Sea can no longer be viewed as separate, isolated problems. They are all part of the delicate chain in which our national well-being is intimately bound up with the protection and sustainable management of ecosystems and natural resources around the world.

In publishing this work and through the many public outreach activities that will follow, the WWF seeks to expand the circle of corporate, civil society, and academic partners who find common cause in addressing these urgent challenges. Above all, we hope to find ever-broadening avenues for collaboration with our government so that promoting sustainability becomes a central pillar of U.S. foreign policy.

Carter Roberts, President and CEO
World Wildlife Fund
February 2014

ACKNOWLEDGMENTS

The seven country studies and two regional studies on which this publication is based have been carried out at a time when international negotiations to reach a global climate agreement have been stalled for several years. Those difficulties have generated considerable uncertainty as to whether the international community will be able to respond to the mounting environmental challenges facing our planet. And, while some countries have intensified efforts to adapt to increased weather variability and others have increased financial resources to forestall anticipated costs, real-time impacts of global environmental change and natural resource scarcities continue to rise. Economic costs and social dislocations are being felt by producers, governments, and communities around the world, whether through accelerated thawing of the Arctic permafrost; more acute water scarcities in India, China, Pakistan, and along the U.S.-Mexico border; or declining fish stocks in Coastal East Africa and the South China Sea.

In parallel, domestic political gridlock in the United States has forestalled decisive action by the world's leading economy to provide urgently needed international leadership to address the underlying causes of global environmental change, much to our own prejudice. In hopes of encouraging more decisive action from our government, this publication is directed toward U.S. policy makers with the purposes of highlighting the attendant impacts on future U.S. prosperity and proposing immediate and longer-term measures by which our government can assume a more active leadership role in international environmental affairs.

The World Wildlife Fund's (WWF) support for the *In Pursuit of Prosperity* endeavor arises directly from the on-the-ground effects that rising natural resource scarcities and accelerating environmental change are now exerting on the many countries in which the WWF has active, sustained operations. WWF colleagues have been uniformly supportive of all activities relating to the research and public dissemination of our findings. First and foremost, I would like to express my gratitude to Brent Nordstrom and Todd Shelton, colleagues in the WWF's Policy Program, who provided day-to-day guidance, critical comments, and a steady flow of materials to facilitate the writing of this book. Brent helped manage many aspects of the research and publishing process and provided frequent suggestions to reframe arguments and recommendations. I would also like to express my sincere appreciation to my WWF colleagues, including Carter Roberts, Marcia Marsh, Steven Chapman, Tom Dillon, Pablo Gutman, Lou Leonard, Nick Sundt, Caroline Cook, Vanessa Dick, Will Gartshore, Bill Eichbaum, Leslie Delagran, Shaun Martin, Margaret Williams, Ali Habib, and Michael Becker, for their continued support. Megan Block managed the many contractual arrangements that allowed the authors and other experts to deliver their contributions in a timely manner.

To Porter Delaney, I extend my thanks for his many contributions in liaising with Ambassador Mark Green, organizing consultative meetings with a wide range of policy and business leaders, and helping balance the political views in the framing and recommendations chapters. Rich Verma, in addition to writing the chapter on India, provided frequent policy guidance, opened many professional contacts, and organized numerous meetings with leaders in the foreign policy community. Sally Donnelly organized several discussions with senior members of the U.S. Armed Forces. Their collective input and guidance helped ensure that the framing, summary, and recommendations chapters employ language that will encourage readership across the full spectrum of American political thought.

I frequently turned to Pamela Stedman-Edwards to provide background analysis on issues of trade, water, and resource scarcities and to suggest text for various chapters. Her contributions are reflected in inclusive framing of the global environmental issues and in the continuity of perspectives offered by the different authors. Diana Ohlbaum helped guide development of the recommendations, notably in analyzing the U.S. Global Change Research Program and proposing practical approaches for internalizing analysis into U.S. government operations. Her understanding of the internal workings of government proved critical in framing our recommendations. David Hunter provided an insightful background analysis on international institutional challenges and opportunities. Bruce Beyer provided up-to-date analysis of environmental conditions and U.S. government operations in Coastal East Africa. Dirk Joldersma provided a steady stream of critical comments, draft text, and advice over the past year.

One of the principal challenges associated with this project has been finding appropriate language that would invite influential thought leaders and policy makers across the American political spectrum to listen to the issues we have raised and to recognize their potential consequences for U.S. prosperity and national security. To that end, I am very grateful to Rich Engel, John Raidt,

Robert Goodland, Rod Schoonover, and Jack May, who reviewed early drafts of the book and, through an informal advisory group, shaped the presentation of ideas and recommendations.

I have had the privilege of working with truly gifted researchers and policy experts specializing in both U.S. foreign policy and environmental issues. These experts include Heather Conley, Lev Neretin, Murray Hiebert, and Greg Poling from the Center for Strategic and International Studies; Shuja Nawaz from the Atlantic Council; Saleem Ali from the University of Vermont; Theodore Trefon from Boston University; Rich Verma, former assistant secretary of state; Ambassador Mark Green; Ricardo Sennes from the Woodrow Wilson Center; Pamela Stedman-Edwards; Chris Sall from Tufts University; and John Norris from the Center for American Progress.

Finally, Sandra Gain, our editor, endured endless revisions and interactions with authors now scattered around the globe. To her, I express my greatest appreciation for her patience, persistence, and good spirit for bringing this project to a successful conclusion.

David Reed

PART I

Changing Landscapes

1

CHANGING LANDSCAPES

David Reed with Brent Nordstrom and Pamela Stedman-Edwards

America's prosperity is built on a strong economy, the ability to project power to ensure a stable international environment, and sustainable management of natural resources and the environment. Ignoring or allowing any one of those pillars to weaken erodes the strength and resiliency of the others and, over time, weakens the broader structure of our society.

America's prosperity—our standard of living, national identity, and sense of having a unique place in the world—is at risk. Clearly, risks arise from the threats of military and terrorist attacks at home and overseas and from economic and financial crises, as exemplified by the recent flirtation with financial implosion. But a longer-term risk of decline also arises from persistent and deepening threats to our environmental sustainability and stability, not only within our borders but also in partner countries around the world. The thesis of this publication is that environmental sustainability must rise to equal status with ensuring national security and economic well-being as a foundational pillar of America's prosperity.

Planet Earth is undergoing environmental changes of historic proportion. As population and economic activity have expanded, so has use of the earth's resources. Agricultural land, for crops and pasture, now covers more than a third of the world's land surface,[1] yet substantial areas are degraded to the point that productivity is reduced on perhaps as much as 40 percent of cropland. Population growth and agricultural intensification, as well as changing consumption patterns, have also driven an enormous increase in withdrawals from rivers and underground aquifers, well beyond sustainable rates. An estimated 2.8 billion people are now living in areas of high water stress, and that number is expected to reach 3.9 billion by 2030.[2] Excessive water drawdown for agriculture, mining, and domestic consumption has dramatically reduced water supplies in some already arid regions, where land degradation is common. Forest cover loss has slowed in recent years, but the past decade still saw a loss of 130 million hectares of forest, of which almost a third was primary forest,[3] driven by demand for food, fodder, fuel, and wood. More than half the world's marine fishery resources are fully fished or fished to the maximum sustainable level, with a third of monitored fish stocks in jeopardy.[4] Both terrestrial and marine biodiversity losses are unprecedented. Most significantly, carbon loading of the earth's atmosphere has triggered an accelerating process of climate change, causing the retreat of mountain glaciers, the rapid retreat of summer sea ice in the Arctic Ocean, sea-level rise, an unprecedented increase in ocean acidification, and an increase in weather variability and intensity in virtually all corners of the world.

The most salient feature of rising environmental change and resource scarcity is that the environmental changes are brought about by human activity, not by long-term climatic or geological trends. So pervasive are human impacts on the planet's environment that scientists posit the entry into a new epoch called the Anthropocene, in which environmental stability is replaced by instability and the prospect of abrupt, irreversible change much less conducive to human development than in the past 10,000 years.[5] Although we have only ourselves to blame for these global changes, we also have the capacity to reshape human use of the earth's enormous environmental resources to prevent disastrous alterations that could lead to economic and social conflicts. The geographic protections afforded to the United States by the Atlantic Ocean on the east and the Pacific Ocean on the west, coupled with our strategic neighbors, Canada and Mexico, to our north and south, no longer spare us from the political, economic, social, and environmental impacts that may unfold in other parts of the world. As we enter this new epoch, we face an array of pressures and forces quite unlike others that we have confronted in earlier periods of our nation's history. Former Secretary of Defense Robert Gates did not overstate the challenge when he asserted, "Over the next 20 years and more, certain pressures—population, energy, climate, economic, environmental—could combine with rapid cultural, social, and technological change to produce new sources of deprivation, rage, and instability."[6]

Having assumed over the past 150 years that America's quite exceptional environmental endowment was inexhaustible, we now have to reckon with the irreducible fact that our economic well-being at home and stability abroad depend on the local and global goods and services that the environment and natural resources provide. More than anytime in U.S. history, our economy and prosperity are interwoven with the expanding international economy and depend on the maintenance of an open trade regime for goods, services, and capital. Entrance into this new epoch in the human experience brings us face-to-face with the reality that disruption of groundwater supply, abrupt change in weather, droughts and floods, rising daytime and nighttime temperatures, collapse of reefs, and a host of other environmental changes directly and immediately affect productivity in economies around the world and could disrupt extensive supply chains among trading partners, including within the United States. In equal measure, those same environmental disruptions can cause economic and social dislocations that fuel demands for greater assistance from central and local governments, induce migrations as people search for means of sustenance, and intensify existing social tensions and conflicts.

Our military leaders have clearly understood the rising security implications of global environmental degradation and climate change, as noted by Admiral Mike Mullen, who, while serving as the chairman of the Joint Chiefs of Staff, further sharpened concerns relating to environmental change:

> Scarcity of water, food and space could not only create a humanitarian crisis but create conditions that could lead to failed states, instability and potentially radicalization. In combination, these strategic constraints related to the economy and energy consumption, combined with the panoply of emerging challenges we see in the headlines, place our nation at what I believe is at a strategic turning point.[7]

Parallel warnings were echoed by John McHugh, secretary of the U.S. Army, and General Dempsey, chief of staff of the U.S. Army, in testimony before the Senate Appropriations Subcommittee on Defense:

> The demand for resources such as water, energy and food will increase competition and the propensity for conflict. Even as countries develop more efficient uses of natural resources, some countries, particularly those with burgeoning middle classes, will exacerbate demands on already scarce resources.[8]

Those environmental pressures and resource scarcities will affect American prosperity in ways that are unpredictable and yet unrelenting. The central thesis of this publication is that while our own prosperity and economic robustness require environmental stability within our boundaries, equally important is the ability of our trading and strategic partners to access water, land, energy, and the full range of environmental services that will ensure their economic productivity and social stability. As the world's wealthiest nation, we will be able to compete confidently in the global marketplace as our businesses seek needed inputs and resources. Yet, while our domestic economy may be dynamic enough to adapt to environmental and economic changes, we cannot ensure our prosperity if we ignore the environmental sustainability of our partners in other regions of the world. America's prosperity is founded on an open trading regime and on the prosperity of our trading and political partners around the world. Their productivity and social stability remain central to our own well being.

One of the paradoxes of the environmental challenges facing our country and the world is that global abundance of some natural resources will be accompanied by local shortages of the resource or environmental service. Take food, for example. The planet has enough arable land and the technology, infrastructure, and water to support the anticipated global population of 9 billion people by 2050.[9] Although those assets are sufficient to feed the world if viewed in the aggregate, the coming environmental changes and scarcities will generate profound, protracted, and often extensive famine in many vulnerable regions of the world because of unequal distribution of wealth, resource management problems, and uneven access to productive technologies. Other resources will be scarce at the global level, providing opportunities for the countries that have abundant access to them. For example, rare earth elements (REE) are found in abundance in the Bolivian altiplano and Mongolia, while demand for those minerals from computer and high-tech communications manufacturers in developed countries remains unmet. In other cases, problems of global magnitude, such as climate change, ocean acidification, and nitrogen cycle change, will have extremely different impacts at the local, national, and regional levels, disrupting economic and social relations in unforeseeable ways.

As these environmental scarcities take deeper hold and are distributed unevenly across different geographic regions of the world, so too will those scarcities fall unevenly on different social groups within many countries. More-affluent social groups are usually better able to absorb or buffer the impacts of environmental change and scarcity through many different measures. In some cases, they will simply move to safer lands or purchase local technological solutions, such as air conditioners or water filters, and thereby protect themselves against some environmental dislocations. In other cases, the wealthy will exert political influence to accumulate more scarce resources or fend off competitors for those same assets. In contrast, the poorer, more vulnerable social groups that lack the economic means to purchase solutions may try to relocate to other parts of a country or region without certainty as to their future. In parallel, lacking the means to mobilize political support, vulnerable populations risk losing all control over their remaining assets, leaving them exposed to social uncertainties. Such social dislocations are factors that intensify social conflict and increase pressure on already fragile states trying to address underlying development and humanitarian issues.

The challenge for the United States is to craft a foreign policy that recognizes the uncertainties and instabilities of this coming period in the human experience. The task is to adjust our engagements with economic and political partners around the world such that in supporting their prosperity and stability, we, in turn, increase the productivity and prosperity of our own nation.

That, indeed, is the purpose of this publication. Our first objective is to enhance understanding of the dynamics of environmental change and rising environmental scarcities in countries of strategic importance to the United States, changes that threaten to undermine American prosperity. Our second objective is to set forth a comprehensive set of recommendations to guide the U.S. government's response to these global challenges. This first chapter in this exploration reviews how environmental issues have figured in U.S. National Security Strategies (NSS), beginning with President Reagan in 1987 and continuing through the Obama administration. The historical overview traces how the United States has responded to rising environmental challenges primarily not only by securing access to nonrenewable resources such as minerals and oil but also through some initiatives to promote productivity and access to renewable resources, such as land, water, forest, and marine resources, and to stabilize the ecosystems provided by the global commons on which our well-being intimately depends.

The second part of this book examines the impacts of environmental change and scarcities on our major economic and strategic partners around the world and explores how those country-level impacts translate into challenges not only to the national prosperity of those countries but also to America's well-being. The nine country and regional chapters examine the impacts of industry-induced environmental degradation and water scarcities. The chapters explore how agricultural expansion and deforestation in the Amazon threaten to disrupt Brazil's economic rise, with direct consequences for U.S. food supplies; how water scarcities in the Chihuahuan Desert of northern Mexico affect immigration and U.S. agricultural productivity; and how increased global competition for mineral wealth and natural resources challenges political stability throughout the Congo Basin. Each chapter investigates the direct links to America's economic growth and prospects for continued stability in the coming decades and suggests specific recommendations by which the United States can strengthen the environmental and economic sustainability of those countries.

The closing chapter sets forth a series of recommendations that constitute a broad platform for reconfiguring U.S. foreign policy to address the environmental changes, uncertainties, and scarcities besetting the planet. Our guiding principle in articulating these recommendations is that by promoting the environmental sustainability and prosperity of other countries, we, in turn, provide the greatest assurance for sustaining the prosperity to which generations of Americans have grown accustomed. We approach the presentation of these recommendations not as a menu of short-term "threat management" tools but rather as a new basis for building U.S. foreign policy through implementation of long-overdue changes that will strengthen America's standing in the world while greatly benefiting U.S. enterprise and the country as a whole.

Shifts in U.S. Foreign Policy

The core locus for supporting global environmental sustainability and America's prosperity resides in the realm of U.S. foreign policy, where a wide range of military, financial, development, and diplomatic resources can be brought to bear in a concerted, strategic manner. While setting out our proposals for reorienting U.S. foreign policy to address global environmental challenges, we also recognize that other immediate pressures and changes are currently reshaping U.S. foreign policy.

First, U.S. fiscal policy and our weakening global economic posture impose very real constraints on the ability of the United States to influence outcomes in international affairs. U.S. indebtedness is attributable not only to the $9 trillion owed to foreign lenders but equally also to the additional $11 trillion in obligations held by the U.S. Treasury for Fannie Mae and Freddie Mac and accumulated by state and local governments.[10] Despite the growing ranks of America's poor and the increasing economic gap between rich and poor, considerable reductions in domestic programs, including entitlements, will eventually be required to reduce the scale of public indebtedness. In turn, hard choices await policy makers as they balance the trade-offs between deeper domestic spending cuts and reductions in military expenditures, which, whether deep or deeper, will undoubtedly constrain American options in international affairs.

Certain facets of U.S. global security strategy will be reshaped or sacrificed as a sharper triage separates optional from essential foreign engagements. For example, support for longer-term stability operations requiring a protracted, multifaceted presence on the ground similar to engagements sponsored in Iraq and Afghanistan has decidedly waned. There is greater reluctance to embrace overseas interventions driven by humanitarian concerns or even genocidal atrocities, such as those undertaken previously in Somalia, Bosnia, and Kosovo. Direct military support for countries and regions gripped by civil war and major political transitions, such as Libya, Tunisia, Syria, and other countries of the Middle East, will likely be carried out at arm's length. Further reductions in Europe and North Atlantic Treaty Organization forces could well follow.[11] As for the Middle East, public proclamations of unwavering commitments to the Saudi Kingdom and Israel and the regional threat posed by Iran may be recalibrated in light of declining U.S. dependence on Gulf oil.[12] Likely to remain a priority under the new triage will be efforts to combat terrorism across the "arc of instability" that runs from the Middle East to the Indian subcontinent and in northern Africa, as well as investments in cyber security. Yet, if viewed through a lens of opportunity, resisting engagements in peripheral areas, reducing overseas deployments, and further prioritizing weapons acquisition can facilitate America's alignment with the rapid changes and new priorities in the international sphere.[13]

The second major realignment in U.S. foreign policy is the "strategic pivot" that rebalances the deployment of American military and diplomatic assets. East and South Asia will be the economic power center of the world.[14] More than half of the world's population lives in the region. The economies of Japan, Korea, and Thailand coupled with the emerging economies of China, India, and Indonesia will position Asia as the center of global production and commerce, a status it held some 250 years ago when China and India alone produced half of the world's wealth. China's rise as a global power will demand expanded access to energy sources, minerals, food commodities, and outlets for manufactured goods, increasing competition for those resources across the region. Many assert that the American pivot is intended to balance China's growing economic and political influence across the region while encouraging mutually supportive trade relations and maintenance of commercial shipping routes. In light of recent Chinese efforts to reassert claims over the Paracel and Spratly Islands and other small but strategically placed islands in the South China Sea, the challenge will be to ensure that America's "forward-deployed diplomacy" will encourage understanding and cooperation on the security, economic, and diplomatic fronts rather than deepen military confrontations across the region.[15]

The Environment Through the Lens of National Security Strategies

Although pockets of the security and intelligence communities have increased their analytical work to understand the threats posed by the destabilizing forces of climate change, resource scarcity, and social inequalities, there has been no government-wide response to those challenges. Resource scarcities and environmental change remain on the margins of U.S. foreign policy. Apart from oil and, to a lesser extent, minerals, which have driven both diplomatic and military interventions, resource scarcities—and degradation, deforestation, water scarcity, overfishing, and climate change—have been placed principally under the purview of development assistance programs, with no apparent systemic relation to national security concerns. To understand better the ebb and flow and ultimately the marginalization of environmental issues in U.S. foreign policy, we turn to the NSS, the most consistent statements of U.S. foreign policy direction over the past quarter century. Although these strategy statements cannot capture the full breadth of U.S. foreign engagements, they bring into sharp focus the main threats, priorities, and strategies highlighted by five presidents over that period.

Presidential statements on national security were mandated by the Goldwater-Nichols Act (known also as the Department of Defense Reorganization Act of 1986). The NSS establish a basis for a president's dialogue with Congress about U.S. foreign policy, by setting the foundation for subsequent budgetary requests to meet national security challenges. The document also serves to notify foreign governments, friends and foes, of U.S. strategic objectives and explain the approach by which the United States intends to accomplish its objectives. In addition, the NSS provides a platform for dialogue and engagement with important domestic political and economic constituencies. This centerpiece of national security is frequently accompanied by subsidiary documents, including the National Military Strategy, the National Defense Strategy, and other policy statements that provide greater detail on anticipated U.S. objectives and operations.

The five presidents have used the platform provided by the NSS differently over the past 25 years. President Ronald Reagan issued two NSS during the last years of his eight-year tenure (1987 and 1988), signaling his intention not only to confront but also to negotiate with the Soviet Union. President George H. W. Bush issued two strategy statements in his four-year term (1991 and 1993) to highlight how the United States anticipated responding to the fundamental realignments in global power leading up to and following the dissolution of the Soviet Union. President Bill Clinton turned to the NSS seven times to signal his policy intentions to strengthen U.S. global economic influence while also addressing multiple challenges, from regional conflicts to global environmental degradation. President George W. Bush provided one policy statement during each of his four-year terms (2002 and 2006), underscoring his focus on combating terrorism. President Barack Obama issued his only national security statement in 2010 to contrast his multilateral, alliance-building approach with his predecessor's international policies. As detailed below, there has been stark unevenness and discontinuity across these NSS on global environmental issues and their challenges to U.S. national security.

President Reagan's NSS centered on containment of the Soviet Union through three complementary approaches: strategic deterrence to "reestablish nuclear parity" with the competing superpower; conventional deterrence to forestall and, if necessary, repel movement of Warsaw Pact ground forces into Western Europe; and rollback of Soviet-inspired or supported regimes in the developing world, emphasizing development of new capabilities to wage low-intensity conflicts. Preceded by the largest peacetime military buildup in U.S. history, President Reagan, taking note in the 1988 NSS of the "new thinking" in the Kremlin, reached an agreement with then Soviet President Gorbachev to reduce intermediate-range nuclear forces. President Gorbachev, in turn, was shedding the policy dictates of the Brezhnev Doctrine. The agreement on reducing nuclear forces marked the critical turning point in the Cold War, from which point forward the foundation of the Truman and Eisenhower Doctrines—containment of the Soviet Union's military prowess and ideological influence—steadily loosened its grip on U.S. foreign policy.

Immediately following the presentation of his strategy to respond to threats posed by the Soviet Union, President Reagan turned his attention to the challenges of the global economy. He recognized that, "since our resource dependence has grown, the potential vulnerability of our supply lines is an issue of concern." In response to that concern, he highlighted the need to "ensure U.S. access to foreign markets, and to ensure the U.S. and its allies and friends access to foreign energy and mineral resources." He further stated, "We have encouraged market-based energy policies and more open energy trade with the International Energy Agency."[16]

Environmental and sustainability issues were raised near the end of President Reagan's 1988 NSS in the discussion of a range of factors that threatened world peace and American prosperity. The 1988 NSS states,

> Critical shortages of food, a lack of health services, and inabilities to meet other basic needs will keep millions of people, particularly in Africa, in peril. The dangerous depletion or contamination of the natural endowments of some nations—soil, forest, water, air—will add to their environmental and health problems, and increasingly to those of the global community.[17]

Beyond underscoring the centrality of open markets and expanding global trade as the principal means for ensuring U.S. access to critical energy and mineral resources, President Reagan offered no prescriptive response to those noted problems. Of importance, however, were his sharply critical comments regarding Congress's cuts to U.S. foreign assistance programs:

> The cuts signal a policy of retreat. Clearly, in the next few months the Congress and the Executive Branch must work together to find solutions. These programs are a key part of our first line of defense in protecting American freedoms.[18]

President George H. W. Bush was the first president to inject an environmental agenda into his NSS. President Bush framed his 1991 NSS with a note of caution about the uncertain intentions of the Soviet Union during the transitional months of glasnost and perestroika. That uncertainty continued in the U.S. approach to its superpower rival despite the fact that East German borders had been opened and the Berlin Wall torn down a year earlier, thereby marking the effective end of communist rule in Eastern Europe. While those events also marked the symbolic end of the Cold War, its operational end followed shortly thereafter when the Soviet Union joined the United States and the international community in condemning Saddam Hussein's invasion of Kuwait. The Soviet signals supporting the expulsion of the Iraqi army through Operation Desert Storm marked the finale to superpower antagonisms that had dominated international relations for more than 50 years.

The signing of the Strategic Arms Reduction Treaty (START) with the Soviet Union in 1991 signaled the beginning of a new period of U.S. foreign policy.[19] The new approach was articulated in President Bush's call for a New World Order predicated on a collective security regime to be provided through multinational cooperation to promote human rights, defend and promote democratic governance, and promote humanitarian needs around the world. Having mobilized a broad international alliance to expel Iraqi forces from Kuwait, President Bush strongly affirmed his commitment to supporting international institutions and to resisting pressures to retreat behind national borders, stating, "At a time when the world is far more interdependent—economically, technologically, environmentally—any attempt to isolate ourselves militarily and politically would be folly."[20] Still framed by the success in defeating the Iraqi forces, President

Bush carried that commitment beyond the realm of military intervention, further stating,

> Our national power, for example, rests on the strength and resilience of our economy, and our security would be badly served if we allowed fiscal irresponsibility at home to erode our ability to protect our interests abroad, to aid new democracies, or to help find solutions to other global problems. The environmental depredations of Saddam Hussein have underscored that protecting the global ecology is a top priority on the agenda of international cooperation—from extinguishing oil fires in Kuwait to preserving the rain forests to solving water disputes to assessing climate change.[21]

The commitment to bolster engagements with the international community was reflected in President Bush's 1991 NSS as he anticipated the United Nations Conference on Environment and Development, which was held in Rio de Janeiro in June the following year. He explicitly raised environmental issues to the level of an emerging global concern for the United States, asserting,

> Global environmental concerns include such diverse but interrelated issues as stratospheric ozone depletion, climate change, food security, water supply, deforestation, biodiversity and treatment of wastes. A common ingredient in each is that they respect no international boundaries. The stress from these environmental challenges is already contributing to political conflict. Recognizing a shared responsibility for global stewardship is a necessary step for global progress. Our partners will find the United States a ready and active participant in this effort.[22]

President Bush further affirmed that the United States was playing and should continue to play an "active role in supporting multinational environmental programs, population control initiatives, and research on global problems."[23] At the Rio Conference, President Bush, on behalf of the United States, was the first signatory of the United Nations Framework Convention on Climate Change, followed thereafter by 153 other heads of state.[24]

The dissolution of the Soviet Union in 1991 and his predecessor's increasing support for multilateral approaches to global security issues allowed President Clinton to further shift U.S. foreign policy away from superpower rivalry and toward a national security strategy that coupled enhanced military strength with promoting U.S. economic interests abroad through expanded international trade and investment. The signature trade agreements—the North American Free Trade Agreement (NAFTA) and completion of the Uruguay Round of trade talks of the General Agreement on Tariffs and Trade—were followed by a succession of bilateral and regional agreements as the president sought to open markets and investment opportunities for American goods and services. The "economization" of U.S. foreign policy through global economic integration and expansion of American economic opportunity was integral to national security: President Clinton viewed economic strength as the primary determinant of global power and influence. As stated in *A National Security Strategy for a New Century,* the 1999 NSS,

> The second core objective of our national security strategy is to promote America's prosperity through efforts at home and abroad. Our economic and security interests are inextricably linked. Prosperity at home depends on stability in key regions with which we trade or from which we import critical commodities, such as oil and natural gas.[25]

Energy security lay at the heart of his strategic view.

> The United States will continue to have a vital interest in ensuring access to foreign oil sources. We must continue to be mindful of the need for regional stability and security in producing areas to ensure our access to, and the free flow of, these resources.[26]

President Clinton also recognized the changes in geographic interests in pursuing that goal.

> The United States is undergoing a fundamental shift away from reliance on Middle East oil. Venezuela is our number one foreign supplier, and Africa supplies 15% of our imported oil. Canada, Mexico and Venezuela combined supply almost twice as much oil to the United States as the Arab OPEC countries. The Caspian Basin promises to play an increasingly important role in meeting rising world energy demand in coming decades.[27]

The Clinton administration further reinforced the saliency of sustainable development as reflected in a steady rise in that issue's prominence in subsequent NSS. Playing off the international agreements reached during the Rio Conference in 1992, including the signing of three multilateral environmental agreements on climate change, biodiversity, and land degradation, and the creation of the Global Environment Facility (GEF), President Clinton integrated the environmental theme into his focus on expanding American economic interests across the globe. With separate sections dedicated to the environment and promoting sustainable development abroad, President Clinton identified the rising environmental challenges in these terms:

> Increasing competition for the dwindling resources of uncontaminated air, arable land, fisheries and other food sources, and water, once considered "free" goods, is already a very real risk to regional stability around the world.

> The range of environmental risks, serious enough to jeopardize international stability, extends to massive population flight from man-made or natural catastrophes, such as Chernobyl or the East African drought, to large-scale ecosystem damage caused by industrial pollution, deforestation, loss of biodiversity, ozone depletion and ultimately climate change.[28]

By the end of his presidency, Clinton's NSS fully embraced the view that promoting sustainable development was a fundamental pillar of U.S. foreign policy.

> Sustainable development brings higher incomes and more open markets that create steadily expanding opportunities for U.S. trade and investment. It improves the prospects for democracy and social stability in developing countries and increases global economic growth, on which the demand for U.S. exports depends. It alleviates pressure on the global environment, reduces the attraction of the illegal drug trade and other illicit commerce, and improves health and economic productivity.[29]

A National Security Strategy for a Global Age, President Clinton's last NSS, released in 2000, affirms that the future prosperity of the United States will reside in "*encouraging democratization, open markets, free trade, and sustainable development.*" (emphasis in the original)[30]

President George W. Bush articulated his initial national security policy in terms of expanding America's core values of freedom, open markets, and democratic systems to the rest of the world. The terrorist attacks of September 11, 2001, rapidly transformed that value-based policy to one dominated by unilateralism and preemption with a trained focus on eradicating the "axis of evil" located in Iraq, Iran, and North Korea. Justified on the premise of removing Saddam Hussein's weapons of mass destruction, the Second Gulf War, the occupation of Iraq, and intervention in Afghanistan left no doubt that muscled interventionism was the hallmark of President Bush's foreign policy.

President George W. Bush released his first NSS in 2002. The contrast to the previous administration was stark. President Bush's first articulation of national security was framed by "terrorist violence and chaos" wherein "the greatest danger our Nation faces lies at the crossroads of radicalism and technology. Our enemies have openly declared that they are seeking weapons of mass destruction."[31] The subsequent brief sections of his NSS framed national priorities in terms of championing human dignity, strengthening alliances to defeat global terrorism, defusing regional conflicts, igniting a new era of free markets and free trade, and building the infrastructure of democracy. He set out his energy security agenda and a six-point agenda for reducing greenhouse gas emissions, stating,

> We will strengthen our own energy security and the shared prosperity of the global economy working with our allies, trading partners and energy producers to expand the sources and types of global energy supplied, especially in the Western Hemisphere, Africa, Central Asia, and the Caspian region.[32]

President Bush's second NSS, in 2006, made no mention of environmental sustainability or the range of emerging environmental issues being addressed in international forums. The overarching message of his second NSS was the threat posed by Saddam Hussein's acquisition of weapons of mass destruction and the imperative to eliminate terrorist threats. Natural resources and the environment were referenced in terms of securing America's energy supply and ensuring "energy independence" by diversifying energy sourcing.

> The world's dependence on these few suppliers is neither responsible nor sustainable over the long term. The key to ensuring our energy security is diversity in the regions from which energy resources come and the types of energy resources on which we rely.[33]

However, one of the singular features of President Bush's first NSS, reaffirmed in his second NSS, was to establish development in Africa and other developing countries as a central priority in U.S. foreign policy, recognizing foreign aid as the indispensable mechanism for supporting that mission. Thereafter, the Millennium Challenge Corporation (MCC) and the President's Emergency Plan for AIDS Relief were singular examples of the Bush administration's commitment to translate development assistance into effective, sustained instruments of U.S. foreign policy.

The overarching framework of President Obama's NSS, released in 2010, was to "pursue our interests through an international system in which all nations have certain rights and responsibilities."[34] Strengthened international institutions, the rule of law, and multilateralism were key operational tenets of President Obama's foreign engagement strategy. He reengaged the great powers to impose sanctions on Iran, continued efforts to isolate North Korea, and ignored Venezuela and other regional provocations, although his early efforts to find a solution to the Israeli-Palestinian conflict yielded no tangible results. President Obama drew down troop levels and declared an end to the U.S. occupation in Iraq and set a timetable for the final U.S. withdrawal from Afghanistan. In 2011, the United States signed the New START treaty with Russia and provided measured support for the Arab Spring transitions in countries across the Middle East. Although Congress approved pending trade agreements with South Korea, Colombia, and Singapore during the Obama administration, expanding U.S. trade relations on a bilateral or multilateral basis was a secondary priority.

A closing section of President Obama's 2010 NSS, "Sustain Broad Cooperation on Key Global Challenges," set forth a strategy for addressing the dangers associated with climate change at home and abroad:

> The change wrought by a warming planet will lead to new conflicts over refugees and resources; new suffering from drought and famine; catastrophic natural disasters; and the degradation of land across the globe. The United States will therefore confront climate change based upon clear guidance from the science, and in cooperation with all nations—for there is no effective solution to climate change that does not depend upon all nations taking responsibility for their own actions and for the planet we will leave behind.[35]

Other than the statement offered above, the striking lacuna in President Obama's 2010 NSS was the virtual absence of recognition of the growing challenges to U.S. economic and security interests posed by increasing degradation of the planet's physical environment with the attendant negative impacts on the productivity and stability of emerging and developing economies. Sustainable development, a strategic point of reference in President Clinton's security strategy, was briefly mentioned in President Obama's strategic assessment of U.S. interests as consisting of three components: increasing investment in development, investing in the political capacity of developing country partners, and providing global public goods, such as increasing Africa's capacity to adapt to climate change.[36] The issue of rising environmental scarcities, which was prominent in President Clinton's multiple strategy papers, did not even figure as an underlying concern. Despite the emergence of the Quadrennial Diplomacy and Development Review as a policy tool employed by the Obama administration, it is difficult to point to hallmark initiatives used to elevate development assistance or promote environmental sustainability as a central pillar of President Obama's foreign policy.

The Rise of Natural Resource and Environmental Scarcities

Presidents have used the NSS in varying ways and for differing audiences. Moreover, the relative significance and impact of the strategy statements have varied among the five presidents. Yet, perhaps the most salient conclusion to be drawn from this brief overview of some 14 NSS is the stark unevenness across presidencies in regard to the importance of environmental change and scarcities in national security affairs. Even as international attention and pressures steadily grew in the new millennium, the second Bush administration accorded little significance to immediate and longer-term consequences of environmental degradation. Despite important research activities in the security and intelligence communities, sustainability and environmental scarcity have not been mainstreamed into U.S. foreign policy even under President Obama, whose administration faces ever sharper environmental challenges.

In the NSS references to natural resource and environmental issues, two distinct but intertwined environmental issues are brought into central focus. The first is the increasing scarcity of and competition for nonrenewable natural resources, principally minerals and energy sources. The second, most notable under President Clinton, is the rising concern about societal risk associated with environmental change, largely, but not exclusively, with climate change and scarcity of renewable resources (water, land, and forests). These two intersecting environmental issues and their real and potential impacts on American society are the central concerns of this publication.

Historically, the priorities established in the NSS and subsequently translated into U.S. interventions around the world, whether through military actions or muscled economic policy, have been tied to securing steady delivery of energy and mineral inputs to support U.S. industry. The first major shift away from securing those industrial inputs and toward addressing scarcities of renewable resources and protecting the global commons was signaled in President Clinton's strategic review. That change in emphasis was reversed under President George W. Bush and, in some ways, equally neglected under the Obama administration. Strategic statements now vacillate between or attempt to straddle those two complementary forms of environmental scarcities. However, as described in detail later in this chapter, there is increased attention and concern in the U.S. military, intelligence, and development communities about the impact of disruption and scarcity of goods and services provided by renewable resources. Although we provide ample discussion of U.S. policy responses to both energy and mineral scarcities, since they have been historically important, the principal focus of this publication will be the need for a new direction in U.S. foreign policy, namely to address the security and stability threats posed by renewable resource scarcities in the developing world that pose long-term challenges to American prosperity.

There are fundamental differences—physical, environmental, economic, and political—between nonrenewable and renewable resources. Given these differences, policy responses to the problems of scarcity for renewables and for the global commons will have to diverge from the models applied over the past century for managing stocks of oil and other nonrenewables. The following sections look in greater detail at these differences. However, although scarcities of nonrenewable and renewable resources are discussed separately, it is important to recognize that environmental changes and scarcities in one are intimately intertwined with changes and scarcities in the other. For example, extraction of hydrocarbons and their subsequent use in generating modern energy services depend directly on access to water. Extraction of natural gas from limestone formations is impossible without staggering volumes of water. By the same token, disposal of water used in hydraulic fracturing has immediate impacts on freshwater quality and availability. Coal mining relies on the availability of water for many phases of the mining process, as well as for cooling coal-fired power plants. Similarly, extraction of hard rock minerals and processing of placer ores require huge volumes of water that must be disposed of following extraction of the sought-after minerals. Each of these extractive and associated industrial processes increases pressures on renewable resources including land, forests, mangroves, and freshwater, often generating scarcities and increasing competition among local users. Ultimately, scarcities of renewable and nonrenewable resources must be addressed through approaches that recognize their distinctiveness and the inseparable linkages between the two. As discussed below, failure to do so increases the prospects for increased social conflicts with the associated implications for U.S. prosperity and security.

Nonrenewable Resources

Strategic Minerals

Not surprisingly, the issue of scarcity of nonrenewable resources, including minerals and oil, has figured prominently in U.S. domestic and foreign policy, beginning before World War II up to the present day. With the passage of the Strategic Materials Act of 1939 and its subsequent expansion through the Critical Materials Stockpiling Act of 1946, Congress mandated the creation and retention of national stockpiles of strategic minerals to "decrease and prevent wherever possible a dangerous and costly dependence upon foreign nations for supplies of these materials in times of national emergency."[37]

Following World War II, the threatening fog of the Cold War stirred concerns about the ability of the United States to ensure provision of raw materials to sustain our economy as the Soviet Union expanded its sphere of military, economic, and ideological control across Eastern Europe and thereafter into the countries of the developing world. President Truman, invoking the threats posed by expanded Soviet economic influence, created the Paley Commission to undertake a study, released as *Resources for Freedom,* to assess that threat. President Truman stated, "The United States has changed from a net exporter to a net importer of material, and projects an increasing dependence on imports for the future."[38] Composed of leading academic, political, and military leaders, the Paley Commission set forth some 70 recommendations that would "best assure the mounting supplies of materials and energy which our economic progress and security will require in the next quarter century."[39] Although strategic stockpiling had provided an adequate security hedge through the end of World War II, the commission recommended that the United States should acquire strategic minerals "at the least cost possible for equivalent values."[40] That recommendation triggered a reduction in strategic mineral stockpiles from a five-year capacity, then to a three-year capacity, and finally to a one-year capacity, thereafter placing emphasis on using global markets to provide the resources that our defense and industry might need. In 1974, Congress also authorized the president to trade military supplies for materials provided by other countries.

The sourcing of critical minerals through global markets from the mid-1950s onward intersected with the rising Cold War ideology and provided the rationale for U.S. intervention in many countries of Latin America, Africa, and other developing regions. Calls to "keep the Americas safe from communism" provided the justification for U.S. actions, including supporting right-wing coups, backing military strongmen and caudillos across the Americas, sending military support, and enforcing muscled economic aggression to ensure a steady flow of materials to the growing American industrial economy. Whether for tin, lead, antimony, and zinc in Bolivia, petroleum in Peru, iron ore and manganese in Brazil, aluminum in Guyana, nickel and manganese in Cuba, or copper in Chile, U.S. government policy ensured that nationalist and often democratically elected governments were replaced with dictators and oligarchs committed to protecting U.S. business and security interests. Interventions in the Congo, Angola, and Chile were prompted by Cold War threats and justified to install and maintain governments sympathetic to U.S. economic interests, notably for minerals. There was little light between official U.S. government policy and the interests of American corporations, such as W. R. Grace & Co., Alcoa, and Bethlehem Steel, in securing access to strategic minerals over the 30-year Cold War.[41]

Focusing on global markets to address perceived security threats to strategic industrial inputs worked well through the end of the twentieth century, but that approach was challenged when China's steady rise as a leading manufacturing power changed market dynamics that previously responded principally to U.S. economic signals. The most immediate change in market dynamics was reflected in the rising demand for more than a score of strategic industrial inputs. The five most important minerals and mineral groups included indium, manganese-group metals, niobium, platinum-group metals, and REE, to which a group of six additional elements are added, including copper, gallium, lithium, tantalum, titanium, and vanadium.[42] China's average 9.9 percent annual growth in gross domestic product (GDP) since 1978, reaching a peak of 13 percent just before the global recession of 2008, intensified pressure on copper, nickel, zinc, lead, and a host of other mineral markets. Aggressive market penetration in Africa, Latin America, and the Asia-Pacific region signaled an increasingly competitive Chinese sourcing strategy driven by comingled Chinese commercial interests and Chinese government initiatives in negotiating agreements with client countries. As a consequence, in reaching commercial agreements with government officials or private companies, the full range of financial, technical, and development assistance resources of the Chinese government, which were holding foreign reserves in excess of $3 trillion, were brought to bear to support companies, including the Aluminum Corporation of China (Chinalco), China Metallurgical

Group Corporation, and China Nonferrous Metal Mining Group, as they acquired equity ownership in companies around the world.

The impact of China's entry into minerals markets at such a scale has been felt on three complementary levels. First, there has been a steady rise in commodity prices over the past decade, resulting in increases of more than 300 percent for some metals, such as copper, and, on average, a doubling in price.[43] While the rapid rise in prices, particularly during 2002–2008, cannot be entirely attributed to China's expansion, during this period China became the world's largest consumer of aluminum, copper, lead, nickel, zinc, tin, and iron ore. Second, the Chinese government has acquired a growing array of publicly traded metals and mining companies in order to secure access to needed raw materials, thereby constraining access by other buyers. In the case of REE—elements with strategic applications in defense, telecommunications, and information technology—China currently enjoys a dominant market position. Approximately 90 percent of rare earth minerals are mined in China, and China has tried to extend its control over this market.[44] A recent example that struck a nerve with U.S. policy makers was China's 2005 attempt to purchase the Mountain Pass REE mine owned by Unocal. Direct political pressure from Congress pushed then President Bush to block the deal on the grounds of threats posed to U.S. national security. Third, the Chinese government, working with commercial Chinese ventures, has tried to consolidate control over strategic materials, in which they already have considerable market influence, and use that influence to shape geopolitical relations. The most notable occurrence unfolded when China halted shipments of REE to Japan, resulting in a maritime confrontation between China and Japan in September 2010. The situation was defused but not before signaling an aggressive Chinese policy to countries trading in the South China Sea.[45]

In response, the United States intensified analysis and monitoring of efforts to restrict free market access to these critical minerals, and slowly the Department of Defense initiated plans to expand stockpiles of critical minerals. These efforts have been accompanied by calls from within the U.S. military to rebuild critical stockpiles in keeping with the Paley Commission Report of 1952, an approach abandoned almost 20 years prior.[46] Intensified competition for strategic minerals, coupled with the fusion of Chinese commercial and government resources, prompted other governments, notably Japan through the Japan Oil, Gas and Metals National Corporation, to establish comparable mechanisms to support privately held companies as they seek access to strategic minerals in a tightened global materials market.

The key factor to bear in mind in this intensifying competition for strategic materials is that, although some countries have greater and more diversified natural resource wealth, no major economy has self-sufficiency in strategic materials. Our shared reliance on markets encourages transparency, stability, and cooperation among competitors and reduces overt hostility and economic aggression. Moreover, previous responses from economic actors and governments to mineral scarcities have proven adequate to address potential economic disruptions. Those responses include (a) exploration, discovery, and more-complete extraction of new sources of the scarce material; (b) the use of substitute materials that are available in greater abundance; (c) introduction of new technologies that fundamentally alter the need for and use of the scarce resource; and (d) more recently, recycling of previously used mineral materials.[47] Less-benign perspectives predict that resource scarcities and intensified competition for dwindling supplies will push a wide range of countries, large and small, into conflict, precipitating a new period of international relations characterized by resource wars.[48] The situation in the Democratic Republic of the Congo, where valuable minerals contribute to continued domestic and regional instability, is just one example of the role that "conflict minerals" and "blood diamonds" have played in aggravating conflict at the national and regional levels over the past decade as these scarce resources have grown in value.

Petroleum

While America's efforts to ensure a steady supply of strategic minerals covered the entire globe, its efforts to secure oil supplies gave primary focus to one geographic region, the Persian Gulf. The concentration of oil reserves and oil production in the Middle East has meant that frequent regional conflicts have disrupted global petroleum markets, and the major oil-producing countries, because they were so few, were able to exert disproportionate control over global markets. The fact that oil reserves are national property and largely exploited by state-owned companies has shaped these problems, making petroleum access a foreign policy issue. Today, markets have become increasingly less subject to control by a few countries, but still the number of oil-producing countries and private companies involved is limited. This has raised issues for the security of the U.S. supply and the stability of prices, which have enormous impacts on the United States and the global economy.

Given the dependence on Middle East oil following World War II, it is not surprising that the region also became the pivot point of Cold War superpower rivalry. That rivalry prompted President Truman in 1947, President Eisenhower in 1957, and President Nixon in 1969 to reaffirm U.S. commitment to send military aid or troops to Persian Gulf countries, notably Saudi Arabia and Iran, if they were threatened by Soviet aggression. There was remarkable continuity in the policies of President Nixon, President Ford, and President Carter toward the region as they sought to stabilize access to this strategic commodity, drawing a proverbial "line in the sand" in regard to Soviet influence and penetration in the region. Even as late as 1979, when the Soviet Union invaded Afghanistan, President Carter declared that any military aggression in the Persian Gulf region would constitute "an assault on the vital interests of the United States of America, and such an assault will be repelled by any means necessary, including military force."[49] Complementing its containment policy during that period, the United States employed a "surrogate strategy" that relied on increasing the military capacity of friendly governments in the Persian Gulf. That policy first emerged in 1971 when the British government announced that it would no longer maintain its military presence "East of Suez," which had provided a stabilizing pro-Western presence in the Indian Ocean and Southeast Asia. With the Vietnam War raging, the Nixon administration decided against replacing the withdrawing British forces or building up U.S. military bases in the region, opting instead to support U.S. allies, namely Iran and Saudi Arabia, with hundreds of billions of dollars during the 1970s.[50]

Between 1950 and 1991, there were several major supply disruptions emanating from the region, each sparking significant price jumps with attendant global economic effects. The Arab-Israeli War of 1973 provoked a pivotal disruption when the Organization of the Petroleum Exporting Countries (OPEC) withheld oil shipments to the United States and other Western powers to punish them for siding with Israel in the conflict. Global oil prices quadrupled. The Arab oil embargo was eased in March 1974 but not before it had created oil shortages in many countries, depressed global industrial output, and precipitated a global recession.[51] Domestically, responding to growing political pressures, President Nixon, followed by President Ford, imposed price controls to contain inflationary pressures rippling across the economy that were triggered by oil shortages. As the U.S. government expanded its oil stocks in the Strategic Petroleum Reserve, transnational oil companies unleashed a frantic search for new petroleum deposits, including in the North Slope of Alaska, the North Sea, and the Gulf of Mexico. In addition, 28 industrialized countries created an energy security system, the International Energy Agency, to anticipate, forestall, and coordinate the response of industrialized countries to future oil shocks.

Another pivotal moment unfolded in November 1979, following the Iranian revolution that led to the overthrow of the Shah and the seizure of American hostages. The $20 billion provided by the United States to the Shah for armaments during the 1970s were now turned against the United States and shortly thereafter Iraq. Even as global markets adjusted to the temporary loss of Iranian oil, Iraq invaded Iran, unleashing an eight-year war that killed more than half a million soldiers and civilians and destroyed the oil facilities of both countries. In response to this regional conflict, non-OPEC countries, including Mexico, Egypt, Malaysia, the Soviet Union, Norway, Angola, and others, moved into global markets and, by increasing total supply, unintentionally altered global oil markets in a fundamental way. Saudi Arabia, sensing opportunity and under pressure from the United States, also increased exports substantially. Likewise, the multinational oil companies scrambled to adjust to the supply disruption from the Gulf, building their inventories to full capacity. What started as a price spike caused by supply disruptions in the Persian Gulf resulted, over the course of several years, in a glut of oil on the world market. By the mid-1980s, global oil prices collapsed, as did oil revenues for many OPEC countries. Only sustained negotiations among OPEC and non-OPEC producers for control over production levels allowed global prices to recover and stabilize by the beginning of 1987. The following year, Iran and Iraq finally signed a peace accord.

The repeated price swings, the addition of new producers trying to bypass a market structure dominated by the major petroleum companies, and the development of new market outlets weakened OPEC's domination over global supplies. No sooner were markets adjusting to these new dynamics than Iraq invaded Kuwait in January 1991, delivering the next shock. At stake in the Iraqi occupation was the prospect that Saddam Hussein would control 20 percent of OPEC production along with control of 20 percent of the world's known oil reserves.[52] Resuming their gyrations, prices doubled almost immediately, reinforcing economic contraction in the United States and other industrialized countries. The day the U.S.-led coalition launched its first air strikes on the Iraqi invasion forces, oil prices dropped dramatically. When the war ended in February 1991, one visible legacy of the war was the sight of 600 flaming Kuwaiti oil wells, burning more than 1 million barrels of oil a day.

The second U.S. war in Iraq, launched against Saddam Hussein in March 2003, likewise affected oil markets throughout the decade. However, a far more significant shock to oil markets in the first decade of the new century was the "demand shock" induced principally by China's rise as the manufacturing center of the world.[53] Certainly President Bush's war unsettled markets by disrupting Iraq's supplies, and civil unrest and political instability in the Niger Delta and Venezuela further disrupted global markets. But the real destabilizing impact was delivered by a sharp increase in global demand in 2004–2005, driven largely by China's steadily rising demand for oil, which it needed to sustain its high growth rate. China's domestic consumption of oil doubled between 2000 and 2010, while growing demand from other countries of East and Southeast Asia, including India, Indonesia, Thailand, and Vietnam, further increased pressures on oil supplies.[54]

As global oil consumption continues to grow, oil companies are turning to increasingly sophisticated methods of extraction and refining in order to exploit petroleum in increasingly difficult environments. In response to the rising cost of exploration and extraction, as well as the expansion of international oil markets, the major private oil companies experienced a series of megamergers, creating vertically integrated behemoths.[55] These private companies, however, still accounted for only 15 percent of the world's total supply at the end of the century. Dwarfing the reserves of those privately owned giants were the state-owned oil companies, which were no longer confined to the Middle East, and that constituted 15 of the 20 largest producers in the world. Pemex of Mexico, Gazprom and Rosneft of Russia, PetroChina, StatoilHydro of Norway, Saudi Aramco of Saudi Arabia, KazMunayGas in Kazakhstan, SOCAR in Azerbaijan, and Petronas in Malaysia shaped international oil markets in parallel to the corporate giants. In addition, new discoveries of reserves off the coast of Brazil, in the North Sea, and in Africa; drilling in the Arctic; and rapidly expanding extraction programs in the Caspian Sea further opened global markets that were once dominated by a few corporations and their governmental counterparts in OPEC countries.

The Cry for Energy Independence in the United States

The 1974 OPEC boycott, long lines at the pump, and repeated volatile swings in the price of gasoline unleashed a public cry for President Nixon and Congress alike to ensure our "energy independence" and "end America's being held hostage to foreign powers," particularly in the Middle East. President Nixon, on imposing price controls in 1973, launched "Project Independence," declaring that "by the end of this decade we will have developed the potential to meet our own energy needs without depending on any foreign energy source."[56] With each price disruption thereafter, Congress and successive presidents up to the present have invoked the specter of Middle East sheikhs throttling America's prosperity and threatening our dominant place in the world economy. More recently, a spate of books warning of "resource wars," "Chinese domination of world oil markets," and "military confrontation with China in the South China Sea" to control oil flows have become part of a steady drumbeat of threats provoked by China's rising global influence. Perhaps the reality is far less ominous because China and the United States share a strategic interest in maintaining stable oil prices. China relies on coal for 71 percent of its domestic energy, with oil constituting only 19 percent of total energy consumption.[57] Of that 19 percent contribution, only half is provided by imports, the same percentage required to satisfy domestic U.S. demand. Moreover, the United States imports about 28 percent from Canada and, according to a 2012 Citibank study, if Canada's contribution remains steady, the United States will become an oil-exporting nation by 2020.[58]

The bottom line is that both countries depend on stable global oil markets to fuel their economies. The optimal scenario relies on a broad range of producers and consumers that can adjust for disruptions in one region of the world or another. In addition, a recent study by the RAND Corporation concluded,

> Because oil is traded through a global market, the U.S. economy will continue to be vulnerable to global shifts in the supply and demand for oil for the foreseeable future, regardless of how much oil or what percentage of its oil the United States imports. Energy prices that are free to adjust to changes in supply and demand, undistorted by subsidies or price controls, offer the most effective mechanism for allocating petroleum in a time of increased scarcity.[59]

Price jumps in petroleum markets have been induced by scarcities caused by conflicts and deliberate control of output—in other words, they have a political or economic basis rather than an environmental basis. As for actually running out of oil, Yergin states that there are "at least 5 trillion barrels of petroleum resources, of which 1.4 trillion is sufficiently developed and technically and economically accessible to count as proved plus probable reserves."[60] That volume of proven reserves acquires meaning when compared with total production since the beginning of the industrial revolution, which amounts to approximately 1 billion barrels. There is no escaping the fact that oil will remain very much a part of the global energy mix for a considerable time, making the key to U.S. and global price stability a steady diversification of supplies until such time as renewable energy can replace hydrocarbons.

Renewable Environmental Goods and Services

Although nonrenewables—oil and to a lesser extent metals and minerals—have been considered critical to U.S. strategic interests for decades, in today's changing world, renewable resources are increasingly critical too, particularly as scarcities of water, land, forests, and fisheries worsen in many parts of the world. There are fundamental differences in the characteristics of renewable and nonrenewable resources. Foremost, access to and use of most nonrenewables are governed by market dynamics. Minerals, metals, and hydrocarbons are priced and subject to the dynamics of supply and demand. Admittedly, as we have seen above, market dynamics have been shaped by muscled diplomacy, military actions, and a wide range of nonmarket interventions that reflect the interests of more-powerful nations or producers. Many renewable resources, in contrast, have remained unpriced and external to the calculus of market interactions. They are often considered "free" goods and services. To the extent that renewables are subject to market forces, they are shaped principally by local or regional supply and demand. While local scarcity of nonrenewables is resolved through global markets, local scarcity of renewables can generate profound local and regional impacts on environmental conditions and productive capacity that cannot be resolved through international markets.

As our brief review of the NSS indicated, over the past 25 years, renewable resources have had no consistent place in strategic policy concerns. Their relegation to the margins of our national security interests is beginning to change now that increasing scarcities of a wide range of renewables are posing direct challenges to U.S. prosperity, albeit frequently through indirect paths and supply chain disruptions.

The central framework for our treatment of environmental change and scarcity is provided by Thomas Homer-Dixon. Writing in his groundbreaking work, *Environment, Scarcity, and Violence,* Homer-Dixon underscores three highly interactive causes of renewable resource scarcities. The first cause is the set of institutions, social relations, governance systems, and cultural norms that societies use in determining how to manage and use natural resources.[61] Prevailing customary uses, regulations, and governance arrangements play a major role in determining if and how a society will use more environmental goods and services than the surrounding environment can provide. The second cause of environmental scarcity is the rise in demand for renewable resources. There are many examples of growing demographic pressure or rising standards of living leading societies to increase consumption of available resources. Structural changes in the economy can likewise reduce demand for one set of renewables while increasing pressures on others, disrupting a previous balance between need and availability. For example, rising prices for kerosene may trigger a return to biomass energy sources that contributes to deforestation. The third cause is the unequal distribution of renewable resources. Some groups in a society may, for historical or cultural reasons, have greater access to land, water, fishing grounds, or forests, while other groups in that same social order are relegated to inferior resources or are allocated a smaller share.

As Homer-Dixon suggests, the manifestations and causes of environmental scarcity are of rising significance for U.S. foreign policy:

> These environmental scarcities usually do not cause wars among countries, but they can generate severe social stresses within countries, helping to stimulate subnational insurgencies, ethnic clashes and urban unrest. Although this violence affects developing societies most, policymakers and citizens in the industrialized world ignore it at their peril. It can harm rich countries' national interests by threatening their trade and economic relations, entangling them in complex humanitarian emergencies, provoking distress migrations, and destabilizing pivotal countries in the developing world.[62]

Resource Capture and Ecological Marginalization: Land Grabs

The distribution and equality, or inequality, of access to resources profoundly shape the way in which resource scarcities affect societies and states. Homer-Dixon points out two dynamics that lead to increased inequality in access and which, in turn, have serious consequences for the stability of societies and states. As he explains,

> Two kinds of interaction are particularly important: *resource capture* and *ecological marginalization* [italics in the original]. Resource capture occurs when the degradation and depletion of renewable resources interacts with population growth to encourage powerful groups within a society to shift resource distribution in their favor. Ecological marginalization occurs when unequal resource access combines with population growth to cause long-term migrations of people dependent on renewable resources for their livelihood.[63]

No clearer example of the dynamics of resource capture and marginalization can be provided than the recent phenomenon dubbed by the press as "land grabs." The basic contours of the issue involve acquisition, usually by lease, of extensive tracts of arable land by governments, investors, multinational corporations, and military services in developing countries. Perhaps the most infamous example arose in 2008 when Daewoo, the Korean multinational conglomerate, acquired a 99-year lease in Madagascar for 1.3 million hectares, or one-third of the country's total agricultural land. News of the secretive agreement converged with broader public discontent over presidential corruption, leading to political turmoil and ultimately the deposing of President Ravalomanana. Beyond that headline-grabbing deal, dozens of other contracts have been signed in recent years that warrant mention to indicate the extent of land grabbing and the partners involved in the transactions. Sime Darby, a Malaysian commodity producer and one of the world's largest producers of palm oil, acquired a 63-year lease to convert 545,000 acres of Liberian tropical forests to palm oil plantations. Egypt acquired the rights to grow grain on 840,000 hectares in Uganda. The Democratic Republic of the Congo has offered South Africa a lease agreement for more than 10 million hectares to produce crops ranging from corn to millet and rice. The Ethiopian government opened 2.7 million hectares to governments and private investors from East Asia and the Gulf States.[64] According to the International Food Policy Research Institute, between 2006 and 2009, between 15 million and 20 million hectares of African land were secured by external agents through some 50 deals.[65] In Asia, major leasing agreements have been reached in Cambodia, Indonesia, Pakistan, and the Philippines with governments and companies from South Korea, India, and China. More recently, acquisition agreements have multiplied in Russia, Ukraine, and Moldova, driven largely by investment companies from Great Britain, Norway, and the United States.[66]

The underlying driver of this growing phenomenon is quite simply food security. The principal concern driving these acquisitions by governments of high- or middle-income countries is their search for long-term access to productive land to ensure a stable supply of basic commodities for their national populations. By providing these commodities through their own supplies, albeit grown overseas, governments hope to bypass world food markets, protect national budgets, moderate price fluctuations, and prevent social unrest. Although large-scale land acquisitions began shortly after the turn of the millennium, the food riots that broke out in scores of developing countries following the global agricultural commodity crisis of 2008 provided the spark that led to a larger search for cheap land in willing developing countries. Private companies, supporting policies set by developed-country governments, have identified land acquisitions as a new source of profits and opportunities to increase market share.

A prima facie case can be made for the beneficial aspects of the acquisition deals, although actual delivery of those benefits is far from guaranteed. If properly executed, land acquisition arrangements should provide a platform through which smallholder producers can interact with capital-intensive operations and receive benefits through improved production techniques and access to improved infra structure financing and improved seed stocks, as well as creation of jobs through backward and forward linkages to the agricultural sector. If those factors are properly tended to, food security in the host country could also improve. As an important sample of acquisition experiences illustrates, however, these outcomes are not delivered with any consistency. In some situations, capital and technology-intensive production regimes are set up as veritable enclaves, neither generating improvements for the traditional farming systems that surround them nor creating links to the national economy. In addition, these capital-intensive enclaves create widespread environmental damage to surrounding areas and divert water to support their agribusiness activities, thereby disrupting local livelihoods and production systems.[67]

One widespread problem threatens not only the viability of the implanted production systems but also the stability of the host governments. Frequently, lands leased to foreign investors are areas managed under traditional or communal ownership patterns, tenure, and usufruct rights. Host governments often claim that the areas are unused or marginal lands, arguing that the lands should be put into production for the benefit of the nation. At play in these "legal" transactions is the exercise of power relations in which elites make decisions with frequent disregard for the communities that have cultivated the land for decades, if not centuries. In addition, not only has control of land been a source of major social conflicts in developing countries around the world, but, as is the case in many African countries, land acquisition agreements are also imposed on vulnerable communities at the very time governments are implementing comprehensive land titling and reform programs. What is in evidence are the dynamics of resource capture and ecological marginalization described by Homer-Dixon. In the case of land acquisitions, the power relationship is between concentrations of global wealth and influence expressed through international investment companies or governments, on one side, and the vulnerable, often impoverished communities of countries beset by infrastructure deficiencies, political instability, and civil strife, on the other. Straddling the exercise of these power dynamics are national government officials who, often for their personal benefit, accede to financial transactions conducted without consultation with the vulnerable communities.

Despite these notable examples, land grabs are not a widespread phenomenon at the present time. They are, however, a symptom of the underlying problem of resource scarcity. The point to be made is that food scarcity has become a source of instability for many countries and, as such, poses rising threats to U.S. security interests around the world. Arable land per person is shrinking, decreasing from 0.38 hectares in 1970 to 0.23 in 2000, with a projected decline to 0.15 hectares per person by 2050.[68] The general process of land degradation that affects more than 900 million people around the globe also reduces the agricultural productivity of as much as two-thirds of the world's arable land.[69]

When the phenomenon of land degradation is combined with the fact that 1.8 billion people will face water scarcity by 2025 and two-thirds will face water-stressed conditions, the outcomes can be explosive and destabilizing.[70] These trends are occurring in all the major resource sectors—land, water, oceans, and forests.

Water: Governance, Demand, and Access

The governance of renewable resources in the face of growing populations and rising demand is shaped, as Homer-Dixon discusses, by traditional and new institutions and cultural and governance norms that shape patterns of distribution and use. Here we review the case of freshwater scarcity to illustrate this understanding of the drivers of scarcity. Freshwater scarcity and degradation affect health, food security, environmental sustainability, and the potential for economic growth in many countries. Although substitutes have been found for many natural resources, there is no substitute for water for either human consumption or agriculture. Because adequate water is essential not only for human health but also for agricultural production, energy production, and industrial development, water mismanagement, overuse, and unequal distribution probably have greater implications for international security than is the case for any other renewable resource.

While the world's population increased fourfold in the twentieth century, freshwater use increased ninefold. Many major rivers are vastly reduced by extraction primarily for agriculture but also for industry and domestic use;[71] many rivers now run dry before they reach the sea. In addition to the extraction of aboveground water, groundwater is being pumped at well above the normal replenishment rate, depleting aquifers and the base flow of rivers in many regions.[72] Twenty-eight countries experienced shortages of freshwater in 1998, and this number is expected to increase to 56 countries by 2026.[73] A recent study surveying month-by-month water consumption rates[74] in more than 400 major river basins[75] found that some 200 river basins experienced water scarcity during at least one month of the year (these basins support about 2.67 billion people); 35 basins suffered scarcity for half the year (483 million people); and 12 suffered year-round scarcity. The most heavily populated basin suffering severe scarcity year-round is the Yongding River in northern China, which serves Beijing and supports a population density of 425 people per square kilometer. A number of other major cities face water scarcity, including Mexico City, with a population of more than 20 million. Built on a lake bed, which has long since dried up as a result of the growing population, the city has depleted its aquifers to the point that buildings are sinking. Yet Mexico City might well have enough water if investments were made to capture and store rainfall and prevent massive leaks and theft from the existing infrastructure.

Like other natural resources, water scarcity is driven by the three factors described by Homer-Dixon. First are the institutions, systems, and norms that govern water use. Inefficient use or poor management of available supplies is often rooted in these systems: overuse of irrigation water that leads to salinization or poorly designed or maintained systems that lead to large water losses are prime examples. Failure to price water often aggravates inefficient use. Second is rising demand, created by growing populations, particularly in Africa, and increased consumption by industry and the world's expanding middle class. Meat consumption in particular is rising; producing a pound of meat requires at least 450 gallons of water.[76] The third factor is unequal distribution. Many people do not have access to potable water or must walk for hours to obtain it. One in six people in the world today lacks access to safe drinking water and two in six lack adequate sanitation, while agriculture claims the lion's share of freshwater. Irrigation claims two-thirds of extracted freshwater globally, and in arid regions it claims as much as 90 percent.[77] Smallholders are less likely to have access to irrigation and freshwater, aggravating problems of aridity and poverty.

Beyond these causes of water scarcity, global warming is expected to exacerbate water shortages in regions that are already water stressed, such as the Sahel and other dry regions of Africa. Accelerated melting of glaciers and snow cover, which supply water for 1 billion people and support power generation in many countries, may increase water flow in the short term, but over the longer term they will reduce water availability. Glaciers in the Andes are likely to disappear within a few decades, eliminating dry season water flows.

Water withdrawals not only affect the amount of water available for immediate human use but also have serious impacts on aquatic ecosystems, sometimes including complete desiccation in dry seasons. This stress leads to eutrophication, pollution concentration, saline intrusion, and species loss. The coincidence of ecological stress and economic stress is clear in a number of river basins, including the Indus River and the Rio Grande.[78] The Indus River, which supports a population of 212 million, suffers severe scarcity for eight months of the year; local groundwater is also being seriously depleted. The combination of pressures is threatening potable water supplies and agricultural output, which could have profound effects on India's food supplies and welfare programs. Low water levels in the Rio Grande/Rio Bravo have led to concentrations of pollution high enough to cause fish kills. The lower river suffers from such high salinity levels that some 32 fish species have been displaced. And regional economic losses in irrigated agriculture resulting from water shortages are estimated at $135 million a year.[79]

Over the past decade, numerous studies have warned that growing water scarcity will be the cause of conflict or even war.[80] Several analysts have asserted that the next war will be over water in the Middle East. Nevertheless, a number of reviews have found that, although water disputes have led to local conflicts, they have not, historically, been the driving force behind international conflicts.

The point made by Homer-Dixon, however, is that although resource scarcity may not be the key driver of conflict, it can certainly contribute to security problems.

The U.S. intelligence community's concerns are reflected in the 2012 Global Water Security Assessment. This review predicts that by 2030 the world's annual global water requirements will exceed current sustainable water supplies by 40 percent. Absent any intervention, the report warns of widespread social and political instability and possible state failure. Four key points draw direct links between worsening water scarcity and U.S. security interests.

1. We assess that during the next 10 years, water problems will contribute to instability in states important to U.S. national security interests. Water shortages, poor water quality, and floods by themselves are unlikely to result in state failure. However, when combined with poverty, social tensions, environmental degradation, ineffectual leadership, and weak political institutions, water problems contribute to social disruption that can result in state failure.
2. We assess that a water-related state-on-state conflict is unlikely during the next 10 years. Historically, water tensions have led to more water-sharing agreements than violent conflicts. However, we judge that as water shortages become more acute beyond the next 10 years, water in shared basins will increasingly be used as leverage: the use of water as a weapon or to further terrorist objectives also will become more likely beyond 10 years.
3. We judge that during the next 10 years the depletion of groundwater supplies in some agricultural areas—owing to poor management—will pose a risk to both national and global food markets.
4. We assess that from now through 2040, water shortages and pollution probably will harm the economic performance of important trading partners.[81]

Short of war, in other words, water scarcity may have important effects on the sustainability and prosperity of many of the world's economies. In 2009, the World Economic Forum warned that lack of water will "soon tear into various parts of the global economic system."[82] Economic growth may already be constrained by water scarcity in California, China, India, Australia, and Indonesia,[83] and conflicts may arise in hard-hit places, including the Middle East and Haiti.

China and India, in particular, need to address problems of water scarcity and degradation in order to ensure food security and continued industrial growth. Water may prove to be the Achilles' heel of these rapidly growing countries. With 40 percent of the world's population, how these two countries address water scarcity matters at a global level. Of China's nearly 700 cities, some 60 percent are short of water; the Yellow River, China's second longest, now has only 10 percent of its natural flow. China has redeployed massive amounts of water from agriculture to industry to fuel growth and has invested heavily in dams and water transport systems. Nevertheless, surface water is insufficient and the country now draws on groundwater for one-fifth of its usage. Much less has been invested in efficiency. Industry uses an estimated 4 to 10 times as much water per unit of GDP as in other competitive economies. A full 20 percent of China's water use is to produce energy from coal. Agricultural use is also inefficient. About half of China's farmland is in the north of the country, a region that receives only 12 percent of the country's normal precipitation. Despite large investments, an estimated 45 percent of irrigation water is lost before reaching the farm. The large-scale infrastructure solutions that China has used to solve its water problems seem to be reaching their limits as dams, wells, and water diversions face increasing technical and political problems. Water conflicts have occurred at the local and regional levels in China.[84] In both India and China, water scarcity, if not adequately addressed, may lead to a decrease of 30–50 percent in production of rice and wheat.[85] Declines in agricultural or industrial production resulting from degradation or depletion of water supplies will affect global markets. Domestic shortages of water and food or even a substantial slowdown in economic growth could contribute to political instability. This issue is, of course, related to the issue of land grabs discussed above. As agricultural land in these heavily populated countries becomes less productive, they will need to turn elsewhere for food supplies.

While water use and allocation can lead to serious domestic disputes, they can also provoke international conflicts. More than 260 important river basins are shared by two or more countries; without good governance agreements, tensions are likely as supplies are reduced.[86] Places where tensions may run high include the United States and Mexico over the Colorado River; Bangladesh and India over the Ganges and Brahmaputra Rivers; China and Southeast Asia over the Mekong River; and Ethiopia and Egypt over the Nile River. However, some analysts assert that transnational water issues, rather than leading inevitably to conflict, can fuel cooperation and foment international agreements that help cement friendly relations between countries.[87] The very act of negotiating a treaty over water sharing can bring countries closer together on other issues.

Global Fish Stocks

The world's fisheries provide another example of the ways in which environmental scarcities and degradation can lead to economic constraints and instability. Marine and inland fisheries provide an important source of nutritious food, as well as livelihoods and income for much of the world's population. Capture fisheries and aquaculture together yielded 148 million tons of fish, worth about $217.5 billion, in 2010. Fish provide about 3 billion people with about 20 percent of their intake of animal protein and another 4.3 billion with 15 percent.

Fish and fishery products account for 10 percent of the world's agricultural trade and 1 percent of world trade.[88]

Yet, current use of the world's fisheries is not biologically sustainable. Production from capture fisheries has plateaued, and the quality of the catch is declining. There are no new major fishing grounds yet to be exploited.[89] A recent global assessment of the state of the world's fish stocks found 30 percent of fisheries overexploited, including stocks of most of the top 10 species, and 57 percent fully exploited.[90] Formal assessments, however, cover just the major stocks. A recent study found that 10,000 smaller fisheries account for 80 percent of the global fish catch.[91] Large predatory fish populations are down dramatically. Coral reefs are dying off, accompanied by the loss of many associated fish communities, and coastal and habitat degradation is taking a further toll.

Scarcity of fisheries resources is driven by the trio of drivers cited by Homer-Dixon—growing demand, institutions and governance systems inadequate to the task, and unequal access to fisheries. Population growth and economic growth have played a key role in the growing demand for fish and fishery products and will continue to drive increased demand. Fish supply, however, has outpaced population growth over the past five decades, as rising incomes have created growing local and global markets. The world per capita fish supply grew from 9.9 kilograms in 1960 to 18.4 kilograms in 2009. Asia accounts for the bulk of consumption, at 20.7 kilograms per capita.[92] Until the 1990s, this demand was largely met by capture fisheries. Over the past decade, growth in fish production has reflected rapidly expanding aquaculture, particularly in Asia, up twelvefold since 1980,[93] which entails its own set of environmental damages.

The globalization of commercial fishing, acceleration of the expansion of fishing into the high seas, and geographical expansion of infrastructure, operations, trade flows, and markets have been major factors driving increased global supply. Fish and fishery products are among the most widely traded food products, reaching a market value of over $100 billion.[94] The world's oversized fishing fleet, new technologies, and the rapid growth of aquaculture have allowed for this growth even as stocks have shrunk in many of the world's fisheries.

The 1982 United Nations Convention on the Law of the Sea (UNCLOS) lays out the rules of the game for international fisheries.[95] Under this treaty, the legal recognition of exclusive economic zones (EEZs) of 200 nautical miles vastly changed the situation for fisheries management. Although EEZs in many cases create the necessary resource rights for fisheries management, they have also created numerous conflicts where international boundaries overlap or are not recognized.[96] The famous Cod Wars between the United Kingdom and Iceland in the 1970s hinged on the question of the legal right of Iceland to exclude British fishing vessels from its EEZ.[97]

Coastal and inland fisheries are common pool resources, meaning that they are naturally open-access resources. A variety of governance mechanisms at the local, national, and international levels have been developed to define user rights for fisheries and to impose limits that are intended to prevent degradation. However, many fisheries remain open access and are suffering the consequences. Effective institutions for fisheries management must include a clear definition of resource rights and scientific knowledge of sustainable yields.

Small-scale fisheries, notably those within 10 miles of the coast, which account for half of the world's catch, are rarely assessed and are often subject to competing fishing efforts. Small-scale fishers often lose out to industrial fishers because they have less-powerful boats, less capital, and often less political clout that would enable them to protect their fishing rights.[98] Tropical resources may be the most threatened, given high human demand, emigration of fish resources, weak governance, and growing coastal populations. Climate change is likely to have disproportionate impacts on small-scale, local fisheries, further threatening communities that will face increased flooding, loss of infrastructure, and extreme weather events.

Fisheries ensure global food security. To continue to meet the world's expanding food requirements as the population heads toward 9 billion by 2050, fish landings will have to grow by 50 percent.[99] Given the constraints on agricultural production, increasing capture fisheries and aquaculture production by some 75 million tons of fish is a necessary element of ensuring future food security. Should climate change drag down production of grains, fisheries may need to grow even more.[100] Overexploited fisheries will only be able to produce more if they are allowed some time to recover. However, there is great uncertainty about how long recovery might take; the extent to which stocks will be able to recover, even under strong management schemes; and what the eventual maximum sustainable yield might be. Canadian cod fisheries are only now recovering after a 20-year moratorium. Economically and politically, many small-scale fisheries would not be able to bear the necessary reduction in catch and income required to allow for stock recovery.[101] In fact, pressures on these fisheries are likely to increase as populations continue to expand and as scarcity of agricultural resources drives more people to engage in fishing.

Further decline of the world's fisheries will have global consequences. Declining fisheries will reduce food security, particularly in some of the lowest-income countries, and contribute to rising food prices. Reduced income and employment in the fisheries sector will affect not only coastal communities but also broader economies. Instabilities and tensions arising from scarcity of this critical resource could lead to conflict. A recent study of the vulnerability of fishing nations, which considered the combination of dependence on fisheries, weak governance, and the likely impacts of climate change, ranked a number of countries of concern to the United States among the most vulnerable, including Pakistan, Eritrea, Haiti, Libya, North Korea, and the Gulf states.[102]

For the poor, degradation of local fish stocks will reduce food security directly. In the world's low-income, food-deficient countries, fish provides 22 percent of animal protein. Especially in coastal areas and near river systems, fish provide a low-cost food for the poor.[103] Of the 30 countries most dependent on fish as a protein source, all but four are developing countries.[104] Growing scarcity will be accompanied by rising prices, and declining availability of fish will affect nutrition, income, and employment, in turn affecting the ability to purchase food, in some of the world's most vulnerable countries. Already in many parts of sub-Saharan Africa and South Asia, fish consumption is low; expanding fisheries production is not increasing food security, as fish are being exported. In the case of the West African countries, access agreements with European and Asian countries allow those countries to harvest fish from Africa's EEZs,[105] decreasing the fish available to the local population.

To take one instance, depletion of near-shore fisheries in Southeast Asia has led to increased conflicts and social tensions that have been labeled "fish wars."[106] The coastal waters of the region are among the most productive and diverse in the world and are heavily used by small-scale fishers. With heavy local reliance on fish for food and income, fish stocks are down to 5–30 percent of the unexploited levels. Declining catches lead to more-destructive fishing efforts and greater competition among the users of the fishery. Disputes have become common, including at the international level, between Vietnam and Cambodia, and between the Philippines and China, over access to territorial waters.[107]

Such disputes may be caught up with larger claims on maritime resources, as they are in the South China Sea. Although the depletion of fisheries is affecting much of East and Southeast Asia, the South China Sea remains relatively rich in marine living resources. However, given the geography of the region, there is substantial overlap and controversy over the legal EEZs. With various countries, including China, the Philippines, Taiwan, Vietnam, Malaysia, and Brunei, claiming rights to small islands in the South China Sea, fishing rights in the EEZs and territorial waters are disputed. Interest in claiming these waters is high given that, in addition to rich fisheries, they likely contain valuable petroleum resources and allow for control of trade routes. Small-scale fishing incidents are common as declining fish stocks lead fishermen into disputed areas and to the capture of illegal species. In 2012, the Philippine Navy intercepted eight Chinese fishing boats in a disputed region, leading to a two-month standoff between the two countries. Fishing bans and arrests are often used as a proxy for sovereignty claims.[108] Increased militarization of the region makes disputes more difficult to resolve, and diplomatic standoffs are increasingly frequent. More than 500 million people live within 100 miles of the South China Sea coastline, an area that has been the hub of the Asian industrial revolution, and conflicts in the region can have major repercussions.[109]

In unstable countries, where communities lose their fisheries rights, more-serious security issues can arise. In Somalia, government collapse has been linked with loss of national control over the EEZ. The resulting influx of foreign vessels, conflicts between local fishers and outsiders, a devastating tsunami, and exorbitant prices charged by Somali warlords for fishing licenses led to a complete breakdown in fisheries management.[110] This governance collapse may well have led many fishers to turn to piracy as their fishing income fell and the economic benefits of piracy became clear. Beyond the problems created for international commerce, piracy in the region is now linked with Islamic fundamentalist groups.

Climate change will only aggravate the damage done by overfishing and coastal degradation. Already-rising ocean temperatures are disrupting ecosystems and forcing warm-water fish populations to shift their ranges toward the poles. Ocean acidification is threatening coral reefs and shellfish. Sea-level rise will also disturb fish habitats. Overfishing may be changing ecosystems in ways that may make them less resilient to further disturbance or climate change.[111] According to one projection, the United States may lose as much as 12 percent of its fisheries catch potential by 2050 as a result of climate change.[112] Although the long-term impact of these changes on fish populations is disputed, shifts and fluctuations in populations will certainly increase the difficulty of managing stocks for sustainability, and the risk exists of entire fisheries collapsing.

Homer-Dixon is cautious about making direct links between environmental scarcities, social conflicts, and violence.

> Although environmental scarcity has often spurred violence in the past, in coming decades the incidence of such violence will probably increase as scarcities of cropland, freshwater, and forests worsen in many parts of the developing world. Scarcity's role in such violence, however, is often obscure and indirect. It interacts with political, economic and other factors to generate harsh social effects that in turn help produce violence. Analysts often interpret these social effects as the conflicts' principal causes, thus overlooking scarcity's influence as an underlying stress.[113]

Cautious as Homer-Dixon may be, the impact of these scarcities is not lost on the U.S. intelligence community, which recognizes these stresses as underlying causalities of social conflict and potential state collapse.

Policy Response from the U.S. Government

Despite clear statements of concern from the military, the current U.S. government response to the growing scarcity of renewable environmental resources is as uneven and spotty as the presidential declarations expressed in the NSS. One of the most focused and perhaps productive U.S. government responses is coordinated under the aegis of the Senator Paul Simon Water for the Poor Act of 2005, which addresses water scarcities through a cross-agency program designed to increase "affordable and equitable access to safe drinking water and sanitation within the context of sound water resources management in developing countries." The program is implemented through the U.S. Agency for International Development (USAID), the MCC, and other government agencies working in

Asia, Latin America, and Africa. In 2009 alone, the U.S. government channeled $774 million for water and sanitation-related activities through USAID and MCC and provided additional assistance through 13 international organizations and seven multilateral development institutions as part of our international development assistance program. Since its creation in 2005, the MCC has invested "almost $1.3 billion in country-led water sector and sanitation related activities."[114]

The Feed the Future (FTF) initiative, which was launched by President Obama in 2010, coupled with the G-8's New Alliance for Food Security and Nutrition, provides another example of the U.S. government's commitment to address the causes of global poverty and the underlying issues related to the management of land and water. FTF is a $3.5 billion USAID program, to be implemented over 10 years, that focuses on investing in smallholder farmers, primarily in Africa but also in a few Asian countries and Central America. FTF takes the Green Revolution as its model, works to increase incomes through increased productivity, and aims to strengthen the entire agricultural food chain. The program recognizes that in order to sustainably meet the growing demand for food, productivity will need to increase with less water and other natural resource inputs, in the context of increased weather variability.[115] The program partners with governments, nongovernmental organizations, the private sector, and stakeholders to achieve its goals. The New Alliance was established by a pledge of $22 billion made by the G-8 in 2009. The New Alliance aims to support country-led agriculture and food security plans; links small-scale agriculturalists to the production capacities, technologies, and capital of larger agribusinesses to increase production; creates on-farm employment; and addresses the looming challenges of food security in vulnerable developing countries. Through partnership of the G-8 governments with African countries and the private sector, the Alliance has leveraged an additional $3 billion in private-sector investment to support agricultural development in Africa.

The U.S. government makes other substantial international investments in the conservation of natural resources primarily through USAID but also through the U.S. Fish and Wildlife Service, the U.S. Forest Service, and the U.S. National Park Service. These investments support sustainable use of natural resources, including biodiversity, timber, and fisheries. USAID's conservation investments for 2012 alone amounted to $200 million, much of it invested in Africa, Asia, and Latin America to support local and regional development through sustainable use of natural resources, with a strong focus on developing local capacity to govern and manage those resources. The United States also invests in international institutions and mechanisms that support sound resource use, notably the GEF, which was allocated almost $90 million in 2012. The GEF works to protect natural resources by helping countries improve environmental governance and seeking innovative ways to promote the sustainable use of natural resources in 155 countries.

Apart from international development assistance, the U.S. government is addressing resource depletion through a number of pieces of legislation, such as the Lacey Act, which seeks to control illegal logging. The United States also has treaties with several countries, including China and Indonesia, regarding cooperation on illegal logging. Trade agreements have provided another innovative means of addressing resource mismanagement. While trade agreements and sanctions have traditionally been used as a tool of foreign policy, beginning with NAFTA in the early 1990s, environmental chapters have been included in most bilateral and multilateral trade agreements. Intended primarily to prevent unfair competition from countries willing to degrade their own resources (with a view to pollution rather than overuse), these agreements oblige the participating countries to enforce their own environmental regulations and provide for public participation in environmental matters. However, countries still set their own regulations and, when it comes to enforcement, the agreements have few teeth. A few of the most recent agreements, notably the U.S.-Chile agreement and the U.S.-Peru agreement, have gone a step further, including measures to support cooperation on resource management and control illegal trade in timber and wildlife.

These signature programs are important both for their potential impacts on the ground and for galvanizing international support to address global environmental issues. Moreover, we need to recognize the leadership of the United States in shaping international environmental mechanisms, notably the GEF, whose formation was actively supported by the first Bush administration in 1992. But, however woven together and however portrayed to the public, these initiatives constitute, at best, a thin patchwork of separate programs and initiatives that lack continuity and cohesion. Even the most focused programs, for instance, those that address global water scarcity under the Water for the Poor Act, are channeled through a dozen or more entities with confusing, if not competing, approaches and implementation plans. The links between FTF and broader U.S. trade policy are nonexistent, as are the nigh invisible links to U.S.-supported programs managed under the multilateral development banks, including the World Bank. And more important is the lack of links with national security issues.

The Global Commons

Beyond nonrenewable and renewable resources lies a larger set of environmental resources known as the global commons: the oceans, the planet's atmosphere, biodiversity, and other environmental goods and services that are valuable to everyone. Scarcities of minerals and energy sources are driven by global markets; scarcities of renewable resources are caused largely by local practices, national policies and institutions, and a wide range of economic activities with very uneven influence. The global commons are transnational in nature although they are influenced by an infinite number of local and national actions that generate, in the aggregate, global impacts. Scarcities in the global commons create profound, life-altering impacts that affect all citizens albeit to different degrees and in different ways.

Environmental changes occurring at the planetary level have been analyzed through a remarkable research endeavor, headed by Johan Rockström and joined by 28 renowned scientists. The research concludes that the planet is now entering a new epoch in which "humans constitute the dominant driver of change to the Earth System."[116] They posit that we are now leaving the Holocene Epoch, a period having lasted some 10,000 years and characterized by a stable environment that allowed agriculture and stable societies to flourish. We are in full transition from that period of stability to the Anthropocene, whose beginning was marked by the Industrial Revolution in the mid-nineteenth century. In the Anthropocene, human behavior threatens to push the earth's ecological systems past dangerous thresholds into zones of ecological uncertainty characterized by abrupt, nonlinear ecological change. In their article "Planetary Boundaries: Exploring the Safe Operating Space for Humanity," Rockström et al. identify nine planetary boundaries that are normative judgments regarding what constitutes unacceptable human-induced global environmental change to the biophysical processes of the earth's systems.[117] Three of the planetary boundaries—climate change, ocean acidification, and stratospheric ozone—are systemic processes at the planetary level. The remaining six are global processes that are aggregated from local and regional changes. Following a careful presentation of the scientific data and normative judgments on which the planetary boundaries are established, the article concludes that

> on condition that these [planetary boundaries] are not transgressed for too long, humanity appears to have freedom to maneuver in the pursuit of long-term social and economic development with the stability domain provided by the observed resilience of the Earth System in the Holocene. [However] our preliminary analysis indicates that humanity has already transgressed three boundaries (climate change, the rate of biodiversity loss, and the rate of interference with the nitrogen cycle). There is significant uncertainty surrounding the duration over which boundaries can be transgressed before causing unacceptable environmental change and before triggering feedbacks that may result in crossing of thresholds that drastically reduce the ability to return to safe levels.[118]

Public resistance remains high in the United States to accepting the overwhelming scientific evidence that the planetary boundary of climate change has been crossed. The rest of the world has accepted the reality that human-generated carbon atmospheric loading will drive an increased rate of sea-level rise, increased bleaching and mortality of coral reefs, retreat of mountain glaciers and summer sea ice in the Arctic Ocean, loss of ice sheets in Greenland and the West Antarctic, and an increase in droughts and floods. The transgression of a second planetary boundary—global nitrogen and phosphorous cycles—is beyond dispute. Disruption of the global nitrogen and phosphorus cycles is a clear and deliberate outcome of human activity in that industrial-scale production of nitrogen, for example, was purposefully encouraged by governments around the world to increase the supply of food. Relative to a century ago, humans have increased the annual amount of nitrogen fixed on land by 150 percent, such that 40 percent of nitrogen in the protein we consume comes directly from deliberate applications of fertilizers along many global food chains.[119] Although industrial-scale nitrogen fixing has allowed steady growth of the global population, the downside of disrupting local, regional, and global biogeochemical balances is eutrophication and aquatic dead zones in river deltas, lakes, and rivers. Those changes, in turn, can contribute to nonlinear changes in terrestrial, aquatic, and marine systems and accelerate climate change. These changes are expressed in the alarming rate of biodiversity loss that constitutes the sixth major extinction process in the earth's history, although the current process is the first to be driven by the impacts of human activities. "Species loss affects both the functioning of ecosystems and their potential to respond and adapt to changes in physical and biotic conditions."[120]

The implications of transgressing the planetary boundaries are considerable. Transgressing one boundary, such as climate change, can generate unforeseen and dramatic changes in other boundaries, such as freshwater use and ocean acidification. Such changes can be abrupt and nonlinear, meaning that resulting changes can be immediate and at scales not suggested by gradual, linear changes. Transgressions signify a steady erosion of the planet's resiliency and ability to recover from severe impacts caused by extreme natural events. Taken as a whole, exceeding the planetary boundaries alters the self-regulating capacities of the earth's systems and poses direct yet unknown threats to the basic character and dynamics of the human enterprise.

The planetary boundaries analysis was complemented by an earlier international research program, the Millennium Ecosystem Assessment (MEA). That study, which involved thousands of scientists, contributes to our understanding of the link between environmental scarcity and security issues and, in particular, differential impacts of environmental degradation on the world's poor. The relation is framed by the MEA's first finding, which is supported by the planetary boundaries assessments and states that "humans have changed ecosystems more rapidly and extensively than in any comparable period of time in human history, largely to meet rapidly growing demands for food, fresh water, timber, fiber, and fuel."[121] The MEA affirms that ecosystem changes have played a central role in raising living standards and improving human well-being, although granted, future generations will not enjoy the same level of environmental benefits as those of us living today. A central conclusion of the study is that the overuse and degradation of ecosystems comes at a considerable cost not only for future generations but also for the poor and vulnerable today who live in communities across the developing world.

> The harmful effects of the degradation of ecosystem services (the persistent decrease in the capacity of an ecosystem to deliver services) are being borne disproportionately by the poor, are contributing to growing inequities and disparities across groups of people, and are sometimes the principal factor causing poverty and social conflict.[122]

This assessment elaborates on Homer-Dixon's analysis on two levels. First, it highlights the dynamics of resource capture and ecological marginalization, particularly given that the livelihoods of some 2 billion rural poor around the planet largely depend on direct access to ecosystem services provided by forests, mangroves, pastures, watersheds, and fishing grounds. Second, it underlines the complex dynamics between environmental scarcity, poverty, social conflict, and international security issues. The MEA's conclusion that degradation of ecosystems around the world "could grow significantly worse" during the coming decades does not bode well for either the environmental integrity of the planet or social stability in many countries.

The consequences of these environmental transgressions and differential impacts on human societies are becoming more clearly understood by the national intelligence community. Remarking on one of those planetary boundaries, climate change, Dr. Thomas Fingar, chairman of the National Intelligence Council, in testimony before the House Permanent Select Committee on Intelligence in June 2008, stated,

> We judge that global climate change will have wide-ranging implications for U.S. national security interests over the next 20 years. Although the United States will be less affected and is better equipped than most nations to deal with climate change, and may even see a benefit owing to increases in agriculture productivity, infrastructure repair and replacement will be costly. We judge that the most significant impact for the United States will be indirect and result from climate-driven effects on many other countries and their potential to seriously affect U.S. national security interests. From a national security perspective, climate change has the potential to affect lives (for example, through food and water shortages, increased health problems including the spread of disease and increased potential for conflict), property (for example, through ground subsidence, flooding, coastal erosion, and extreme weather events), and other security interests. The United States depends on a smooth-functioning international system ensuring the flow of trade and market access to critical raw materials such as oil and gas, and security for its allies and partners. Climate change and climate change policies could affect all of these—domestic

stability in a number of key states, the opening of new sea lanes and access to raw materials, and the global economy more broadly with significant geopolitical consequences.[123]

U.S. Policy and the Global Commons

President George H.W. Bush responded to the problems of the global commons in the early 1990s by actively contributing to the international community's efforts to craft international agreements and financial mechanisms to address environmental degradation and climate change. President Bill Clinton, in turn, framed his strategic response by elevating sustainable development as a strategic pillar of U.S. security. But since the presidency of George W. Bush, the United States not only has remained on the margins of the international response to the burgeoning global environmental crisis but also has resisted active participation in a range of international initiatives. Such initiatives include the international efforts that embrace the MEA recommendations and international climate change negotiations.

Early in his administration, President Obama sent promising signs of U.S. reengagement in international climate negotiations and other global environmental initiatives. His policies were announced through the Global Climate Change Initiative that was issued in the lead-up to the 2009 Copenhagen Conference and set forth ambitious goals for promoting clean energy, reducing emissions from deforestation and degradation, and increasing climate resilience. Action on that major policy initiative pivoted on the passage of a domestic energy and climate bill that would provide the resources, incentives, and strategy to diminish U.S. greenhouse gas emissions and increase use of nonfossil fuels. Congressional defeat of comprehensive climate and energy policy in 2010 obliged the Obama administration to temporarily pull back from its international commitments and to scale back a range of domestic policies designed to shift the country's energy foundations away from petroleum and imported oil in particular. That initial setback notwithstanding, in subsequent years President Obama has pursued a domestic climate policy that relies on regulatory change to reduce greenhouse gas (GHG) emissions from new and old power plants, strengthen fuel economy standards, incentivize innovation in renewable energy, and prepare the country for the domestic impacts of climate change. Despite intense domestic polarization on environmental issues, including concerted efforts to discredit the scientific foundations of climate change, these regulatory efforts coupled with technological innovation on shale gas extraction have allowed the U.S. to stay on track to meet international climate obligations. While remaining a viable partner in global environmental issues, the United States faces innumerable environmental challenges at home and abroad that pose direct and growing threats to our prosperity. Overcoming domestic political polarization on environmental issues remains the principal obstacle to allowing our government to assume a global leadership function to address the new challenges to our economic well-being and national security.

Notes

1 www.fao.org/climatechange/54270/en/.
2 A country is said to experience water stress when annual water supplies fall below 1,700 cubic meters per person. Levels below 1,000 cubic meters per person are considered water scarcity. Today this includes about 37 countries (World Water Council).
3 www.fao.org/worldfoodsummit/english/fsheets/environment.pdf.
4 www.fao.org/newsroom/common/ecg/1000505/en/stocks.pdf.
5 Johan Rockström et al., "Planetary Boundaries: Exploring the Safe Operating Space for Humanity," *Ecology and Society* 14, no. 2 (2009), www.ecologyandsociety.org/vol14/iss2/art32/main.html.
6 Jonathan Foley, "Boundaries for a Healthy Planet," *Scientific American* 302, no. 4 (2010): 54–7.
7 Admiral Mike Mullen, "Rostov Lecture Series on International Affairs," Lecture (Johns Hopkins School of Advanced International Studies, March 3, 2011).
8 John McHugh, Testimony before the Senate Committee on Appropriations, Subcommittee on Defense, May 18, 2011.
9 Jorgen Randers, *2052: A Global Forecast for the Next Forty Years* (Chelsea Green, White River Junction, VT, 2012).
10 Roger Altman and Richard Haass, "American Profligacy and American Power," *Foreign Affairs* 89, no. 6 (2010): 25–34.
11 Michael Mandelbaum, *Frugal Superpower* (Perseus Books, New York, 2010); Adam Quinn, "The Art of Declining Politely: Obama's Prudent Presidency and the Waning of American Power," *International Affairs* 87, no. 4 (2011): 803–24.
12 David Rothkopf, "Justify My Love," *Foreign Policy* (July 24, 2010), www.foreignpolicy.com/articles/2010/07/24/Justifymylove.
13 Joseph Parent and Paul MacDonald, "The Wisdom of Retrenchment," *Foreign Affairs* 90, no. 6 (2011): 32–50.
14 Dennis Blair, Testimony before the Senate Select Committee on Intelligence, Feb. 12, 2009.
15 Hillary Clinton, "America's Pacific Century: The Future of Politics Will Be Decided in Asia, Not Afghanistan or Iraq, and the United States Will Be Right at the Center of the Action," *Foreign Policy* (Nov. 2011), 1–14.
16 Ronald Reagan, *National Security Strategy of the United States* (White House, Washington, D.C., 1987): 5.
17 Ronald Reagan, *National Security Strategy of the United States* (White House, Washington, D.C., 1988): 6.
18 Reagan, *National Security Strategy of the United States* (1988): 37.
19 George H. W. Bush, *National Security Strategy of the United States* (White House, Washington, D.C., 1991): 2.
20 Bush, *National Security Strategy of the United States* (1991).
21 Bush, *National Security Strategy of the United States* (1991): 2.
22 Bush, *National Security Strategy of the United States* (1991): 22.
23 Bush, *National Security Strategy of the United States* (1991).
24 Daniel Yergin, *The Quest* (Penguin Books, New York, 2011): 469.
25 William Clinton, *A National Security Strategy for a New Century* (White House, Washington, D.C., 1999): 21.
26 Clinton, *A National Security Strategy for a New Century* (1999): 25.

27 Clinton, *A National Security Strategy for a New Century* (1999): 24.
28 William Clinton, *A National Security Strategy of Engagement and Enlargement* (White House, Washington, D.C., 1994): 15.
29 Clinton, *A National Security Strategy for a New Century* (1999): 25.
30 William Clinton, *A National Security Strategy for a Global Age* (White House, Washington, D.C., 2000).
31 George W. Bush, *National Security Strategy* (White House, Washington, D.C., 2002): 2.
32 G.W. Bush, *National Security Strategy* (2002): 19.
33 George W. Bush, *The National Security Strategy of the United States of America* (White House, Washington, D.C., 2006): 28.
34 Barack Obama, *National Security Strategy* (White House, Washington, D.C., 2010).
35 Obama, *National Security Strategy,* 47.
36 Obama, *National Security Strategy,* 34.
37 U.S. Congress, *President's Materials Policy Commission (Paley Commission)* (U.S. Congress, Washington, D.C., U.S. Printing Office, 1952).
38 U.S. Congress, *Paley Commission,* 1.
39 U.S. Congress, *Paley Commission.*
40 Larry Bradfish, "United States Strategic Mineral Policy," *Loyola of Los Angeles Law Review* (Nov. 1987): 113.
41 Eduardo Galeano, *Open Veins of Latin America* (Monthly Review Press, New York, 1997).
42 Michael Klare, *Resource Wars* (Henry Holt, New York, 2001).
43 "Downhill Cycling: A Peak May Be in Sight for Commodity Prices," *Economist* (July 28, 2012).
44 Stephen Morse, "China's Monopoly on Rare Earth Mining and Exports Erodes," *Atlantic* (Sept. 27, 2012).
45 Kent Butts, Brent Bankus, and Adam Norris, "Strategic Minerals: Is China's Consumption a Threat to United States Security?" (Center for Strategic Leadership, U.S. Army War College, 2011).
46 Butts et al., "Strategic Minerals."
47 Jeffrey Krautkraemer, "Economics of Natural Resource Scarcity: The State of the Debate," RFF Discussion Paper 05–14 (Resources for the Future, Washington, D.C., 2005).
48 Michael Klare, *The Race for What's Left* (Metropolitan Books, New York, 2012); Dambisa Moyo, *Winner Takes All* (Basic Books, New York, 2012).
49 Jimmy Carter, State of the Union address (Washington, D.C., Jan. 23, 1980).
50 On military transfers to the Gulf, see Klare, *Resource Wars,* 66–7. See also Daniel Yergin, *The Prize* (Simon & Schuster, New York, 2009): 626.
51 Yergin, *The Prize.*
52 Yergin, *The Prize,* 754.
53 Yergin, *The Prize,* 160–88.
54 Yergin, *The Quest,* 192.
55 Yergin, *The Prize,* 8–105.
56 Yergin, *The Prize,* 599.
57 Hydro, natural gas, and nuclear power add the remaining 10 percent.
58 Clifford Krauss, "U.S. Reliance on Saudi Oil Goes Back Up," *New York Times* (Aug. 17, 2012).
59 RAND Corporation, "Does Imported Oil Threaten U.S. National Security?" Research Brief (RAND Corporation, Santa Monica, CA, 2009).

60 Yergin, *The Prize,* 239.
61 Thomas Homer-Dixon, *Environment, Scarcity, and Violence* (Princeton University Press, Princeton, NJ, 1999).
62 Homer-Dixon, *Environment, Scarcity, and Violence,* 12.
63 Homer-Dixon, *Environment, Scarcity, and Violence,* 177.
64 Michael Kugelman and Susan Levenstein, eds., "Land Grabs? The Race for the World's Farmland" (Woodrow Wilson Center, Washington, D.C., 2012): 10, www.wilsoncenter.org/publication/land-grab-the-race-for-the-worlds-farmland-0; Fred Pearce, *The Land Grabbers* (Random House, New York, 2012).
65 Joachim von Braun, *Are Food-Security Risks for Poor People on the Rise?* (International Food Policy Research Institute, Washington, D.C., 2009).
66 Klare, *The Race for What's Left,* 183–208.
67 Kugelman and Levenstein, "Land Grabs?"
68 www.fao.org/worldfoodsummit/english/fsheets/environment.pdf.
69 Joachim von Braun et al., *The Economics of Land Degradation* (University of Bonn, Bonn, 2012).
70 Kugelman and Levenstein, "Land Grabs?", 53.
71 A.Y. Hoekstra et al., "Global Monthly Water Scarcity: Blue Water Footprints versus Blue Water Availability," *PLOS ONE* (Feb. 29, 2012), www.plosone.org/article/info%3Adoi%2F10.1371%2Fjournal.pone.0032688.
72 Hoekstra et al., "Global Monthly Water Scarcity."
73 World Resources Institute (WRI), *Millennium Ecosystem Assessment* (WRI, Washington, D.C., 2005), www.maweb.org/documents/document.358.aspx.pdf.
74 The more standard measure is extraction rates, but this does not account for water that is returned to the natural system. Studies estimating extraction rates credit about 70 percent to agriculture, 20 percent to industry, and 10 percent to domestic consumption.
75 These 400 rivers account for 65 percent of the world's population and 75 percent of the world's irrigated area.
76 www.water.usgs.gov/edu/sc1.html.
77 http://articles.mercola.com/sites/articles/archive/2008/09/09/world-water-crisis-underlies-world-food-crisis.aspx.
78 Hoekstra et al., "Global Monthly Water Scarcity."
79 Hoekstra et al., "Global Monthly Water Scarcity."
80 See, for example, Klare, *Resource Wars*; Pearce, *The Land Grabbers*; Ken Conca, *Governing Water: Contentious Transnational Politics and Global Institution Building* (MIT Press, Cambridge, MA, 2006); Peter Rogers and Susan Leal, *Running Out of Water: The Looming Crisis and Solutions to Conserve Our Most Precious Resource* (St. Martin's Press, New York, 2010); Steven Solomon, *Water: The Epic Struggle for Wealth, Power and Civilization* (HarperCollins, New York, 2010).
81 National Intelligence Council (NIC), *Global Water Security* (NIC, Washington, D.C., 2012).
82 *The Bubble Is Close to Bursting: A Forecast of the Main Economic and Geopolitical Water Issues Likely to Arise in the World during the Next Two Decades.* 2009 World Economic Forum Annual Meeting.
83 www.unesco.org/new/en/natural-sciences/environment/water/wwap/wwdr/wwdr3–2009/downloads-wwdr3/.
84 Alex Crawford, Oli Brown, and Van Yand, *Growing into Risk: Emerging Environment and Security Issues in China* (IISD Publications Center, Winnipeg, 2006).

85 Roger Thurow, "The Fertile Continent: Africa, Agriculture's Final Frontier," *Foreign Affairs* (Nov./Dec. 2010), www.foreignaffairs.com/articles/66827/roger-thurow/the-fertile-continent.
86 Stewart Patrick, "The Coming Global Water Crisis," *Atlantic* (May 9, 2012), www.theatlantic.com/international/archive/2012/05/the-coming-global-water-crisis/256896/.
87 Geoffrey Dabelko et al., "Navigating Peace Initiative Briefs" (Woodrow Wilson Center, Washington, D.C., 2006): 200, www.wilsoncenter.org/sites/default/files/ECSPReport13_NavigatingPeace.pdf.
88 Food and Agriculture Organization (FAO), *State of World Fisheries and Aquaculture* (FAO, Rome, 2012).
89 C. Frid and O. Paramor, "Feeding the World: What Role for Fisheries?" *ICES Journal of Marine Science* 69, no. 2 (2012): 145–50.
90 FAO, *State of World Fisheries and Aquaculture.*
91 C. Costello et al., "Status and Solutions for the World's Unassessed Fisheries," *Science* 338, no. 6106 (2012): 517–20.
92 FAO, *State of World Fisheries and Aquaculture.*
93 FAO, *State of World Fisheries and Aquaculture.* Because some aquaculture production relies on inputs (fish meal) from the capture fisheries sector, the increase in available food fish is less (Frid and Paramor, "Feeding the World").
94 FAO, *State of World Fisheries and Aquaculture.*
95 The United States has not ratified UNCLOS but recognizes the treaty as a codification of customary international law.
96 R. Pomeroy et al., "Fish Wars: Conflict and Collaboration in Fisheries Management in Southeast Asia," *Marine Policy* 31 (2007): 645–56; K. Miller and G. Munro, "Cooperation and Conflict in the Management of Transboundary Fishery Resources," paper prepared for the 2nd World Congress of the American and European Association of Environmental and Resource Economics, Monterey, CA (June 2002); Morse, "China's Monopoly on Rare Earth Mining."
97 Trade and Environment Database, "The Cod War," Case Study No. 402, www1.american.edu/ted/icefish.htm.
98 Marine Resources Assessment Group (MRAG), "Fisheries and Food Security," Policy Brief 3 (Department for International Development, United Kingdom, 2010), www.mrag.co.uk/Documents/PolicyBrief3_Food_Security.pdf.
99 J. Rice and S. Garcia, "Fisheries, Food Security, Climate Change, and Biodiversity: Characteristics of the Sector and Perspectives on Emerging Issues," *ICES Journal of Marine Science* 68 (2011): 1343–53.
100 Rice and Garcia, "Fisheries, Food Security."
101 Rice and Garcia, "Fisheries, Food Security."
102 M. Huelsenbeck, "Ocean-Based Food Security Threatened in a High CO_2 World: A Ranking of Nations' Vulnerability to Climate Change and Ocean Acidification," *Oceana* (Sept. 2012).
103 MRAG, "Fisheries and Food Security."
104 FAO, *State of World Fisheries and Aquaculture.*
105 M. Smith et al., "Policy Forum: Sustainability and Global Seafood," *Science* 327 (12, 2010): 784–86.
106 Pomeroy et al., "Fish Wars."
107 Pomeroy et al., "Fish Wars."

108 Beina Xu, "South China Sea Tensions," Council on Foreign Relations (Jan. 11, 2013), www.cfr.org/china/south-china-sea-tensions/p29790.
109 Xu, "South China Sea Tensions."
110 A. Arky, "Trading Nets for Guns: The Impact of Illegal Fishing on Piracy in Somalia," Security Studies thesis, Naval Postgraduate School (2010).
111 G.T. Crothers and L. Nelson, "High Seas Fisheries Governance: A Framework for the Future?" *Marine Resource Economics* 21 (2007): 341–53.
112 Huelsenbeck, "Ocean-Based Food Security Threatened."
113 Homer-Dixon, *Environment, Scarcity, and Violence,* 177.
114 U.S. Department of State, *Senator Paul Simon Water for the Poor Act: Report to Congress,* June 2010.
115 Towards the Future We Want, End Hunger and Make the Transition to Sustainable Agricultural and Food Systems, www.feedthefuture.gov/.
116 Johan Rockström et al., "A Safe Operating Space for Humanity," *Nature* 461 (2009): 472–75, www.nature.com/nature/journal/v461/n7263/full/461472a.html.
117 Rockström et al., "Planetary Boundaries."
118 The nine planetary boundaries are atmospheric aerosol loading, chemical pollution, climate change, ocean acidification, stratospheric ozone depletion, nitrogen/phosphorous cycles, global freshwater use, change in land use, and biodiversity loss.
119 Rockström et al., "Planetary Boundaries"; Jonathan Foley et al., "Solutions for a Cultivated Planet," *Nature* 478, no. 7369 (2011), www.nature.com/nature/journal/v478/n7369/full/nature10452.html.
120 Rockström et al., "A Safe Operating Space."
121 WRI, *Millennium Ecosystem Assessment,* v.
122 WRI, *Millennium Ecosystem Assessment,* 2.
123 Statement for the Record of Dr. Thomas Fingar before the Permanent Select Committee on Intelligence and the Select Committee on Energy Independence and Global Warming, June 25, 2008.

PART II

Country and Regional Studies

INTRODUCTION

David Reed

Guaranteeing America's prosperity requires ensuring the country's geostrategic security in the face of external threats, ensuring the sustained provision of the goods and services needed to provide U.S. citizens with a high standard of living, and maintaining international coordination and market mechanisms built on democratic and transparent governance arrangements.

In the past, the United States was able to obtain nonrenewable resources for its industrial economy thanks to its dominant position in the global economy, which was reinforced by the ability to project power around the globe. The evidence presented in the preceding chapter emphasizes a new set of challenges arising from environmental change and natural resource scarcities that pose immediate and longer-term threats to the country's prosperity and national security. The principal challenge today arises not from nonrenewable resource constraints but rather from global environmental changes and diminished provision of renewable resources—notably water, productive soils, forests, clean air, fisheries, and mangroves, among others.

In this new context, America's prosperity depends directly on the prosperity and stability of the full range of its trading and political partners, which, in turn, depend on the integrity and sustainability of their respective national and regional environments. Unless partner and competing countries ensure the sustainability of the environmental goods and services on which their economic productivity and social cohesion depend, America's prosperity will be diminished. Water depletion in China and India, deforestation in Brazil and Congo, exhaustion of fishing stocks in the South China Sea and along the coast of East Africa, and the melting tundra in the Russian Arctic are among the environmental changes besetting vital contributors to the global economy. Such environmental issues pose long-term challenges to America's prosperity because they promise to weaken the economic fabric and undermine the social stability of these key U.S. trading and political partners and the stability of the regional cooperation on which America's prosperity depends.

This section of the book presents the research of analysts having combined expertise in international affairs and environmental policy in nine selected countries and regions. The four major emerging economies of China, India, Mexico, and Brazil, each with unique and growing environmental problems, are of strategic importance to the United States and the world economy more generally. Several developing countries, including Pakistan, the Democratic Republic of Congo, and the countries on the coast of East Africa, must address growing environmental and social stability challenges that have direct effects on U.S. regional interests. In addition, studies on the Russian Arctic and the South China Sea describe dramatic environmental and geostrategic changes in two regions of vital importance to the United States. Although these countries and regions are not fully inclusive of U.S. interests overseas, they bring into focus the key issues and challenges the United States will continue to face in the coming years.

The authors of the case studies were provided five guiding issues to analyze, as follows:

1. Review the main contours of past and current U.S. foreign policy toward the country.
2. Provide an analysis of ongoing and anticipated environmental changes that are likely to take hold in the country.
3. Provide an analysis of the impacts and consequences of those changes on the specific country or region.
4. Evaluate the direct impacts and longer-term significance of those changes for U.S. economic, security, and social interests.
5. In light of this analysis, provide recommendations for changes or improvements in U.S. foreign policy toward the country or region.

The experts followed analytical paths tailored to the history and conditions in their respective country or region. Their unique findings delineate a broader mosaic of impacts and consequences for the United States, which are summarized in Section III, "Changing Landscapes," and support the development of the specific recommendations provided in the concluding chapter.

2

THROUGH THE ARCTIC LOOKING GLASS AND WHAT THE U.S.-RUSSIAN RELATIONSHIP FOUND THERE

*Heather A. Conley and Lev Neretin**

One of the greatest strategic accomplishments of U.S. domestic and foreign policy occurred in 1867 when, for a mere $7.2 million (roughly $120 million in today's dollars), the United States purchased the Territory of Alaska from Russia. This move both significantly increased the country's size, adding a territory nearly twice the size of Texas, and substantially increased America's wealth as gold and North Slope oil were later discovered in the new territory. The Alaska Purchase, as it was known, also allowed the United States to become an Arctic coastal state with the added benefit of having a mere 53 miles separating the borders of the United States and Russia in the Bering Strait.

America's Arctic acquisition has added new dimensions to the complex U.S.-Russian relationship and significantly shaped its course over nearly two centuries, turning the Arctic into an accurate bellwether of bilateral relations. From the earliest days of the gold rush of the 1890s to the new twenty-first century rush to discover oil, gas, and mineral resources in a rapidly melting Arctic, economic interests have proven to be a powerful force for development in the region and motivation for advancing Arctic policy in both countries. The estimated 90 billion barrels of oil and 47 trillion cubic meters of natural gas now believed to be located in the Arctic have heightened the region's significance.[1]

Overview of U.S. Foreign Policy Toward the Russian Arctic

Geopolitical and military dynamics and the Arctic's geostrategic location have profoundly shaped the Arctic during the past 70 years. During World War II, the Arctic symbolized the close wartime alliance between the then Soviet Union and the United States, serving as a supply lifeline to the Russian Eastern Front via the Port of Murmansk. However, as the wartime allies transformed into Cold War archenemies, the Arctic region again reflected contemporary geopolitical times, serving as an "Ice Curtain" between the two superpowers. The United States constructed the distant early warning line, which provided continental defense against Soviet attack. Likewise, the Soviets developed their strategic submarine-based nuclear deterrent in the Murmansk-based Northern Fleet. U.S. and Soviet strategic bombers patrolled over the Arctic ice and their submarines stealthily hid beneath the ice cover.

However, as the Berlin Wall fell and Soviet President Mikhail Gorbachev's perestroika reforms were undertaken, the geopolitical ice in the Arctic began to melt figuratively between the two superpowers, and the region reflected both the increased uncertainty and the promise of a new direction in the relationship. Shortly before the dissolution of the Soviet Union, the United States and the Union of Soviet Socialist Republics (USSR) negotiated the Baker-Shevardnadze Agreement, a clear boundary delimitation treaty for the Arctic Ocean, the Bering Sea, and the northern Pacific Ocean. The agreement represented a compromise for both countries, with both sides signaling willingness to reduce the extent of previous territorial claims. Nevertheless, the agreement granted the United States control of a larger area in the Bering Sea than it would have if the agreement had been based on the equidistant line principle normally used in boundary disputes.[2] Signed on June 1, 1990, and ratified by the U.S. Senate on September 16, 1991, the agreement was not subsequently ratified by the Russian Duma, which cited this inequity and the loss of rich fishing grounds.[3] Later, the Duma argued that USSR Foreign Minister Eduard Shevardnadze failed to effectively represent Russian interests in the negotiations. The Duma called for the Russian need to secure cross-border quotas for its vessels and to gain access to Alaska's pollack stocks.[4] The United States ultimately rejected the Russian requests to renegotiate these aspects of the agreement. However, the Russian Federation informed the U.S. government on January 13, 1992, that the Russian Federation "continues to perform the rights and fulfill the obligations flowing from the international agreements" signed by the Soviet Union, making clear that Russia applies the maritime boundary agreement on a provisional basis.[5]

After the collapse of the Soviet Union in December 1991, the United States and Russia had largely abandoned, yet by no means completely, their Cold War military architecture and hardware in the Arctic. The Russian military atrophied because of the collapse of the Soviet economy, and the United States significantly downsized its military presence in Alaska. As the United States and Russia began a new era in bilateral relations, economic and people-to-people projects were developed between the state of Alaska and the oblasts of the Russian Far East, in particular the Chukotka region. International efforts were also undertaken to remediate the Cold War's environmental legacy, particularly in the Russian Arctic. One such example was the Arctic Military Environmental Cooperation Program (AMEC). Created in 1996, AMEC was a collaborative effort between the United States, Norway, and Russia that sought to

> advance U.S. national security interests through the environmentally safe, accountable reduction of Russian naval nuclear forces in Northwest Russia, constructive engagement between U.S., the United Kingdom, Norwegian and Russian military forces and the advancement of sustainable military use of the Arctic region.[6]

AMEC focused on developing technology and capacity for transportation and treatment of radioactive waste. A decade later, AMEC had successfully completed eight initial projects in the region, although the United States and Norway were no longer active participants.[7]

For Russia, the Arctic is a key driver of twenty-first-century Russian policy. As Russian President Medvedev noted in 2008, "Our first and main task is to turn the Arctic into a resource base for Russia in the twenty-first century. . . . Using these resources will guarantee energy security for Russia as a whole."[8] Home to Russia's strategic nuclear fleet, as well as 14 percent of Russia's gross domestic product (GDP) and 25 percent of its exports,[9] the Russian Arctic holds

80 percent of Russia's natural gas, 90 percent of its nickel and cobalt, and 60 percent of its copper.[10] Russia's economic development and security strategies in this resource-rich territory will be an important bellwether as to how Russia's leadership will steer its economy and, subsequently, its future.

The American Arctic also holds economic significance. Between 1980 and 2000, the North Slope oil fields generated an average of 20 percent of the nation's domestic oil production, and Alaska currently accounts for 13.2 percent of U.S. production.[11] The Alaskan Arctic is believed to be home to 17.6 percent of the world's undiscovered hydrocarbon resources, roughly 72.7 billion barrels of oil equivalent, making it the second most prospective Arctic province behind the West Siberian Basin.[12] The Bureau of Ocean Energy Management estimates that approximately 26 billion barrels of oil and 131 trillion cubic feet of gas resources are technically recoverable in undiscovered fields within Alaska's outer continental shelf.[13] Mineral resources are also a critical component of the Alaskan Arctic, with exports of these materials generating $1.3 billion and accounting for 36.8 percent of Alaska's foreign export earnings in 2010.[14] The Red Dog Mine in Alaska is the second-largest producer of zinc in the world, accounting for 79 percent of U.S. zinc production. It is also the fourth-largest producer of lead in the world (33 percent of U.S. production).[15] Alaska's commercial fisheries bring in $5.8 billion annually to the state's economy,[16] and Alaskan tourism generates more than $2 billion annually.[17] These figures illustrate the extent and richness of the economic drivers and resources in this vast U.S. territory.

Increased economic activity in the Arctic will physically draw both the United States and Russia into closer coordination and cooperation. This is especially the case where the U.S. and Russian borders meet in the Bering Strait, a major passage for ship traffic to and from the resource-rich Arctic and the Diomede Islands. Managing the increase in human and commercial traffic through this strait will be a key test to the relationship between the two countries, requiring mutual understanding and the establishment of a comprehensive approach to environmental regulations and safety. Clear governance of the maritime border on the Bering Sea, the Bering Strait, and the Chukchi Sea will be paramount to U.S. policies toward the Russian Arctic throughout the twenty-first century.

Encouragingly, there already has been extensive cooperation for and coordination of management of the Bering Strait between the Russian Federal Border Service (RFBS) and the U.S. Coast Guard (USCG), particularly USCG District 17, which operates in Alaska and the North Pacific. Since 1991, there have been numerous port visits along with extensive joint operations.[18] The signing of an October 1995 memorandum of understanding by Admiral Robert E. Kramek of the USCG and General Nikolayev, director of the RFBS, set the framework for maritime cooperation between the two countries, particularly with regard to search and rescue and maritime law enforcement, which continues to this day.[19] The USCG and the RFBS have developed a combined operations manual to facilitate bilateral operations between the two organizations regarding use-of-force policies, communications, logistics, and other substantive operational issues.[20] In 1997, both services agreed to start sharing law enforcement information pertaining to fisheries, such as vessel locations, and planned for 1998 fisheries law enforcement operations in the Bering Sea and the northwest Pacific Ocean.[21] Coordination was further refined following the 2001 protocol to the 1995 pact, which more effectively combined maritime law enforcement in the North Pacific. This included improvements in search-and-rescue operations, protection of the 200-mile exclusive economic zones, prevention of terrorism and smuggling at sea, and maritime border security.[22] To optimize this cooperation in the Bering Strait, both nations continue to exchange personnel and conduct combined training operations in the area.[23]

On August 6, 2012, while testifying before the Senate Appropriations Subcommittee on Homeland Security in Alaska, USCG Commandant Admiral Robert Papp reiterated this cooperation. He stated that the USCG

> maintains communications and working relationships with Canadian and Russian agencies responsible for regional operations including search and rescue, law enforcement and oil spill response. We maintain bilateral response relationships with Canada and Russia, and last month we hosted representatives from the Russian State Marine Pollution Control Salvage and Rescue Administration (SMPCSRA) to sign an expanded Memorandum of Understanding and Joint Contingency Plan to foster closer cooperation in oil spill response. We will continue to engage Arctic nations, international organizations, industry, academia and Alaskan state, local and tribal governments to strengthen our partnerships and inter-operability.[24]

These statements drive home the importance of the mutually beneficial collaboration between the United States and Russia in the Arctic.

Long-standing bilateral cooperation in the search-and-rescue arena was both the foundation for and a driver of the larger multilateral effort by the member states of the Arctic Council to develop an international search-and-rescue agreement. At the Arctic Council Ministerial in Nuuk, Greenland, on May 12, 2011, the intergovernmental forum delivered the Agreement on Cooperation on Aeronautical and Maritime Search and Rescue in the Arctic. The signing of the Search and Rescue (SAR) agreement was a landmark event, as it represented the first legally binding instrument negotiated under the auspices of the Arctic Council and the first time such a document had been negotiated by all eight Arctic states.[25,26] Russia and the United States co-chaired the task force that negotiated this agreement, which was first introduced at the April 2009 Arctic Council ministerial meeting. The agreement defines regions of the Arctic where each signatory has primary responsibility for organizing SAR response. It also commits each party to provide SAR assistance, case-specific details, and information on

SAR facilities. In addition, each party is required to exchange knowledge regarding fueling, supply, and medical facilities, and to train relevant personnel.[27] The first Arctic Council SAR exercise took place on October 4–6, 2011, in Whitehorse, Yukon. The exercise focused on strategic and operational aspects of aeronautical and maritime SAR in the Arctic.[28] During September 10–14, 2012, the eight Arctic states participated in SAREX 2012, the first live SAR exercise held in "stormy weather and high seas in a remote area along Greenland's east coast."[29] The exercise, which consisted of a full-scale operation to locate a cruise ship in distress and evacuate its passengers and crew, tested not only the countries' SAR assets and equipment but also multilateral coordination with respect to communication and operational procedures.[30]

Given the positive momentum of the SAR agreement, the Arctic Council has pushed forward plans to create a second legally binding agreement dealing with oil spill response cooperation. The May 2012 Nuuk Declaration called for the establishment of a task force to develop "an international instrument on Arctic marine oil pollution preparedness and response" and called for relevant working groups to formulate recommendations and best practices to prevent marine oil pollution.[31] Co-chaired by the United States, Russia, and Norway, initial meetings of the oil spill task force took place in Anchorage, St. Petersburg, and Oslo, respectively.[32] USCG Rear Admiral Cari Thomas, in charge of the U.S. delegation, has expressed her belief that the agreement will require all eight Arctic nations to develop response systems, notification procedures, and joint training and exercises for oil spill response.[33] At the May 2013 Arctic Council Ministerial in Kiruna, a second internationally binding agreement, the Agreement on Cooperation on Marine Oil Pollution Preparedness and Response in the Arctic, was signed by the eight member states and commits the signatories to work together to clean up any oil spill that may take place in the Arctic region. The Arctic Council ministers from each nation signed the agreement, and the process of treaty ratification and deposit, which is required for the treaty to go into force. Ambassador David Balton, the U.S. co-chair of the task force that produced the agreement, expressed confidence that the ratification process would be concluded within a year.[34]

Both the SAR agreement and the oil spill response agreement highlight an increasingly multilateral approach to resolving Arctic challenges by utilizing the framework of the Arctic Council. Although direct bilateral relations between Russia and the United States will continue at the local, state, and federal levels through joint operations between District 17 and Russia's North-East Border Guard, as well as scientific endeavors, it is likely the Arctic Council will be the primary venue for confronting large challenges that impact the entire region moving forward, with policy momentum provided by the Arctic coastal states.

In an effort to reposition the bilateral relationship following an acrimonious period between the two powers as a result of the 2008 Georgian-Russian conflict, U.S. President Barack Obama and then Russian President Dmitry Medvedev created a Bilateral Presidential Commission in July 2009. As part of the Commission, a U.S.-Russia Environmental Working Group, co-chaired by the U.S. Department of State and the Russian Ministry of Natural Resources and Ecology (MNRE), has focused on the Arctic. The key areas identified for cooperation were reduction of black carbon emissions, management and disposal of waste, protected area management, and wildlife conservation for species such as polar bears and salmon.[35] A 2011 joint workshop between the MNRE and the U.S. Environmental Protection Agency resulted in the preparation and implementation of joint demonstration projects to reduce black carbon, as well as to identify joint research into the pollution of Arctic territories in the United States and Russia.[36]

The working group has also examined ways to coordinate initiatives in the Bering Strait, particularly those that focus on conservation assessments and protected areas in Alaska and Chukotka.[37] The Shared Beringian Heritage Program, established in 1991, is a key example of an existing successful initiative in this arena. The program seeks to foster cooperation between the United States, Russia, and the indigenous people on both sides of the Bering Strait on issues of environmental protection and historic preservation. The program promotes research and supports cultural exchanges and other bilateral initiatives. The program remains active, with 19 continuing and 3 new research projects underway, on topics including indigenous language study, knowledge of ocean currents, and monitoring of animal populations.[38]

Although there have been many U.S.-Russian policy successes in the Arctic, there have also been some sobering developments that continue to reflect geostrategic uncertainties for both powers. In August 2007, Russian strategic bombers threatened Norwegian, Icelandic, and American airspace in the Arctic.[39] Shortly thereafter, Russian explorer and Arctic envoy Artur Chilingarov instigated a publicity stunt by planting a Russian flag on the Arctic seabed at the North Pole. Between December 2007 and February 2008, two Russian nuclear submarines inexplicably appeared in the North Atlantic.[40] Four years later, Russian domestic opposition to Vladimir Putin's return to the Kremlin as Russian president gained momentum, and tensions between Moscow and Washington were once again on the rise. In June 2012, Russia conducted exercises over the central Arctic Ocean, deploying approximately 30 strategic nuclear bombers and support aircraft, including refueling tankers and airborne warning and control aircraft. According to the U.S. Northern Command and joint U.S.-Canadian North American Aerospace Defense Command, two Russian strategic nuclear bombers violated U.S. airspace near Alaska and F-15 jets responded by intercepting the aircraft. It is believed that Moscow was simulating strikes against the U.S. missile defense interceptor base at Fort Greely, Alaska, and strategic radar systems on the Aleutian Islands. This symbolic exercise was likely a response to two separate but intimately intertwined issues: the potential involvement of the North Atlantic Treaty Organization (NATO) in the Arctic and increased Russian angst over

NATO's European missile defense architecture. The Russian Foreign Ministry has complained that increased NATO activity in the Arctic could "erode constructive cooperation."[41]

Russia is also raising flags with its increased military presence in the Arctic. In August 2012, Russian Security Council Secretary Nikolai Patrushev announced plans to build several naval bases along the Northern Sea Route for the "temporary stationing of Russian Navy warships and vessels operated by the Federal Security Service's Border Guard Department."[42] This was part of a plan to deploy, by 2020, a combined arms force consisting of military, border, and coastal guard units to protect Russia's economic and security interests. In September 2012, plans were announced for a squadron of MiG-31 supersonic interceptor aircraft to be based in the Novaya Zemlya archipelago as part of an antimissile defense system in the region. In February 2013, however, Minister of Defense Sergey Shoygu scrapped his predecessor's plans, which were reportedly based on political, rather than military, motivations.[43] With the Northern Fleet slated to receive four new Borei-class nuclear-powered submarines in the next decade, there will be a significant increase in the number of strategic nuclear warheads in the Russian Arctic.[44] The increased military presence and infrastructure investment in the Russian Arctic will likely continue to fuel tensions with the United States and other Arctic states.

Today, the U.S.-Russian bilateral relationship stands at a political and economic crossroads. The Arctic reflects this crossroads position, as both the bilateral relationship and the physical Arctic are undergoing profound transformation and transition.

Environmental Change and the Russian Arctic

The Arctic Ocean and its surrounding seas are not only economically and strategically significant but also influential in relation to global atmospheric and oceanic circulation and biodiversity. The Arctic is indispensable for maintaining a balanced carbon cycle and stable global climate, conserving bio-cultural diversity, and preserving the cultures and ways of life of indigenous peoples. The Arctic experiences extensive seasonal migration of marine mammals, especially whales, walruses, and other cetaceans, and approximately 300 species of migratory birds travel to the Arctic to breed annually.[45] The Russian Arctic hosts about half of all land and a third of all marine ecological regions identified in the circumpolar Arctic, representing areas of significant biological diversity and unique ecosystems.[46] Without question, the Arctic region—in particular, the Russian Arctic—plays critical roles in the global environment.

Increased warming in the Arctic is acting as a profound driver of environmental change. Average temperatures in the Russian Arctic have increased by 0.2°C to 2.5°C since the 1960s, about twice the global average.[47] Sea ice reduction has averaged approximately 3 percent per decade since 1979. By 2050, there may be a 30 percent reduction in ice extent in the Arctic, equivalent to 3.5 million square kilometers. By that time, it is possible that the entire Russian coast could become free of ice in the late summer months. Although significant ice will remain in the central Arctic Ocean, it will be only 1.5 meters thick and less compact.[48]

Over the past 10–20 years, Russia has experienced an increased number of extreme meteorological events linked to climate change, including extreme heat waves, floods, fires, and winter snowfall. A significant increase in the number of fires was observed not only in European Russia but also in Siberian peatlands. There have been recurrent outbreaks of flooding in the Russian Arctic caused by heavy rain and premature river ice breakup.[49] Outbreaks of infectious diseases are also taking place with greater frequency, a consequence associated with the increased number of floods on major Siberian rivers and the subsequent damage to wastewater treatment infrastructure.[50] By some estimates, the frequency of high winds and squalls in the Russian Arctic will likely double between 2005 and 2015.[51]

The Arctic Ocean is more dramatically affected by river runoff than other oceanic regions because the Arctic Ocean receives approximately 11 percent of the world's river runoff. The combined basin area of the Arctic rivers Ob, Yenisei, and Lena, which form the Russian Arctic delta, is 8 million square kilometers, an area two and a half times larger than the Mississippi River Basin (3.2 million square kilometers).[52] Runoff from these three Russian Arctic rivers, along with the Mackenzie River and the Northern Dvina, comprises more than 4,300 cubic kilometers. Annual river discharge to the Arctic Ocean increased by an average of 7 cubic kilometers annually between 1964 and 2000. River runoff not only causes erosion of the earth's surface but also has been associated with transport of water pollutants to groundwater, surface water, and soil. In some cases, runoff can lead to flooding.

The Arctic Ocean and adjacent Arctic shelves are also becoming increasingly affected by ocean acidification. The absorption of anthropogenic carbon dioxide emissions, which occurs more rapidly in cold surface waters, is changing the Arctic Ocean's chemistry by reducing its pH level. The pH level is predicted to drop from 8.1 to 7.8 by 2100, raising the acidity of the water.[53] The increase in acidity could reduce shell formation, which is required by many calcifying organisms, thus posing a threat to food chains and disrupting ecosystems and habitats.[54] For example, the decline in pteropod populations (marine snails) could affect the pink salmon fisheries in the North Pacific.[55]

Coastal retreat, the process by which coastal material (sediment) wears away and erodes, is also transpiring in the Russian Arctic. Mean averages of coastal retreat are currently 1–2 meters per year, although in the East Siberian and Laptev Seas, coastal retreat reaches up to 10–30 meters per year.[56] This retreat impacts not only coastal and river communities but also the coastal Arctic food web, as land and marine mammals seasonally inhabit shorelines and are affected by drift ice conditions.[57] For example, the Arctic polar bear is vulnerable to changes in sea ice because the species uses the ice as a platform for hunting seals, traveling, finding mates, and breeding.[58] Walruses also have sea ice requirements, and as the coastline retreats, much of the remaining sea ice that is suitable for habitation shifts to areas too deep for these mammals to utilize. Arctic coasts are also affected by thermal abrasion, wave erosion, storm-surge flooding, and sea ice grounding in the shore zone, with important implications for coastal populations and species distribution.[59]

Clearly, all of these changes deeply affect biodiversity, populations, and habitat loss of rare Arctic species. Although the majority of Arctic species populations are currently stable or increasing, a number of iconic Arctic species of global significance are on the decline.[60] For example, 7 of 19 polar bear subpopulations are declining, and Russian Arctic reindeer populations are also dwindling.[61] The Pacific walrus population is currently estimated at 129,000, almost 50 percent fewer than the estimated 250,000 in the early 1980s.[62] The reduction in these animal populations raises concern about the future of the species and also has broader implications regarding food security for the Inuit and indigenous populations of the region, who rely on subsistence hunting of marine mammals to survive.

Increased warming in the Russian Arctic also affects the Russian permafrost zone, which covers 60 percent of Russia, or roughly 4 million square miles.[63] The permafrost zone is becoming warmer, and the permafrost active layer, factoring in seasonal freeze-thaw cycles, will become 15–25 percent thicker (in some coastal areas and in western Siberia, the permafrost active layer will become 50 percent thicker).[64] It is projected that by 2050, the permafrost area in the Russian Arctic will shrink by 12–15 percent and its south boundary will move by 150–200 kilometers to the northeast.[65] Arctic permafrost contains an amount of carbon equivalent to, or even more than, the existing carbon dioxide in the atmosphere. As permafrost thaws and the decomposition of organic matter accelerates, the release of methane into the atmosphere also increases. A warming Arctic may lead to the release of large amounts of carbon dioxide and methane at a scale that significantly exceeds current global emissions of these gases. Although more scientific research in this area is urgently needed, estimates suggest that global carbon emissions resulting from Russian permafrost thaw could double during this century.[66]

Significant amounts of methane are also trapped in the sub-seafloor permafrost. With increasing water temperatures in the warming Arctic, the stability of undersea methane hydrates could also be compromised. Increasing scientific evidence suggests that the Arctic Sea and particularly the East Siberian Arctic Shelf (ESAS) are releasing significant amounts of methane into the atmosphere. By some estimates, approximately 50 gigatons of methane could be released from the ESAS alone, causing the global methane level to rise by 11 or 12 times.[67] This would rapidly accelerate global warming and lead to potentially catastrophic consequences within a few decades.[68] Scientists estimate that even lower emissions (e.g., a 1 percent increase of potential methane over 20 years) could "erase" existing climate mitigation efforts to limit global warming. There is evidence that methane has been increasing in the atmosphere since 2007, after a relatively stable period, and this tendency could at least partially be explained by the accelerating emissions of methane in the Arctic. Increasing methane emissions from the Arctic could trigger further climate warming through feedback mechanisms.

Recent global attention to the problem of short-lived climate forcers (SLCFs) is of utmost importance to the circumpolar Arctic because the reduction of these sources (black carbon, methane, and ozone) could provide the best opportunity to slow Arctic warming in the near term.[69] The Arctic Council has been particularly active in this space by conducting assessments, such as the July 2011 report, *An Assessment of Emissions and Mitigation Options for Black Carbon for the Arctic Council,* undertaken by the Council's Task Force on Short-Lived Climate Forcers. Among other findings, the report identifies the largest sources of black carbon emissions in the Arctic Council nations and recommends the best options to curb these emissions.[70] Although there are no authoritative inventories of black carbon and other SLCF emissions in the Russian Arctic, indirect estimates suggest that total black carbon emissions in Russia are 150 kilotons (gigagrams) per year.[71] This makes up approximately 2 percent of global black carbon emissions and nearly half of total black carbon emissions in the circumpolar region north of 60°N. Black carbon emissions mainly come from Russian sources such as small-scale boilers, stoves, and diesel generators; on- and off-road transport emissions; and industrial emissions. An unknown amount of black carbon is emitted from gas flaring and could be brought to the Arctic after massive forest and agricultural fires in the southern latitudes. With Arctic shipping projected to increase to 2 percent of global traffic by 2030, black carbon emissions could increase fivefold to 4.5 gigagrams, causing an increase of 17–78 percent in global warming from ships.[72]

Moreover, the polar region attracts global pollution because of the tropospheric transport of atmospheric emissions from western Europe, North America, and Asia. In the Arctic Zone, the Kola Peninsula and Norilsk emit an annual average of 4 million metric tons of sulfur dioxide and hundreds of thousands of metric tons of carbon monoxide and nitrogen oxides. These large pollution centers could significantly contribute to the transboundary transport of air pollutants from the Arctic to other regions.

Challenges in the Russian Arctic

Russian legislation[73] defines the Arctic Zone of the Russian Federation (AZRF) as the area encompassing fully or partially the territories of Murmansk Oblast, Sakha (Yakutia) Republic, Arkhangelsk Oblast, Yamalo-Nenets Autonomous, and

Chukotka Autonomous Okrug, as well as islands in the Arctic Ocean.[74] Closely connected physically and economically, the Russian Subarctic includes the adjacent territories of Khanty-Mansiysk Autonomous Okrug, southern Yakutia, the Komi Republic, and some areas in Khabarovsk Kray far in the east. The AZRF is approximately 9 million square kilometers in size, has a population of 2.5 million people, produces 12–15 percent of Russia's GDP, and generates about one-quarter of all export revenues. Among the population, approximately 140,000 individuals are from indigenous populations, representing 16 indigenous groups of the north (Saami, Nentsy, Khanty, Mansi, Selkup, Kety, Entsy, Nganasany, Dolgany, Evenki, Eveny, Yukagiry, Chukchi, Eskimos, Kereki, and Chuvantsy). Most residents in the Russian Arctic live in cities and urban settlements, with only a few cities having populations of more than 100,000.

The Russian government has been abundantly clear—by the articulation of its policies and its actions thus far—that Russia's economic future is in the Arctic. Of the five Arctic coastal states,[75] Russia has the most to gain economically and strategically from the Arctic's rapidly melting ice cap. It also has the most to lose environmentally. The economic benefits are clear: new transportation routes, such as the important Northern Sea Route, will carry exports of Russian natural resources to eager markets, and the exploration of potentially vast oil and gas fields will increase Russia's budget coffers. In its most significant policy document, "Foundations of the Russian Federation's State Policy in the Arctic until 2020 and Beyond," the Russian government declared in 2010 its main strategic imperatives for the Russian Arctic. The document makes clear that the Arctic is a strategic resource base that will improve Russia's social and economic development, the Arctic is a zone of peace and cooperation, the Arctic's unique ecosystems must be conserved, and the Northern Sea Route is a *national* transit passage and not an international strait.[76]

Today's Russian Arctic economy was largely inherited from the Soviet era and the initial period of industrialization in the 1920s and 1930s. Significant regional infrastructure, such as railroads, ports, and industrial complexes, was established during this time frame and has not received significant investment since that era.[77] The Russian Arctic economy is dominated by extractive industries, particularly oil and gas, and mineral resources, such as diamonds, antimony, apatite, barite, phlogopite, vermiculite, rare earth metals, nickel and cobalt (90 percent of Russian domestic production[78]), copper (60 percent of domestic production[79]), gold, and other metals and minerals. The region also provides about one-third of all fisheries in the country, primarily concentrated in the Barents Sea and the Bering Sea.

Although there are regional economic differences within the Russian Arctic, the importance of and reliance on extractive industries for Russia compared with the other Arctic coastal states is stark. Despite statements by Russian government officials about the increasing need to diversify its economy, Russian extractive industries remain the backbone of the Russian economy, providing more than

50 percent of the federal budget and approximately 65 percent of export revenue. The five major Russian oil companies account for 60 percent of the Russian stock market.[80] With increased access to the vast Arctic resources, it is clear that the Russian economy will continue to rely heavily on Arctic extractive industries. At the same time, these industries must build new coastal infrastructure, storage terminals, underwater and land pipelines, additional sea transport and auxiliary ships, search-and-rescue capabilities, and satellite networks to enhance knowledge related to weather and sea ice conditions. These capabilities will require sophisticated technologies and practices that are often not available domestically.

In addition to the need to construct new Arctic infrastructure, the Russian Arctic's existing infrastructure is literally sinking. Instability and changes in the integrity of the permafrost are shifting the ground on which this infrastructure is built, which significantly increases the risk of oil spills and gas leaks. For example, approximately 20 percent of accidents on oil and gas pipelines in West Siberia are caused by loss of fixity and deformation.[81] The carrying capacity of pipeline pile foundations is expected to decrease by 50 percent.[82] Increased annual and seasonal river discharge from Russian rivers and ice regime change will also stress underwater pipelines. New roads and railways, as well as aboveground pipelines, will need to be constructed to withstand thermokarst, the land surface depressions that are often filled with water and result from the thawing of the permafrost. Power transmission lines, similar to other land-based infrastructure, will be susceptible to collapsing ground caused by permafrost melt. In addition, higher winds, which have been forecasted for the regions of Murmansk, Arkhangelsk, Leningrad, portions of Sakha (Yakutia), Irkutsk, Magadan, Khanty-Mansiysk, and Evenkia, will stress power transmission lines and cause regional electricity power shortages.[83]

The Russian Arctic is extremely vulnerable to environmental pollution, as Russia has an extensive legacy of residual contamination from past industrial and state-administered activities. This has resulted in perhaps the world's largest inventory of past environmental liabilities.[84] Industrial production and military decline in the 1990s left thousands of facilities and sites abandoned in the Russian Arctic with high levels of contamination of soil and groundwater. For example, steel drums and tanks containing up to 50,000 tons of petrol and lubricants were left behind at the decommissioned military bases on the Franz Josef Land archipelago northeast of the Barents Sea.[85] These past environmental liabilities are posing a large and growing threat to the Arctic environment and its inhabitants, as well as placing constraints on economic growth.

The most challenging and dangerous environmental problems in the Russian Arctic are the presence of "hotspots" in areas of intensive economic activity, notably resource extraction. As of this writing, more than 100 hotspots have been identified throughout the Arctic Zone, 30 of which are considered to have severe environmental problems.[86] Chemical contamination by heavy metals, petroleum and petroleum products, persistent organic pollutants (POPs), solid waste, and radiation contamination are among the most dangerous pollutants found in the region. These problems are exacerbated by the warming climate, as thawing permafrost leads to the increased release of hitherto trapped contaminants.[87] POPs tend to accumulate in the fatty tissues of species along the food chain, with the highest concentrations observed in polar bears, seals, and whales. This is especially dangerous for indigenous populations of the Arctic, who, by hunting and fishing, consume significant amounts of lipid-rich food products. In the Russian Arctic Zone, the concentrations of POPs found in the blood and breast milk of small indigenous populations are the highest in the circumpolar Arctic.[88]

The Russian Arctic has also been affected by nuclear weapons testing carried out by the former Soviet Union, as well as the United States, China, the United Kingdom, and France during the Cold War. The nuclear test site on the Novaya Zemlya archipelago holds about 12 percent of the 273 megatons of radioactive materials tested, a large majority of which has entered the circumpolar environment. The Arctic environment was also contaminated by radionuclides from the 1986 Chernobyl accident. Additional potential sources of radiation contamination in the Russian Arctic are spent nuclear fuel storage sites located along the northern shore of the Kola Peninsula and in the Severodvinsk region on the White Sea. Another concern is potential leakages from the radioisotope thermoelectric generators (RITEGs) sunk in the bays off Novaya Zemlya, which could pose a lethal radiation danger if they are mishandled. Although most RITEGs stored in the western part of the Russian Arctic have been replaced, environmentally sound disposal of outdated RITEGs remains an issue in the Sakhalin Republic and the Chukchi Autonomous Okrug.

These challenges will impact the future development of the Russian Arctic and the country's economic growth. The geographic scope of the region and the important role it plays in Russian GDP and export revenues, notably through extractive industries, mean that Arctic climate change cannot be ignored. Beyond the need for building new infrastructure and reinforcing existing capabilities, Moscow must take aggressive strides toward addressing dangerous hotspots and safely disposing of dangerous pollutants that remain in the region from past generations. This effort can be achieved only through a forward-thinking strategy that involves cooperation with and support from other state and non-state actors with the expertise and capabilities required to assist. Such a strategy must also consider the rights and desires of the significant populations that are indigenous to the Russian Arctic region. Unfortunately, although the Russian strategy for the development of the Arctic Zone discusses Russia's approach to regional sustainable development, at the most senior government level, there has been limited capacity and policy interest to pursue, let alone implement, robust Arctic environmental activities.[89]

Even if the most conducive political and policy conditions were present within Russia today, Russian authorities would face numerous and daunting challenges.

Implementing remediation projects would be extremely difficult because of the immense size of the Russian Arctic, the dated infrastructure, the lack of connectivity between the regions, and the limited availability of human capital. Based on the country's adaptive capacity to respond to the multiple economic, social, and environmental challenges of climate change in the Arctic, Russia is currently close to the bottom of the world ranking in the Global Competitiveness Index.[90] This index includes factors such as the quality of roads, the development of financial markets, the availability of the latest technologies, and a favorable climate for technology transfer. The quality of the country's institutions, including government policy making, use of public funds, and a number of criteria defining technological readiness, are particularly alarming given the magnitude, scope, and pace of the required capacities to develop the Russian Arctic in the face of climate change.

Moreover, Russian regional and central authorities lack adequate monitoring and forecasting technologies as rapid economic and societal change occurs. Moscow's overreliance on extractive industries to bolster economic growth in the Russian Arctic makes the region vulnerable to global market forces (which may drive greater or lesser demand) and private-sector practices related to safety and environmental protection.

To compound these challenges, recent domestic policies from Moscow could adversely affect the safe future development of the Russian Arctic. In July 2012, the Russian Duma approved and President Putin signed a law on noncommercial organizations. According to the law, nongovernmental organizations (NGOs) that receive foreign funds must register with a governmental authority as "foreign agents" and provide detailed financial reports to the Russian authorities.[91] This law has already affected the Arctic region, most notably with the government-ordered closure of RAIPON, the Russian Association of Indigenous Peoples of the North, Siberia, and Far East, which had received funding from a number of international entities.[92] An NGO representing 41 indigenous groups (more than 300,000 people), RAIPON is one of six indigenous organizations that have permanent participant status in the Arctic Council.[93] The closure could severely affect the livelihood of indigenous groups, stifle their political voice in decisions regarding economic development of the Russian Arctic, and limit opportunities for international cooperation in indigenous affairs. In fact, the closure of RAIPON has already put an end to an existing cooperation agreement between the group and the Norwegian Barents Secretariat to promote and fund Norwegian-Russian cooperation projects.[94]

The NGO law could also have widespread effects on environmental organizations operating throughout Russia, because 70 percent of environmental NGOs there are funded through grants from foreign governments and organizations.[95] Although environmental organizations such as Greenpeace Russia and Ecodefense have tried to resist the law to this point by refusing to be listed as foreign agents, there are serious concerns that the law could silence environmental opposition to poorly planned and potentially dangerous oil and gas development in the Arctic.[96] The law could also constrain U.S. and international efforts to help Russia become more resilient in the face of environmental change.

Russian Arctic policy making is a paradox. Moscow is "open" to greater Western engagement in the form of Western investment and technology, which Russia needs to allow it to exploit its oil and gas resources in the Arctic. However, at the same time, Russia wishes to keep the Arctic "closed" to non-Arctic states, NATO, and other outside interests that could potentially challenge Russia militarily or economically in the region. Russian Arctic policy is also at once highly centralized and highly decentralized. Policy orders emanate from Moscow through elaborate strategic documents, and President Putin addresses Arctic events personally. Simultaneously, implementation of these policies is often decentralized at the local and regional levels. To successfully engage Russia in the Arctic region would require effectively balancing this duality and fully understanding that Russia will not be deterred from fully exploring and exploiting the economic potential of its vast Arctic resources.

Development of the Russian Arctic and Strategic Interests of the United States

The strategic interests of the United States in the Arctic have most recently been articulated in the 2009 National Security Presidential Directive 66 (NSPD-66). The directive includes seven key focus areas: (1) meeting national security needs; (2) strengthening international governance; (3) resolving outer continental shelf and boundary issues; (4) promoting international scientific cooperation; (5) prioritizing maritime transportation; (6) promoting economic and energy issues; and (7) ensuring environmental protection, conservation, and stewardship. Moscow's strategy for developing its Arctic region has the potential to affect every one of these priorities. Although the United States cannot deter Russia from developing or exploring its Arctic resources, the United States can try to work with Russia to drive best practices and seek outcomes that benefit both countries and the region as a whole.

There is a broad array of national security needs in the Arctic. A critical area of focus for the United States related to the Russian Arctic will remain vessel traffic passing through the Bering Strait, an important choke point for shipping along the Northern Sea Route. The strait has seen a steady increase in shipping traffic, up from 245 vessels in 2008 to more than 400 vessels in 2011.[97] In addition to the potential economic benefits that come with this increase, there are also increased security concerns. Issues ranging from the need for search and rescue to the potential for illegal smuggling mean that the development of the Northern Sea Route will require increased U.S. capabilities and cooperation with regional partners to monitor and police this narrow section of the passage. Fortunately, the USCG's District 17 in Alaska and the RFBS have a strong history of collaboration; this cooperation will need to be reinforced as development continues.

Russia's implementation of its Arctic development strategy must strive to avoid potential pitfalls that could increase tensions with the United States or other Arctic states. Beyond an environmental disaster with international implications, Moscow should avoid a strategy that aggravates border disputes or prompts legal battles and security risks over establishing sovereignty in the region. There are some historical tensions in the region, with Russia threatened by U.S. missile defense architecture in Alaska and Moscow's positioning of its Northern Fleet above the Arctic Circle at Severomorsk and Kola Bay. Both states must continue to keep bilateral communications open while also working through the existing international governing bodies, such as the Arctic Council, to strengthen ties and prevent tensions from escalating.

The United Nations Convention on the Law of the Sea (UNCLOS) plays a major role in several of the focus areas of NSPD-66, notably in both strengthening international governance and resolving outer continental shelf and boundary issues. Russia has ratified the convention and is currently working to submit its claims to the United Nations by December 2013.[98] The United States has yet to formally ratify the treaty. This means not only that the United States is unable to submit claims for its own outer continental shelf but also that it would be unable to challenge boundary claims from Moscow that the United States finds contentious within the UNCLOS framework. Until the United States ratifies the treaty, the chair for the United States at the international body that will determine the claims, the International Tribunal for the Law of the Sea, will remain empty.

Moscow's development of its domestic Arctic resources will have foreign policy implications, intended or otherwise. These could affect U.S. objectives with regard to maritime transportation, specifically how Russia develops its infrastructure—such as deepwater ports and icebreakers—along the Northern Sea Route. These decisions will have a profound influence on the viability of the North Sea Route as a competitive shipping route for traffic between Europe and Asia. And they will affect both trade relations and security, with the potential to foster economic growth and promote global trade as the route would reduce travel times and cut fuel costs. In addition, increased shipping along the Northern Sea Route could allow transporters to sidestep involvement in politically volatile or dangerous shipping routes, such as the Suez Canal, where piracy in the Gulf of Aden has disrupted supply lines. Increased traffic along the route would also increase the need for coordination between the United States, Russia, and the other Arctic states, likely through the Arctic Council, on matters such as search and rescue and oil spill response.

The U.S. goal of promoting economic and energy issues in the Arctic could be enhanced by further development of the Russian Arctic and may provide an impetus for a U.S. and Russian bilateral investment treaty. Both countries have expressed interest in pursuing such an agreement, with the United States releasing template documents for such a bilateral investment treaty in April 2012 and Moscow publicly expressing interest in resuming negotiations as recently as May 2012.[99] Development of the Russian Arctic could also create opportunities for further cross-border investment between multinational companies and their Russian counterparts, such as the joint venture between Russia's Rosneft and the ExxonMobil Corporation of the United States to explore the Kara Sea. Rosneft has already established relationships with Norwegian Statoil to explore the Okhotsk and Barents Seas, in addition to other joint ventures with Italian (Eni), French (Total), and United Kingdom (BP) companies to explore other parts of the Arctic. This openness toward international cooperation in the Arctic among multinational actors for economic ventures could provide an opportunity for non-Russian companies to help set standards on issues such as environmental regulations in the Russian Arctic. As such ventures become more commonplace, there may be an opportunity for the Arctic Council to play a role in coordinating best practices for the private sector.

Related to this, the U.S. objective of promoting environmental protection, conservation, and stewardship in the Arctic could be affected by Russia's decision making about developing its vast Arctic resources. Given the fragility of the region's ecosystem, an incident such as an oil spill in the Russian Arctic shelf would likely result in environmental damage that crosses sovereign boundaries. Beyond the environmental impact, such an incident could result in other nations reconsidering their regulatory frameworks, imposing stricter standards, and possibly denying drilling permits, postponing lease sales, or imposing a moratorium on drilling in the Arctic. Conversely, the development of strong regulation, perhaps encouraged through partnerships with private industry or standards set by the Arctic Council, could provide models for other Arctic actors in the region. Cooperation between the United States and Russia in conducting scientific research, such as joint oceanographic expeditions as part of the Russian-American Long-Term Census of the Arctic or environmental monitoring research projects funded by the Shared Beringian Heritage Program, would also be mutually beneficial. Such work would foster collaboration, build relationships, and improve shared understanding of the rapid changes facing the fragile Arctic ecosystem.

Recommended U.S. Policy Approaches to the Russian Arctic

If Russian Arctic policy is considered a paradox, then U.S. policy toward the Russian Arctic must be considered "missing in action" or perhaps simply missing an important opportunity. There has been little official thought given to how best to leverage U.S. expertise and assistance bilaterally and multilaterally or the private sector to focus on environmental resiliency in the Russian Arctic.

What permits the U.S.-Russian relationship to be successful in the Arctic is that the relationship is dichotomous: Russia's economic potential and its strategic military strength make Russia an unquestioned Arctic "superpower." Russian Arctic identity is strong. The United States is an Arctic "science power" that spends most of its resources in the Arctic on economic development, environmental protection, and scientific research. Beyond the state of Alaska, America's Arctic identity is weak. Therefore, the United States will not be a strategic competitor to Russia in the Arctic, but it could be a valuable partner in a region that Russia prioritizes.

The most logical place to begin to strengthen bilateral cooperation is in the Bering Strait, where the U.S. and Russian borders come together. Strengthening cooperation in ecosystem-based management, traffic management schemes, and enhanced marine and coastal area protection in the Bering Strait would be important measures. This cooperation could occur at the state and regional level, such as between Alaska and Chukotka.

Another opportunity to strengthen the bilateral relationship would be to take advantage of the important role that the private sector will play in developing the Russian Arctic. The United States should seek to develop innovative public-private partnership arrangements with U.S. or multinational companies—in the oil and gas, mining, shipping, fishing, and cruise industries—that conduct activities in the Russian Arctic or have entered into joint ventures with their Russian counterparts. By leveraging both international and Russian corporate expertise, environmental practice standards could be enhanced for a range of Arctic operations, particularly along the Northern Sea Route and near onshore and offshore fields.

Russian authorities lack adequate monitoring and forecasting technologies and urgently need better tools to increase resilience to the dramatic environmental changes that are already underway in the Russian Arctic. More U.S.-Russian scientific collaboration could be fostered in developing integrated assessment capabilities for climate resilience and an early warning system. The United States and other Arctic Council states should also invest in Russia's regional and local emergency capacity for disaster preparedness and response. Perhaps available multilateral funds from the United Nations or international financial institutions, such as the World Bank and the European Bank for Reconstruction and Development, could also be used to strengthen Russian environmental security and resilience. Existing efforts include those undertaken by the United Nations and the World Bank's Global Facility for Disaster Reduction and Recovery, which seeks to reduce vulnerabilities to natural hazards and enhance climate change adaptation capacity in high-risk countries.[100] A specific example of an ongoing project in the Russian Arctic is the Russian Federation Partnership on Sustainable Environmental Management in the Arctic under a Rapidly Changing Climate (known as Arctic Agenda 2020). This $300 million project is funded by the United Nations' Global Environment Facility and targets Arctic marine ecosystems, protected areas, and river basins.[101]

It is important to note that Russia's recently adopted NGO law could be a potentially major stumbling block that would prevent American and European investment from helping Russia develop and implement an environmental security plan in the Arctic. Although the law exempts organizations engaged in work related to "flora and fauna," it is unclear whether some nongovernmental Russian organizations would be reluctant to accept international funds to help mitigate the effects of climate change in the Russian Arctic. This potential uncertainty strengthens the argument for public-private partnerships to improve environmental resilience while also pursuing engagement with Russian civil society and NGOs in the Russian Arctic.

Finally, as Russia joins the World Trade Organization (WTO) and potential action is taken by the U.S. Congress to recognize permanent normal trade relations status for Russia, the economic dimension of the U.S.-Russian relationship, particularly in the Arctic, could reach new levels. WTO membership may allow U.S. exports to Russia to more than double over the next five years, from $9 billion in 2010 to $19 billion by 2016. WTO membership would open new opportunities for U.S. companies in foreign direct investment and particularly trade in services. Given the significant demand for developing a knowledge-based economy in the Russian Arctic, U.S. investments in this region could become a particularly attractive area of cooperation between the two countries.

Successful U.S.-Russian cooperation is already occurring within the Arctic Council, utilizing the council's framework for securing legally binding multilateral agreements in the Arctic, such as the 2011 international search-and-rescue agreement and the May 2013 international oil spill response agreement, negotiated by the trilateral-led (United States, Russia, and Norway) Task Force on Arctic Marine Oil Pollution Preparedness and Response. However, further bilateral engagement in the Russian Arctic would not only enhance multilateral collaborative efforts but also provide some needed balance in an increasingly complex and often negative U.S.-Russian agenda.

The future contours of U.S.-Russian relations are not clear. However, it is clear that the Russian Arctic and environmental security will play a more prominent role in the future. If the Arctic continues to be an accurate reflection of the state of the U.S.-Russian relationship, as it has in the past, the future holds the promise of a cooperative partnership. However, the future will be severely tested by rapid climatic change and its potentially devastating impact in the Russian Arctic. Both nations will need to work together to develop best practices and secure infrastructure to mitigate the worst effects of this environmental change. To succeed, future U.S. Arctic strategy must be based on operational and actionable tactics, such as public-private partnerships and security cooperation, which take into account these changes in the Russian Arctic and ensure environmentally safe and secure development of the region.

Notes

* The authors thank Terry Toland, research associate of the Center for Strategic and International Studies (CSIS), Europe Program, and Mihaela David, formerly associated with the CSIS Europe Program, for their countless hours of research, meticulous attention to detail, and editing prowess.

1 James Kraska, "From Pariah to Partner—Russian-American Security Cooperation in the Arctic Ocean," *ILSA Journal of International & Comparative Law* 16, no. 2 (2009), http://ssrn.com/abstract=1648907.

2 Vlad M. Kaczynski, "US-Russian Bering Sea Marine Border Dispute: Conflict over Strategic Assets, Fisheries and Energy Resources," *Russian Analytical Digest* 20, no. 7 (May 20, 2007), www.css.ethz.ch/publications/pdfs/RAD-20–2-5.pdf.

3 Bureau of European and Eurasian Affairs, "Status of Wrangel and Other Arctic Islands" Fact Sheet (U.S. Department of State, 2009), www.state.gov/p/eur/rls/fs/128740.htm.

4 Kaczynski, "US-Russian Bering Sea Marine Border Dispute."

5 Bureau of European and Eurasian Affairs, "Status of Wrangel and Other Arctic Islands."

6 Todd Margrave, "Arctic Military Environmental Cooperation," www.toddmargrave.com/amecprogram.htm.

7 U.S. Government Accountability Office, *Russian Nuclear Submarines: U.S. Participation in the Arctic Military Environmental Cooperation Program Needs Better Justification,* Report to Congressional Committees (U.S. Government, 2004), www.gao.gov/assets/250/243985.pdf.

8 "Medvedev: Arctic Resources Are Key to Russia's Future," *Seattle Times* (Sept. 18, 2008), http://seattletimes.nwsource.com/html/nationworld/2008187217_russia18.html.

9 Sergio Vecchi, *European Union-Russian Federation: Sustainable Proximity* (EU-Russia Centre, 2011), www.eu-russiacentre.org/wp-content/uploads/2012/03/European-Union-Russian-Federation-sustainable-proximity.pdf.

10 Russian Federation, "Second Arctic International Economic Forum in Murmansk" (Oct. 1, 2010), www.minregion.ru/press_office/news/799.html.

11 "Alaska's Oil & Gas Industry," Resource Development Council for Alaska, www.akrdc.org/issues/oilgas/overview.html.

12 U.S. Geological Survey, "Circum-Arctic Resource Appraisal: Estimates of Undiscovered Oil and Gas North of the Arctic Circle" (2008), http://pubs.usgs.gov/fs/2008/3049/fs2008–3049.pdf.

13 Bureau of Ocean Energy Management, "Assessment of Undiscovered Technically Recoverable Oil and Gas Resources of the Nation's Outer Continental Shelf, 2011" (2011), www.boem.gov/Oil-and-Gas-Energy-Program/Resource-Evaluation/Resource-Assessment/2011-FA-Assessments.aspx.

14 Charles Emmerson and Glada Lahn, "Arctic Opening: Opportunity and Risk in the High North" (Lloyd's and Chatham House, 2012), www.lloyds.com/~/media/Files/News%20and%20Insight/360%20Risk%20Insight/Arctic_Risk_Report_20120412.pdf.

15 Red Dog Alaska, "Red Dog Operations" (2009), www.reddogalaska.com/Generic.aspx?PAGE=Red+Dog+Site%2fZinc+and+Lead&portalName=tc.

16 Alaska Department of Fish and Game, "Commercial Fisheries" (2013), www.adfg.alaska.gov/index.cfm?adfg=fishingcommercial.main.

17 "Alaska's Tourism Industry" (Resource Development Council for Alaska), www.akrdc.org/issues/tourism/overview.html.
18 Robert E. Kramek, "Steaming with the Russians," *U.S. Naval Institute* 123, no. 12 (1997): 1, 138, www.usni.org/magazines/proceedings/1997–12/steaming-russians.
19 Kramek, "Steaming with the Russians."
20 Kramek, "Steaming with the Russians."
21 Kramek, "Steaming with the Russians."
22 Kraska, "From Pariah to Partner."
23 Kraska, "From Pariah to Partner."
24 U.S. Department of Homeland Security, "Written Testimony of U.S. Coast Guard Commandant Admiral Robert Papp, Jr. for a Senate Committee on Appropriations, Subcommittee on Homeland Security Field Hearing" (2012), www.dhs.gov/news/2012/08/06/written-testimony-us-coast-guard-commandant-admiral-robert-papp-jr-senate-committee.
25 The Arctic Eight (A8) are Canada, Denmark (via Greenland), Finland, Iceland, Norway, Russia, Sweden, and the United States.
26 U.S. Department of State, "Secretary Clinton Signs the Arctic Search and Rescue Agreement with Other Arctic Nations," Fact Sheet (Office of the Spokesman 2011), www.state.gov/r/pa/prs/ps/2011/05/163285.htm.
27 International Federation of Red Cross and Red Crescent Societies, "Agreement on Cooperation on Aeronautical and Maritime Search and Rescue in the Arctic" (May 12, 2011), www.ifr.org/docs/idrl/N813EN.pdf.
28 Arctic Council, "First Arctic Council SAR Exercise in Whitehorse, Canada" (Oct. 17, 2011), www.arctic-council.org/index.php/en/about/general-news-archive/209-sar-exercise-whitehorse.
29 Arctic Council, *First Live Arctic Search and Rescue Exercise—SAREX 2012* (2012), www.arctic-council.org/index.php/en/environment-and-people/oceans/search-and-rescue/620-first-arctic-search-and-rescue-exercise-sarex-2012.
30 Arctic Council, *First Live Arctic Search and Rescue Exercise.*
31 Arctic Council Indigenous Peoples Secretariat, "Arctic Oil Spill Agreement Progressing" (May 31, 2012), http://ips.arcticportal.org/index.php?option=com_k2&view=item&id=480:arctic-oil-spill-agreement&Itemid=2.
32 Arctic Council Indigenous Peoples Secretariat, "Arctic Oil Spill Agreement Progressing."
33 Dan Joling, "Arctic Council Group Works on Spill Response Plan," Associated Press (March 23, 2012), www.adn.com/2012/03/22/2386370/arctic-council-group-works-on.html.
34 Alex Boyd, "Arctic Ministers Sign New Agreement to Tackle Oil Spills" (May 17, 2013), www.nunatsiaqonline.ca/stories/article/65674arctic_ministers_sign_new_agreement_to_tackle_oil_spills/.
35 Bureau of European and Eurasian Affairs, *U.S.-Russia Bilateral Presidential Commission: Spring 2012 Joint Report* (U.S. Department of State, 2012), www.state.gov/p/eur/ci/rs/usrussiabilat/186831.htm#13.
36 Bureau of European and Eurasian Affairs, *U.S.-Russia Bilateral Presidential Commission.*
37 Bureau of European and Eurasian Affairs, *U.S.-Russia Bilateral Presidential Commission.*
38 U.S. National Park Service, "Shared Beringian Heritage Program: Current Projects" (Aug. 7, 2013), www.nps.gov/akso/beringia/projects/currentprojects.cfm.

39 Bill Gertz, "The Bear at the Door," *Washington Free Beacon* (June 26, 2012), http://freebeacon.com/the-bear-at-the-door/.

40 Gertz, "The Bear at the Door."

41 Kraska, "From Pariah to Partner."

42 "Russia to Set Up Naval Infrastructure in Arctic—Patrushev," *RIA Novosti* (Aug. 6, 2012), http://en.rian.ru/military_news/20120806/175015455.html.

43 "Russia Drops Arctic Air Force Plans," *Barents Observer* (Feb. 4, 2012), http://barentsobserver.com/en/security/2013/02/russia-drops-arctic-air-force-plans-04–02.

44 "More Nukes on Kola," *Barents Observer* (Jan. 10, 2013), http://barentsobserver.com/en/security/2013/01/more-nukes-kola-10–01.

45 International Council for Game and Wildlife Conservation, "Migratory Birds Commission," www.cic-wildlife.org/index.php?id=76.

46 Peter Christie and Martin Sommerkorn, *Rapid Assessment of Circumarctic Ecosystem Resilience,* 2nd ed. (World Wildlife Fund Global Arctic Programme, Washington, D.C., 2012), http://awsassets.panda.org/downloads/racer_handbook.pdf.

47 Projected 2°C to 4°C increases in the mean global temperature by the end of the century are translated into 2°C to 9°C in the Arctic. See Global Environment Facility, "Project Framework Document: GEF-Russian Federation Partnership on Sustainable Environmental Management in the Arctic under a Rapidly Changing Climate" (Sept. 6, 2011), www.thegef.org/gef/sites/thegef.org/files/gef_prj_docs/GEFProjectDocuments/Multi%20Focal%20Area/Russian%20Federation%20-%20(4664)%20-%20GEF-Russian%20Federation%20Partnership%20on%20Sustainable/10-7-11%20-%20Revised%20PFD%20doc.pdf.

48 New estimates suggest it might happen even earlier. In 2011, 34 vessels traversed the North Sea Route and shipped 820,000 tonnes of cargo; Russian estimates for 2012 projected 1.5 million tons of cargo, and U.S. estimates projected 64 million tons by 2020. See Trude Pettersen, "Rosatomflot Is Ready for More Cargo on Northern Sea Route," *Barents Observer* (Dec. 14, 2011), www.barentsobserver.com/rosatomflot-is-ready-for-more-cargo-on-northern-sea-route.4998361–116320.html.

49 World Wildlife Fund, "Climate Change Impacts in the Russian Federation," http://wwf.panda.org/about_our_earth/aboutcc/problems/rising_temperatures/hotspot_map/russian_federation.cfm.

50 Frequent and more severe than earlier floods, the Lena River flood affected Yakutia more than any other region in the Russian Arctic, causing multiple incidents of damage to infrastructure and collapse of vital sanitation and health services along the river basin. See Lynn Berry and Sergey Ponomarev, "Russia Flooding Raises Questions of Government Response" (July 9, 2012), www.huffingtonpost.com/2012/07/09/russia-flooding-government-response_n_1658996.html.

51 World Wildlife Fund-Russia, *The Impact of Climate Change on the Russian Arctic: Analysis and Paths to Solving the Problem* (WWF-Russia, Moscow, 2008), www.wwf.ru/resources/publ/book/eng/308/.

52 Caytlin Antrim, "The Next Geographical Pivot: The Russian Arctic in the Twenty-First Century," *U.S. Naval War College Review* 63, no. 6 (2010), www.usnwc.edu/getattachment/f8217b41-afd2–4649–8378–7b6c8a7e61d2/The-Next-Geographical-Pivot—The-Russian-Arctic-in.

53 United Kingdom Ocean Acidification Research Programme, "Acidification Impacts on the Surface Ocean," www.arcticoacruise.org/?page_id=455.

54 Lisa Robbins, "Studying Ocean Acidification in the Arctic Ocean" (Fact Sheet 2012-3058), U.S. Geological Survey (2012), http://pubs.usgs.gov/fs/2012/3058/.

55 Steeve Comeau, Ross Jeffree, Jean-Louis Teyssié, and Jean-Pierre Gattuso, "Response of the Arctic Pteropod Limacina Helicina to Projected Future Environmental Conditions," *PLOS ONE* 5, no. 6 (2010), www.plosone.org/article/info:doi/10.1371/journal.pone.0011362.

56 International Permafrost Association, *State of the Arctic Coast 2010: Scientific Review and Outlook* (2011), http://ipa.arcticportal.org/files/sac/state%20of%20the%20arctic%20rept.pdf.

57 United Nations Environment Programme (UNEP), "Coastal Arctic Food Web (Drift Ice)" (UNEP/GRID-Arendal, 2005), www.grida.no/graphicslib/detail/coastal-arctic-food-web-drift-ice_a0af.

58 Ian Stirling and Andrew Derocher, "Melting Under Pressure: The Real Scoop on Climate Warming and Polar Bears," *Wildlife Professional,* Fall (2007): 24–43, www.polarbearsinternational.org/sites/default/files/stirling_derocher_climate_wildlife_professional_2007.pdf.

59 Stirling and Derocher, "Melting Under Pressure."

60 Polar bear, Atlantic walrus, whales, other cetaceans, snow sheep, certain species and subspecies of whitefish and salmon, and migratory species of waterfowl and shorebirds such as geese, brant, and waders. "Strategic Action Plan," University of the Arctic, www.luarctic.org/RussianEnvironment_SpuoC.pdf.file.

61 World Wildlife Fund, "Polar Bear Status, Distribution, and Population," http://wwf.panda.org/what_we_do/where_we_work/arctic/wildlife/polar_bear/population/.

62 Alaska Sea Grant, "Walrus Numbers Decline" (Jan. 12, 2000), http://seagrant.uaf.edu/news/00ASJ/01.12.00_WalrusDecline.html.

63 Met Office, "Permafrost in Northern Russia: Understanding the Impact of Thawing Permafrost on Global Climate Change" (2010), www.metoffice.gov.uk/media/pdf/k/5/Permafrost_in_Russia.pdf.

64 Oleg Anisimov and Svetlanda Reneva, "Permafrost and Changing Climate: The Russian Perspective," *Ambio* 35 (2006): 169–75, www.ncbi.nlm.nih.gov/pubmed/16944641.

65 Anisimov and Reneva, "Permafrost and Changing Climate."

66 Terra Nature Trust, "Melting Permafrost Methane Emissions: Another Threat to Climate Change" (Sept. 15, 2006), http://terranature.org/methaneSiberia.htm.

67 Natalia Shakhova and Igor Semiletov, "Methane Release and Coastal Environment in the East Siberian Arctic Shelf," *Journal of Marine Systems* 66 (2007): 227–43, http://ic.ucsc.edu/~acr/BeringResources/Articles%20of%20interest/Eurasian%20Basin/Shakova%20and%20Semiletov%202007.pdf.

68 Natalia Shakhova, Igor Semiletov, Anatoly Salyuk, Vladimir Yusupov, Denis Kosmach, and Örjan Gustafsson, "Extensive Methane Venting to the Atmosphere from Sediments of the East Siberian Arctic Shelf," *Science* 327 (March 5, 2010), www.sciencemag.org/content/327/5970/1246.full.

69 United Nations Environment Program (UNEP), *Integrated Assessment of Black Carbon and Tropospheric Ozone* (2011), www.unep.org/dewa/Portals/67/pdf/Black_Carbon.pdf.

70 Arctic Portal, "Technical Report of the Arctic Council Task Force on Short-Lived Climate Forcers" (July 22, 2011), http://library.arcticportal.org/1210/1/ACTF_Report_22July2011.pdf.

71 Karen Bice, Andrew Eil, Bilal Habib, Pamela Heijmans, Robert Kopp, Juan Nogues, Frank Norcross, Maragaret Sweitzer-Hamilton, and Alex Whitworth, "Black Carbon: A Review and Policy Recommendations" (Woodrow Wilson School of Public and

International Affairs, Princeton University, 2009), http://wws.princeton.edu/research/PWReports/F08/wws591e.pdf.

72 James Corbett, Daniel Lack, James Winebrake, Susie Harder, Jordan Silberman, and Maya Gold, "Arctic Shipping Emissions Inventories and Future Scenarios," *Atmospheric Chemistry and Physics* 10 (2010): 9689–704, www.atmos-chem-phys.net/10/9689/2010/acp-10–9689–2010.pdf.

73 "Foundations of the Russian Federation's State Policy in the Arctic until 2020 and Beyond," Order 1969, approved by the president of the Russian Federation on Sept. 18, 2008, www.rg.ru/2009/03/30/arktika-osnovy-dok.html.

74 For a map of the AZRF, go to http://ic.pics.livejournal.com/miniku/12604377/67704/original.jpg.

75 The five Arctic coastal states (A5) are Canada, Denmark (via Greenland), Norway, Russia, and the United States.

76 Arctic Portal, "Foundations of the Russian Federation's State Policy in the Arctic until 2020 and Beyond" (Dec. 1, 2010), http://icr.arcticportal.org/index.php?option=com_content&view=article&id=1791:foundations-of-the-russian-federations-state-policy-in-the-arctic-until-2020-and-beyond&catid=45:news-2007&Itemid=111&lang=sa.

77 Solveig Glomsrød and Iulie Aslaksen, "The Economy of the North 2008," *Statistics Norway* (2009), www.ssb.no/english/subjects/00/00/30/sa_economy_north/sa112_en/sa112_en.pdf.

78 MBendi Information Services, "Nickel and Cobalt Mining in Asia—Overview," www.mbendi.com/indy/ming/nkcb/as/p0005.htm.

79 Mining World Russia, "Russian Federation—Mining Overview" (2013), www.miningworld-russia.com/pages/Russia.htm.

80 Oil and Gas Eurasia, "Russia's Oil Production and Global Developments" (May 2011), www.oilandgasEurasia.com/articles/p/140/article/1494/.

81 Vladimir Pavlenko and Elena Glukhareva, "Environmental Changes and the Economic Growth in Regions of the Russian Arctic," *Studies on Russian Economic Development* 21(2) (2010): 158–64, www.springerlink.com/content/3p5074g431574671/.

82 Pavlenko and Glukhareva, "Environmental Changes and the Economic Growth."

83 World Bank, *How Resilient Is the Energy Sector to Climate Change?* (Europe and Central Asia Region, World Bank, Washington, D.C., 2008), http://siteresources.worldbank.org/INTECA/Resources/AdaptationandEnergy11032009.pdf.

84 World Bank, *Past Environmental Liabilities in the Russian Federation* (2013), http://siteresources.worldbank.org/INTECAREGTOPENVIRONMENT/Resources/10843-Brochure3.pdf.

85 "Demonstration Project: Environmental Remediation of Decommissioned Military Bases on Franz Josef Land Archipelago," http://archive.iwlearn.net/npa-arctic.ru/publications/booklet_bases.pdf.

86 http://archive.iwlearn.net/npa-arctic.ru/Picture/hs_in_ra.jpg.pdf.

87 R.W. Macdonald, T. Harner, and J. Fyfe, "Recent Climate Change in the Arctic and Its Impact on Contaminant Pathways and Interpretation of Temporal Trend Data," *Science of the Total Environment* 342, no. 1–3 (2005): 5–86.

88 United Nations Russia, *Climate Change Impact on Public Health in the Russian Arctic* (2008), www.unrussia.ru/sites/default/files/doc/Arctic-eng.pdf.

89 Russian Federation, "Strategy for the Development of the Arctic Zone of the Russian Federation and Assuring National Security for the Period up to 2020" (Ministry of

Regional Development, Russian Federation, 2009), www.city-strateg.ru/UserFiles/File/strategar.doc.

90 World Economic Forum, *The Global Competitiveness Report 2011–2012* (2011), http://reports.weforum.org/global-competitiveness-2011–2012//.

91 United Nations, "UN Human Rights Experts Warn of Potential Damage by Russia's Draft Law to Civil Society" (July 12, 2012), www.un.org/apps/news/story.asp?NewsID=42457&Cr=russia&Cr1=.

92 "Russia Strangles International Indigenous Peoples Organization as War on NGOs Continues," *Bellona* (Nov. 15, 2012), www.bellona.org/articles/articles_2012/raipon_closure.

93 Arctic Council, "Permanent Participation Article Series: RAIPON," (Aug. 29, 2012), www.arctic-council.org/index.php/en/arctic-peoples/indigenous-people/596-permanent-participant-article-series-raipon.

94 "Moscow Orders Closure of Indigenous Peoples Organization," *Barents Observer* (Nov. 12, 2012), http://barentsobserver.com/en/arctic/moscow-orders-closure-indigenous-people-organization-12–11.

95 "NGOs to Be Called 'Foreign Agents' in Devastating New Bill under Consideration in Russia's Duma," *Bellona* (July 2, 2012), www.bellona.org/articles/articles_2012/NGO_foreign_agents.

96 "NGOs Vandalized and Intimidated by Pro-Kremlin Youth Groups as New Law Takes Effect," *Bellona* (Nov. 23, 2012), www.bellona.org/articles/articles_2012/ngo_vandals.

97 "Alaska Sprints to Build up Arctic Infrastructure as Development Looms," *Alaska Dispatch* (Aug. 25, 2012), www.alaskadispatch.com/article/alaska-sprints-build-arctic-infrastructure-development-looms.

98 Trude Pettersen, "Russia to Submit Arctic Claims by Year's End," *Barents Observer* (Jan. 24, 2013), http://barentsobserver.com/en/arctic/2013/01/russia-submit-arctic-claims-years-end-24–01.

99 Kelley Drye & Warren LLP, "The Obama Administration Releases New Model Bilateral Investment Treaty with Enhanced Disciplines" (May 7, 2012), www.kelleydrye.com/publications/client_advisories/0742.

100 The Global Facility for Disaster Reduction and Recovery is a global partnership that was established in 2006 and is led by the World Bank and the United Nations in partnership with 41 countries and six other international organizations. See Global Facility for Disaster Reduction and Recovery, "About GFDRR" (2013), http://gfdrr.org/gfdrr/node/1.

101 The Global Environment Facility was established by the World Bank in 1991; it partners with 182 countries, international institutions, civil society organizations, and the private sector. See Global Environment Facility, "Detail of GEF Project #4664" (2013), www.thegef.org/gef/project_detail?projID=4664, and Global Environment Facility, "What Is the GEF" (2013), www.thegef.org/gef/whatisgef.

3

BRAZIL AND THE UNITED STATES

Cooperation on Sustainable Development

Ricardo Ubiraci Sennes

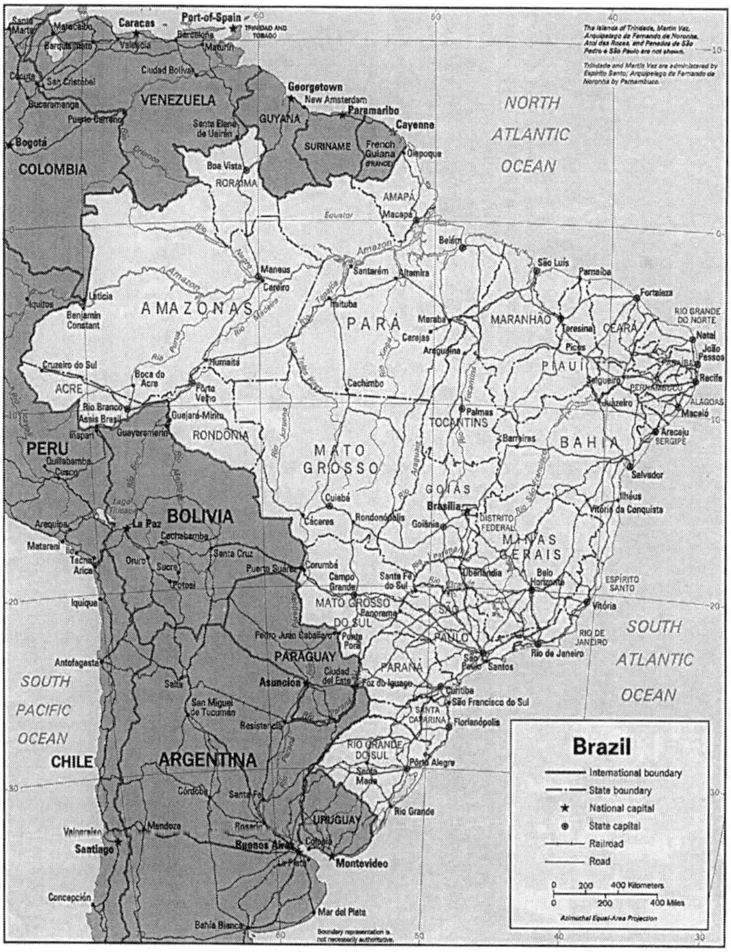

Over the past decade, Brazil has assumed a growing role on the world stage as a major economy and a leader in South America and the developing world. Economic growth has been strong, the economy has been stable, and the country has achieved substantial reductions in poverty. Brazil is now the world's eighth-largest economy and a top producer of agricultural products, energy, and manufactured goods. Poverty is down 24 percent since 2003 as a result of growth and strong social programs. These social gains have made Brazil a model for the developing world. Brazil has enormous natural resources, including land, water, minerals, and biodiversity. It is well known as the home of the Amazon, which is of great global value for its biodiversity and its role in storing carbon and regulating the global climate. With its vast territory, Brazil is also home to other critical ecosystems that play a central role in global food and energy production and sustainability.

The Brazilian economy's heavy reliance on natural resources, including hydropower, iron ore, and agriculture, generates pressure on the environment. Although Brazil has made substantial strides to develop clean and renewable energy and to protect its tropical forests, conflicts between economic growth and sustainability are becoming increasingly pronounced. Opposition to new hydroelectric dams, disagreements over the causes of deforestation, concerns about the expansion of agriculture, the threat of climate change, and a recent political battle over revision of the country's Forest Code all bring this tension to the forefront of Brazil's domestic political debates. Parallel to these conflicts is the tension between Brazil's international position as a leader among developing countries and its frequent opposition to the developed countries in international forums.

The recent diplomatic relationship between Brazil and the United States has more often been characterized by tension than by cooperation, particularly in international forums. Economic and social ties have been more effective in bringing the two countries together than political or strategic efforts; relationships among private entities from the two countries have often been more positive than that between the governments. The gulf between the two governments has a long history.[1] After World War II, asymmetries in political and economic power led to growing political opposition and a series of misunderstandings on both sides. This conflict has continued as Brazil has positioned itself as a leader in Latin America and among the world's emerging economies and still affects the day-to-day relationship between the two governments on some issues. Brazil's official positions on many global issues, in forums such as the Group of Twenty (G-20), Rio+20, and the United Nations, diverge from those of the United States. Although there have been collaboration and joint projects in a number of areas, there has been little interest in significant cooperation on issues such as the global order, regional security, and sustainable development.

Economic and social links between the two countries have been increasing, but bilateral political and strategic cooperation has lagged. However, the emergence of Brazil as a regional leader and its stable and growing economy could open new opportunities for strategic partnership between Brazil and the United States. Brazil has been an ally on a number of issues, including international peacekeeping missions, and has recently established a "global partnership dialogue" with the Obama administration. Today, both countries have a strong interest in clean energy and sustainable development that could provide the basis for forging a more collaborative engagement, beginning with existing civil society links. Fostering these informal links in the realm of sustainable development could open new opportunities to overcome current obstacles to intergovernmental cooperation.

This chapter explores the potential for Brazil-U.S. cooperation on sustainable development. The first section discusses Brazil's economic policies and the shape of its economy. The second section focuses on Brazil's development model and the environment. The third section analyzes the positions that Brazil has taken in international forums and illustrates the differences between the two countries. The last section explores ways in which cooperation on sustainable development, particularly in the areas of biofuels, climate change, and green technology, could be fostered and the United States' stake in ensuring environmental sustainability in Brazil enhanced.

Brazil's Economic Growth

Brazil's largely state-driven economic development has relied heavily on expansion of the domestic market and use of the country's extensive natural resources. Although this model has enjoyed some success, Brazil's dependence on state investment currently impedes further growth. At the same time, tensions between Brazil's economic path and development policies and the demands of sustainability are becoming increasingly apparent.

In the 1950s, Brazil's development strategy was one of import-substitution industrialization, which successfully built basic industries. This strategy went largely unchanged under the military dictatorship (1964–1985) and was only partially dismantled in the 1990s, when economic and state reforms were implemented in the wake of the financial crises of the 1980s. Throughout this period, Brazil focused on protecting its economy from international rules that could have forced economic liberalization and from direct economic competition with developed countries. Protectionism fostered an urban industrial economy dominated by a network of medium- and low-tech companies catering to the domestic market. These companies still play an outsized role in the economy.

As the impacts of debt crises in the 1980s and 1990s spread through developing countries, structural adjustment was a key component of the neoliberal solution. In Brazil, following years of high inflation, the 1990 *Plano Real* macroeconomic stabilization program succeeded where previous plans had failed. This stabilization plan, instituted by the Collor de Mello administration, included an important privatization agenda, government reforms, and the creation of regulatory agencies related to the infrastructure sector (telecom, oil and gas, water resources, etc.) in addition to significant economic opening. Industrial policy centered on an across-the-board reduction in tariffs. The *Plano Real* had the support of the International Monetary Fund (IMF), the World Bank, and the Group of Eight (G-8). In 1994, Brazil participated in the Brady Plan, which restructured the external debt with U.S. Treasury support. Until 2002, Brazil used agreements with the IMF as insurance against a crisis of confidence in the financial market, pledging to achieve primary surpluses—that is, to save money to pay the interest on its debts. After 2002, Brazil stopped drawing money from the IMF; in 2005, Brazil did not renew its agreement and settled its debt with an early payment of $15.5 billion. This phase in Brazilian economic history was critical for establishing stability; however, the adoption of neoliberal macroeconomic policies was at odds with Brazil's statist tradition.

With macroeconomic stability established, economic policy shifted to focus on growth (2002–2010) by strengthening the domestic market, domestic companies, economic competitiveness, and innovation. Although the country achieved success on the first two objectives, the latter two met with less than impressive results. Brazil's economic growth has been strong, averaging 3.7 percent from 2001 to 2008, peaking at 6 percent in 2007. During the global economic crisis year of 2009, performance was well above the world average, decreasing only 0.2 percent and returning to 7.5 percent in 2010. However, growth slowed in 2011 and 2012, averaging 2.7 percent and 0.7 percent, respectively. The first quarter of 2013 also registered weak performance: 0.6 percent.

Domestic demand has driven growth in Brazil's gross domestic product (GDP) (Figure 3.1). In other emerging economies, high rates of investment have driven growth. In Brazil, the key factor has been a high level of demand for durable and nondurable consumer goods.

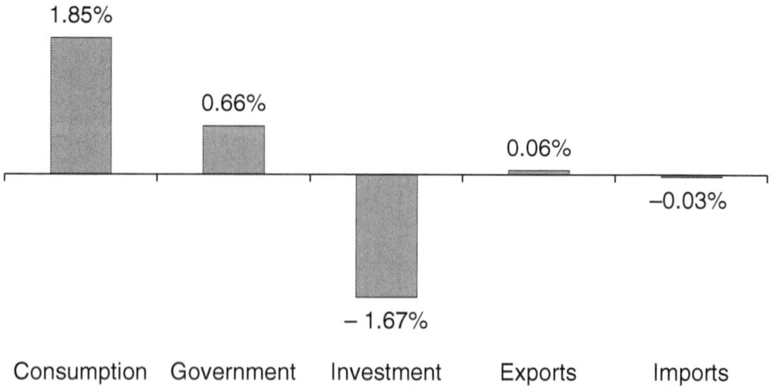

FIGURE 3.1 GDP Growth in Brazil, Demand Side, 2012

Source: IPEADATA.

In 2002, under the first administration of President Lula da Silva, the Brazilian government returned to the promotion of industrial policies, with varying degrees of protection for selected sectors. The past decade has seen three industrial policy cycles, coinciding with the first and second administrations of Lula da Silva and the 2011 election of President Dilma Rousseff. The latest plan promoting industrial growth in Brazil, the *Plano Brasil Maior* (Greater Brazil), is a continuation of previous policies, although it puts more stress on innovation for development. The plan aims to increase the competitiveness of the Brazilian economy and sets specific goals, including (a) expanding different forms of investment, (b) working with the business sector to increase investment in research and development, (c) building workforce capacity, (d) increasing national value-added in manufacturing, (e) increasing the share of knowledge-intensive industries in GDP, (f) diversifying exports, (g) increasing access to goods and services that improve the quality of life, and (h) promoting sustainable development.[2] To achieve these goals, the government is relying heavily on the use of government procurement to support domestic industries and services. Another relevant policy initiative, the Growth Acceleration Program (PAC), is a $500 billion investment program that combines management initiatives and public projects, focusing on investments in logistics, energy, and social development. Launched in 2007 during President Lula da Silva's second term and since led by President Rousseff, the program aims to encourage public and private investments. The most recent official report on the PAC concluded that only 53 percent of the project has been implemented.[3]

Several social programs, in combination with improved access to credit and strengthening of the labor market, have improved social indicators. Conditional cash transfer programs were expanded under President Lula da Silva, starting in 2000. *Fome Zero* and *Bolsa Família* are the two main programs, benefiting some 30 million of Brazil's poorest through four subprograms: educational stipends to boost school attendance, maternal nutrition, food supplements, and a domestic gas subsidy.

Domestic demand for goods and services has been stimulated by credit expansion,[4] an increase in workers' wages, and growing household consumption (Figure 3.2). Consumption has increased not only for essential goods but also for high-tech goods and luxury items. The Lula da Silva administration made an effort to expand the country's credit supply, which has largely taken effect in the past few years. Total credit as a share of GDP increased from 22 percent in 2002 to 54 percent by 2012, according to the Central Bank of Brazil. Public-sector banks (e.g., Banco do Brasil and Caixa Econômica Federal) have played a central role in credit expansion.

Lula da Silva's and Dilma Rousseff's economic plans aimed to sustain the current growth cycle by expanding Brazil's internal market, promoting demand for basic household consumption and durable goods, and providing incentives in the housing sector, as well as focusing on basic industries and infrastructure. These priorities are reflected in economic projections (Table 3.1). According to Brazilian Development Bank (BNDES) reports, investment in Brazil in the coming years will be driven by five major sectors: oil and gas, electricity, logistics, housing

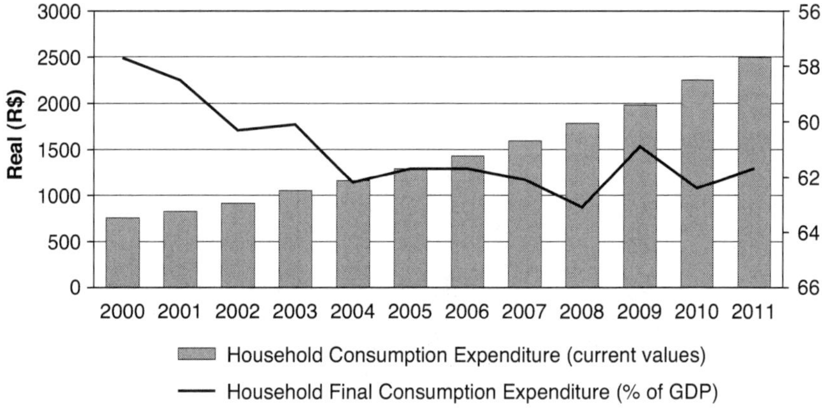

FIGURE 3.2 Household Consumption in Brazil, 2000–2011

Source: Brazilian Institute of Geography and Statistics.

TABLE 3.1 Investment Projections for Brazil, 2008–2011 and 2013–2016

Sectors	*2008–2011*	*2013–2016*	*Accumulated variation*	*Growth rate*
	in 2012 US$ billion		*(in %)*	*Linear average (in % per year)*
Industry	434.4	529.7	21.9	4.0
Infrastructure	184.3	250.8	39.2	6.4
Services	81.5	111.5	36.7	6.5
Housing	305.6	394.9	29.2	5.2
Other Sectors	507.7	664.6	30.9	5.5
Total	1513.5	1951.5	29.0	5.2

Source: BNDES.

construction, and agribusiness. The largest share of investment is expected to go to the oil and gas and electricity sectors; the highest investment growth rate is expected to be in the oil and gas and infrastructure, not only for railways and ports sectors.

The weakness of the long-term investment credit supply is a threat to current economic growth. The Brazilian investment rate did rise from historic levels of 14–15 percent to 19.1 percent in 2011, but at the current rate of 19 percent it is considered low by international standards.

The public sector still dominates investment lending. BNDES accounted for 39.6 percent of total industrial investment in 2011, and together the three state-owned banks (BNDES, Banco do Brasil, and Caixa Econômica Federal) represent 87 percent of the credit supply, while foreign direct investment (FDI) has been directed toward the service sector. Between 2007 and 20012, the share of services in FDI inflows and industry increased; however, the share of the mining, agriculture, and livestock industries fell from 14 percent to 13 percent of total FDI. Industry was the most negatively affected by this process of turning the economy toward the domestic market.

The country's low investment rate has been one of the most critical problems in its development policy. Brazil invests a very small proportion of its GDP compared with the other BRICS (Brazil, Russia, India, China, and South Africa). Growth of public-sector investment, particularly investment in the state oil and gas company, Petrobras, has been the main driver of the increase in investment, leaving the private sector to play a supporting role. Public investment for 2011–2014 is allocated largely to the oil and gas and electricity sectors. Some R$614 billion, or 61 percent, will be invested in the oil and gas sector, primarily Petrobras, and R$380 billion, or 36 percent, will be invested in infrastructure for the energy sector, with Eletrobras and BNDES as the main drivers.

The low rate of private-sector participation is another weakness, limiting Brazil's capacity to compete internationally. The balance of trade has been positive since 2000; however, the gap between exports and imports has been shrinking since 2006 (Figure 3.3). Exports of high value-added goods have lost some of their dynamism, and imports—particularly high value-added imports—have

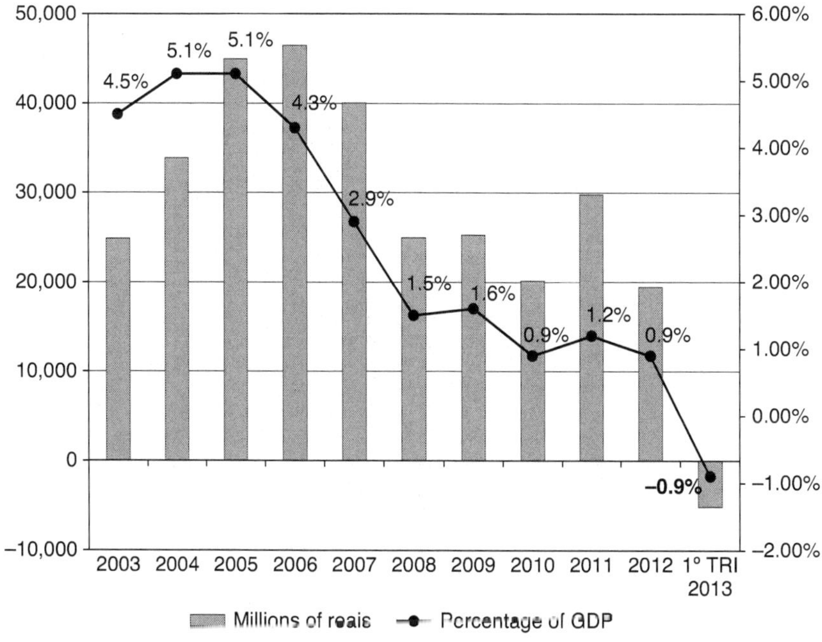

FIGURE 3.3 Brazil's Trade Balance, 2003–2013

Source: Central Bank of Brazil (2013).

grown at significant rates. Brazilian exports are increasingly concentrated among commodities. More critically, 30 percent of exports are accounted for by just three products—iron ore, oil, and soybeans. In the cases of iron ore and oil, two companies account for virtually all production, increasing the fragility of Brazil's current account surplus.

These sectors at the core of the Brazilian economy—which are the main focus of investment and provide most of the country's exports—have major environmental impacts. Already, increases in domestic consumption and Brazil's growing energy needs have put a wedge between the resource demands of economic growth and environmental protection. Large hydroelectric projects, which account for 80 percent of the country's energy use, are at capacity. At the same time, rising food prices have led to an expansion in agricultural production, often achieved through illegal land acquisition rather than increases in efficiency. With the weak trade balance and dependence on iron ore, oil, and soybeans, actions and policies aimed at environmental sustainability often arouse serious controversy in Brazil. Such has been the case with the recent battle over the Forest Code, which will be discussed below. Conflict between the agribusiness lobby and environmentalists resulted in a standoff between the president and the Chamber of Deputies. Because the dependence on natural resources creates tension between economic policies that seek to bolster economic growth and environmental policies that may affect production, it has been difficult to balance economic and environmental objectives.

Brazil's Development Model and the Environment

Brazil's development model has had an enormous impact on the environment because of the central role of the natural resource sectors, including iron ore, hydroelectric plants, and extensive agribusiness, as well as the intense urbanization the country has faced in the past decades. This section reviews some of the effects on the Amazon rainforest at the hands of the agriculture and energy sectors and evaluates Brazil's response to those impacts.

Deforestation and Climate Change

The Amazon is the largest rainforest on Earth, covering 40 percent of the South American continent. More than 60 percent of the Amazon rainforest is in Brazil, and that area of Brazil is home to more than 20 million inhabitants. Although still extensively forested, the region has passed through an intense period of development through a combination of energy projects, land speculation, cattle ranching, commercial and subsistence agriculture, and mining.

During the 1970s and 1980s, intense deforestation and extraction activities were driven by an expansion of agricultural and pasture land and by informal settlement. These activities were supported by government monetary incentives in the agricultural sector, as well as substantial investments in infrastructure, such as the Trans-Amazonian Highway, an ambitious project built under the military regime to connect northern Brazil with the rest of the country. Deforestation continues today but at a much lower rate (Figure 3.4). Cattle ranches and commercial agriculture remain the largest culprits, although soybean production now contributes to the direct clearing of the forest and has pushed cattle ranching into forested areas, increasing the level of deforestation.

The use of new monitoring technologies has contributed to the reduced deforestation rate in recent years. The PRODES Project (Surveillance of the Brazilian Amazonian Forest by Satellite), coordinated by the National Institute of Space Technology (INPE), has used satellite images to provide bimonthly surveys to monitor Amazon deforestation since 1989. Satellite images show, for example, that large burn areas are now less common in the Amazon than they were 10 years ago. Although there were fewer burns (102,841) in 2000, they were highly concentrated. Given this new monitoring capacity and the government's efforts to fine lawbreakers, the nature of deforestation has changed. On the one hand, the increase in burn spot numbers for 2012 (150,367) reflects an increase in deforestation in the Cerrado grassland region rather than the forest itself. On the other hand, fires extend into the forest in areas that previously had limited access.

In 2005, the Amazon region suffered what was considered the worst drought in 100 years. The effects were so grave that scientists predicted another such event would not occur for another century. But in 2010, drought struck the region again. According to studies by the Amazon Environmental Research Institute, in

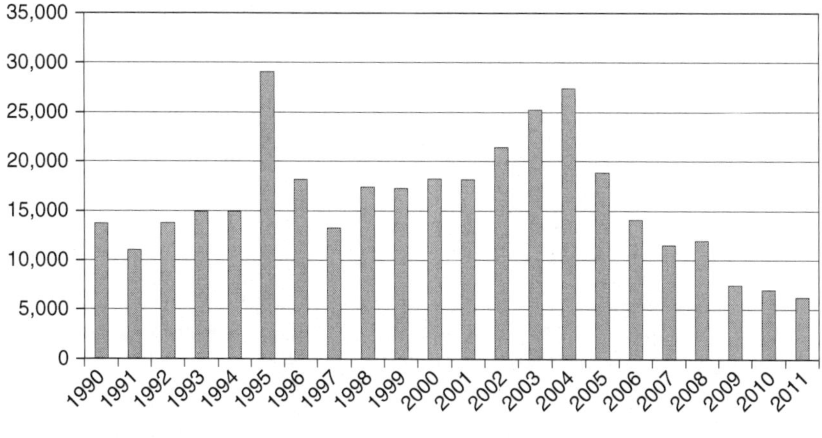

FIGURE 3.4 Deforestation in the Brazilian Amazon, 1990–2011

Source: National Institute for Space Research.

Note: Values are square kilometers of deforestation per year.

partnership with the University of Leeds, the drought of 2010 was even more severe. In 2005, 37 percent of forest in the region suffered severe rainfall deficit; in 2010, 57 percent was affected. Although less severe, the 2011–2012 period also showed atypical rainfall, with less precipitation than usual.

Reduced rainfall directly affects a large range of social groups whose commercial and subsistence activities depend on the forest. Lack of rain has caused problems for farmers in several regions near the Amazon rainforest. In the state of Piauí, 48 municipalities declared a state of emergency because of drought at the beginning of 2012. In the municipality of Jata in Goias, 40 percent of the banana crop failed. In Bahia, the soybean harvest fell by approximately 10 percent and cotton by 6.3 percent. The reduction in water levels has affected river transport, fishing, and subsistence activities for river-dependent communities.

Deforestation can significantly impact tropical rainfall. According to a study by the University of Leeds and the Natural Environment Research Council's Centre for Ecology and Hydrology, air passing over extensive tropical forest produces twice as much rain as air passing over land with little vegetation.[5] In some cases, forest vegetation generates increases in rainfall thousands of kilometers away. By combining observational data with predictions of future deforestation, the researchers estimate that destruction of tropical forests could reduce rain across the Amazon Basin by up to a fifth by the year 2050. Drought impacts extend beyond Brazil to affect the rest of the world. In addition to environmental costs, such as biodiversity loss, reduced water availability leads to higher tree mortality. According to climate studies, the world's remaining tropical forests remove 4.8 billion tons of carbon dioxide (CO_2) from the atmosphere each year, roughly equivalent to annual U.S. emissions from fossil fuels.[6] If this vegetation dies, billions of tons of CO_2 will not be absorbed, thus accelerating climate change.

A scientific report published in *Nature* magazine suggests that the world's remaining tropical forests remove 4.8 billion tons of CO_2 emissions from the atmosphere each year. This includes a previously unknown carbon sink in Africa, which annually absorbs 1.2 billion tons of CO_2.

Brazilian Forest Code

Brazil has projected itself as a champion of sustainability and an agent for sustainable development on the international stage. Brazil has promoted this image in multilateral forums and meetings on the environment, as Conferences of the Parties meetings in Copenhagen have shown. Nevertheless, at home, Brazil has had difficulty overcoming conflicts between the country's current pragmatic, resource-based development model and the concerns of environmentalists. This conflict has come to a head in the debate over the new Forest Code.

Congress has been debating the revision of the 1965 Forest Code, particularly as it affects agriculture and livestock production, since 1999. The 1965 code set limits on the clearing of land parcels, requiring that 80 percent of native vegetation be maintained as "legal reserves" in the Amazon, 35 percent in the savannah, and 20 percent in other biomes. The code also set requirements for protection of forests along riverbanks, other bodies of water, and hillsides, known as permanent preservation areas, with larger areas required for larger landholdings. However, enforcement has always been lax and incentives for compliance few. As enforcement of the Forest Code became stricter in the 1990s, particularly with the implementation of satellite surveillance in 2008, opposition began to grow among farmers and agribusiness operations. Strongly influenced by the agricultural lobby, Congress favored reducing the conservation requirements, with the Chamber of Deputies favoring even greater reduction than the Senate, while the administration has pushed to keep stringent laws for medium and large property owners. The Chamber of Deputies approved a new text in May 2011, representing a defeat for the administration's position. When the new text reached the Senate in December, the Senate modified it to align with the administration's position. Because of the substantial differences between the two versions, the code returned to the Chamber, which rejected the Senate's changes before approving the law. Several organizations, including the World Wildlife Fund, Greenpeace, the Brazilian Academy of Sciences, and the Catholic Church, pressed President Rousseff to veto the new code. Stakeholders favoring the congressional version organized to override any presidential vetoes.

As expected, President Rousseff was dissatisfied with the new code. She vetoed 12 items and altered several others in the text approved by the Chamber of Deputies, partially restoring the conservation requirements for medium and large property holders. In essence, the new law reduces the 80 percent requirement for native vegetation in the Amazon for some states, reduces the amount of land that must be kept forested along riverbanks and hillsides, and grants an amnesty to small farmers who have already overstepped the limits on clearing.

The new law displeases both environmentalists and the rural lobby. Environmentalists believe that even with the line-item vetoes, the new law is too weak. The Committee in Defense of the Forests and Sustainable Development, an umbrella organization for 163 civil society groups, called the law "environmentally backward," because it allows amnesty for deforesters and reduces the size of protected areas. One study by the University of São Paulo concluded that the proposed changes, in addition to abolishing the need to restore, which was already defined by the original Forest Code, would put an additional 22 million hectares at risk of deforestation.[7] Environmentalists are concerned that large landholders, who control the lion's share of Brazil's agricultural land, may subdivide their properties to take advantage of the amnesty intended for smallholders.

The rural lobby believes that the law is too strict and will negatively impact agribusiness productivity. The Ministry of Agriculture predicts a 24.7 percent decrease in coffee production and a 27.3 percent reduction in cereal, legume, and oilseed cultivation. For the Chamber of Deputies and for organizations such as the Confederation of Agriculture and Livestock of Brazil, weak GDP performance means that economic criteria, not environmental concerns, should guide the debate. Moreover, farmers argue that compliance is difficult—there are too many obstacles to the public registration of reserves and to meet preservation requirements.

Given the technical and pragmatic approach preferred by President Rousseff, the new Forest Code takes a middle-of-the-road approach, favoring neither the agricultural nor the environmental lobby. The new law will most likely be contested in the Supreme Court, but clearly the environment is not an issue on which the current government is willing to spend its political capital.

Agribusiness

Brazil has emerged as a major agricultural producer. A net importer of agricultural products in the 1970s, the country now ranks among the world's five largest agricultural producers, third among the world's agricultural exporters, and fourth for food products. Agriculture remains a driving force in the Brazilian economy, accounting for 5.5 percent of GDP, and agribusiness accounts for 23 percent of GDP.[8]

Between 1990 and 2005, Brazilian agricultural production increased by more than 100 percent, driven primarily by export markets. In the case of soybeans, Brazil has increased production by 110 percent over the past 10 years. Brazil is now the world's largest exporter of sugarcane, poultry, beef, and orange juice and accounts for one-third of the world's soybean exports. In the case of soybeans, it is interesting to note that Brazil has not taken any market share from its main competitors, the United States and Argentina; all three were able to increase production because of growing Chinese demand. However, productivity gains in the agricultural sector have been driven by the introduction of new machinery, equipment, and agricultural inputs.

Rapid expansion of soybean production in Brazil's savannah, the Cerrado, has resulted from new techniques to overcome the high acidity and low nutrient levels in Cerrado soils and the development of crops and pasture grass that are suited to that particular climate. Together these innovations have turned the Cerrado into an agricultural powerhouse accounting for 70 percent of Brazil's farm output. Since 1996, land in production in the Cerrado has increased by a third. Spurred by strong demand, soybeans have done well and, as a result, production is expanding into the Amazon region. The development of a new variety of soybean that flourishes in the rainforest climate has enabled this expansion. Infrastructure, including highways, has gone hand in hand with the shift to agricultural production.

In addition to changes in production techniques, important changes have occurred in the marketing of agricultural products. In the 1970s, large-scale agribusiness began to develop toward international markets, particularly for grains and meat. Since the 1990s, a series of mergers and acquisitions has led to concentration of the export sector in the hands of a few large multinational agribusiness companies. This consolidation has increased the political strength of the sector.

These changes have aggravated some social conflicts, leading to the expansion of a number of social movements, including the Movement of Landless Workers (*Movimento dos Trabalhadores Sem Terra*), Rural Unionism (*Sindicalismo Rural*), and the Women's Farmer Movement (*Movimento das Mulheres Agricultores*). Nongovernmental organizations (NGOs) have emerged with renewed strength and a solid basis for questioning the current development model.

The controversy over the Forest Code is just one example of the tensions arising from conflicts between economic and environmental goals. Another example, widely discussed by NGOs and research institutions, is the root cause of deforestation. The agribusiness sector maintains that commercial agriculture is not the primary driver of deforestation, despite the assertion of environmental groups that soybean expansion is directly linked to deforestation in the Amazon.

According to a study by two business organizations, the Institute for International Trade Negotiations (ICONE) and the São Paulo State Federation of Industries (FIESP), livestock and other intensive crops will not be the main drivers of deforestation over the next 10 years.[9] The study finds that demand for new land for agriculture and livestock production will be lower than it was in past years; by 2022, the need for additional land could fall by as much as 63 percent in comparison with 2002–2011.

According to Rodrigo C. A. Lima, ICONES general manager and a researcher at RedeAgro, agribusiness is not solely responsible for deforestation. He blames small farmers and agrarian reform settlers, who are largely subsistence producers, for much of the small-scale deforestation of the Amazon. Deforestation of small plots may escape satellite monitoring systems and enforcement of forest policies. According to Lima, other issues that deserve attention are the lack of effective incentives for sustainable forest management and for reducing illegal logging, which often opens lands to small farmers, and the failure of land documenting claims throughout Brazil.

A joint survey by INPE and the Brazilian Agricultural Research Corporation (EMBRAPA) shows that more than 60 percent of the deforested area in the Amazon has been turned into pasture. The study categorized the deforested area in 10 classes of use, including livestock, agriculture, mining, secondary vegetation, and urban occupations (Figure 3.5).[10] Agricultural production occupies only about 5 percent of the total deforested area in the Amazon. According to INPE's director, Gilberto Câmara, the large percentage of deforestation that is linked to

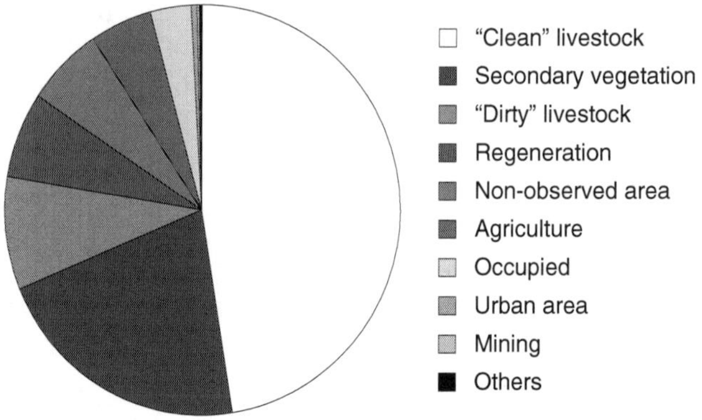

FIGURE 3.5 Land Use in Deforested Areas of the Amazon, 2010

Source: TerraClass (2011).

Note: "Clean" livestock refers to productive pasture areas with a predominance of herbaceous vegetation and grass species covering between 50 percent and 80 percent, associated with the presence of sparse scrub coverage (between 20 percent and 50 percent). "Dirty" livestock refers to productive pasture areas with a predominance of herbaceous vegetation and grass species covering between 90 percent and 100 percent. See TerraClass (2011).

pasture (60 percent) shows that in Brazil livestock is still an activity based on a system that requires public policies to foster intensive system models. It is not, even from the economic point of view, the best production option for those areas. Agriculture would be the most productive use of this deforested land.

On the other side of the issue, an article published in the *Proceedings of the National Academy of Sciences* found that expanding soybean production is not confined to areas that have previously been cleared for pasture.[11] After cross-referencing satellite data, maps of changes in vegetation cover, and field research, a team of Brazilian and U.S. scientists estimated that 5,400 square kilometers of forest in the state of Mato Grosso was converted directly to soybean cultivation between 2001 and 2004. Deforestation for grain cultivation increased 10 percent over this period, while clearing for pastures declined by 12 percent. Rapidly expanding soybean cultivation uses extensive technologies and has the potential to spread to other forested regions. This interpretation is broadly confirmed by NGOs such as Greenpeace and Mongabay.

Studies by environmental organizations,[12] by contrast, find that intensive crops such as sugarcane and soybeans are putting pressure on the land now used for cattle, pushing cattle ranching into protected areas.[13] The argument is that sugarcane and soybean production are indirectly linked to increasing deforestation of the Amazon and the Cerrado despite the fact that production is not expanding in those regions. However, according to a study by ICONE and

FIESP, sugarcane and soybeans are expanding only in already cleared areas, primarily pasturelands.[14] In the case of sugarcane, the study finds that land area will actually shrink because of an increase in productivity (tons per hectare) that is projected to reach 1.3 percent per year between 2011 and 2023. One of the incentives for that process would be the strong increase in agricultural land in the country.

Although these studies were conceived and interpreted independently, it is clear that the production of some Brazilian crop yields will not meet increasing global demand without expanding the amount of land used for cultivation and livestock. Demand from emerging trade partners, particularly China, is growing so rapidly as to outstrip any yield gains. High prices for agricultural products, lack of regulation, and the remoteness of some undeveloped areas all promote incursion into forested areas. The perpetrators are not generally large agribusiness operations but rather small- and medium-size rural producers. These producers operate in the informal sector but benefit from opportunities created by the rapid growth of the agribusiness sector. For example, small informal ranchers sell their meat in local markets, avoiding inspections and the taxes that go with them, or they sell meat to larger meat processors through intermediaries that use false inspections and certificates of origin.

In the absence of consensus on the main causes of deforestation, civil society movements have begun to engage producer groups on the matter. Initiatives bringing together NGOs and large private enterprises are underway. In 2009, a project proposed by Greenpeace brought together the four largest companies to combat deforestation, slave labor, and the invasion of forested lands in the Amazon linked to cattle production.[15] In 2010, those Brazilian companies became signatories of a Conduct Adjustment Contract (*Termo de Ajuste de Conduta*) with the Federal Public Ministry committing not to buy meat or leather from cattle ranches engaged in these activities. In addition, the meat industry will adopt a program that includes rigorous monitoring of deforestation along the production chain. In March 2013, the Brazilian Supermarket Association, Supermercados, sealed a similar pact with the Federal Public Ministry, promising not to purchase meat unless it was certified that it was not produced in the Amazon or other unsustainable environs.

The debate over the causes of deforestation has made it clear that the lack of state monitoring and enforcement capacity over extensive areas is detrimental to efforts to reduce deforestation. Civil society engagement with consumers and industry can help establish good practices, but alone it will not solve the problem of deforestation. Brazilian society must choose between expanding agriculture and protecting the environment. As discussed above, increased clearing of the Amazon may ultimately harm agriculture by reducing the availability of water and reducing productivity not only in the Amazon region but also elsewhere.

Renewable Energy

The Brazilian energy matrix is one of the cleanest in the world.[16] Renewable sources supply more than 45 percent of Brazil's energy needs, while the global average is 13 percent and only 8 percent in high-income countries.[17] The bulk of Brazil's electricity is generated by hydroelectric projects, which account for 71 percent of installed capacity. Thermoelectric power accounts for 28 percent of installed capacity (of which 11.4 percent is gas, 7.3 percent thermal biomass, 1.7 percent nuclear, and 1.7 percent coal). Wind power provides just less than 1 percent of Brazil's energy.[18]

Brazil is the world's tenth-largest consumer of electricity.[19] Since 2001, Brazil's energy use has increased by 38 percent, faster than the world energy use average of 30 percent.[20] According to studies of energy supply conducted by the Ministry of Mines and Energy, the Brazilian economy is expected to grow by 5 percent per year between 2010 and 2020, which will require a significant increase in energy infrastructure.[21] Investments of $475 billion in energy expansion are planned (2012–2020), of which 63 percent will be in oil and gas, 22 percent in electricity, and 15 percent in biomass, together representing 2.6 percent of GDP.

Hydroelectric Power

Hydropower will continue to be Brazil's primary source of electricity, and it is expected to account for more than half of new production capacity.[22] However, some of the locations with the greatest potential for hydropower production are in remote regions and subject to strong environmental restrictions. Existing hydropower plants are near capacity and new hydro projects—Belo Monte, Jirau, and Santo Antônio—are facing serious opposition on environmental and social grounds. Other renewable sources are growing in importance in part because of socioeconomic and environmental concerns over hydro projects. The following are two examples:

- *Belo Monte (planned).* The government approved construction of this controversial hydroelectric dam on the Amazon's Xingu River despite strong opposition from environmentalists and indigenous activists who assert that the project will cause environmental damage and displace indigenous tribes. It will be the world's third-largest hydro plant. According to the Brazilian Energy Ministry, the R$20 billion dam will come online in 2015 and will eventually produce 11 gigawatts of electricity. However, it will flood about 500 square kilometers, which activists believe will displace thousands of people.
- *Itaipú (operating).* This enormous dam on the Paraná River, with a total production capacity of 14 gigawatts, provides 20 percent of Brazil's

> electricity and 94 percent of Paraguay's electricity supply. The dam is almost 8,000 meters long and reaches a height of 196 meters, equivalent to a 65-story building. Negative impacts of dam construction did occur on the surrounding wildlife. Large amounts of forest along the Paraguayan side of the river were destroyed, and several waterfalls and dips have been overrun by the development of the reservoir. Almost 60,000 people were displaced and relocated as a result of the construction of the dam.

The federal government continues to bet on the rapid expansion of hydroelectric companies, as evidenced by the ambitious schedule of rights auctions listed in Table 3.2. Many of the scheduled auctions are in or close to the Amazon region.

TABLE 3.2 Scheduled Hydroelectric Auctions, 2013–2017

Leilão	*Hibrelétrica*	*Rio/UF*	*Capacidade (MW)*	*Capacidade Total (MW)*	*Investimentos estimados em Dez/2012 (R$bilhões)*
2013	SINOP	Teles Pires/MT	400	1,407	6,2
	Davinópolis	Paranaíba/MG-GO	74		
	São Manoel	Teles Pires/MT-PA	700		
	Apertados	Piquiri/PR	136		
	Ercilândia	Piquiri/PR	97		
2014	S. Luiz Tapajós	Tapajós/PA	6,133	7,241	24,4
	Água Limpa	das Mortes/MT	380		
	Comissário	Piquiri/PR	105		
	Foz Piquiri	Piquiri/PR	101		
	Telêmaco Borba	Tibagi/PR	109		
	Paranhos	Chopim/PR	63		
	Tabajara	Ji-Paraná/RO	350		
2015	Jatobá	Tapajós/PA	2,336	3,249	12,4
	Castanhiera	Arinos/MT	192		
	Itapiranga	Uruguai/SC-RS	721		
2016	Torixoréu	Araguaia/GO-MT	408	1,117	5,3
	Bem Querer	Branco/RR	709		

Source: EPE (Energy Planning Company)

Column heads: Year, Hydroelectric company, Location, Capacity (megawatts), Total capacity (megawatts), Estimated investment (billions of reals).

Biofuels

Two liquid biofuels are widely used in Brazil: ethanol made from sugarcane and used in light vehicles and, more recently, biodiesel made from vegetable oils and animal fats and mainly used in buses and trucks. Biofuel production surged in the 1970s in the wake of the first oil crisis. The government's *Proálcool* Program introduced ethanol on a large scale with the aim of replacing gasoline-powered vehicles. By 1980, the initial production target of 3 billion liters had been met. The program was given a boost when flex-fuel cars were introduced in 2003 (Figure 3.6); by 2008, about 92 percent of the cars sold in Brazil were flex-fuel vehicles.[23] Investments in flex-fuel vehicles and in the ethanol supply chain led to a large increase in domestic ethanol production, which reached a peak of 27.9 billion liters in 2010. Currently about 90 percent of Brazil's ethanol is produced in the mid-south, with the state of São Paulo alone accounting for 60 percent, and the remainder in the northeast.

The National Program for Production and Use of Biodiesel was launched in 2004, with the goal of generating employment and promoting regional development. Biodiesel fuel is blended with petroleum diesel fuel and, beginning in 2008, a blend containing 2 percent biodiesel was made mandatory throughout the country. The percentage was increased to 5 percent in 2010. This biodiesel blend is now sold at more than 30,000 gas stations in Brazil. Production of

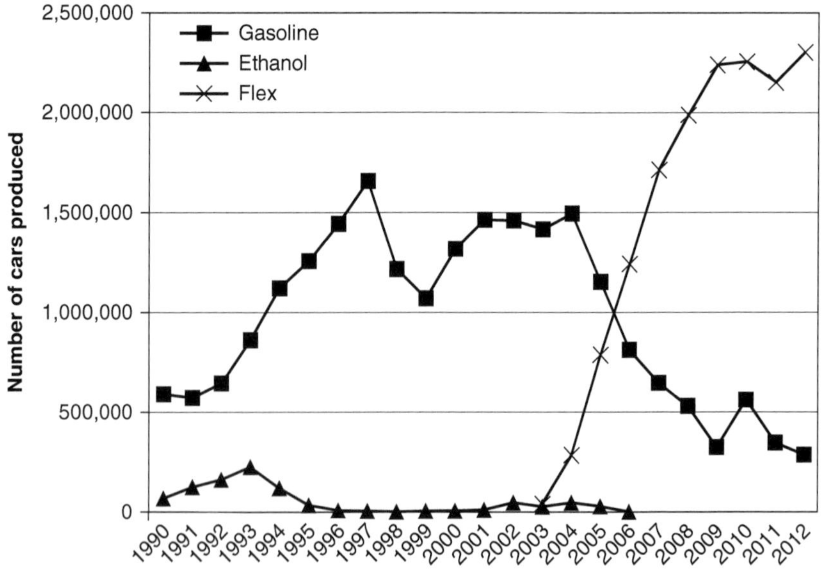

FIGURE 3.6 Evolution of Flex-Fuel Cars, 1990–2012

Source: ANFAVEA (2013).

biodiesel jumped from 69 million liters in 2006 to 2.4 billion liters in 2010, making Brazil the second-largest biodiesel market worldwide, behind only Germany. Since the launch of the biodiesel program, Brazil has reduced imports of diesel fuel by 7.9 billion liters, worth about $5.2 billion.

Although both ethanol and biodiesel are important to Brazil's energy autonomy, these markets are in different stages of development. Since its beginning with the *Proálcool* Program in the 1970s, ethanol production has evolved to become competitive with fossil fuels and now provides a significant share of the energy supply for the transport sector. The introduction of biodiesel has been more recent, and the sector is still evolving in terms of technology, business structure, and marketing.

A third energy alternative has also emerged: biomass. Thermoelectric plants, which are integrated with ethanol plants, use bagasse, the fibrous matter left after the juice is extracted from sugarcane, to generate energy. Crop residues from soybeans and the wood industry are also being used as fuel for thermoelectric plants.

Brazil as an International Player

Brazil is not an easy player to deal with in the international arena, and it has a distinct approach to multilateral organizations, such as the IMF and the United Nations, when compared with the United States. The United States has a long history of bilateral engagement and rarely relies on multilateral institutions, especially the United Nations, to achieve its international or foreign policy objectives. Brazil, for a variety of historical and internal political reasons, does rely on multilateral institutions. Many of the following observations draw this juxtaposition in sharp relief.

As a developing power and emergent market with leadership ambitions and strong views on sovereignty, Brazil has not fit easily into coalitions that include the Organisation for Economic Co-operation and Development (OECD) countries. Brazil's international stance has evolved in recent years, moving away from its opposition to the international financial institutions toward greater integration. Traditionally aligned with the G-77 within the General Agreement on Tariffs and Trade–World Trade Organization, Brazil has now enlarged its alliance network beyond the developing countries. For example, it has joined the Cairns Group of agricultural exporters, which brings together both developed and developing countries. Brazil has accepted observer status at the OECD and has also signed on to some important international regimes, most notably the Nuclear Non-Proliferation Treaty in the security field. Historically taking a firm position in international negotiations, Brazil has softened its opposition to the developed world, drawing somewhat closer to the United States and the European Union. However, recent history has shown that Brazil prefers to ally itself with South America or the other BRICS countries.[24]

Brazil's international engagement is often defined in defensive terms—avoiding international commitments that could reduce its scope for managing its economy or expose it to the instabilities of the international system. Brazil has been able to maintain this position because of its relative economic strength and stability. Brazil also pushes for international recognition as a representative or leader of the developing countries. A brief analysis of recent international events related to the global order—economic, political, and environmental—illustrates how Brazil defines itself, its interests, and its alliances.

United Nations

Brazil's role in the United Nations provides an illustrative example. The United Nations has been the forum where Brazil has most clearly voiced its differences—symbolic and otherwise—with the United States. Brazil's votes in the General Assembly are consistent with the country's efforts to define itself in opposition to the United States. One study has found a pattern of increasing divergence between Brazil and the United States in General Assembly votes.[25] Until 1959, the two countries' voting aligned between 80 percent and 100 percent of the time. From 1960 to 1980, the numbers consistently decreased until reaching their lowest point of alignment in 1980. Over the past 20 years, Brazil and the United States have voted differently in more than 80 percent of the United Nations votes almost every year.

Brazil, India, and Japan are the countries that have most often held the nonpermanent seats in the United Nations Security Council. The importance of these seats has increased since the late 1990s, buoyed by the possibility of reform of the composition of the Security Council, which could create more permanent seats. Brazil held a nonpermanent seat in the 2010–2011 biennium, during which time the country positioned itself assertively in several cases that came before the Council:

- United Nations Stabilization Mission in Haiti leadership effort to stabilize Haiti.
- Recognition of the Palestinian state. Exercising its prerogative, Brazil officially recognized the Palestinian state on December 1, 2010.
- Support for extending the mandate of the United Nations in Guinea-Bissau, maintaining that the United Nations should be committed to the African country's economic and institutional development and to the construction and maintenance of peace.
- Abstained on resolution against Libya. Despite acknowledging the undemocratic character of the Libyan regime, Brazil insisted on a negotiated peace settlement with local authorities and argued that an intervention could inflict more harm than good for the civilian population.
- Attempted bilateral agreement with Iran over its nuclear program.

With the exception of the Haiti case, Brazil led the other discussions without support from the United States. Likewise, at the 2012 United Nations Conference on Sustainable Development, known as Rio+20, Brazil found itself in opposition to the United States because Brazil insisted on the principle of "common but differentiated," arguing that each country must define measures to achieve a green economy within its own particular context.

G-20

The G-20 was established in 1999 in response to a series of crises in emerging economies in the second half of the 1990s. The aim was to foster cooperation on economic and financial issues among the relevant developed and developing countries. The G-20 gained in prominence after the 2008 financial crisis, when the apparent exhaustion of the macroeconomic model advocated by developed countries opened space for discussion of new policies, led by new actors. Brazil has been working to consolidate the G-20 as the main forum for dealing with international economic issues, arguing that it is more legitimate and efficient than the traditional G-8 or the OECD. Working primarily with China and India, Brazil has taken positions that bring together issues of international financial reform with issues of reforms in governance and voting within international economic institutions. Brazil has increased the forum's degree of politicization and often brings issues of North-South relations and developing country interests into the debate.

Brazil's agenda has similarities with those of China and India; however, the three countries differ in some important areas. As a result, the agenda set by Brazil at the G-20 is restricted to the points of convergence, supporting a tactical alignment among the three large developing countries, geared toward reforming the voting and representation rules in international economic agencies, particularly the IMF. Arguably, Brazil's interests have been more closely aligned with those of the United States than with the BRICS in many G-20 debates, including, for example, the need to strengthen laws on domestic banking systems. However, Brazil has preferred to maintain its policy of alignment with developing countries, in opposition to the United States, in view of the asymmetries in the international order. Table 3.3 illustrates how BIC (Brazil, India, and China) have defined their strategies in the case of several critical G-20 debates.

IMF Reform

The relationship between Brazil and the IMF has always been difficult, with the prominent role of the United States on the IMF Board of Directors particularly irksome for Brazil. In Brazil's official view, the IMF, whose mandate was to provide financial support to countries in deficit for the short term, vastly overstepped when it began promoting substantial structural changes in developing countries,

TABLE 3.3 BIC Positions on Important Global Issues

Theme	*Position*
Recovery and global unbalance	*Divergent interests.* Brazil and India have been negatively affected by depreciation of the yuan, but they have avoided putting public pressure on China.
International financial market reform	*Moderately divergent interests.* BIC are working together to implement international financial market reform; however, there are important differences on details, which reflect the specific characteristics of the internal system in each country.
Reform of international financial institutions	*Converging interests.* BIC all favor reform on quotas, voice, and governance.
Climate change	*Divergent interests in climate change negotiations but converging positions within the G-20.* BIC have different energy matrices, as well as different interests, but they try to present similar positions. Recently, Brazil has moved toward a more "progressive" approach. The three countries prefer to keep negotiations on this matter at the United Nations.
Global trade	*Divergent interests, attempt to coordinate positions.* BIC tried to maintain a shared stance on global trade, but the coalition was broken up when the "Lamy Package" was questioned by some of them.

Source: CINDES (2010).

interfering in the restructuring of those economies, and requiring cuts and modifications to social benefits. The last agreement signed by Brazil with the IMF was in 2003, under the Lula da Silva administration. With significant improvements in the Brazilian economy, renewal became unnecessary and Brazil was able to redefine its relationship with the IMF.

The heart of Brazil's position has been a demand for change in the IMF's governing structure. Brazil has been demanding a greater voice in the institution, alleging that the distortions related to the existing quota system exclude the emerging economies and favor the United States, which held about 17 percent of the shares.[26] In 2006, a first round of reforms was approved, which increased the quota of only four countries that the IMF considered underrepresented: China, South Korea, Mexico, and Turkey. Brazil, along with Argentina, Egypt, and India, opposed this reform, demanding immediate expansion for all developing countries.

Brazil benefitted in the second round of reforms, which were approved in 2008 and increased the country's share from 1.38 percent to 1.78 percent. More recently, Brazil's shares should have been increased to 2.32 percent,[27] but this has not taken effect, so the Brazilian quota remains at 1.78 percent in the IMF voting process.[28] The participation of the BRICS increased by 6.4 percent, reaching 14.18 percent, still leaving them with less than the 15 percent of the votes necessary to exercise veto power. In the next phase of reforms, scheduled for 2014, the entire voting system will be revisited. The formula for granting quotas is expected to give greater weight to GDP in defining country contributions.

The United States, resisting IMF reforms, used its enormous weight in the institution to stall the agreed measures in 2010. This behavior is contradictory, because the United States was one of the main promoters of reform at the 2010 Seoul Summit, where it criticized the overrepresentation of the European countries. As the largest contributor to the IMF, the United States is the only G-8 country that has not ratified the agreed increase in contributions. The increase would double the IMF's resources but would also entail structural reform for greater representation of emerging countries. According to a former IMF staff member, Washington has resisted the reforms for two reasons: first, it is opposed to enlarging China's power within the IMF because of differences between the two countries over trade; and second, the administration has been reluctant to send the reform to Congress during an election year.[29]

A joint communiqué that emerged from developing-country discussions in early 2012 shows the frustration of the emerging economies with the failure of the United States to ratify the reforms in the IMF decision-making process demanded by emerging countries: "This dynamic process of reform is needed to ensure the legitimacy and effectiveness of the Fund," affirmed the representatives of the BRICS countries.[30] The five BRICS confirmed their willingness to contribute to the IMF anti-crisis fund, but only on the condition that the voting reforms be implemented. Situations like this reinforce the divergences between Brazil and the United States: Brazil wants these reforms approved in order to increase its representation, which it believes is merited by the size of its economy; the United States has been unwilling to accept the changes. Although U.S. inaction on the reform agenda is not a direct attempt to slight Brazil, tangentially repeated inaction nonetheless increases the likelihood of spillover and collateral damage in other international forums.

In short, there have been few points of agreement between the United States and Brazil over major issues related to the international order. Brazil's position in these international discussions differs from that of the United States on these issues. Perhaps the broader point is that the United States has a long history of bilateral engagement and rarely relies on multilateral institutions, especially the United Nations, to achieve U.S. international and foreign policy objectives, whereas Brazil—for a variety of reasons—does. Nevertheless, there is potential for cooperation. The following section discusses some areas in which the two countries could work together on environmental issues.

Agenda for Cooperation on Sustainable Development

The conflict between economic growth and environmental sustainability that Brazil faces is one that has global ramifications. The United States should take a strong interest in supporting Brazil's capacity to protect its natural resources and to use them sustainably because deforestation, whether linked to expansion of soybean production, cattle ranching, or landless farmers, contributes to the loss of important global commons. Climate change, aggravated by deforestation, will have major effects on the world's food supply. Given Brazil's new role as one of the world's primary food producers, it is critical to the country's strategic interests to ensure that agricultural productivity will not suffer from rising temperatures and deforestation. Brazil is also one of the world's major consumers of energy, which has important environmental impacts. Brazil has already undertaken some important initiatives both in terms of reducing deforestation and in terms of developing the technologies, institutions, and markets needed to promote sustainable energy sources. The United States would do well to support these initiatives on a broader scale and foster or support Brazil to take an international leadership role where it can make a global contribution to sustainability rooted in its own successful experiences. Cooperation on innovations in sustainable development could help reduce the tension between economic growth and environmental protection that endangers the environment in both Brazil and the United States.

As the discussion above has shown, there has been little scope for alignment between the United States and Brazil on sustainable development topics in the multilateral political sphere. The differences between both the vision and the diplomatic practices of the two countries are quite entrenched, although some efforts at rapprochement have been seen recently and the reelection of President Obama may create a window of opportunity, as a recent slate of official visits between the leaders of the two countries suggests.[31]

Collaboration with Brazil will be best pursued bilaterally and perhaps by nongovernmental entities rather than in global forums. Academic groups, joint research projects, innovative enterprises, business organizations, and NGOs may have the greatest potential to pursue cooperation. Interactions between official entities are most likely to be successful if there are concrete terms of reference for the cooperation, such as specific technological support or financial agreements. Otherwise, political constraints and historical opposition on both sides, in some issues, and historic indifference on behalf of the United States rather than opposition, in others, are likely to create serious obstacles.

A few initiatives have been pursued by the United States and Brazil, and some new formats have been tried with positive results. For instance, some initiatives were designed to be led by government institutions with close links to the private sector and NGOs, other than foreign affairs ministries. Successful projects in the area of higher education involving both the public and private sectors to address topics in the fields of science, technology, and innovation are a good start.[32] One particularly interesting set of bilateral initiatives is being developed in the energy field. Climate change and green technology are two other areas (discussed below) in which bilateral cooperation could be a boon for both the United States and Brazil.

The following subsections discuss environmental areas where bilateral cooperation has already begun and where such initiatives hold promise for broader cooperation on sustainability.

Biofuels and Clean Energy

Biofuels, particularly the shared interest in promoting the development of an international market, could provide a productive area of cooperation. Both countries have important initiatives in the area of biofuels. The U.S. Department of Energy has developed a biomass program that will work with a broad range of industrial, academic, agricultural, and nonprofit partners across the country to develop and deploy commercially viable, high-performance biofuels, bioproducts, and biopower from U.S. renewable biomass resources, as a means to reduce dependence on imported oil. A good example is the U.S. Renewable Fuels Standards passed in 2005 and strengthened in 2007, when mandates were put in place for annual increases in blend rates through 2022 and caps were placed on corn ethanol production in favor of second-generation ethanol. The Brazilian Cane Producers Association (União da Indústria de Cana-de-Açúcar) and others in Brazil have been pushing this model as a way to break the linkage with Petrobras-controlled gas prices that depress ethanol consumption. Brazil, for its part, has also been active in the field of promoting second-generation biofuel innovation through the Joint Plan for Supporting Industrial Technological Innovation in the Sugar-Based Energy and Chemical Sectors (PAISS). The PAISS program is coordinated by two agencies, the Studies and Projects Finance Organization and BNDES. The program serves as a single point of government contact for business proposals for biofuels investment and has funded 35 business plans to the tune of R$3.1 billion (about $1.5 billion). To access funds, foreign firms only have to form a joint venture with a Brazilian company or establish a local subsidiary. The program has now closed, but there is an ongoing mechanism to replicate its success.[33]

To expand the bioenergy industry and make it sustainable, the PAISS program invests in research, technology development, and financing. Because the biofuels sector has shown some significant advances in Brazil, there is substantial room for cooperation, particularly on matters of logistics and infrastructure for the production of biodiesel, and for technological cooperation to increase efficiency gains in the use of second-generation biofuels, such as cellulose.

The Brazilian government, together with local enterprises, has initiated biofuels programs in some African countries, with strong support from President Lula da Silva. Brazil's agricultural research agency, EMBRAPA, has opened offices in several countries in sub-Saharan Africa in order to adapt varieties of sugarcane, soybeans, and other crops to local conditions. Companies such as Odebrecht have started large agribusiness projects focused on biofuels. These investments are being made on the premise that technology and plant adaptations developed in Brazil can easily be replicated in countries with a similar climate. Biomass energy production is an area in which the United States has been weak, and Brazil has been able to make some important advances. Brazil's initiatives in Africa could be complemented or expanded with support from the U.S. government, with benefits for the United States and sustainability in Africa's developing countries.

Brazil and the United States have agreed on a broad program for cooperation on energy issues, known as the Brazil-U.S. Strategic Energy Dialogue (SED). This forum was agreed on in a meeting between President Rousseff and President Obama in 2010, based on an understanding that the two countries should act as strategic partners to promote economic growth, energy security, and the transition to a clean-energy economy. To date, the United States and Brazil have undertaken collaborative activities with the following goals: (a) strengthening the energy relationship, (b) increasing bilateral trade in energy-related goods and services, and (c) enhancing national and shared energy security. The two governments also committed to develop a work plan related to the energy sector to further enhance the private sector's role in SED. Some initial steps have been taken:

- *Oil and natural gas.* The United States and Brazil are committed to identifying and implementing solutions to key challenges for the safe and efficient development of oil and natural gas reserves in both countries through technical, policy, and regulatory cooperation. To this end, they have organized technical workshops and events for government regulators and private industry to exchange information and share best practices on common oil and gas issues.
- *Biofuels.* Progress has been made on two levels: bilaterally, through the Memorandum of Understanding to Advance Cooperation on Biofuels and the Binational Energy Working Group, and multilaterally, through the Global Bioenergy Partnership. Under SED, biofuels cooperation focuses on four main areas: (1) bilateral research activities and cooperation on establishing standards, (2) joint work with other nations in the Americas and Africa, (3) multilateral efforts related to sustainable production and modernizing of bioenergy use, and (4) a Partnership for Aviation Biofuels to establish common standards and specifications and facilitate the commercialization and expansion of aviation biofuels. Embraer and Boeing have a joint research facility in São José dos Campos for biofuels in aviation. Both governments have also been working to improve life cycle modeling of biofuels, including greenhouse gases and land-use change, and to exchange information on maximizing the fuel economy of ethanol-optimized engines in flex-fuel vehicles. To expand the current work, the U.S. National Renewable Energy Laboratory and Petrobras are preparing to sign a Cooperative Research and Development Agreement on next-generation biofuels.
- *Hydropower, wind, and solar energy.* Partnership has not advanced in this area, although there are plans to work together through the Sustainable Development

of Hydropower Initiative under the Clean Energy ministerial process. The goal is for interested counterparts from both the public and private sectors to explore the technical feasibility, potential benefits, and market opportunities for developing and distributing wind energy in Brazilian communities. Wind power has the potential to improve energy access in rural areas and to reduce the dependence on fossil fuels in both countries.

- *Nuclear energy.* Technical and regulatory agencies continue to collaborate to help ensure that nuclear power for peaceful purposes is generated safely, securely, and responsibly. The United States intends to explore some areas for technical cooperation with Brazil, namely, site selection and licensing criteria for long-term sustainability of reactors, increased life span of reactors, and management of severe accidents and radioactive waste, among other potential activities. The United States is also interested in cooperating with Brazil to strengthen global efforts for the safe, secure, and peaceful development of civilian nuclear power and sharing U.S. experience in supporting nuclear security Centers of Excellence globally.

A good starting point to expand this cooperation on sustainable energy would be an initiative to develop an international market for biofuels, beginning with the definition of international standards—for example, defining what constitutes a biofuel in terms of quality, composition, or other relevant classifications—necessary for an international market. This step could be carried out under the aegis of the World Trade Organization (WTO) or the International Energy Agency, or through a plurilateral agreement. Negotiations with the WTO could establish the regulatory basis for open markets for biofuels. Finally, Brazil and the United States could collaborate to establish special funds or programs with the international development banks that would support initiatives in biofuel production and commercialization.

Climate Change and Deforestation

The issues of climate change and deforestation are closely linked. In addition to the local changes wrought by deforestation, such as changes in rainfall patterns and biodiversity loss, global climate change poses a significant threat to Brazil's prosperity and contribution to the global food supply. Rising temperatures and changing rainfall patterns will affect agricultural production both in Brazil's arid northeast, which suffers perennial drought problems, and in the newly established agricultural lands in the Cerrado. Although temperate crops have been adapted to the tropical savannah conditions, they are less likely to thrive as temperatures rise. One study indicated that even moderate temperature increases would cause significant damage to a range of agricultural products in Brazil—including rice, coffee, beans, manioc, maize, and soya—with declines of perhaps 25 percent in soybean production in the short term. Of great concern is the potential for drying of the Amazon with rising world temperatures, which could cause regional and even global changes in rainfall patterns. Collaboration between the U.S. and Brazilian federal governments, or states and municipalities, could contribute in the areas of remote monitoring technologies and equipment and training and financial support for the environmental agencies. This collaboration, both to reduce deforestation and to ensure that increases in agricultural production do not come at the expense of the forest, could enhance global food security and reduce the impact of climate change.

Although not a Kyoto Protocol signatory and still quite refractory in international forums that deal with the reduction of carbon emissions, the United States has sought to establish bilateral agreements and research conventions with other international actors to develop mitigating technology for carbon emissions. The United States has agreements with Brazil in this field. In 2012, the United States significantly increased its climate change funding to a total of $1.7 billion, composed of $1.3 billion for aid and $400 million for financing development and export credits. The goal was to develop strategies for sustainable forest management and to promote the necessary agreements for a forest carbon market. These activities are in accord with the conservation policies launched by Brazil's government to protect biodiversity and reduce emissions throughout the country.

The United States has already invested in conservation in Brazil. Under the terms of the U.S. Tropical Forest Conservation Act of 1998 (TFCA), the United States and Brazil reached an agreement in 2010 by which the United States would reduce Brazil's debt payments (by approximately $21 million) over the next five years; in return, the Brazilian government committed to allocate those resources to conservation programs in the Atlantic Forest, Cerrado, and Caatinga biomes. Resources allocated through the TFCA have supported initiatives in the conservation of protected areas, the management of natural resources, and the development of sustainable activities for forest-dwelling communities. This TFCA is the first debt-for-nature swap between the United States and Brazil and the sixteenth TFCA agreement signed by the United States.[34] The TFCA mechanism is expected to release more than $239 million to protect tropical forests globally.

Cooperation between the United States and Brazil could support multilateral efforts. Commercial and subsistence agricultural pressure on tropical forests and other biomes, as seen in Brazil, is common in other tropical and semitropical countries in South America, Africa, and South and Southeast Asia. Although only partially successful, Brazil's experience in monitoring and controlling this process could engender a global initiative to address this problem in concert with the United States. A set of policies would be necessary that could be formally supported by international organizations, whether through credits, grants, monitoring technology, or initiatives with private enterprises.

The United States could also provide support to ensure continuing high levels of agricultural productivity. For example, an area of mutual interest could be the establishment of a specialized agency or a program within the Food and Agriculture Organization, United Nations, or World Bank to map, monitor, and provide alerts on major climatic oscillations that could affect food production. An institution ensuring international awareness of these threats would help countries and international agencies promote necessary measures to mitigate or manage these changes.

Green Technology

A number of partnerships have been initiated to support green technology. In 2010, U.S. Assistant Secretary of Commerce Nicole Lamb-Hale led a trade mission to Brazil focused on partnering Brazilian and U.S. firms in construction, architecture, water, and landscaping, with a view to developing green technologies. The assistant secretary stated that the United States could invest as much as $10.5 billion in Brazil for green technology applications, including traditional areas such as water and wastewater treatment, as well as green building, engineering, and consulting. In early 2012, John Holdren, the president's advisor on science and technology, laid the foundations for an enlarged partnership in scientific exchange with Brazil under the auspices of the Brazil-U.S. Joint Science and Technology Cooperation Meeting. The partnership will foster collaboration on the use of satellites to gather data, particularly related to the hydrological cycle, which will be important for sustainable agriculture and advanced biofuels, areas in which Brazil is considered a world leader.

Academic exchanges are another important part of the growing partnership. Brazil will send more than 100,000 graduate students and researchers abroad to study over the next four years through Brazil's Science Without Borders Program, with financing from the government and the private sector. Of these, some 20,000 will study in the United States. The program is expected to foster international exchange of knowledge and research. To encourage Brazilian scientists to return to Brazil to work after participating in the program, the government is investing in scientific infrastructure, including laboratories, scientific personnel, and research facilities.

Finally, the technology sector is highly relevant to many environmental issues: monitoring satellites, fixed and mobile radar, drones, airplanes, and other equipment. Brazil's capacity in these areas, particularly observation satellites, lags behind the other BRICS. The United States, which has substantial capacity in this area, could be an important partner in helping Brazil advance, focusing particularly on monitoring technologies and satellites. These can be useful in monitoring and managing deforestation, climate change, and agricultural production. There is naturally some political resistance to cooperation in this field, given its potential for both civilian and military use, so it would be necessary to clearly define the scope and goals of any such collaboration.

Addressing Broader Sustainability Issues

Brazil's economic dynamism in recent years has enabled the country to implement important socioeconomic policies for reduction of poverty and inequality. Although these policies have been relatively successful, it will be challenging to maintain current growth and social gains, given the economy's dependence on state enterprises, domestic consumption, and heavy use of natural resources. Brazil's development model puts pressures—direct and indirect—on the environment. Energy consumption is increasing rapidly, and agribusiness development pressures many ecosystems, most notably the Amazon and Cerrado. The rate of deforestation in the Amazon has fallen in recent years, and some renewable energy programs, mainly hydropower and biofuels, are reducing the impact of economic growth on national ecosystems and reducing Brazil's emissions of greenhouse gases. However, these initiatives are still modest in comparison with the change that is needed to ensure sustainable growth. For Brazil to maintain its strong economic performance, the country will have to move away from its heavy dependence on commodities and state investment, which could open opportunities for more sustainable approaches.

In Brazil, the risks that environmental degradation poses for economic growth and stability are not yet on the political agenda. Policies for economic growth and social improvements, particularly poverty reduction, have had strong political and electoral support. The environment, however, is treated as a secondary issue. The risks that environmental degradation poses to the country's economic model are largely ignored.

The role that Brazil has played in international debates reflects a phase of democratic consolidation and economic growth, which has established Brazil as a leader among emerging economies. It also reflects Brazil's diplomatic history of opposition to multilateral commitments dominated by developed countries and a highly politicized approach to North-South issues. There is little room for agreement between the United States and Brazil in many of these forums. Designing agendas and political strategies that could foster stronger links will demand creativity and new approaches.

Partnerships between the United States and Brazil are most likely to thrive and create significant impacts if they can circumvent the political and diplomatic barriers between the two governments. Mobilization of nongovernmental actors, such as business associations, research centers, and NGOs, could engender initiatives and foster a positive joint agenda on sustainable development. Clean energy, monitoring of sustainable use of the Amazon, and the environmental impacts of agribusiness are all key issues that could be addressed cooperatively.

In the multilateral field, a dialogue between the United States, China, Brazil, and India could reduce Brazil's resistance to international commitments on sustainable development. Brazil has a strong preference for alliances with its neighbors in South America and for strategic alignment with the other BRICS. Recognizing and supporting Brazil's political role within the BRICS would certainly encourage more feasible multilateral agendas. Although this has not been the usual U.S. strategy—and it is likely to meet with some resistance from the U.S. Congress—the United States has already improved its strategic approach with India and other emerging countries on several issues with positive results, as is the case with Indian nuclear cooperation and general support for Vietnam and South Korea. Perhaps this experience can be replicated in the environmental arena.

Moreover, given Brazil's political role among developing countries, not only in Africa but also in South America and the Middle East, especially in the areas of basic health, including vaccine production, and agricultural research and development, Brazil could be a valuable ally for the United States in dialogues with other developing countries. The United States also has an interest in supporting Brazil's contributions to crop development for tropical environments and clean energy development around the world.

The United States has an interest in maintaining and increasing Brazil's agricultural output to ensure global food security and in protecting the Amazon for both climate change mitigation and biodiversity conservation. Any decrease in Brazilian agricultural production or rainfall regime changes in Amazonia could create a global food security threat. Because Brazil is one of the world's agricultural powerhouses, any substantial decline in Brazilian production would reduce the world's food supply and lead to increasing food prices. If drought also occurs simultaneously in other productive regions, as happened in the United States in 2012, these international pressures on the system could create a global food crisis. Likewise, the world has a major stake in ensuring the continued functioning of the Amazon ecosystem, often described as the lungs of the world. Evaporation and condensation over the Amazon are "engines" of the global atmosphere and strongly affect precipitation patterns in South America and the Northern Hemisphere. Drying of the Amazon would change weather patterns significantly and lead to a loss of forest biomass. This loss of biomass would entail the release of stored carbon into the atmosphere, creating a positive feedback loop for climate change. The Amazon is home to an estimated one-quarter of Earth's terrestrial species. With rising temperatures, large-scale extinctions are expected. Moreover, if much of the CO_2 stored in the tropical rainforest is released, either through deforestation or forest drying, global temperatures will rise much more quickly, affecting everyone. The value of this loss cannot be calculated. Moving beyond the current pattern of limited bilateral engagement will be essential to promote a sustainable development path for Brazil that will prevent these losses to the global commons. Energy, climate, agricultural development, and biofuels are clearly key points for engagement.

Notes

1 Several issues illustrate this dynamic. See, for example, Octavio Amorim, *De Dutra a Lula—a Condução e os Determinantes da Política Externa Brasileira* (Editora Campus, São Paulo, 2011); Gelson Fonseca, Jr., "Política externa brasileira: padrões e descontinuidades no período republican," *Relações Internacionais* 29 (March 2011), Lisboa.

2 For detailed percentages and other numerical targets, go to "metas" at www.brasilmaior.mdic.gov.br.

3 Government of Brazil, "Relatório PAC 2, 5° Balanço—Ano 2" (Ministry of Planning, Government of Brazil, Brasilia, 2012), www.planejamento.gov.br.

4 An example of these policies is the R$15 billion program called "Minha Casa Melhor," which provides official subsidized loans for the purchase of ovens, refrigerators, and other home appliances. It is a type of innovative credit facility that aims to stimulate production and consumption of durable goods while attempting to fight inflation.

5 D.V. Spracklen, S.R. Arnold, and C.M. Taylor, "Observations of Increased Tropical Rainfall Preceded by Air Passage over Forests," *Nature* 489 (Sept. 13, 2012): 282–85, doi: 10.1038/nature11390.

6 Simon Lewis, G. Lopez-Gonzalez, B. Sonké, K. Affum-Baffoe, L. Ojo, L. White, T. Hart, A. Hladik, D. Sheil, M. Swaine, D. Taylor, and O. Phillips, "Increasing Carbon Storage in Intact African Tropical Forests," *Nature* 457 (Feb. 19, 2009): 1003–1006, doi: 10.1038/nature07771.

7 Gerd Sparovek, "O Código Florestal proposto," Working Paper (Escola de Agronomia da USP (ESALQ), 2011).

8 World Bank data for January 2012.

9 São Paulo State Federation of Industries (FIESP) and Institute for International Trade Negotiations (ICONE), *Outlook Brazil* (2012), www.fiesp.com.br/publicacoes-agronegocio/tendencias-do-agronegocio-em-2022/.

10 The project, called TerraClass, categorized the Amazon's deforested areas based on satellite images as the basis for a map depicting land use and cover in 2008. See TerraClass, "Levantamento de informações de uso e cobertura da terra na Amazônia" (Empresa Brasileira de Pesquisa Agropecuária (EMBRAPA) and Instituto Nacional de Pesquisas Espaciais (INPE), Sept. 2011).

11 Marcia N. Macedo, Ruth S. DeFries, Douglas C. Morton, Claudia M. Stickler, Gillian L. Galford, and Yosio E. Shimabukuro, "Decoupling of Deforestation and Soy Production in the Southern Amazon during the Late 2000s," *Proceedings of the National Academy of Sciences* 109, no. 4 (2012): 1341–46, www.pnas.org/cgi/doi/10.1073/pnas.1111374109.

12 Visão Brasil, "Caminhos para o agronegócio sustentável," *Análise Integrada* (April 2010), www.visaobrasil.org/wp-content/uploads/2010/04/focus_abril2010_analise-integrada_final1.pdf.

13 Greenpeace, Comendo a Amazônia, Brasil (April 2006), www.greenpeace.org.br/amazonia/comendoamz.pdf.

14 FIESP and ICONE, *Outlook Brazil.*

15 The first three signatories were Independência, JBS, and Marfrig. Brazil Foods and 29 other small- and medium-size meat processors later joined the group.

16 The benefits of a clean energy matrix include reduced particle emissions from energy use and greater economic sustainability. While Brazil emits 1.4 tons of CO_2 per ton equivalent of oil, the world average for this indicator is 2.4.

17 World Bank data.

18 Agência Nacional de Energia Eléctrica data.
19 International Energy Agency data.
20 International Energy Agency data.
21 Government of Brazil, *Plano Decenal de Expansão de Energia 2019* (Ministério de Minas e Energia, Empresa de Pesquisa Energética. Brasília: MME/EPE, 2009).
22 Government of Brazil, *Plano Decenal de Expansão de Energia 2019.*
23 National Association of Automobile Manufacturers (ANFAVEA), *Year Book* (ANFAVEA, 2013), www.virapagina.com.br/anfavea2013/.
24 The BRICS countries—Brazil, Russia, India, China, and South Africa—are developing countries characterized by their large, fast-growing economies.
25 Amorim, *De Dutra a Lula.*
26 IMF data.
27 This new quota was defined at the Gyeongju meeting in South Korea.
28 IMF data.
29 Interview cited in Centro de Estudos de Integração e Desenvolvimento (CINDES), "Brazil, India and China (BICs) in the G-20," *Breves CINDES* 31 (June 2010), Rio de Janeiro.
30 Joint communiqué (Brazil, Russia, India, China, and South Africa) at the Fourth BRICS Summit in 2012 in New Delhi, India.
31 President Barack Obama visited Brazil in March 2011, and President Dilma Rousseff visited the United States in April 2012. Vice President Joseph Biden visited Brazil in 2013, and President Dilma Rousseff planned a state visit to the United States for September 2013. (Rousseff later cancelled this engagement.)
32 For example, the United States has supported technical training programs for Brazil's Patent and Trademark Office.
33 BNDES Presentation, "PAISS—BNDES/Finep Joint Plan to Support Industrial-Technology Innovation for the Sugarcane Industry" (Feb. 2013).
34 Other agreements are with Bangladesh, Belize, Botswana, Colombia, Costa Rica, El Salvador, Guatemala, Indonesia, Jamaica, Panama (two agreements), Paraguay, Peru (two agreements), and the Philippines.

4

CHINA

Christopher Sall and Katrina Brandon

The China of tomorrow will be vastly different from the China of today.[1] By 2030, China will be among the world's high-income countries, with the world's largest economy. It will have a highly skilled workforce with more than 200 million college graduates, but also a shrinking labor pool. Its gross domestic product (GDP) will grow between 4 and 5 percent per year compared with the 10 percent growth rate it has achieved on average over the past 15 years. With 270 million more Chinese expected to leave the countryside, China will be a predominantly urban society with a large middle class that will consume far more resources per capita than the average Chinese person today (although still far fewer than today's average American). The educated, urban middle class will demand open information, public accountability, and a cleaner environment. Yet, China will also be a country still grappling with poverty—especially insensitive border regions—and a persistent rural-urban divide.

The coming decades will be laden with both opportunities and risks for China. The country's ascendance to high-income status is far from a sure thing. A prosperous, sustainable, and responsible China is undoubtedly in the interests of the United States. Making the transition to a path of resource-efficient, low-carbon, and sustainable development is a choice that the Chinese must make themselves. But the United States can play a role in facilitating this transition through a range of bilateral and multilateral policies that will build a stronger basis for cooperation between China and the United States on climate, energy, and environmental issues while also integrating China more securely into the existing international system.

Background: Evolution of U.S.-China Relations and the Opening of Opportunity for Cooperation

Since the United States and China first set out on the uncertain path to rapprochement 40 years ago, the exchange of goods, people, and ideas between the two countries has grown phenomenally. In 1971, two-way trade volumes between the United States and China were only $5 million. Direct airline flights and shipments between the United States and China were prohibited; Chinese companies could not receive payments from U.S. banks; and restrictive export policies severely limited the technologies that U.S. companies could sell to China.[2] Since diplomatic relations were reestablished in 1979 and the barriers preventing commerce between the two countries have been gradually lifted, the total value of goods and services traded between the United States and China each year had soared to nearly $582 billion by 2012, including $142 billion in U.S. exports.[3] China has become the largest foreign investor in U.S. Treasury securities, with holdings valued at $1.317 trillion.[4] Similarly, while only a handful of U.S. trade delegations, artists, journalists, and scholars were allowed to enter China during the tumultuous years of China's Cultural Revolution (1966–1976), visits by Americans to China each year topped

2 million in 2011.[5] Nearly 158,000 Chinese students are now studying in the United States—more than from any other country—and the number of students learning Mandarin in public elementary and secondary schools in the United States tripled from 20,000 in 2004 to 60,000 in 2008.[6]

Interdependence has brought the United States and China closer together. Yet, the relationship continues to be rife with tensions. Until 2008, the U.S. Department of State, in its annual reports, consistently accused China of being one of the world's worst human rights violators and sponsored numerous resolutions against China in the United Nations Commission on Human Rights (UNCHR).[7] China responded in kind by issuing its own annual condemnations, charging repeatedly that the United States has "turned a blind eye to its own woeful human rights situation."[8]

While the United States decided early on not to let concerns over human rights interfere with granting China most-favored nation status,[9] China's model of state-led growth has drawn increased criticism by U.S. politicians and precipitated disputes on trade and currency issues. In May 2012, the U.S. Department of Commerce announced that antidumping tariffs of more than 31 percent would be imposed on Chinese-made solar photovoltaic (PV) panels.[10] Chinese solar panel manufacturers reacted to the move by saying the complaint was a "political farce" and a "publicity show."[11] China's Ministry of Commerce responded in 2013 by saying it would impose tariffs of more than 50 percent on imports of materials from the United States used to make PV panels.[12] As anti-China rhetoric intensified in the United States prior to the 2012 elections, American candidates in both parties called for labeling China a "currency manipulator."[13] Meanwhile, China has made known its interest in diversifying away from the U.S. dollar as the main international currency and introduced new rules in early 2012 to allow importers and exporters in China to settle cross-border trade accounts with renminbi.

On the military front, the United States has grown leery of China's rising military spending and its ability to project power beyond its borders. In a 2011 report to Congress, the U.S. Department of Defense noted, "The pace and scope of China's military development, combined with a relative lack of transparency, remains a point of concern in the United States and among our regional allies and partners."[14] The department reiterated in a 2013 report to Congress that "these concerns will likely intensify as the PLA modernization progresses."[15] Meanwhile, China has consistently blasted the United States for its continued arms sales to Taiwan, at times refusing U.S. naval vessels entry to port or canceling joint military exercises in retaliation. Responding to the Obama administration's "Pivot to Asia," voices in the Chinese media accused the United States of "stifling China's influence in Asia so as to obstruct China from rising to become a global power that can counterbalance the United States."[16]

Tensions in the U.S.-China relationship stem partly from a deep-seated and historic sense of "strategic distrust."[17] Thankfully, the United States and China have been able to manage this distrust and prevent delicate situations, such as the 1999 U.S. bombing of the Chinese Embassy in Belgrade or the 2001 collision of an American reconnaissance plane with a Chinese fighter off Hainan Island, from escalating out of control. To improve bilateral coordination, the Obama administration has focused on increasing channels for dialogue and upgrading official-to-official exchanges.[18]

U.S.-China relations on environmental sustainability have followed the basic contours of the larger bilateral relationship. China and the United States have become the world's number one and number two users of energy and emitters of greenhouse gases (GHGs)[19] and the world's largest consumers of timber,[20] metals and minerals,[21] water,[22] ocean-caught fish,[23] and livestock.[24] Given their size and influence, the indispensable role of the two countries in solving the environmental challenges of the twenty-first century is undeniable, as is their mutual dependence and the need to act in concert. The two countries are sharply divided as to the appropriate responsibilities and actions each should assume in tackling sustainability, and both countries are constrained by other domestic priorities. Nevertheless, by virtue of expanding dialogue, officials in the United States and China have come to better understand each other's circumstances and have made progress in ways that are less headline-grabbing.

Since 1979, the United States and China have signed more than 30 bilateral agreements and memorandums of understanding on climate change, energy, and the environment.[25] Most bilateral initiatives have focused on collaborative research and efforts to solve technological problems, from monitoring urban air pollution, to developing biofuels for passenger jets, to carbon capture and storage for advanced coal-fired power plants, to strengthening the capacity of regulators to enforce environmental laws, to labeling standards for energy-efficient appliances. The number of programs initiated over the years has been impressive, but it has drawn criticism for being "miscellaneous and episodic rather than sustained" and "undermined by insufficient funding, shifting policy priorities, and failure to significantly 'scale-up' promising projects."[26] President Obama has sought to address this problem by giving higher priority to climate change, energy, and the environment as part of his administration's China policy.[27] In July 2009, formal working groups on electricity, water, air, transportation, wetlands, protected areas, and energy efficiency were incorporated into the Strategic and Economic Dialogues (S&ED). The S&ED, which originated during the years of President George W. Bush, have become the single most important venue for discussions between the two countries on a range of core issues. As a product of the S&ED, in 2009 the United States and China announced reinvigorated cooperation on the research and development of cutting-edge clean energy, energy efficiency, and clean transportation technologies. The new package of agreements, which was finalized during President Obama's visit to Beijing in November 2009, included creating a U.S.-China Clean Energy Research Center (CERC), which has received $150 million in public and private funding commitments split evenly between the two countries.

Bilateral initiatives have played a crucial role in forging new partnerships between U.S. and Chinese companies. CERC, for example, has brought together American industry leaders, such as General Electric, Honeywell, Dow Chemical, Duke Energy, Ford, and GM, with major Chinese companies, such as Huaneng, Shenhua, and Geely Automobile. GE has signed five agreements with Chinese partners since 2011, which the company expects to bring in $2 billion in revenue, generate $1 billion in exports from the United States, and create 4,500 new jobs in the United States.[28]

The emerging bilateral partnership has been particularly instrumental in helping the United States and China regain some momentum on climate change issues after the two countries' engagement in the United Nations climate talks hit a low point in Copenhagen in 2009. The much-hyped 15th Conference of Parties (COP15) to the United Nations Framework Convention on Climate Change failed to produce a legally binding agreement to reduce global GHG emissions beyond 2012. In the wake of COP15, a flurry of stories appeared in the international press singling out China for standing in the way of a global target for long-term emissions reductions and sending a low-level official rather than Premier Wen Jiabao to a meeting with heads of state, including President Obama, in what was a diplomatic snub to all.[29] Ed Miliband, who was the United Kingdom's secretary of state for energy and climate at the time and who participated in the talks, publicly accused that China and its allied countries (e.g., Sudan) had "hijacked" COP15 and tried to "block global progress."[30]

Developments since COP15 have suggested an opening for compromise and greater willingness by the United States and China to overcome some sticking points. Like their U.S. counterparts, China's leaders have been keen to avoid the appearance of holding up progress on climate change and are sensitive to the effects of international negotiations on their country's image.[31] China played a quieter, more positive role at COP16 in Cancun in 2010,[32] agreeing to greater transparency in emissions reporting (a key concern of the United States) and to register its domestic carbon dioxide (CO_2) reduction targets under the United Nations Framework Convention on Climate Change.[33] At COP17 in Durban, China and India backed off from their outright refusal of mandatory commitments and agreed to a new platform for negotiating a legally binding instrument on climate change that will cover both developing and developed countries by 2020.[34] Domestically, China has set binding targets to reduce its CO_2 emissions per unit of GDP by 2015 and announced its intention to cap annual energy use at around 2.8 billion tons oil equivalent (TOE).[35] It is also experimenting with carbon cap-and-trade initiatives in seven major cities and provinces, which may later be scaled up into a national exchange.[36]

While the outcomes of the most recent United Nations climate talks in Warsaw (COP19) were uninspiring, the United States and China nonetheless made considerable headway in 2013 through other forums. In April, during

Secretary of State John Kerry's visit to Beijing, the two countries announced the creation of a high-level Climate Change Working Group as part of the S&ED.[37] In June, at the summit between Presidents Obama and Xi Jinping in California, the United States and China unveiled a new accord to phase down potent GHGs known as hydrofluorocarbons.[38] In July, the joint Climate Change Working Group launched five new initiatives to reduce pollution from heavy-duty vehicles, accelerate development of carbon capture and storage, enhance monitoring and reporting of GHG emissions data, and cooperate on policies and technologies for smart grids. Work plans to implement the initiatives were scheduled to be completed by October.[39]

Apart from improved bilateral cooperation on climate change, 2012 marked an important turning point for top leaders of both countries. In the United States, Barack Obama entered his second term in office with a greater imperative to deliver successes in his foreign policy despite the rancor and dysfunction of U.S. congressional politics. In China, President Xi Jinping cemented his authority as paramount leader as a vigorous debate continued among political elites and in society at large about China's role in the international community. Across the growing multiplicity of views, many have realized that China's problems are now the world's problems and that the country is reaching a new juncture in its foreign policy. China's mantra has long been to "keep a low profile" while also "accomplishing something (or playing a positive role)." Now, emphasis has shifted more firmly to the latter. In a June 2013 speech outlining the basic tenets of China's "new model of major country diplomacy," Foreign Minister Wang Yi affirmed that China is ready "to undertake its due responsibilities and to make a greater contribution to world peace and common development . . . through more proactive diplomacy."[40] The Chinese want to be seen as upstanding, constructive members of international society in an increasingly multipolar world.[41] Although uncertain, this longer-term trajectory in China's foreign policy points toward greater cooperation with the United States and other countries on the environment and climate change.[42]

At this juncture, confrontational, zero-sum thinking is the largest threat to strengthening the U.S.-China bilateral relationship and must be avoided.[43] As China grows, it will have a greater stake in the integrity of the emerging international institutions, such as the climate change regime, and in ensuring that they align with its perceived national interests. In asking China to be a "responsible stakeholder," the United States must be prepared for China to be more assertive in expressing its preferences in shaping those institutions.[44] Feelings of distrust between the United States and China will no doubt persist into this next phase of their relations, but as the United States has repeatedly assured, a "strong, prosperous, and successful China" is in the interests of the United States.[45] Now more than ever, leaders in the two countries must capitalize on the pragmatic, productive nature of the relationship. Working together to solve environmental problems of common concern marks a path forward.

COMMON PROSPERITY IN THE U.S.-CHINA RELATIONSHIP

"We want to see China not only deliver economic prosperity for its large population, but also play a key role in world affairs. And our countries and our peoples gain far more from cooperation than from competition, so we are committed to pursuing a positive, cooperative, comprehensive relationship." ***Former U.S. Secretary of State Hillary Clinton***

"The Sino-U.S. relationship should not be considered a zero-sum game. . . . The essence of the challenge is that the two great societies are obliged to deal with each other amid pressures and transformations no previous generation has faced at all, much less on such a global scale." ***Former U.S. Secretary of State and National Security Advisor Henry Kissinger***

China's Environmental Challenges

Although China faces many formidable environmental challenges that threaten the long-term viability of its economic growth, it has made remarkable progress on measures of sustainable development. China has already met or is on track to achieve all the United Nations Millennium Development Goals by 2015.[46] Access to proper sanitation facilities and clean drinking water in rural areas has improved. Government spending on reducing industrial pollution has achieved parity with high-income European countries as a percentage of GDP,[47] and new standards for air pollution in major cities have been set to meet World Health Organization (WHO) interim targets for developing countries. Logging in the natural forests in the upper catchments of the Yellow and Yangtze Rivers has largely been halted, and forest coverage has rapidly expanded (although mainly in monoculture plantations and nonnative species). Gains in economy-wide energy efficiency have surpassed those achieved by any other country in recent history. For the past two years, China has invested more than any other country in renewable energy.[48]

Despite this progress, measures of ecosystem health, biodiversity, and natural habitat show that overall environmental health is still worsening. As China's Ministry of Environmental Protection (MEP) reports, "China's environment continues to deteriorate, environmental conflicts are apparent, and pressures on the environment are growing."[49]

Acknowledging the scale of its problems, China has committed itself to a broad array of policy goals for the future.[50] The current Five-Year Plan makes resource efficiency and environmental protection a key feature of economic policy for 2011–2015 and mandates that by 2015 China will have "slowed the deterioration of [its] ecological environment."[51] By 2030, long-term policy goals commit the country to halting widespread biodiversity loss, ensuring the sustainability of its natural resource base, stabilizing the health of vital but degraded ecosystems, and expanding protection for all forms of natural habitat.[52] To say these goals are ambitious would be an understatement.

The following subsections summarize some of the main challenges that China must overcome to realize its long-term goals for sustainability. These challenges include resource insecurity, the rising burden of pollution on society, climate change, policy risks, and internal institutional weaknesses.

Challenge: Insecurity of Natural Resource Supplies

China became the world's largest energy consumer in 2009, and its appetite for energy will only grow.[53] According to projections by the International Energy Agency (IEA), even if China reduces the carbon intensity of its GDP and meets the current policy target to increase the share of nonfossil fuel sources in its energy supply by 2030,[54] China's demand for coal will rise 30 percent compared with 2009 and demand for oil will increase by 79 percent (Figure 4.1). Overall, in 2030 China will use nearly 71 percent more energy than the United States did in 2009 and 63 percent more than what Americans are expected to use in 2030 (although on a per capita basis, the Chinese will still use 62 percent *less* energy than Americans did in 2009 and 58 percent *less* than what Americans are projected to use in 2030).[55]

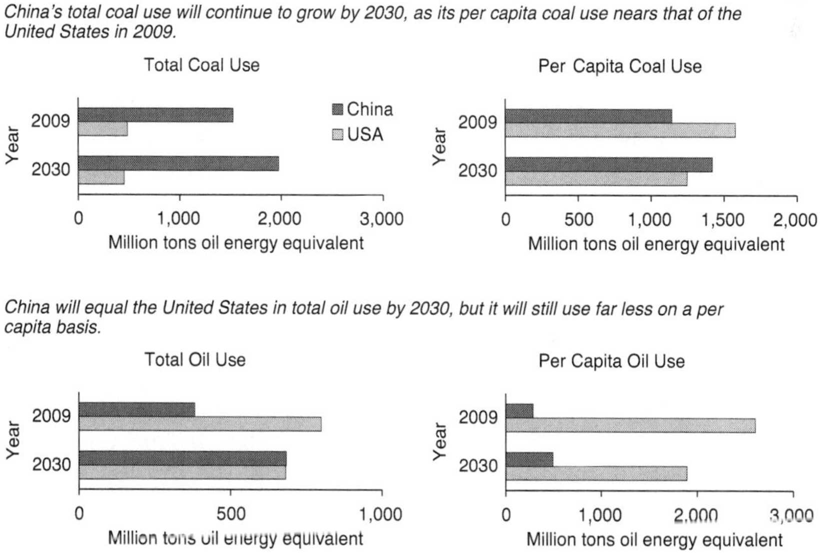

FIGURE 4.1 Coal and Oil Consumption in China and the United States, 2009 and 2030

Source: Based on data and projections for the reference ("New Policies") scenario in IEA (2011b).

Given the dramatic growth projected for China's energy demand, the Chinese are faced with the dilemma of how to transport huge amounts of energy from where it is sourced to where it is consumed. China has some of the world's most abundant coal reserves and is one of the most coal-dependent economies. Coal satisfies 70 percent of the country's total demand for energy and supplies 79 percent of its electricity.[56] About 95 percent of the coal China consumes each year is mined domestically—a trend projected to continue during the next 20 years.[57] Coal reserves are located mainly in the hinterlands, while demand is concentrated along the Eastern Seaboard. Transporting coal has placed severe strain on the country's railways,[58] highways, ports, and other infrastructure, causing such bottlenecks to emerge as the infamous 11-day, 70-mile traffic jam that occurred in 2010 along the highway from coal-rich Inner Mongolia into Beijing.[59] Disruptions in the energy supply system have been exacerbated by heavy-handed government actions, such as restricted access to state-owned railways and rigid price controls on electricity.[60] The result has been wasteful electricity use in some sectors and recurring power shortages during times of high fuel prices, such as in 2011. China has sought to relieve these energy supply strains by investing heavily in transport infrastructure and building a number of "bases" where large coal-fired power plants are sited next to mines. Yet, without significant pricing reforms, periodic shortages are likely to continue.[61]

As China faces growing pressures on its domestic energy supply, its increasing dependence on external energy resources has exposed it more to the vagaries of the international commodities markets and caused it to incur a higher level of political and military risk.[62] Since 1990, the share of imported crude oil and refined oil products in China's total oil consumption has risen from 8 percent to 65 percent.[63] China's crude oil imports originate principally from countries in Africa and the Middle East, including Saudi Arabia (19 percent of its total imports), Angola (17 percent), Iran (9 percent), Oman (7 percent), and Sudan (5 percent).[64] Sourcing from faraway lands means that more than four-fifths of China's imports must be shipped long distances by sea and eventually cross the Straits of Malacca, leaving the economy potentially vulnerable to disruptions.[65] China's dependence on unsavory countries for resources has drawn it more deeply into a number of sticky international situations, such as the Iranian nuclear crisis, and has called into question its policy of supposed noninterference in the internal political dealings of these countries.

China has sought to improve the security of its energy supply through a multipronged strategy. In the short term, the Chinese have concentrated on diversifying supplies by investing in oil- and gas-producing countries outside the Middle East and northern Africa.[66] Much of the $75 billion in loans the Chinese Development Bank has provided to Russia, Venezuela, Brazil, Ecuador, and Turkmenistan since 2009 is backed by revenue from oil and gas sales to Chinese state-owned enterprises. (These loans should not be viewed as a grand strategy orchestrated by Beijing but rather as profit-seeking ventures by Chinese firms that also support national interests).[67] The Chinese have constructed a system of strategic petroleum reserves, with plans to boost capacity to 500 million barrels by 2020,[68] and have invested in pipelines to deliver oil and natural gas overland from Russia and central Asia. In the mid- to long term, China's leaders hope to alleviate energy insecurity by restructuring the country's economy away from heavy industry, pursuing further gains in energy efficiency, and increasing the share of natural gas and nonfossil fuel sources in energy supply. Yet, even under the most optimistic scenario, China's coal use is expected to grow another 20 percent by 2020, while oil demand is projected to grow 58 percent by 2030.[69]

Water insecurity represents an even more difficult constraint on China's growth. Like energy, water is critical for the entire spectrum of economic activity, but, unlike energy, it is expensive to transport long distances and importing it is often impractical (except for "virtual" water embodied in imported crops).

China is already a water-poor country, with per capita freshwater resources of 2,310 cubic meters,[70] one-quarter the world average. China's drier regions have both higher demand and scarcity. The provincial-level territories comprising the North China Plain have per capita resources of only 395 cubic meters,[71] far below the international threshold for "severe" water stress.[72] Despite only having 4 percent of China's freshwater supplies, these provinces are home to 15 percent of the country's population and produce 26 percent of its grain.[73] High grain output is made possible largely through irrigated agriculture, which has expanded in the North China Plain by nearly 8 million hectares over the past 30 years. As surface water and groundwater resources have been depleted, farmers have made up for shortfalls by drilling deeper and deeper wells to tap reserves of water in underground aquifers, causing the water table to drop by hundreds of feet in some places.[74] Groundwater depletion has caused problems such as land subsidence, saltwater contamination of drinking water supplies in coastal areas, and the loss of natural ecosystems in dried-up lakes, rivers, streams, and wetlands.

Water shortages and poor water quality have been aggravated by the growth of water-intensive industry and large cities. More than 100 cities around the country experience frequent water shortages each year,[75] costing urban businesses an estimated $30 billion in losses.[76] Poor water quality has added to these losses by repressing productive activities. About 53 percent of the water sampled in the northern river basins in 2011, for example, was graded Class V or below, making it unsuitable for drinking water, aquaculture, or even industrial use.[77]

Attempts to ease water shortages have placed overwhelming priority on supply-side infrastructure. China has initiated a huge South-to-North Water Transfer Project that is designed to divert 12 trillion gallons of water annually north from the Yangtze River Basin along three different routes, each more than 1,000 kilometers long.[78] The eastern and central legs are under construction, while the controversial western leg is still in the planning phase.[79] When the government announced a $60 billion investment last year to complete sustainable water use projects over the next decade, the focus was still on large infrastructure—new reservoirs, wells, and inter-basin water transfers.[80] Yet, if *demand* for water is not successfully reduced,[81] shortages will intensify. Over the next 20 years, booming demand from urban industries and households (which use twice the per capita water as rural households) will wipe away the gains made from shifts to more-efficient irrigation agriculture and in the composition of China's economic activity toward higher value-added sectors.[82] Consequently, in a reference case scenario, total water requirements are expected to rise from 602 billion cubic meters in 2010 to 667 billion cubic meters in 2015 and 818 billion cubic meters in 2030.[83] Water stress in the Yellow, Hai, and Liao basins will likely worsen,[84] and between 15 million hectares and 27 million hectares of irrigated land may go dry nationwide by 2050.[85] Larger areas of wetlands, lakes, and even rivers will also go dry, as water withdrawals in the northern basins already far exceed what is needed to ensure minimum environmental flows.[86]

Challenge: Rising Burden of Pollution on Society

According to official statistics, air quality in China's major cities has improved, but not fast enough. With an aging population and rapid urban growth, exposure rates for environmental illnesses are growing faster than pollution is decreasing (see Figure 4.2). According to the WHO, deaths attributable each year to outdoor air pollution in China's cities rose from 356,000 in 2004 to around 470,000 in 2008.[87] Average concentrations of small particulates (PM_{10}) in urban areas,

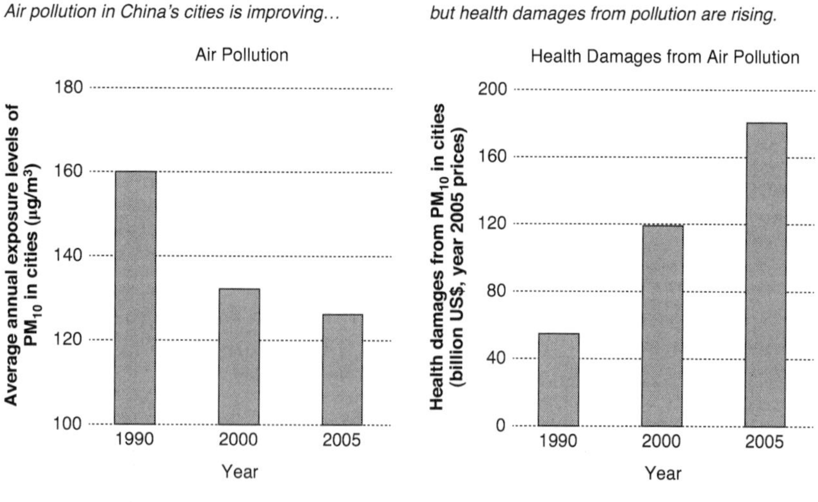

FIGURE 4.2 Air Pollution and Health Damages in China, 1990, 2000, and 2005

Notes and sources: PM_{10} concentrations are estimated values modeled by the World Bank (http://data.worldbank.org); damages include consumption and welfare losses, as estimated by Matus et al. (2012).

meanwhile, fell from 115 to 85 micrograms per cubic meter.[88] So, although the air was relatively cleaner, pollution was still far above what WHO considers healthy—and with more urban residents in 2008 than in 2004, more people were breathing in polluted air and getting sick. Since 2009, monitoring of PM_{10} and extremely small particulates ($PM_{2.5}$) in major urban areas reveals that improvements in air quality have stagnated.[89]

Even more disconcerting than overall levels of pollution in China is the contribution of pollution to existing social inequalities. As in the United States,[90] pollution in China disproportionately affects poor people. Studies from two provinces in the urban southeast reveal that large point sources of air pollution, such as factory smokestacks, tend to be sited in areas that are inhabited by larger numbers of migrant workers, such as the peripheries of cities where land is cheaper and monitoring by environmental protection authorities is more lax.[91] China's 300 million rural-to-urban migrants are at the bottom rungs of urban society. They are at greater danger from unsafe environmental conditions in the workplace; they are often forced to cope with poor sanitation; and they are largely excluded from social services such as public health insurance.[92] Thus, they are more likely to suffer from pollution-related illnesses as a result of exposure.

Pollution has fueled social protest and discontent with China's uneven growth. Approximately 90,000 "illegal mass incidents" (a Chinese epithet for public disturbances or protests) involving nearly 4 million people occur in China each year.[93] In 2009, a high-ranking official from the Central Committee, Chen Xiwen, cited pollution as a top cause of public protest in China.[94] One recent example of unrest occurred during July 2012 in Sichuan province, where some 5,000 angry students took to the streets and were joined by 10,000 more in opposing a project to build a molybdenum-copper processing plant in their city. After violent clashes between protesters and police, the local government backed down and declared that it would cancel the $1.6 billion project.[95]

China's leaders are aware of the growing threat of environmental degradation to social stability and long-term growth. Reflecting on this threat, Minister of Environmental Protection Zhou Shengxian said in a press conference in 2012, China has entered a peak period in which environmental risks are becoming clear and pollution accidents are occurring frequently. . . . Added to the fact that the public is incredibly sensitive at a time when many kinds of social tensions are mounting, *environmental risks may go from being scattered, discrete problems to becoming an all-encompassing problem.*[96]

The government's more aggressive stance on reducing pollution is reflected in recent policies. In January 2012, new emissions standards for coal-fired power plants that are on par with standards in Europe and the United States went into effect.[97] A month later, the State Council approved air-quality standards for $PM_{2.5}$—which are the most damaging to human health and had not been regulated before—along with plans to build an extensive nationwide $PM_{2.5}$ monitoring network.[98] The new air-quality standards were to go into effect in

Beijing, Shanghai, and other major cities by the end of 2012 and nationwide by 2016. Mid-term targets introduced by MEP in April 2011 called for all of China's cities to meet WHO interim targets for $PM_{2.5}$ in developing countries by 2020.[99] After a winter of recurring incidents of emergency-level air pollution in Beijing and other cities, in September 2013 the State Council released an ambitious national action plan to curb pollution and said it would invest nearly $281 billion (RMB 1.7 trillion) in prevention, monitoring, and control.[100]

The MEP's targets for 2020 indicate that the Chinese government is cautiously optimistic that China can solve its air pollution problems. Although they fall short of current standards in high-income countries for what is considered healthy, the targets will still be challenging to meet. Inventories of air pollution sources in China's major cities show that about 15–30 percent of suspended particulate matter (PM_{10}) comes from burning coal; about 5–20 percent from motor vehicles; and about 30–60 percent from suspended dust that is blown from roadways, construction sites, and other areas.[101] Emissions of PM from any or all of these sources are in danger of increasing over the next two decades.[102] Under a business-as-usual scenario, by around 2030 another 550 gigawatts of coal power plants will be built,[103] another 300 million private vehicles will be added to the roads,[104] and another 430 billion square feet of floor space in new buildings will be constructed.[105] Without more aggressive policies and the widespread adoption of control measures, these projected trends could spell worse pollution.

Greater attention must also be given to reducing nonpoint sources of pollution, such as the runoff of pesticides, fertilizers, and excrement into rivers, lakes, and groundwater sources from farms, fields, and livestock operations.[106] Researchers from China's MEP project that these nonpoint-source emissions will further increase over the next 20 years, mainly because of shifts in people's diets toward more meat, milk, eggs, and other animal products as people become wealthier. Even with better technologies and higher reutilization rates for waste from large-scale feed operations, by 2030 effluents from livestock are projected to increase by 12 percent in an optimistic scenario and 74 percent in a pessimistic scenario.[107] Wastewater discharged from urban households is also expected to grow—by as much as threefold between 2000 and 2030, according to the Organisation for Economic Co-operation and Development (OECD).[108] Considering that, as of 2006 less than one-third of China's cities had wastewater treatment facilities, significant additional investment will be required.[109]

Challenge: Impacts of Climate Change in China[110]

The growing body of scientific evidence in China shows that climate change will be a "threat multiplier," increasing pressure on ecosystems and species that are already under tremendous pressure.[111] In southern Yunnan province, for example, natural forest area declined by 20 percent between 1976 and 2003 as large areas were cleared and converted to rubber tree farms.[112] Rubber plantations require a lot of water, and the trees are unable to store water during dry periods. The frequency and severity of drought in the region has significantly increased since the mid-twentieth century, causing massive tree mortality and making forests more susceptible to pests and disease.[113] Projections for Yunnan, one of the most biodiverse and threatened places, show that more severe droughts and floods will increase the risk of extinction for many species.[114]

Climate change will exacerbate water scarcity in China's arid regions (and partially alleviate it in other regions).[115] Summer runoff may decrease by 2 percent for the mid-to-lower Yellow River basin and 21 percent for the Liao River basin by the 2030s under a middle-of-the-road emissions scenario.[116] Accounting for future land-use changes and rising demand from agriculture, cities, and industry, drier conditions in the Yellow River basin alone may increase annual water shortages by more than 12 billion cubic meters.[117] Interannual variability in rainfall in the Yellow and Huai River basins is expected to increase; and more precipitation each year will come from short, severe storms rather than being spread evenly.[118] The result of this "lumpy" hydrology for the North China Plain may be worse agricultural droughts, as more rain will come between peak growing seasons and soils will be unable to capture large amounts of water all at once from severe storms.[119]

Climate change will also increase economic losses from extreme weather events. China's government estimates that annual damages from extreme weather such as floods, droughts, and tropical cyclones are already 1–3 percent of GDP.[120] Losses from floods alone have averaged $42.6 billion each year since 2006,[121] and drought affects one-quarter to one-third of the nation's cropland each year.[122] Future damages from extreme weather are likely to arise, especially in the densely populated and high-value industrial centers along the coast, as the asset value of these areas and the frequency of storms both increase.[123] These valuable coastal areas will also face other hazards, such as sea-level rise. China is one of the world's most vulnerable countries to sea-level rise and storm surges, with some 80 million people living in low-lying coastal areas.[124] By the government's estimates, coastal sea walls need to be raised by 50 percent to protect against higher seas in the 2030s. If coastal defenses are not significantly improved by the 2080s, some 18,000 square kilometers of land in China's heavily populated deltas will be under water.[125]

Challenge: External Policy Risks to China and Lock-in Effects

China's deepening trade connections with other countries present greater risk of increased economic costs from policy changes beyond China's borders and outside its control. Risks arising from climate change policies are becoming more acute as countries signal greater willingness to take unilateral action to reduce emissions. In 2009, European leaders committed to the European Union to reducing its emissions to 20 percent below 1990 levels by 2020. As part of its effort to meet its target, in January 2012 the European Union included aviation as part of its cap-and-trade regime (the Emissions Trading System) and began charging airlines for the price of CO_2 emitted by all planes flying into the European Union. Although more than 99 percent of the world's major airlines have agreed to comply with the new rules,[126] the Chinese government responded to the European Union's decision by reportedly blocking an order for 10 new Airbus A380 aircraft worth $3.8 billion by a subsidiary of Hainan Airlines[127] and forbade Chinese airlines from paying fees or increasing ticket prices in response to the European Union's new rules.[128]

The row over CO_2 emissions from aviation may foretell future disputes and potentially damaging impacts on Chinese industry from delaying more ambitious emissions cuts. Concerns about World Trade Organization (WTO) trade rules aside, one recent study estimated that if the United States and the European Union were to suddenly impose border taxes based on the carbon content of their imports, the result would equal a tariff greater than 20 percent on Chinese goods and would reduce the country's total manufacturing exports by about 21 percent, leading to a sizeable loss in welfare.[129] Of course, whether and how border taxes would be imposed depends on how countries design their CO_2 reduction policies. If a climate change law is enacted in the United States someday, the legislative history suggests it will very likely include provisions to prevent the "leakage" of high-polluting industries to other countries that do not have equivalent reduction measures.[130]

Policy risks will magnify the potentially damaging effects of China becoming "locked into" a high-emissions development pathway. According to the IEA, more than 4 billion tons of the CO_2 emissions that will be emitted each year by Chinese power plants in 2020 are essentially already guaranteed.[131] This is because coal-fired power plants have an average functional lifespan of around 40 years and many of China's power plants are relatively new. Nearly 420 gigawatts of thermal generating capacity was added to the grid in China between 2000 and 2009—a figure roughly equal to three times Canada's entire capacity—and will continue to be in service for a long time to come.[132] China is expected to invest nearly $400 billion in its power generation infrastructure and build another 550 gigawatts of coal-fired power plants over the next 20 years.[133] If carbon emissions are priced later rather than sooner, China will risk having to retire valuable assets before they reach the end of their useful lives, further upping the costs of mitigating climate change.

Challenge: Internal Institutional Weaknesses

According to the latest reports by the United Nations Environment Programme (UNEP), global emissions will need to peak before 2020 and then decline thereafter for the world to have a "likely" (not guaranteed) chance of avoiding warming of more than 2°C.[134] For China, scenarios that are consistent with this pathway show emissions from fossil fuels growing from around 8 billion tons of CO_2 in 2011, reaching 8.6 billion tons just before 2020, and then eventually falling to 6.1 billion tons in 2030.[135]

Achieving such reductions will require decisive action in China (and the United States) to retool and restructure its economy and transition to low-carbon development in less than a decade. Each year that more ambitious reductions are delayed, the gap between current policies and what is actually needed widens. Although the political commitment of China's central authorities to this transition is clear—and greater than that shown by leaders in many other countries—it is uncertain whether China can complete this transition in the timeframe needed to avoid dangerous human-caused climate change.

Certain institutional features of the Chinese state run counter to making large changes in a short time.[136] Over the past two decades, China's system of government evolved into a kind of "*de facto* federalism" as decision-making powers and control over resources have gradually devolved to the provinces, cities, counties, and townships.[137] These governments have assumed primary responsibility for providing a wide range of services such as education, health care, and environmental protection, as well as building local infrastructure.[138] Although the central government has at times taken measures to recentralize authority, its control over local affairs is often limited. New policies are decided by a process of bargaining that occurs largely behind closed doors, as proposed measures must be negotiated both vertically, with officials up and down different levels of government, and horizontally across different agencies. This "fragmented" and "authoritarian" system has led to disjointed policies between sectors, a lack of transparency, rent-seeking behavior, feigned or incomplete compliance, and a relatively high level of individual discretion by bureaucrats at different levels of the political chain of command—all contributing to slow, incremental policy change and weak enforcement of environmental protections that are perceived as detrimental to local industrial growth.[139]

China's energy sector illustrates some of the institutional impediments to low-carbon development. As Richard Lester and Ed Steinfeld of the Massachusetts Institute of Technology write,

> What many outsiders take to be the deliberate result of Chinese national "energy strategy" is in fact better understood as an agglomeration of ad hoc decisions by local governments, local power producers, and local industrial concerns, few if any whom have the national interest in mind and most of whom are rushing to fill a void left by the absence of national-level energy strategy.[140]

At times, the government's flexibility in allowing the provinces greater autonomy has helped. In the 1990s and 2000s, when the country's industry was booming, gaps in state lending for infrastructure were filled by provincial investment funds, local government-owned companies, and subsidiaries of the state grid company. They provided much-needed capital to build power plants and other infrastructure that was needed to drive economic growth.[141] So many local entities went off the books entirely and engaged in self-help that, by 2006, about one-quarter of the country's generating capacity came from "illegal" power plants that were never approved by central government planners or regulators.[142] Yet, the lack of coordination and the preference for heavy-handed administrative measures by the central authorities have also been a hindrance. For example, to meet the energy savings targets dictated by the Five-Year Plan, many local governments literally turned the lights off in the final months before the 2010 deadline. The press was filled with stories of local authorities enforcing daily blackouts; forcing businesses to cut back operations or close up shop; and leaving streets, schools, offices, residences, and even hospitals in the dark.[143] Because China's goals to become a resource-efficient, low-carbon society will require broad-based changes in industry and consumer behavior across many sectors, overcoming these pitfalls will be crucial.

Risks to the United States and the World

China's environmental challenges present several intertwined layers of risk to U.S. interests, ranging from direct risks to U.S. economic and foreign policy interests to regional risks and risks borne by the global community. Following this widening progression, this section looks at the risks of a political or economic meltdown in China, shocks to world food prices, instability along China's periphery, the potential undermining of long-term growth in developing countries in other regions, and the erosion of global goods caused by climate change and the loss of marine biodiversity.

Importantly, such risks should not be interpreted as a deliberate affront by China to the supremacy of the United States. Contrary to the views of a vocal minority, centrist political leaders and mainstream academics in China do not think China will unseat the United States as the world's superpower over the next few decades, nor do they think such a change would be desirable.[144] What the Chinese seek is an equal seat at the table with the United States and other major countries and a greater voice in deciding the rules of the existing international system that has largely been shaped by the United States. If China *does* threaten the United States, it will not be by design but rather as a consequence of China's environmental decline and its inability to ensure greater sustainability both at home and in its dealings abroad.

Risk: Environmental Meltdown in China

China watchers have long debated if and when China's economy and polity will implode under the weight of its environmental deficit.[145] In *The River Runs Black*, for example, Elizabeth Economy[146] describes a spectrum of future scenarios for

China, ranging from a green renaissance to an "environmental meltdown." In the worst-case scenario, pollution worsens, agricultural output falls, economic growth becomes sluggish, local governments are buried under debt and corruption, social services crumble, violent protests spread, foreign investors withdraw, and the state turns in on itself, becoming increasingly isolated from the rest of the world and teetering on collapse.

On balance, it is highly unlikely that environmental problems will lead to China's collapse in the next couple of decades. The Communist Party state is very resilient and has a long history of weathering tumult, much of it self-inflicted.[147] And, as China has become more deeply integrated into the world economic system, the stakes of a massive state failure are simply too high for all parties.

However, a meltdown is not impossible. A sudden, cataclysmic event such as the bursting of the Three Gorges Dam (described by Economy), catastrophic flooding in a megacity such as Guangzhou because of inadequate investment in basic infrastructure,[148] or a string of major industrial pollution accidents in major river basins leading to water shortages for tens of millions of people could trigger widespread discontent, forcing a series of deep-reaching changes.

The upheavals that China went through during the 1980s provide an analogy for the kind of unrest that could be precipitated by environmental degradation and resource depletion.[149] During that time, the dividends of early economic reforms began to wear off. Farmers were resentful of grain production quotas that forced them to sell at artificially low prices, and many farmers began to leave the land. Rampant inflation was unleashed by the lifting of price controls. Student demonstrations erupted, fueled by grievances over poor living conditions and lethargic political reforms. By 1988, inflation was the worst it had ever been in history, farmers were facing increasingly volatile grain prices, workers were being laid off, state employees were seeing their living standards fall, intellectuals were dismayed by the lack of reform, and fractures were widening in the upper echelons of the party. Then, in 1989, the sudden, unexplained death of a reformer named Hu Yaobang spurred a new wave of protests in cities across the country. In Beijing, students gathered in Tiananmen Square and were soon joined by workers, officials, teachers, and others. While the ending to the protests in Tiananmen and elsewhere was tragic, these events nonetheless illustrate how grievances may build under the right conditions. In the 1980s, it was a setting of macroeconomic weakness; in the 2010s or 2020s, it could be environmental weakness.

Environmental weaknesses also heighten the risk of China's economy making a "hard landing" as it enters a new, slower period of GDP growth. Depleted resources, degraded ecosystems, and unhealthy living conditions lead to productivity losses that are a real drag on growth. Already, wages lost by urban residents who die or miss work because of respiratory illnesses linked to air pollution cost the country about 1.1 percent of its GDP every year.[150] Damages from acid rain falling on crops, wastewater being used for irrigation, deserts encroaching on rangelands, and soil nutrients lost due to erosion reduce farm productivity by 1.6 percent of GDP each year.[151] Further declines in environmental quality and worsening shortages will add to growth constraints and produce an even stronger drag on productivity. When combined with other constraints (e.g., a shrinking, aging workforce), it is possible that resource depletion and environmental degradation may create a strong enough downward pull to force a hard landing. The potential shock of an accelerated slowdown over the next 5 to 10 years will only increase in magnitude as China locks itself into a high-carbon development pathway and increases the costs of adjustments needed to relieve environmental constraints.

Risk: Sudden Shocks to Prices of Commodities Such as Grains

Rising commodity prices and volatile markets have made headline news in recent years. Trends in food prices have been particularly worrying, as food price volatility during the period from 2008 to 2011 was the worst in 50 years.[152] During the 2008 food crisis, world grain prices rose by 60 percent within a month, which caused upward of 105 million people around the world to fall into poverty and increased the number of undernourished people by some 44 million (reaching a total of 967 million worldwide by the end of 2008).[153] Global food prices spiked again in early 2011, as the food price index surpassed levels seen during the 2008 crisis and reached a record high.[154]

In explaining why such dramatic food price spikes have occurred over the past few years, analysts have pointed to a number of factors: higher oil prices, policies that encourage the use of farmland to grow biofuels, weather disasters in grain-producing regions, thinner grain reserves to buffer against shocks, growing industrial demand for grains and oilseeds by the emerging economies, counterproductive export bans in response to supply shortages, and a surge in the trading of grain futures.[155]

In light of the above, there is strong reason to believe that environmental stress in China may contribute to more-volatile food prices. The size of this effect is uncertain, but the fundamental pressures are well known. As China's demand for oil continues to increase, prices of fuels and petroleum-based agricultural inputs will also increase.[156] Population growth, higher income levels, and a corresponding change in diets will substantially raise China's per capita consumption of agricultural products such as meat and dairy, in turn increasing the demand for animal feed (e.g., soybeans). The area of farmland in China will continue shrinking as cities expand and labor shifts away from farming, but the ability of Chinese farmers to raise yields will be limited by more-severe water stress in the northern river basins and the worsening quality of land caused by erosion, loss of natural soil fertility, salinization, and pollution.[157] Together, these constraints will cause China's imports of wheat, maize, rice, and soybeans to rise. Increasingly, volatile prices may also occur as a result of more-frequent droughts, floods, and other extreme weather events.[158] Although global food markets should be able to accommodate a "moderate" and "predictable" adjustment in Chinese grain imports,[159] they may struggle to cope with a spike caused by acute water shortages and weather disasters, especially as climate change increases the severity and frequency of extreme events in other grain-producing parts of the world.[160]

Risk: Instability in China's Borderlands

China's borderlands are characterized by a unique fragility. Half of the 14 countries sharing a land border with China were listed in the top quartile of the 2010 Failed States Index; half are afflicted by ongoing insurgencies; and half have been cited as highly or extremely risky for business.[161] Political instability has been mirrored by high levels of ecological sensitivity. This is particularly true for the western part of China, which has already shown dramatic effects from climate change because of the region's high altitudes and rugged topography.

The United States and China have a common interest in managing this fragility on China's periphery, although for differing reasons. The United States desires to stem the rise of extremism and militancy in South Asia and maintains strong political and economic alliances with countries such as India and Thailand. China views South and Southeast Asia as important parts of a broader regional development strategy and stable relations with these countries as being integral to their mutual economic prosperity.[162]

Chinese trade and investment have contributed greatly to the economies of its border countries, but China's appetite for resources has also been a destabilizing factor. For example, China is the world's leading supplier and user of wood products sourced from illegally harvested timber.[163] Along China's southern border, strong demand from neighboring Chinese provinces combined with porous borders and weak law enforcement capacity has fed a thriving black market for tropical hardwoods smuggled from neighboring Burma (Myanmar). Profits from trafficking timber, gems, and drugs have sustained insurgent ethnic militia groups in the northern and eastern parts of the country, which remain outside government control.[164] Immersed in conflict and lawlessness, this area of Burma has nevertheless been the focus of large-scale investments by China Power Investment, which has plans to build seven dams along the upper Irrawaddy River to produce and sell electricity across the border. One of these projects, the Myitsone Dam, which would have cost $3.6 billion and sent 90 percent of the electricity it generated to China, was abruptly called to a halt in 2011 by the Burmese president. Burmese civil society strongly opposed the project because they were concerned that it would displace some 8,000 villagers and flood a large area of natural forest and cropland. But the decision of Burma's leaders to cancel the project may have ultimately been motivated by fears over intensified fighting with the Kachin Independence Army, which continues to control the area where the dam was being built.[165]

Concerns about the security of water resources flowing out of China have also fueled tensions.[166] China is home to the headwaters of the Mekong, Irrawaddy, Brahmaputra, Irtysh, and other rivers, which supply freshwater to hundreds of millions of people living downstream and outside China's borders. China has found itself embroiled in numerous water disputes with Russia, India, Burma, Kazakhstan, North Korea, and others because of China's dam-building activities and increasing water withdrawals.[167]

Cross-border tensions could be heightened by climate change. Although future projections are highly uncertain, current expectations are that the incidence and severity of drought along China's side of the Himalayas will worsen as summer rainfall decreases.[168] With further warming, some studies warn that by the 2050s, meltwater from snow and glacier ice in China's western and northwestern mountain ranges may drop below a critical threshold and cause abrupt shortages.[169] Warming will also increase the likelihood of geologic disasters, such as landslides and flooding caused by the sudden outburst of glacial lakes, leading to the loss of life and property downstream. These changes in the environment will most directly affect the rural and traditional peoples in China's border regions whose livelihoods depend directly on the crops, livestock, forest products, and other natural goods that come from the ecosystems they inhabit.[170] Environmental changes and the resulting loss of livelihoods may intensify the movement of people across borders. The potential for environmental refugees will be heightened by ongoing conflict, lack of basic public services, low levels of development, and inability to cope with weather-related disasters in border countries such as Pakistan and Burma.[171]

The ability of the United States and China to stabilize China's periphery has been hampered by a lack of strong regional institutions. In the Greater Mekong subregion, China has joined a cooperation program organized by the Asian Development Bank and is taking part in an initiative to set up a series of biodiversity conservation corridors.[172] China has also agreed to share data on water discharges from its upstream ladder of dams, water level, and rainfall with the downstream countries in the Mekong River Commission (MRC).[173] Yet, China has no interest in signing on as a full-fledged member of the MRC, and thus the commission has continued to be relatively weak and unable to fulfill its mandate of coordinating development in the Greater Mekong. Bilateral and multilateral cooperation between China and the South Asian countries is even more lacking. China has signed agreements with neighboring states, such as India and Kazakhstan, to share data on water. Yet, cross-border flood warnings are sometimes delayed and Indian water authorities have refused access to data for joint scientific research on climate change. The only forum specifically for enhancing cooperation between China and South Asian countries on water issues in the Greater Himalayas is low-level and purely consultative.[174] These regional institutions are simply not up to the task of managing risks emanating from large infrastructure projects on international rivers, transboundary pollution, environmental-induced migration, or climate change.

Risk: Undermining the Sustainability of Developing Countries in the Global South

In "The Coming Anarchy," Center for New American Security fellow and *Atlantic Monthly* correspondent Robert D. Kaplan describes a bleak future of environmental scarcity in which once-resource-rich countries deplete their natural wealth and plunge into poverty, conflict, crime, despair, and disease.[175] Perhaps channeling this vision, anti-China hawks have said that China is engaging in a new form of colonialism by cornering supplies of resources from poor countries and is leading the developing world along the path to environmental wreckage.

The reality is far more complicated. There are still vigorous debates in academic circles as to the extent to which Chinese trade and investment are actually contributing to the long-term development of other countries in the Global South.[176] On balance, the current evidence shows that Chinese trade and investment have indeed brought real benefits. Still, the *environmental* sustainability of its economic activities in the Global South is questionable.

China's investment activities in Africa embody these contradictory dynamics. Between 1995 and 2010, Chinese foreign direct investment in Africa grew from a mere $14 million to $9 billion, while African exports to China increased from $948 million to $80 billion.[177] The Chinese have improved the trade position of resource-rich countries by presenting them with a new buyer for commodity exports and bolstering higher prices. And in times of financial austerity in much of the world, Chinese investors have provided poorer countries with much-needed access to credit lines that would otherwise be difficult to secure. Perhaps even more important, the Chinese are also providing money to build much-lacking infrastructure. China finances about $5 billion worth of infrastructure projects each year in Africa, whereas total financing from the World Bank for infrastructure in Africa between 2003 and 2009 was only $2.5 billion.[178] Although less than one-tenth of this new infrastructure is built directly for use in extractive activities, most projects have been financed with loans paid for with exports of natural resources to China.[179] Chinese-financed projects have included rehabilitating and expanding road and rail networks, building hydropower plants, laying fiber-optic communications lines, and installing high-voltage power lines.[180] In June 2012, China pledged to loan African countries another $20 billion over the next three years for infrastructure, agriculture, and other projects—a promise which President Xi Jinping reiterated during his visit to Africa in 2013.[181]

In other ways, Chinese trade and investment have not been much help. For one, China's presence in Africa continues to be relatively small and concentrated in a few extractive industries. China's share of Africa's total exports is still only about 13 percent (the United States' share is 18 percent). Around 82 percent of Africa's exports to China originate from just four countries and are composed of metals, minerals, gems, and oil (the share is 88 percent for the United States).[182] As a result of such intense focus on resource commodities, Africa's exports to China have created relatively few local jobs.[183] Natural resources are often in more remote places where there is little spillover to the local economy, extractive industries are more capital-intensive than labor-intensive, and Chinese companies have brought workers from China.[184] Finally, Chinese companies have fueled political troubles by offering a lifeline to pariah regimes such as Angola, Zimbabwe, and Sudan. In one study, economists found that, all else being equal, investment by China had a negative effect on measures of human rights in African host countries (the same effect was found for investments by U.S. companies, although it was not as strong).[185]

The natural resource trade with China is taking a heavy environmental toll in Africa, particularly where Chinese companies have engaged in damaging behavior in the absence of strong standards for environmental or social responsibility in host countries. In Gabon, Sinopec began drilling for oil in Loango National Park over the protests of conservation groups and prior to review of the environmental impact assessment for the project by the Gabonese Ministry of Environmental Protection. In Sierra Leone, Chinese timber companies clear-cut forests, displacing forest residents. In Sudan, Chinese developers built a 1,250-megawatt hydropower dam that displaced some 74,000 people from the fertile river valley and caused siltation problems, increased the erosion of riverbanks, and prevented fish from migrating up or downstream. In Zambia, tailings from a Chinese-financed copper mine have contaminated the Kafue River on three separate occasions.[186] Controlling the environmental footprint of Chinese-backed extraction activities has been a relatively low priority for host governments eager to increase investment capital. Many of these countries lack adequate financial resources, skilled employees, and laws to effectively monitor and enforce environmental standards. Oversight has only been weakened by the lack of disclosure requirements for loans made by Chinese state-owned banks.

Admittedly, Chinese investors are taking steps to raise standards for environmental and social responsibility. In 2007, China Exim Bank released guidelines that require social and environmental impact assessments to be conducted for all overseas projects. The guidelines also call for borrowers to "refer to" Chinese or international standards in cases where the host country's environmental protections are insufficient. In 2008, the MEP, the People's Bank of China, and the China Banking Regulatory Commission issued a "green credit" policy, which cut bank financing to energy-intensive and polluting industries and encouraged banks to include environmental performance in credit risk management and lending criteria.[187] That same year, the Industrial and Commercial Bank of China (ICBC) became the first Chinese bank to adopt the Equator Principles, voluntary standards developed by the World Bank, the International Finance Corporation, and others for "determining, assessing, and managing environmental and social risk."[188] ICBC has also signed on to the UNEP Finance Initiative and the United Nations Carbon Disclosure Project.[189] And in 2009, Sinohydro, which claims 50 percent of the world hydropower market, engaged a nongovernmental organization called International Rivers to develop a world-class environmental policy it then adopted.[190]

Despite these promising examples, overall buy-in by Chinese banks and companies in environmental and social responsibility remains low. Few others have joined such international initiatives or formally committed to abide by internationally accepted practices overseas. The Ministry of Commerce and MEP issued guidelines in February 2013 that require all companies investing overseas to complete environmental impact assessments, create management plans for hazardous waste, conduct monitoring, and publish environmental data; however, the guidelines remain voluntary—without penalties for violators—leaving Chinese firms investing overseas to operate in a gray area.[191]

Higher environmental standards for Chinese companies could help reduce the environmental footprint of their overseas activities. But ultimately, whether Chinese trade and investment will actually contribute to sustainable development in the Global South will be determined largely by what the host countries do. Especially in regions such as Latin America, but also in Africa, countries are not investing enough in hands-on policies to promote the formation of human capital, grow industry, spur innovation, and reduce their reliance on primary commodities. As a result, trade with China is not leading to enhancements in productivity and countries are increasingly finding themselves out-competed by China in world markets for higher-value manufactured goods and services.[192]

Risk: Erosion of Shared Global Goods Such as the Atmosphere and Marine Biodiversity

Finally, there are global risks, such as a failure to protect the common atmosphere. The growth of resource-intensive industries and consumer lifestyles in China will play a decisive role in the severity of future climate change. From the standpoint of what is fair, it is difficult to argue that the Chinese should not consume and pollute as much as people in the United States or other high-income countries. Indeed, projections by IEA show that Americans will probably still emit roughly 60 percent more CO_2 per capita than the Chinese well into the 2030s.[193] Yet, what is fair would also be disastrous.[194] As the U.S. Department of Defense concluded in a 2010 review of its operations, in light of emerging security risks to the United States,

> climate change could have significant geopolitical impacts around the world, contributing to poverty, environmental degradation, and the further

> weakening of fragile governments.[195] Climate change will contribute to food and water security, will increase the spread of disease, and may spur or exacerbate mass migration.

Both China and the United States will be crucial players in helping the world avoid the most damaging effects of these projected changes.

The biodiversity contained in marine fisheries offers another example of a global good that is being undermined by China's current pattern of growth. Worldwide, more than 85 percent of fish stocks have either already reached capacity or are being depleted and an estimated 90 percent of the large fish in the oceans are gone.[196] By the middle of this century, stocks of all the species that are currently fished for food may collapse. Overfishing by large commercial fleets, wasteful bycatch, and destructive practices such as bottom trawling are among the factors contributing to the loss of fisheries and declines in marine biodiversity. China shares responsibility for these problems. For example, in 2003, environmentally negative subsidies to China's commercial fishing industry were on the order of $2.19 billion (second only to Japan), including money for discounted fuel, boat construction, pricing support, tax exemptions, and agreements to access fish in other countries' waters—far more than the $1.23 billion in environmentally beneficial spending on fisheries management, research, and protected marine areas.[197] China's government is pouring much of its support into building the capacity of its deepwater fishing fleet. In 2010, the fleet had some 1,990 boats in faraway waters catching 1.116 million tons of fish each year. About 476,000 tons came from the high seas, while 636,000 tons were fished from other countries' offshore waters (exclusive economic zones).[198] Despite its growing catch, as a stakeholder in the global commons that are the world's oceans, China has a mixed record in abiding by the rules of international agreements.[199] A 2008 review by the World Wildlife Fund (WWF) placed China in the middle of the pack in terms of compliance with the Food and Agriculture Organization's Code of Conduct for Responsible Fishing among the world's top capture fishery producers and near the bottom on measures of controlling illegal fishing and flags of convenience.[200]

Recommendations for U.S. Policy Makers

A strategy for China should begin with an understanding that China's leaders are incredibly pragmatic and open to absorbing ideas from the international community on environmental best practices.[201] U.S. policy makers should also realize that the United States has limited influence over China's domestic politics and will not be able to produce a "green transformation" in China. Most of what is needed for this transformation must be achieved by the Chinese themselves. So while the United States cannot *ensure* China's success in greening its growth, a successful U.S. foreign policy will nonetheless be vital to *facilitating* a shift toward more sustainable development. Such a policy should be grounded on the principles of cooperation. The following sections highlight a range of policy responses that seek to minimize zero-sum thinking in the U.S.-China bilateral relationship while maximizing shared benefits. The policy recommendations are categorized by multilateral, bilateral, and domestic actions.

Opportunities for Multilateral Engagement

A narrow focus on ramping up the intensity of U.S. bilateral engagement with China may produce unintended results and be counterproductive. The Chinese are wary that pursuing a "G2" superpower relationship with the United States may isolate China and be used to exert greater pressure on China, adding to existing distrust. Instead, what is needed is a reorientation of policy toward China to focus on multilateral engagement, especially in regional forums.[202] This subsection describes a few of the possibilities.

Encourage China to Join the Trans-Pacific Partnership

The Trans-Pacific Partnership (TPP) is a regional free trade agreement that, as of August 2013, includes the following countries: Australia, Brunei, Chile, Canada, Japan, Malaysia, Mexico, New Zealand, Peru, Singapore, the United States, and Vietnam. The TPP is viewed not only as a way to "shape the regional economic architecture" to standards on par with existing U.S. free trade agreements but also as a way to "positively affect change in the perceptions of Asian states of the U.S. commitment to Asia."[203] China has viewed the TPP with great suspicion, and some Chinese experts have argued that it is a thinly veiled attempt by the United States to weaken Asia-centric frameworks, such as the Association of Southeast Asian Nations (ASEAN), and isolate China from its regional trading partners.[204] Given that two-way trade with China climbed from 3 percent to 11 percent of total international merchandise trade by TPP countries between 2000 and 2011[205]—and that China's share in world trade is projected to double over the next 20 years[206]—going forward with an agreement that excludes China would be wholly inadequate.

Although it will not be easy, the United States should make a genuine effort to bring China on board as a full participant in negotiating the TPP framework and to ensure that the TPP is not seen as an attempt to counterbalance China's influence or derail free trade pacts among ASEAN states. Indeed, economic analysis shows that the mutual development of the TPP and ASEAN-centered negotiating tracks—and their eventual convergence under a comprehensive Asia-Pacific trade agreement in the 2020s—will yield significant benefits to *both* the United States and China in terms of higher income and exports.[207] To ensure greater sustainability, the United States Trade Representative should continue to support efforts under the TPP for promoting better labor and environmental practices in exporting countries, ensuring the sustainability of marine fisheries, introducing sustainable sourcing requirements, and eliminating tariffs on "green" goods and services.[208]

Step Up Efforts to Reach Full Conclusion of the Doha Round of WTO Trade Negotiations

In December 2013, WTO members ended a 12-year deadlock in the Doha Round of negotiations, striking a deal at the Ninth Ministerial Conference in Bali on a package of decisions to simplify customs procedures and improve market access for goods exported by least-developed countries. The Bali Package represents a modest breakthrough, but most of the issues for negotiation on the Doha Development Agenda have yet to be resolved. The United States should continue to push for the full conclusion of Doha. The continued importance of the WTO lies in the fact that it is the most viable option for keeping China anchored in the multilateral system. The United States and other like-minded countries will be more successful in leveraging their negotiating position with China in the WTO than if they rely solely on fragmented regional arrangements.[209] A major effort by the United States to build on the momentum of Bali could help kick-start stalled discussions in the WTO on opening up trade in environmental goods and services, securing ownership of genetic resources, and eliminating perverse fisheries subsidies.

Bolster Existing Commitments to Repeal Fossil Fuel Subsidies Under the G-20

China's subsidies to consumers for oil, coal, and natural gas are on the order of $20 billion.[210] The G-20 countries (including China) pledged in 2009 to eliminate fossil fuel subsidies "over the medium term,"[211] a commitment reiterated by Asia-Pacific Economic Cooperation (APEC) countries that same year. Overall progress toward fulfilling this pledge has been negative so far. According to conservative estimates from the OECD's IEA, fossil fuel consumption subsidies by G-20 member nations climbed to more than $160 billion in 2010, while subsidies in APEC economies increased 40 percent to $105 billion. Worldwide, fuel consumption subsidies surpassed $409 billion (up from $312 billion in 2009), with another $100 billion spent on subsidies for producers.[212] Subsidies may continue to rise to $660 billion by 2020.[213] The United States and China should take the lead in countering these trends by phasing out fossil fuel subsidies completely before 2020[214] and actively encouraging other countries in the G-20 and APEC to follow through with their pledges. China's part in this will demonstrate two things: first, its resolve to be accountable and to ensure others are accountable and, second, willingness to play a more prominent role in promoting environmental sustainability within existing multilateral institutions.

Hold an Anti-Wildlife-Trafficking Summit with China and Its Neighbors

Despite devoting more resources to policing the illegal wildlife trade, tightening regulations on captive animals, improving collection of seizure data by customs officials, and pushing for an increase in public awareness, China continues to be the world's largest buyer of illegal wildlife products. Reducing wildlife trade is vital in its own right, but also for reducing the risks of alien invasive species—which already cost China 1.3 percent of its GDP annually—and pandemic diseases from wildlife, such as severe acute respiratory syndrome.[215] Many illegal wildlife products bought in China are smuggled through border countries, such as Laos and Vietnam, which were cited in a 2012 review by the WWF as two of Asia's worst performers in enforcing international treaty requirements to restrict the trade of elephant, rhino, and tiger products.[216] As WWF wildlife trade expert Leigh Henry has pointed out, "There's a lot that the U.S. government and consumers can do to help stop this illegal trade . . . but right now, the U.S. government is not putting enough manpower and money behind its wildlife crime enforcement efforts."[217]

To start, the United States can enlist China's support in jointly convening a ministerial or presidential-level summit with the Southeast Asian countries to boost efforts aimed at stamping out the illegal wildlife trade. This would be similar to the Heads of State Tiger Summit held by Russia in 2010, where 13 countries launched a recovery program that has led to greater progress in conserving tiger habitat and enforcing laws to limit the tiger trade. In addition, U.S. law enforcement and customs authorities can assist with current efforts by China, the Convention on International Trade in Endangered Species of Wild Fauna and Flora Secretariat, and the United Nations Office on Drugs and Crime to build the capacity of countries to stop cross-border smuggling and improve enforcement at the retail level in domestic markets. As relations between China and its Southeast Asian neighbors have recently soured over competing territorial claims and river disputes, a high-profile anti-wildlife-trafficking initiative would symbolize the commitment of these countries to more constructive dialogue and cooperation.

Opportunities for Bilateral Cooperation

Clean energy has become emblematic of the dangers of the zero-sum thinking that exists in the U.S.-China bilateral relationship, despite the potential for greater mutual gains. The United States and China are often portrayed as being locked in a "clean energy race," with one clear winner and one clear loser. However, the reality is much different. As a report by Bloomberg New Energy Finance has stated, the clean energy industries in the United States and China are "joined at the hip."[218] First, a modest but growing share of the financing mobilized in the

United States is coming from China. Chinese investments in U.S. renewable energy projects have totaled around $6 billion since 2006.[219] Notable investments in 2011 included a $200 million deal by Goldwind, China's leading wind turbine manufacturer, to build a 109.5-megawatt wind farm in northern Illinois that will generate enough power for 25,000 homes.[220] Even more important, due to the global nature of value chains for high-tech goods such as wind turbines or solar PV modules, U.S. companies are still able to capture a significant percentage of value created from the clean energy industry in China. In 2010, U.S. solar companies exported upward of $1.93 billion in materials, capital equipment, and other products to Chinese manufacturers to make solar PV modules, which was $532 million more than the total value of the modules that were then imported into the United States.[221] For a hypothetical wind farm built in Texas using Chinese turbines, Bloomberg estimates that 44 percent of the value created by that project would go to U.S. companies versus 36 percent to Chinese companies. Mutual gains are also achieved in terms of jobs. The U.S. solar industry estimates that for every job created by manufacturing a solar panel in China, two to three jobs are created in the United States by selling, installing, and servicing that panel.[222]

U.S. foreign policy should capitalize on the mutual benefits of green sectors, such as clean energy, for the economies of the United States and China by building a sturdier foundation for companies and research institutions to partner with each other in these sectors. Several candidate policies are described below.

Explore Further Agreements on Intellectual Property Rights and Technology Transfer

As Ed Steinfeld writes in *Playing Our Game: Why China's Rise Doesn't Threaten the West*, as Chinese companies integrate more fully into complex global networks of production, they are increasingly adapting themselves to the legal and regulatory regimes in which multinationals operate.[223] Concerns about intellectual property (IP) rights infringement have "receded" in the most high-tech sectors and are not a significant barrier to cooperation in the long term. Bilateral agreements on technology transfer and the sharing of IP rights, such as the one pioneered under the U.S.-China CERC, will further reduce barriers to joint efforts on the research, development, demonstration, and deployment of new technologies via public-private partnerships.

Complete the Review and Lifting of Selective Restrictions on Technology Exports to China

The review of selective restrictions on technology exports to China, which the Obama administration began during its first year in office, may help smooth negotiations on the transfer of technology from U.S. firms with operations in China.[224]

Incentivize Chinese Companies to Invest in Updating Infrastructure in the United States

Chinese capital investment in the United States has been limited (on the order of only $3.8 billion in assets versus $54.2 billion worth of U.S.-owned assets in China)[225] but can be encouraged as a way to upgrade outdated infrastructure in the United States.[226] Chinese companies are already investing in some basic infrastructure in the United States and, as China's Minister of Commerce Chen Deming told a gathering of U.S. business leaders, they would like to expand this investment.[227] Indeed, the Chinese are also investing in places such as Europe and Canada. In 2011, for example, the Chinese telecomm firm Huawei announced a deal with Telecom Italia to build a nationwide fiber-to-home network in Italy.[228] With the right incentives from the U.S. federal government and a more-predictable, less-politicized process for vetting Chinese investment, such deals may also be possible in the United States. More financial resources can be channeled into building low-carbon infrastructure such as high-speed rail; solar and wind power farms; and smart grids for small, intermittent, and distributed electricity sources.

Complete Negotiations on a Bilateral Investment Treaty

A bilateral investment treaty (BIT) would ensure the free flow of capital between the United States and China. It would also help reduce the interference of political flare-ups on investment activity by ensuring the protection of investors in both countries against expropriation and giving investors the option of neutral arbitration to settle disputes.[229] Three years of deliberation on a model BIT for the United States were completed by the U.S. Trade Representative and the U.S. Department of State in April 2012.[230] At the S&ED in July 2013, China declared its interest in negotiating a wide-ranging BIT with the United States. A successful BIT with China will be a step forward in creating a more predictable business environment. It will also benefit U.S. investors. According to the U.S. Treasury Department and Federal Reserve Board,[231] a BIT "would open up China's highly restrictive system to foreign investment and help create a wide range of opportunities for U.S. firms to participate in the Chinese market."

Opportunities for Technical Assistance and Joint Research

Technical assistance programs and joint research and development initiatives have been a highlight of U.S.-China cooperation on climate change and other environmental issues so far. There are several areas in which greater technical assistance and collaboration could be fostered.

Support Innovation of Low-Carbon Technologies, Particularly at the Stage of Commercial-Scale Demonstration and Deployment

Typically, there are two "valleys of death" that new energy technologies must overcome during the innovation process in order to survive and become commercially successful. The first valley is the time between when new technologies are *developed* in the lab and when they are *demonstrated* on a large, commercial scale.[232] The second valley is between when technologies are demonstrated and when they are *deployed* in the market. Early U.S.-China collaboration on low-carbon technologies focused primarily on the earliest stages of the innovation process by sponsoring basic scientific research and early development in the lab. Recently, more funding and attention have been directed to bridge the valleys preventing clean technologies from being marketed. As part of the U.S.-China CERC, U.S. and Chinese companies are planning to demonstrate technologies to capture and store CO_2 emissions at two low-emission coal gasification plants, the GreenGen plant in Tianjin, China, and the Edwardsport plant in Indiana.[233] Separately, under the U.S.-China Renewable Energy Partnership, scientists, entrepreneurs, and policy makers are working to overcome barriers to deployment through such efforts as identifying new ways to finance solar projects and analyzing import and export policies.[234] These partnerships should be strengthened. In addition, CERC's work plan should be expanded to include a framework strategy for public and private collaboration on the entire energy technology innovation process, from research to marketing. This would help both China and the United States, which has yet to introduce a comprehensive policy for supporting and accelerating technology innovation.[235]

Develop Green Standards for Government Procurement in China

By some estimates, government purchases of goods and services account for as much as 20 percent of China's GDP (compared with 15–20 percent for OECD countries).[236] China has issued a number of administrative rules and guidelines for governments at all levels to purchase environmentally friendly, resource-saving products but has yet to fully develop a legal framework for green procurement under its Government Procurement Law. China can learn from the experience of other countries, including Japan, European Union countries, and the United States in strengthening legal standards, procedures, and incentives for green procurement. Further developing green procurement in China thus has the potential to create a "huge" market for green products and services.[237] The U.S. Environmental Protection Agency (EPA) has developed extensive guidelines for the purchase of environmentally friendly products by federal agencies and may be best positioned to offer collaborative technical assistance in its exchanges with the Chinese MEP. Given the experience of the U.S. Department of Defense in crafting its strategy for green procurement, there is also the possibility for greater military-to-military collaboration.

Promote Institutional Capacity-Building for Energy and the Environment

Over the past decades, the agencies in charge of China's energy policy have been scraped together, torn down, rebuilt, and reworked again and again.[238] The result of this patchwork process is that China's central government still lacks a single institution with unified authority to make cohesive energy policies and manage turf battles between competing sectors of the government and economy.[239] The latest reconfiguration came in 2008, when the National Energy Administration (NEA) and National Energy Commission (NEC) were pieced together from existing bureaus, departments, and a high-level leading group. The NEA and NEC have failed to live up to expectations, in part because they were badly understaffed (NEA has only a couple hundred employees versus the 4,000 employees at the Department of Energy in the United States), but also because they were not given key powers, such as price setting for oil, coal, and electricity.[240] Now there is talk of possibly creating a super Ministry of Energy, and the NEA and others are reported to be undertaking studies for setting up such a ministry.[241] The U.S. Department of Energy is uniquely positioned to provide assistance to the NEA through bilateral exchanges. U.S. agencies have provided similar assistance in the past. The EPA, for example, was instrumental in helping China's State Environmental Protection Agency (now MEP) establish regional environmental protection offices.[242]

Opportunities for Government-to-Government Dialogue

At the level of government-to-government dialogue, bilateral initiatives between the United States and China on energy, climate, and the environment would further benefit from several initiatives.

Ensure That Greater Funding and Political Commitment Are Devoted to Climate, Energy, and Environment Initiatives

Long-term commitments are needed to avoid the pitfalls of short-lived projects in the past. Improving these existing structures for bilateral cooperation, rather than adding new structures, would better communicate ongoing commitment to the importance of institutionalizing and deepening the bilateral relationship.

Lift Restrictions on Bilateral Assistance to China Through the Overseas Private Investment Corporation and Other Aid Agencies

The Chinese have long complained that the United States is the only Western country not to provide official development aid to China. Enabling agencies such as the U.S. Agency for International Development (USAID) to establish an official presence in China would improve technical collaboration with Chinese agencies on biodiversity conservation, climate change adaptation, and other work areas in the USAID portfolio.

Complete Negotiations on a Bilateral Agreement to Combat Illegal Trade in Natural Resources

U.S. and Chinese officials had originally to set a deadline to finish negotiations on the fourth meeting of the S&ED, held in April 2012;[243] however, an agreement has yet to be announced. The United States is one of China's largest export markets for wood products, after Europe. A bilateral agreement to combat illegal logging would define obligations for collecting and sharing data and set requirements for sustainable sourcing and certification of all timber products imported into the United States from China. There should also be agreements to combat illegal fishing and wildlife trafficking. A fisheries agreement could be negotiated as part of consultations between the U.S. National Oceanic and Atmospheric Administration (NOAA) and the Chinese State Oceanic Administration on fisheries management and enforcement.[244]

Create a Forum for Corporate Environmental and Social Responsibility

The past decade has seen a flourishing of voluntary programs for greater transparency, accountability, and sustainability in extractive industries and other areas of overseas investment. These efforts include the Extractive Industries Transparency Initiative, the International Council on Mining and Metals, the Equator Principles, the UNEP Finance Initiative, and the United Nations Carbon Disclosure Project. Few Chinese companies have signed on to these voluntary efforts. Similar to CERC, a public-private partnership could be created under the S&ED in which leading U.S. companies (especially those with operations in China) would collaborate with top Chinese companies and research institutions on strategies to improve corporate performance on measures of social and environmental responsibility. In establishing standards, benchmarks for good performance should be set according to international best practices and could be gleaned from existing programs such as those mentioned above. To complement this effort, in dialogue with Chinese officials from the State-owned Assets Supervision and Administration Commission and Ministry of Commerce, representatives from the U.S. Departments of Treasury and Commerce should emphasize the need for China to require overseas investors and companies to adhere to standards *no less than* those enforced under China's own environmental laws.

Opportunities to Lead by Example at Home

Ultimately, much of what the United States needs to do effectively to engage China on sustainability issues will have to be done domestically in the United States. It is time for the United States to show greater leadership and long-term strategic thinking; otherwise, its leverage with China will substantially diminish. Over the course of the next decade, the United States should demonstrate its leadership on environmental sustainability at home via such ambitious policy actions as outlining a national strategy for "green growth" in a presidential directive; passing comprehensive energy legislation that includes federal mandates for clean electricity; continuing to raise efficiency standards for vehicles, buildings, and appliances; pricing carbon emissions from energy producers and industry; and phasing out harmful subsidies for agriculture, energy, and commercial fishing.

Notes

1 World Bank and Development Research Center, *China 2030: Building a Modern, Harmonious, and Creative High-Income Society* (World Bank and DRC, State Council, People's Republic of China, Washington, D.C., 2012); United Nations, *World Urbanization Prospects: The 2009 Revision*, POP/DB/WUP/Rev.2009/1/F3 (Department of Economic and Social Affairs, Population Division, United Nations, 2009).

2 Harry Harding, *A Fragile Relationship: The United States and China Since 1972* (The Brookings Institution, Washington, D.C., 1992): 58–59.

3 U.S. Bureau of Economic Analysis, "Table 12. U.S. International Transactions by Area—China" (U.S. Bureau of Economic Analysis, Department of Commerce), www.bea.gov/iTable/iTable.cfm?ReqID=6&step=1#reqid=6&step=3&isuri=1&600=52.

4 U.S. Treasury Department and Federal Reserve Board, "Major Foreign Holders of U.S. Treasury Securities," Statistics released Jan. 16, 2014, www.treasury.gov/resource-center/data-chart-center/tic/Documents/mfh.txt.

5 Harding, *A Fragile Relationship*; PRC (People's Republic of China) Bureau of Exit and Entry, "Steady Growth in the Number of Persons and Vehicles Entering and Exiting China in 2011" (in Chinese) (Bureau of Exit and Entry, Administration of the Ministry of Public Security, People's Republic of China, Jan. 14, 2012), www.mps.gov.cn/n16/n84147/n84196/3100875.html.

6 The number of university students learning Mandarin in the United States meanwhile increased from 34,000 in 2002 to 61,000 in 2009. See Institute of International Education, "Open Doors 2011: International Student Enrollment Increased by 5 Percent in 2010/11" (Nov. 14, 2011), www.iie.org/Who-We-Are/News-and-Events/Press-Center/Press-Releases/2011/2011-11-14-Open-Doors-International-Students; American Council on the Teaching of Foreign Languages, "Foreign Language Enrollments in K-12 Public Schools: Are Students Prepared for a Global Society?" (2011), www.actfl.org/files/ReportSummary2011.pdf.

7 Warren I. Cohen, *America's Response to China: A History of Sino-American Relations*, 5th ed. (Columbia University Press, New York, 2010). The one year since 1989 when the United States did not sponsor such a resolution was 2003, when China supported a United Nations Security Council resolution against Iraq and withheld vociferous objections to the U.S. invasion. Since the UNCHR was replaced by the United Nations Human Rights Council and since the United States sought a seat on the council in 2009, no further resolutions have been brought.

8 See, for example, Hui Lu, "Full Text of Human Rights Record of the United States in 2011," *Xinhua* (May 25, 2012), http://news.xinhuanet.com/english/china/2012-05/25/c_131611554.htm; and Ningzhu Zhu, "Full Text of Human Rights Record of the United States in 2012," *Xinhua* (April 21, 2013), http://news.xinhuanet.com/english/world/2013-04/21/c_132327175.htm.

9 Harding, *A Fragile Relationship*.

10 Keith Bradsher, "Trade War in Solar"; New York Times, November 9, 2011. http://www.nytimes.com/2011/11/10/business/global/us-and-china-on-brink-of-trade-war-over-solar-power-industry.html?pagewanted=all&_r=0. Keith Bradsher and Diana Cardwell, "Chinese Solar Panels Face Big Tariffs," *New York Times* (May 18, 2012): Section B.

11 Keith Bradsher, "Trade War in Solar."

12 The tariffs will be imposed on polysilicon. See Diana Cardwell, "In Feud with West, China to Impose Tariffs on Key Solar Panel Material," *International Herald Tribune* (July 20, 2013): 9.

13 "The China-Bashing Syndrome," *Economist* (July 14, 2012).

14 U.S. Department of Defense, *Annual Report to Congress: Military and Security Developments Involving the People's Republic of China, 2011* (Office of the Secretary of Defense, U.S. Department of Defense, Washington, D.C., 2011), www.defense.gov/pubs/pdfs/2011_cmpr_final.pdf.

15 U.S. Department of Defense, *Annual Report to Congress: Military and Security Developments Involving the People's Republic of China, 2013* (Office of the Secretary of Defense, U.S. Department of Defense, Washington, D.C., 2013), www.defense.gov/pubs/2013_china_report_final.pdf.

16 Jingwei Zhang, "Skill and Risk in U.S. Use of 'Smart Power' with China" (美国对华'巧实力'的巧与险), *Xinhua* Development Forum (July 19, 2012), http://forum.home.news.cn/detail/101650980/1.html.

17 Kenneth Lieberthal and Jisi Wang, "Addressing U.S.-China Strategic Distrust," John L. Thornton China Center Monograph Series, The Brookings Institution, Washington, D.C. (2012), www.brookings.edu/~/media/research/files/papers/2012/3/30%20us%20china%20lieberthal/0330_china_lieberthal.pdf; E.C. Economy and A. Segal, "The G-2 Mirage—Why the United States and China Are Not Ready to Upgrade Ties," *Foreign Affairs* 88 (2009): 14.

18 Warren I. Cohen, *America's Response to China*; Michael D. Swaine, *America's Challenge: Engaging a Rising China in the Twenty-First Century* (Carnegie Endowment for International Peace, Washington, D.C., 2011). As evidence of "maturing" U.S.–China ties, commentators have cited the ability of the two governments to quickly resolve the incident in May 2012 when Chinese human rights lawyer Chen Guangcheng escaped house arrest and sought refuge in the U.S. Embassy in Beijing. The Chen Guangcheng incident contrasted sharply with that of Fang Lizhi, a Chinese dissident who sought shelter in the U.S. Embassy in 1989 and remained there for more than a year. See William Wan, "Crisis Required Delicate Dance of Diplomacy," *Washington Post* (May 20, 2012): Section A; William Wan, "End of Chen Saga Suggests Maturing U.S.-China Ties," *Washington Post* (May 21, 2012): Section A; Thomas Kaplan, Andrew Jacobs,

and Steven Lee Myers, "Ordeal Ended, China Activist Lands in the U.S.," *New York Times* (May 20, 2012): Section A.

19 U.S. Energy Information Administration (EIA), "International Energy Statistics" (2011), www.eia.gov/cfapps/ipdbproject/IEDIndex3.cfm.

20 In terms of industrial roundwood. From Food and Agriculture Organization of the United Nations (FAO), FAOSTAT database, www.fao.org/corp/statistics/en/.

21 Based on D. G. Rogich and G. R. Matos, "The Global Flows of Metals and Minerals," *U.S. Geological Survey Open-File Report 2008–1355* (2008), http://pubs.usgs.gov/of/2008/1355/.

22 Based on freshwater withdrawals; UN Statistics Division, *Environmental Indicators Database*, http://unstats.un.org/unsd/environment/qindicators.htm.

23 Based on data for capture fisheries production and landings by country; Food and Agriculture Organization of the United Nations (FAO), *The State of World Fisheries and Aquaculture 2012* (FAO, Rome, 2012); The Pew Charitable Trusts (Pew), Sea Around Us Project Database, http://seaaroundus.org/data/.

24 Based on meat, eggs, and milk supply. See FAO, FAOSTAT database.

25 Joanna Lewis, "The State of U.S.-China Relations on Climate Change: Examining the Bilateral and Multilateral Relationship," *China Environment Series* 11(2011): 7–47.

26 Asia Society Center on U.S.-China Relations and Pew Center on Global Climate Change, "Common Challenge, Collaborative Response: A Roadmap for U.S.-China Cooperation on Energy and Climate Change" (Washington, D.C., 2009), www.c2es.org/docUploads/US-China-Roadmap-Feb09.pdf; Haibin Zhang, "Tackling Climate Change: Comparative Research on Sino-Japanese and Sino-American Cooperation" (应对气候变化：中日合作与中美合作比较研究), in *Global Climate Change Diplomacy and China's Policy* (世界气候变化外交与中国的应对), edited by Jiemian Yang (杨洁勉) (Shi Shi Chu Ban She, Beijing, 2009); Shimo Li and Yunheng Zhou, "U.S. Energy Policy Toward China in the New Century" (论新世纪以来美国对华能源政策), *International Review* (国际观察) 20, no. 2 (2012): 60–65; Swaine, *America's Challenge*.

27 Kenneth Lieberthal, *U.S.-China Clean Energy Cooperation: The Road Ahead* (Brookings Institution, Washington, D.C., 2009), www.brookings.edu/~/media/research/files/papers/2009/9/us%20china%20energy%20cooperation%20lieberthal/09_us_china_energy_cooperation_lieberthal; Deborah Seligsohn, Robert Heilmayr, Xiaomei Tan, and Lutz Weischer, "China, The United States, and the Climate Change Challenge" (Policy Brief, World Resources Institute, Washington, D.C., 2009), http://pdf.wri.org/china_united_states_climate_change_challenge.pdf; Hui Meng and Jiang Haixiao, "The Influence of New Energy Cooperation on the Sino-U.S. Relationship" (中美能源合作对两国关系的影响), *Pacific Journal* (中美新能源合作对两国关系的影响) 19, no. 9 (2011): 33–43; Shaoxue Zhou, "Climate Diplomacy to Become a New Point of Growth for Sino-American Strategic Cooperation" (气候外交将成为中美战略合作新增长点), *Journal of University of International Relations* (国际关系学院学报) 6(2010): 37–42.

28 World Resources Institute (WRI), "Clean Tech's Rise, Part I: Will the U.S. and China Reap the Mutual Benefits?" *China FAQs Issue Brief* (WRI, May 1, 2012), www.chinafaqs.org/files/chinainfo/ChinaFAQs_IssueBrief1_MutualBenefits.pdf; World Resources Institute (WRI), "Clean Tech's Rise, Part II: US-China Collaboration in Public-Private Partnerships," *China FAQs Issue Brief* (WRI, May 1, 2012), www.chinafaqs.org/library/issue-brief-clean-techs-rise-part-ii-us-china-collaboration-public-private-partnerships.

29 The Chinese maintain that Premier Wen was not invited to the unscheduled meeting arranged by President Obama and a few other heads of state. The Chinese say that upon overhearing at a dinner on December 17, 2009, that a meeting would take place later that night, Premier Wen dispatched Vice Foreign Minister He to find out more about the gathering. According to a detailed account of the events, which was published by the *Xinhua* News Agency and *People's Daily*, the Vice Foreign Minister promptly "rushed to the venue of the small-group meeting and raised serious concerns with the host for arranging such a meeting with hidden motives." The article goes on to describe President Obama's subsequent interruption of a meeting between China and the BASIC countries (Brazil, South Africa, India, and China), which was attended by Premier Wen, as "awkward." Others have argued that the talks were spoiled early on by the "Danish Draft," a negotiating text hammered out by the Danish hosts and about a dozen other countries that was leaked to the press in the first days of the summit. As *The Guardian*'s China correspondent Jonathan Watts, who was at the talks, remarked in an interview: "The authority of the chair was undermined. From then on, the talks ground to a halt. Almost the entire two weeks was wasted as a result." In Watts's view, Premier Wen's supposed snub of Obama "was primarily a defensive tactic." Premier Wen "did not want to be strong-armed into a deal" knowing that Obama's hands were tied by the U.S. Congress blocking any climate legislation. See *Xinhua* and *The People's Daily*, "Premier Wen at Copenhagen Conference," *China Daily* online (Dec. 25, 2009), www.chinadaily.com.cn/china/2009-12/25/content_9231783.htm; Mark Lynas, "How Do I Know China Wrecked the Copenhagen Deal? I Was in the Room," *Guardian* (London) (Dec. 22, 2009), www.guardian.co.uk/environment/2009/dec/22/copenhagen-climate-change-mark-lynas; John Lee, "How China Stiffed the World in Copenhagen," *Foreign Policy* (Dec. 21, 2009), www.foreignpolicy.com/articles/2009/12/21/how_china_stiffed_the_world_in_copenhagen; Andrew Revkin and John Broder, "Accord on Climate, Along with Plenty of Discord," *New York Times* (Dec. 20, 2009): A1; Andrew Jacobs, "Chinese and British Officials Tangle in Testy Exchange Over Climate Agreement," *New York Times* (Dec. 23, 2009): A10; Alice Xin Liu, "Danwei Interviews Jonathan Watts, 'Copenhagen Will Shape Our Lives for Years to Come,'" *Danwei* (Dec. 25, 2009), www.danwei.org/foreign_media_on_china/danwei_interviews_jonathan_wat.php.

30 Ed Miliband, "The Road from Copenhagen," *Guardian* (Dec. 20, 2009), www.guardian.co.uk/commentisfree/2009/dec/20/copenhagen-climate-change-accord; Lynas, "How Do I Know."

31 International Institute for Sustainable Development (IISD), "Summary of the Cancun Climate Change Conference: Nov. 29–Dec. 10," *Earth Negotiations Bulletin* 12 (2010): 498, www.iisd.ca/climate/cop16/.

32 See, for example, Suzanne Goldenberg, "China on Path to Redemption in Cancun," *Guardian* (London) (Dec. 7, 2010), www.guardian.co.uk/environment/2010/dec/07/cancun-climate-change-summit-china.

33 IISD, "Summary of the Cancun Climate Change Conference," 498.

34 IISD, "Summary of the Durban Climate Change Conference: Nov. 28–Dec. 11, 2011," *Earth Negotiations Bulletin* 12 (2011): 534, www.iisd.ca/download/pdf/enb12534e.pdf.

35 By comparison, China used 2.5 billion TOE of energy in 2012. Regional pilot programs to cap total coal use in the 12th Five-Year Plan (2011–2015) have been announced (or are already underway) for Beijing, Tianjin, Hebei, and major cities in

the Pearl and Yangtze River deltas. See *Xinhua*, "Interpreting Measures by Standing Committee of State Council to Limit Energy Consumption" (解读国务院常务会议控制能源消费总量措施) (Jan. 30, 2013), http://news.xinhuanet.com/politics/2013-01/30/c_114559953.htm.

36 People's Republic of China National Development and Reform Commission (PRC NDRC), "National Development and Reform Commission Office Notice Regarding Start of Carbon Trading Pilots" (国家发展改革委办公厅关于开展碳排放权交易试点工作的通知). FaGai Ban Qi Hou 2601 Hao 29 (2011), www.ndrc.gov.cn/zcfb/zcfbtz/2011tz/t20120113_456506.htm.

37 U.S. State Department, "Report of the U.S.-China Climate Change Working Group to the Strategic and Economic Dialogue" (July 10, 2013), www.state.gov/e/oes/rls/pr/2013/211842.htm.

38 White House, "United States and China Agree to Work Together on Phase Down of HFCs," Press Release (June 8, 2013), www.whitehouse.gov/the-press-office/2013/06/08/united-states-and-china-agree-work-together-phase-down-hfcs.

39 U.S. State Department, "Report of the U.S.-China Climate Change Working Group."

40 People's Republic of China Ministry of Foreign Affairs (PRC MoFA), "Exploring the Path of Major-Country Diplomacy with Chinese Characteristics," translated text of Foreign Minister Wang Yi's speech at the Second World Peace Forum (June 27, 2013), www.fmprc.gov.cn/eng/zxxx/t1053908.shtml.

41 Kejin Zhao, "Constructive Leadership and China's Diplomatic Transformation" (建设性领导与中国外交转型), *World Economics and Politics* (世界经济与政治) 18, no. 5 (2012): 42–57; Jisi Wang, "China's Search for a Grand Strategy: A Rising Great Power Finds Its Way," *Foreign Affairs* (April 2011), www.foreignaffairs.com/articles/67470/wang-jisi/chinas-search-for-a-grand-strategy; David Shambaugh, "Thinking About China's Future," *International Spectator* 47, no. 2 (2012): 18–23.

42 In this respect, it also helps that China is managed by technocrats and that science is given an incredibly high priority and entrée into policy making. More acute understanding among China's leaders of the potential impacts of climate change, for example, has helped make climate change an issue of increasingly high importance, as evidenced by China's *National Climate Change Program*. See People's Republic of China National Development and Reform Commission (PRC NDRC), "China's National Climate Change Programme" (2007), www.ccchina.gov.cn/WebSite/CCChina/UpFile/File188.pdf; and the latest Five-Year Plan (PRC Central Government, "Outline of the 12th Five Year Plan for the Economic and Social Development of the PRC" (中华人民共和国国民经济和社会发展第十二个五年规划纲要) (March 16, 2011), www.gov.cn/2011lh/content_1825838.htm.

43 Henry Kissinger, *On China* (Penguin Books, New York, 2012); Swaine, *America's Challenge*; Congjun Li, "The World as a Fishbowl: Rebalancing the Global Economy," *New York Times* (July 17, 2012), www.nytimes.com/2012/07/18/opinion/the-world-as-a-fishbowl.html?_r=1&ref=economy.

44 Alan Wachman, Testimony before the US-China Economic and Security Review Commission, *China's Current and Emerging Foreign Relations Policy Priorities* (April 13, 2011), www.uscc.gov/hearings/2011hearings/written_testimonies/11_04_13_wrt/11_04_13_wachman_testimony.pdf; Kissinger, *On China*; Jianyang Hu, "How to Integrate China into the International Community: U.S.-China Relations Under Power Transition in the 21st Century," *Journal of US-China Public Administration* 9, no. 1 (2012): 81–89.

45 U.S. Department of Defense, *Annual Report to Congress: Military and Security Developments Involving the People's Republic of China, 2011*; Hillary Rodham Clinton and Victoria Nuland, Remarks at the Strategic and Economic Dialogue U.S. Press Conference, Beijing, China (May 4, 2012), www.state.gov/secretary/rm/2012/05/189315.htm; Joe Biden, "China's Rise Isn't Our Demise," *New York Times* (Sept. 7, 2011), www.nytimes.com/2011/09/08/opinion/chinas-rise-isnt-our-demise.html.

46 United Nations, *The Millennium Development Goals Report 2012* (United Nations, New York, 2012), http://mdgs.un.org/unsd/mdg/Resources/Static/Products/Progress2012/English2012.pdf; People's Republic of China Ministry of Foreign Affairs (PRC MoFA), *China's Progress Towards the Millennium Development Goals, 2010 Report* (PRC MoFA, 2010), www.un.org.cn/public/resource/China_MDG_Progress_report_2010_e.pdf.

47 World Bank and Development Research Center, *China: Efficient, Inclusive, and Sustainable Urbanization Study* (State Council, People's Republic of China, and World Bank, Washington, D.C., forthcoming).

48 Solar-PV.cn, "China Solar PV Exports to Increase 15% in 2010" (in Chinese) (April 8, 2010), www.solar-pv.cn/article/article_3165.html; Zhongrong Liang, "China's Solar PV Exports Face Contraction" (中国光伏出口面临萎缩), *Morning Whistle* (21世纪经济报道) (Feb. 29, 2012), www.21cbh.com/HTML/2012-2-29/1NMDcyXzQwNTQ1Nw.html; *China Greentech Report 2012*, www.china-greentech.com.

49 People's Republic of China Ministry of Environmental Protection (PRC MEP), "Report on the State of the Environment in 2011" (2011年中国环境状况公报) (June 2, 2012), http://jcs.mep.gov.cn/hjzl/zkgb/.

50 These policy goals are summarized in detail by the authors in a forthcoming World Bank study, *Climate Risk Management and Adaptation in China*.

51 PRC Central Government, "Outline of the 12th Five Year Plan."

52 People's Republic of China Ministry of Environmental Protection (PRC MEP), Report on the State of the Environment in 2010 (2010年中国环境状况公报) (June 3, 2011), http://jcs.mep.gov.cn/hjzl/zkgb/.

53 World Bank, *World Development Indicators Database*, http://data.worldbank.org/.

54 These targets are to reduce carbon emissions per unit of GDP (carbon intensity) by 40–45 percent in 2020 compared with 2005, to raise the share of nonfossil energy in total energy supply to 15 percent by 2020, to bring 70–80 gigawatts of nuclear power online by 2020, and to raise fuel economy standards. Projections for 2030 assume that new, unspecified policies will be introduced in later years so as to follow the same trajectory set by current targets. See International Energy Agency (IEA), "Fossil-Fuel Subsidies in APEC Economies and the Benefits of Reform," IEA background paper for APEC leaders' summit (IEA, OECD, Paris, 2011), http://apecenergy.tier.org.tw/database/db/ewg42/1018/fossil_fuel_subsidy/FOSSIL_FUEL_SUBSIDIES_IN_APEC_ECONOMIES_AND_THE_BENEFITS_OF_REFORM.pdf.

55 IEA, "Fossil-Fuel Subsidies in APEC."

56 BP, *Statistical Review of World Energy* (2012), www.bp.com/statisticalreview; World Bank, *World Development Indicators Database*.

57 U.S. EIA, "International Energy Statistics."

58 In 2009, for example, coal shipments accounted for about one-half of the total volume in freight transported by China's railroads. See Yande Dai, "Outlook of Energy Supply and Demand in China" (能源供需现状及其展望), in *Annual Report on China's Low Carbon Economic Development 2012* (中国低碳经济发展报告2012), edited by Xue Jinjun, Zhao Zhongxiu, et al. (Social Sciences Academic Press, Beijing, 2012): 139–159.

59 Katherine Zhu, "China's Great Wall of Traffic Jam: 11 days, 74.5 miles," *ABC News* (Sept. 3, 2010), http://abcnews.go.com/International/chinas-traffic-jam-lasts-11-days-reaches-74/story?id=11550037#.UBYOr6M-n3U; Jonathan Watts, "China's Mega-Jams Show the True Costs of Coal," *Guardian Environment Blog* (Aug. 25, 2010), www.guardian.co.uk/environment/blog/2010/aug/25/china-mega-jams-coal; Jonathan Watts, *When a Billion Chinese Jump: How China Will Save Mankind—Or Destroy It* (Scribner, New York, 2010).

60 Measures such as strict licensing requirements for producers and traders and limited access to rail and road transport are part of an effort by the central and provincial governments to improve the overall efficiency, safety, and environmental performance of the coal mining industry by shutting down smaller mines and consolidating control of mining under larger state-owned enterprises.

61 Hongbin Li and Weng Shiyou, "Transporting Coal a Freak of Nature" (煤运怪胎), *Caijing* (财经杂志) (Aug. 28, 2011): cover story; L. He, "Analysis: Rising Coal Prices Exacerbate China's Electricity Shortages" (分析: 煤价上涨加剧中国 "电荒"), *Financial Times Chinese Edition* (FT中文网) (May 18, 2011); Ming Zhu, "Worries of 'Hard' Power Shortages Return" ('硬缺电'重来忧虑), *Caijing* (Jan. 2, 2012): 112–15; IEA, "Fossil-Fuel Subsidies in APEC."

62 Weiqi Tang, Wu Libo, and Zhang Zhongxian, "Oil Price Shocks and Their Short- and Long-Term Effects on the Chinese Economy," *Energy Economics* (2010), http://dx.doi.org/10.1016/j.eneco.2010.01.002.

63 Imports and total final consumption include crude oil and refined oil products. See International Energy Agency (IEA), "World Energy Balances," *IEA World Energy Statistics and Balances* (IEA, OECD, Paris), doi: 10.1787/enestats-data-en.

64 U.S. EIA, "International Energy Statistics."

65 Shenlei Tian, Gao Tianming, and Gao Lizhi, "China's Resource Security and Global Strategy" (中国资源安全与全球战略), in *China Sustainable Development Report 2012* (中国可持续发展战略报告) (China Academy of Sciences Sustainable Development Strategy Research Group, China Sciences Press, Beijing, 2012): 62–100. To mitigate the vulnerability to oil imports being disrupted, China is constructing a pipeline to bring oil and natural gas 870 kilometers through Burma to a terminus near Kunming in southwestern China. According to official press reports released by *Xinhua* in June 2013, construction on the natural gas pipeline had already been completed and the oil pipeline was expected to open in October 2013. See *Xinhua*, "Myanmar Energy Minister Says Oil and Gas Pipeline Will Open in October" (in Chinese) (June 14, 2013), http://news.xinhuanet.com/yzyd/world/20130614/c_116146088.htm?prolongation=1.

66 Jian Zhang, "China's Energy Security: Prospects, Challenges, and Opportunities" (The Brookings Institution Center for Northeast Asian Policy Studies Paper, Brookings Institution, Washington, D.C., 2011), www.brookings.edu/research/papers/2011/07/china-energy-zhang; Erica Downs, "Pursuing Policy—and Profit," *China Economic Quarterly* (December 2011): 43–47.

67 Downs, "Pursuing Policy—and Profit."

68 International Energy Agency (IEA), "People's Republic of China," *Oil & Gas Security: Emergency Response of IEA Countries. Environmental Outlook to 2050: The Consequences of Inaction* (IEA, OECD, Paris, 2012), www.iea.org/publications/freepublications/publication/China 2012.pdf.

69 IEA, "Fossil-Fuel Subsidies in APEC."

70 PRC NBS, *China Statistical Yearbook 2011* (中国统计年鉴2011) (China Statistics Press, Beijing, 2009, 2010, 2011).

71 These are the provincial-level territories of Beijing, Tianjin, Hebei, Shanxi, Henan, and Shandong. See PRC NBS, *China Statistical Yearbook 2011.*

72 United Nations Development Programme (UNDP), *Human Development Report 2006* (UNDP, New York, NY, 2006).

73 Grain output in terms of tonnage, not value. See PRC NBS, *China Statistical Yearbook 2011.*

74 World Bank and People's Republic of China State Environmental Protection Administration (PRC SEPA), *Cost of Pollution in China: Economic Estimates of Physical Damages* (World Bank, Washington, D.C., 2007); Jiao Li, "Water Shortages Loom as Northern China's Aquifers Are Sucked Dry," *Science* 328 (June 28, 2010): 1462–63.

75 Shucheng Wang, "China's Water Resources Security Issue and Its Counter Measures" (中国水资源安全问题及对策), *Power Systems and Clean Energy* (电网与清洁能源) 26, no. 9 (2010): 1–3.

76 Liping Zhang, "Situation and Problem Analysis of Water Resource Security in China" (in Chinese), *The Environment and Water Resources of the Yangtze River* 18 (2008): 116–20.

77 Average for water quality in the Yellow, Hai, Huai, Song, and Liao River basins weighted by volume of surface water available in each basin. See PRC MEP, Report on the State of the Environment in 2010; PRC Ministry of Environmental Protection and General Administration of Quality Supervision, Inspection, and Quarantine (MEP and AQSIS), "Environmental Quality Standards for Surface Water" (地表水环境质量标准), GB 3838-2002, issued April 2002, effective June 1, 2002, www.nthb.cn/standard/standard02/20030428174340.html; PRC National Bureau of Statistics and Ministry of Environmental Protection (NBS and MEP), *China Statistical Yearbook on the Environment 2010* (中国环境统计年鉴2010) (China Statistics Press, Beijing, 2010). Unfortunately, although this water is so polluted that it is virtually unable to support any life, it continues to be used in some places because people have no alternative choice. About 7 percent of the country's farmland is irrigated with wastewater. See Jian Xie, *Addressing China's Water Scarcity: Recommendations for Selected Water Resource Management Issues* (World Bank, Washington, D.C., 2009).

78 By way of comparison, this project is 10 times the size of California's water transfer system. The idea for the transfer originated with Mao but was not brought to implementation until water scarcity became more pressing in recent years.

79 A group of some 50 scientists has advised against building the western leg, but the government decision-making process goes on behind closed doors.

80 Gong Peng, Ying Yongyuan, and Yu Chaoqing, "China: Invest Wisely in Sustainable Water Use," *Science* 331, no. 11 (2011): 1264–65.

81 Water authorities in China are just beginning to explore ways to limit water demand through the use of economic tools. In the early 2000s, local governments in Zhejiang, Gansu, Ningxia, and Inner Mongolia began experimenting with trading schemes for water rights. These pilot projects established the basis for introducing tradable water rights into national law in 2006. Developing a functional market for water use rights has been slow in practice, in part because existing water tariffs are either extremely low (for China's largest cities) or nonexistent (in the case of farmers who pump groundwater for irrigation). Thankfully, these problems are attracting greater attention and the Five-Year Plan for 2011–2015 has identified strengthening market institutions for water rights as a priority. See China.com.cn, "China's Experimentation and Experience with Water Rights Trading" (in Chinese) (April 27, 2007), www.china.

com.cn/info/2006zghjzb/2007-04/27/content_8179760.htm; Xie, *Addressing China's Water Scarcity*; World Bank and Development Research Center, *China 2030*; PRC Central Government, "Outline of the 12th Five Year Plan."

82 M.W. Rosegrant, X.M. Cai, and S.A. Cline, *World Water and Food to 2025: Dealing with Scarcity* (International Food Policy Research Institute, Washington, D.C., 2002).

83 The 2030 Water Resources Group, *Charting Our Water Future: Economic Frameworks to Inform Decision-Making* (2009), www.2030waterresourcesgroup.com/water_full/Charting_Our_Water_Future_Final.pdf.

84 Organization for Economic Cooperation and Development (OECD), *Environmental Outlook to 2050: The Consequences of Inaction* (OECD, Paris, 2012); Xiong Wei, Ian Holman, Lin Erda, et al., "Climate Change, Water Availability, and Future Cereal Production in China," *Agriculture, Ecosystems and Environment* 135 (2010): 58–69. "Water stress" is defined as the ratio of total freshwater withdrawals from surface or groundwater sources to total freshwater availability (i.e., annual river discharge or combined surface runoff and groundwater recharge). A water stress score of 0.4 or higher is conventionally seen as "severe water stress." See J. Alcamo, T. Henrichs, and T. Rösch, "World Water in 2025: Global Modeling and Scenario Analysis for the World Commission on Water for the 21st Century," Report No. 2, Kassel World Water Series (2000), www.usf.uni-kassel.de; J. Alcamo, M. Flörke, and M. Märker, "Future Long-Term Changes in Global Water Resources Driven by Socio-Economic and Climatic Changes," *Hydrological Sciences Journal* 52, no. 2 (2007): 247–75.

85 Wei, Holman, Erda, et al., "Climate Change, Water Availability." These projections do not contemplate the effects of climate change, which could either increase water availability for agriculture (by as much as 28 percent in a low-emissions scenario) or decrease it (by as much as 17 percent in a high-emissions scenario).

86 Yong Jiang, "China's Water Scarcity," *Journal of Environmental Management* 90 (2009): 3185–96.

87 World Health Organization (WHO), "Outdoor Air Pollution, Burden of Disease," Global Health Observatory Data Repository, http://apps.who.int/ghodata/.

88 Monitoring data from Renmin University, Environment, Energy, and Economy Network, www.3edata.com.

89 World Bank and (DRC), *China: Efficient, Inclusive, and Sustainable.*

90 For a review, see Richard Brulle and David Pellow, "Environmental Justice: Human Health and Environmental Inequalities," *Annual Review of Public Health* 27 (2006): 103–24.

91 This is true even accounting for a number of confounding factors, such as the percentage of the local population employed in polluting industries. See Ethan D. Schoolman and Chunbo Ma, "Migration, Class and Environmental Inequality: Exposure to Pollution in China's Jiangsu Province," *Ecological Economics* 75 (2012): 140–51; Chunbo Ma, "Who Bears the Environmental Burden in China—An Analysis of the Distribution of Industrial Pollution Sources?" *Ecological Economics* 69, no. 9 (2010): 1869–76.

92 Therese Hesketh, Ye Xuejun, Li Lu, and Wang Hongmei, "Access to Health Care of Migrant Workers in China," *Public Health Reports* 123, no. (2008): 189–97; Shenglan Tang, Meng Qingyue, Lincoln Chen, Henk Bekedam, Tim Evans, and Margaret Whitehead, "Tackling the Challenges to Health Equity in China," *Lancet* 372, no. 9648 (2008): 1493–1501; Xiaojiang Hu, Sarah Cook, and Miguel A Salazar, "Internal Migration and Health in China," *Lancet* 372, no. 9651 (2008): 1717–19; Yuehua Geng, Yuan Haoran, Zhou Chengguang, Dou Jibo, and Liu Jing, "Occupational Hazards

and Control Measures of Migrant Workers in Liaocheng City" (农民工意外伤害的原因分析及预防对策), *Occupation and Health* (职业与健康) 27, no. 1 (2011): 12–15; Ling Zhu, "Food Security and Agricultural Changes in the Course of China's Urbanization," *China & World Economy* 19, no. 2 (2011): 40–59.

93 Data for the number of incidents are for 2005, the most recent year for which Ministry of Public Security statistics were released; data for the number of participants are from 2004. Because the number of annual incidents has more than doubled since then, this should be considered a conservative estimate of the number of people involved. See Lianhe Hu, Angang Hu, and Lei Wang, "Empirical Analysis of Changes in Social Conflicts Influencing Social Stability" (in Chinese), *Front Lines of Social Sciences* 4 (2006): 175–85; *Guangzhou Evening Post* (羊城晚报), "Mass Incidents Reach More Than 90,000 Each Year" (群体性事件上升到每年9万起) (Feb. 27, 2010), www.ycwb.com/epaper/ycwb/html/2010-02/27/content_752762.htm; AiniMi, "Expert Says Mass Incidents a Major Threat to Stability over the Next Decade" (专家称未来10年群体性事件是社会稳定最大威胁), Sina.com.cn (Jan. 25, 2010), http://news.sina.com.cn/c/2010-01-25/124319541548.shtml.

94 Renyi Chen, "Director of Central Rural Work Leading Group Chen Xiwen Explains the Central Committee's No. 1 Document" (中央农村工作领导小组办公室主任解读中央一号文件), *Southern Daily* (南方日报) (Feb. 3, 2009), http://news.nfmedia.com/nanfangdaily/zt/nshiz/fznm/200902030038.asp.

95 Jiangtao Shi and Hanhang Wei, "Factory Axed as Shifang Heeds Protesters' Calls," *South China Morning Post* (July 4, 2012): 1; Jing Li, "Protests Show Rising Green Concerns," *South China Morning Post* (July 4, 2012): 6; Keith Bradsher, "Bolder Protests Against Pollution Win Project's Defeat in China," *New York Times* (July 4, 2012); Keith Bradsher, "Chinese City Suspends Factory Construction After Protests," *New York Times* (July 3, 2012).

96 This is an unofficial translation, with emphasis added by the author. See *People's Daily*, "Important Measures to Transform the Mode of Development—Minister of Environmental Protection Zhou Sheng Xian Explains the 12th Five Year Plan on the Environment" (加快转变经济发展方式的重大举措——环境保护部部长周生贤解读《国家环境保护"十二五"规划》) (Feb. 20, 2012), www.mep.gov.cn/zhxx/hjyw/201202/t20120220_223702.htm.

97 World Resources Institute (WRI), "China Adopts World Class Pollution Emissions Standards for Coal Power Plants," *China FAQs* (June 15, 2012), www.chinafaqs.org/files/chinainfo/China%20FAQs%20Emission%20Standards%20v1.4_0.pdf.

98 $PM_{2.5}$ are small suspended particles with a diameter of 2.5 micrometers or less, which are inhaled deep into the lungs and most closely associated with the damaging effects of air pollution. Standards for $PM_{2.5}$ require that all cities at the prefecture level and above publicly report $PM_{2.5}$ data by 2015. New compliance standards are equivalent to WHO's Interim Target-1 (35 micrograms per cubic meter annual mean concentration) for developing countries. See PRC Central Government, "Wen Jiabao Leads State Council Standing Committee Conference, Agrees to Release Revised Ambient Air Quality Standards and Pursue Major Work on Strengthening Comprehensive Prevention and Reduction of Air Pollution" (温家宝主持召开国务院常务会议同意发布新修订的《环境空气质量标准》部署加强大气污染综合防治重点工作) (Feb. 29, 2012), www.gov.cn/ldhd/2012-02/29/content_2079351.htm; *Xinhua*, "State Council Standing Committee Approves Release of Revised Ambient Air Quality Standards" (国务院常务会同意发布新修订的《环境空气质量标准》) (Feb. 29,

2012), http://news.xinhuanet.com/politics/2012-02/29/c_111585881.htm; PRC Ministry of Environmental Protection (PRC MEP), "Notice Regarding Implementation of Ambient Air Quality Standards" [GB 3095-2012] (关于实施《环境空气质量标准》[GB3095-2012] 的通知), Huan Fa, Hao (Feb. 29, 2012); PRC MEP and AQSIS, "Ambient Air Quality Standards" (环境空气质量标准), GB 3095-2012, issued Feb. 29, 2012, effective Jan. 1, 2016.

99 World Bank and PRC Ministry of Environmental Protection (MEP), *Integrated Air Pollution Management in China: Developing Particulate Matter Control* (World Bank, Washington, D.C., forthcoming).

100 *Xinhua*, "Atmospheric Pollution Prevention and Control Action Plan (Authorized Release)" [(授权发布) 大气污染防治行动计划] (Sept. 12, 2013), http://news.xinhuanet.com/politics/2013-09/12/c_117349304.htm.

101 World Bank and PRC MEP, *Integrated Air Pollution Management.*

102 This is not to say that the source apportionment profile of air pollution in China's cities will remain the same. Indeed, pollution sources are highly site-specific, hence the importance of conducting a pollution source inventory as a first step in any air quality management plan. The numbers here are simply intended to illustrate the danger of increased PM from existing sources. World Bank and PRC MEP, *Integrated Air Pollution Management.*

103 IEA, "Fossil-Fuel Subsidies in APEC."

104 See Hao Han et al., "Hybrid Modeling of China's Vehicle Ownership and Projection Through 2050," *Energy* 36 (2011): 1351–61. They estimate that there will be 295 million private vehicles on the road in China by 2010. See also International Energy Agency (IEA), *World Energy Outlook: China and India Insights* (IEA, OECD, Paris, 2007). They estimate that there will be 270 million private vehicles in China by 2030. On the high end, Y. Wang et al. predict that China's vehicle population will top 419 million by 2022, based on comparative data for historic rates of growth in vehicle ownership for other countries. See Yunshi Wang et al., "China's Soaring Vehicle Population: Even Greater Than Forecasted?" *Energy Policy* 39 (2011): 3296–3306.

105 Projections are for 2025. See McKinsey Global Institute, "Preparing for China's Urban Billion" (2009), www.mckinsey.com/insights/mgi/research/urbanization/preparing_for_urban_billion_in_china.

106 Measured in terms of chemical oxygen demand (COD). See Maxia Guo, Yu Fang, Cao Dong, and Niu Kunyu, "Calculation of Agricultural Non-Point Source Pollution Emissions in China and Long-Term Forecast" (中国农业面源污染排放量计算及中长期预测), *Acta Scientiae Circumstantiae* (环境科学学报) 32, no. 2 (2012): 489–97.

107 Guo, Fang, Dong, and Kunyu, "Calculation of Agricultural Non-Point Source Pollution."

108 Estimated by the OECD in terms of volumes of nutrient effluents (nitrogen and phosphorus) from wastewater. See OECD, *Environmental Outlook to 2050.*

109 Figure from 2006 official SEPA (MEP) review, reported by *Haikou Evening Post*. See "State Environmental Protection Agency: 200 Cities Without Any Centralized Water Treatment" (环保总局：200个城市生活污水集中处理率为零), *Haikou Evening Post*, hosted by Sohu.com.cn (June 12, 2007), http://news.sohu.com/20070612/n250532196.shtml.

110 This section draws extensively from Chris Sall, "Review of Climate Trends and Impacts in China," Sustainable Development Discussion Paper Series (World Bank, Washington, D.C., and Beijing, China, 2013).

111 Joanna Lewis, "Climate Change and Security: Examining China's Challenges in a Warming World," *International Affairs* 85, no. 6 (2009): 1195–1213.

112 L. He et al., cited in Jane Qiu, "China Drought Highlights Future Climate Threats," *Nature* 465, no. 13 (2010): 142–43; "China's Tibetan Nomads Face Uncertain Future" (中国藏族牧民面对着不确定的未来), Radio Netherlands Worldwide (April 30, 2012), www.rnw.nl/chinese/article/659134.

113 National Assessment Report on Climate Change, Editorial Committee (NARCC), *Second National Assessment Report on Climate Change* (第二次气候变化国家评估报告) (Sciences Press, Beijing, 2011); Zhongyan Huang, "Changes of Dry-West Climate in the Dry Season in Yunnan (1961–2007)," *Advances in Climate Change Research* (English version) 2, no. 1 (2011): 49–54; Wenjie Wang, Junsheng Li, Hao Wu, Chao Xu, and Tan Liu, "The Impact of Sustained Drought on Vegetation Ecosystem in Southwest China Based on Remote Sensing," *Procedia Environmental Sciences* 2 (2010): 1679–91; Jane Qiu, "China Drought Highlights Future Climate Threats," *Nature* 465, no. 13 (2010): 142–43; "China's Tibetan Nomads," Radio Netherlands Worldwide.

114 Jianguo Wu and Jiajia Lü, "Potential Effects of Climate Change on the Distributions of Yunnan Snub-Nosed Monkey (PygathrixBieti) in China" (气候变化对滇金丝猴分布的潜在影响), *Journal of Meteorology and Environment* 25, no. 6 (2009): 1–10.

115 NARCC, *Second National Assessment Report.*

116 G.Q. Wang, J.Y. Zhang, J.L. Jin, T.C. Pagano, R. Calow, Z.X. Bao, C.S. Liu, Y.L. Liu, and X.L. Yan, "Assessing Water Resources in China Using PRECIS Projections and a VIC Model," *Hydrology and Earth System Sciences* 16, no. 1 (2012): 231–40.

117 S. Wang and Z. Zhang, "Effects of Climate Change on Water Resources in China," *Climate Research* 47, no. 1 (2011): 77–82.

118 Xuejie Gao, Shi Ying, Zhang Dongfeng, and Giorgi Filippo, "Climate Change in China in the 21st Century as Simulated by a High Resolution Regional Climate Model," *Chinese Science Bulletin* (2012), doi: 10.1007/s11434-011-4935-8; Xuejie Gao, Shi Ying, Zhang Dongfeng, and Giorgi Filippo, "RegCM3 High Resolution Regional Climate Model Simulation of Climate Change in China in the 21st Century" (RegCM3对21世纪中国区域气候变化的高分辨率模拟), *Chinese Science Bulletin* (科学通报) 57, no. 5 (2012): 374–81; Ying Shi, Xuejie Gao, Filippo Giorgi, et al., "High Resolution Simulation of Changes in Different-Intensity Precipitation Events over China Under Global Warming" (全球气候变化下中国区域不同强度降水事件变化的高分辨率数值模拟), *Advances in Climate Change Research* (气候变化研究进展) 6, no. 3 (2010): 164–69; NARCC, *Second National Assessment Report.*

119 J. Woetzel et al., "From Bread Basket to Dust Bowl? Assessing the Economic Impact of Drought in North and Northeast China," (McKinsey & Company, 2009), www.mckinsey.com/locations/chinatraditional/From_Bread_Basket_Dust_Bowl_EN.pdf; NARCC, *Second National Assessment Report.*

120 *Xinhua*, "Weather Disasters Cause RMB 200–300 Billion in Economic Damages Each Year in China" (中国每年由于气象灾害造成经济损失2000–3000亿人民币) (March 30, 2010), http://news.xinhuanet.com/video/2010-03/30/content_13270583.htm.

121 Expressed in year 2010 prices. See PRC Ministry of Water Resources (MWR), *Bulletin of Flood and Drought Disasters in China* (中国水旱灾害公报) (2006–2010), www.mwr.gov.cn/zwzc/hygb/zgshzhgb/; *Xinhua*, "Direct Economic Losses from Drought and Flooding in China Reach RMB 232.9 Billion in 2011" (2011年全国旱涝灾害直接经济损失达2329亿元) (Feb. 2, 2012), http://news.xinhuanet.com/society/2012-02/02/c_111482077.htm.

122 PRC NBS, *China Statistical Yearbook 2011.*

123 For example, even in the absence of climate change, Mendelsohn and coauthors have estimated that the value of damages from tropical cyclones in East Asia is likely to triple by the end of this century. See Robert Mendelsohn, Kerry Emanuel, Shun Chonabayashi, and Laura Bakkensen, "The Impact of Climate Change on Global Tropical Cyclone Damage," *Nature Climate Change* 2, no. 3 (2012): 205–209.

124 G. McGranahan, D. Balk, and B. Anderson, "The Rising Tide: Assessing the Risks of Climate Change and Human Settlements in Low Elevation Coastal Zones," *Environment & Urbanization* 19, no. 1 (2007): 17–37.

125 NARCC, *Second National Assessment Report.*

126 Erin Hale and Damian Carrington, "World Airlines 99% Compliant on Emission Targets," *Guardian* (London) (May 16, 2012).

127 Alison Leung and Fang Yan, "China-Backed HK Airlines May Dump A380 Order," Reuters (March 1, 2012), www.reuters.com/article/2012/03/01/uk-hongkong-airbus-idUSLNE82000X20120301.

128 James Kanter, "Europe Refuses to Budge on Airline Emissions Fee," *New York Times* (Feb. 7, 2012): Section B.

129 Aaditya Mattoo, Arvind Subramanian, Dominique van der Mensbrugghe, and Jianwu He, "Reconciling Climate Change and Trade Policy" (Center for Global Development, Washington, D.C., 2009). Similar levels of border tariffs on Chinese exports are in such a situation where imports are taxed based on embedded carbon content and are estimated by Atkinson et al., although the authors of the latter study do not consider the general equilibrium effects on welfare. See Giles Atkinson, Kirk Hamilton, Giovanni Ruta, and Dominique Van Der Mensbrugghe, "Trade in 'Virtual Carbon': Empirical Results and Implications for Policy," *Global Environmental Change* 21, no. 2 (2011): 563–74.

130 Lewis, "Climate Change and Security."

131 Assumes a reference case scenario (what the IEA calls its "New Policies Scenario," in which all new policies recently announced are enacted). See International Energy Agency (IEA), *World Energy Outlook 2011* (IEA, OECD, Paris, 2011).

132 Only net capacity additions are considered, which do not account for the capacity that was retired during these years. The real figure for how much generating capacity China will actually build during this decade would be larger. See U.S. EIA, "International Energy Statistics."

133 In year 2010 prices. See IEA, "Fossil-Fuel Subsidies in APEC."

134 United Nations Environment Programme (UNEP), "Bridging the Emissions Gap," A UNEP Synthesis Report (2013), www.unep.org/publications/ebooks/emissionsgapreport2013/.

135 International Energy Agency (IEA), *CO_2 Emissions from Fuel Combustion* (IEA, OECD, Paris, 2013); International Energy Agency (IEA), *World Energy Outlook 2013* (IEA, OECD, Paris, 2013).

136 Philip Andrews-Speed, *The Institutions of Energy Governance in China* (*Institut français des relations internationals*, Paris, 2010); Philip Andrews-Speed, "China's Long Road to a Low-Carbon Economy: An Institutional Analysis," Transatlantic Academy Paper Series (Transatlantic Academy, Washington, D.C., 2012), www.transatlanticacademy.org/sites/default/files/publications/AndrewsSpeed_China%27sLongRoad_May12_web.pdf.

137 Yongnian Zheng, "Central-Local Relations: The Power to Dominate," in *China Today, China Tomorrow: Domestic Politics, Economy, and Society*, edited by Joseph Fewsmith (Rowman & Littlefield, Lanham, MD, 2010): 193–309.

138 Christine Wong, "Rebuilding Government for the 21st Century: Can China Incrementally Reform the Public Sector?" *China Quarterly* 200 (2009): 929.

139 Kenneth Lieberthal, "China's Governing System and Its Impact on Environmental Policy Implementation," *China Environment Series* 1 (1997): 3–8; Kenneth Lieberthal, *Governing China: From Revolution through Reform* (W.W. Norton, New York, 2004); Kenneth Lieberthal and Michel Oksenberg, *Policy Making in China: Leaders, Structures, and Processes* (Princeton University Press, Princeton, NJ, 1988).

140 Richard Lester and Ed Steinfeld, "China's Energy Policy: Is Anybody Really Calling the Shots?" (Working Paper Series, Industrial Performance Center, Massachusetts Institute of Technology, 2006): 3–4.

141 Edward Cunningham, "Energy Governance: Fueling the Miracle," in *China Today, China Tomorrow: Domestic Politics, Economy, and Society*, edited by Joseph Fewsmith (Rowman & Littlefield, Lanham, MD, 2010).

142 Lester and Steinfeld, "China's Energy Policy."

143 Zhong Xiao Lu Chen, "Time for Reckoning with Energy Efficiency and Emissions Reductions—'We Won't Mind You for the First Half of the Year, but You Can Bet We Will for the Second Half,'" (in Chinese), *Southern Weekend* (Sept. 25, 2010); Haining He, "We Did It Because It Was Our Duty, With No Shortcuts Left, Only Option Is to Shut Off Power" (in Chinese), *Southern Weekend* (Nov. 12, 2010), www.infzm.com/content/52344; *In Focus* (焦点访谈), "What's the Point in Shutting Off the Power?" (拉闸限电为哪般) (Nov. 15, 2010), http://news.cntv.cn/program/jiaodianfangtan/20101115/107116_print.shtml.

144 For a thoughtful collection of middle-of-the-road and liberal-leaning Chinese experts conversing on this issue, see Jisi Wang, Weiying Zhang, Huaihong He, Haizhou Huang, and Yaxiang Yuan, "China and the United States in the Next 10 Years" (未来10年的中国与美国), *International Economic Review* (国际经济评论) 3 (2011): 15–35.

145 See, for example, Gordon Chang, *The Coming Collapse of China* (Random House, New York, 2001); Gordon Chang, "The Coming Collapse of China: 2012 Edition," *Foreign Policy* (Dec. 29, 2011), www.foreignpolicy.com/articles/2011/12/29/the_coming_collapse_of_china_2012_edition; Brahma Chellaney, *Water: Asia's Next Battleground* (Georgetown University Press, Washington, D.C., 2011).

146 Elizabeth Economy, *The River Runs Black: The Environmental Challenge to China's Future*, 2nd ed. (Cornell University Press, New York, 2004).

147 Indeed, as panelists at a National Intelligence Council workshop in 2009 concluded, "China has a robust capacity to handle the large-scale disruptions that probably will be caused by climate change and that China's trajectory of continued growth is likely to further increase its resilience through 2030" (National Intelligence Council (NIC), "China: The Impact of Climate Change to 2030, Geopolitical Implications," CR 2009-09, Conference report prepared by CENTRA Technology, Inc. and Scitor Corporation (2009): 3).

148 Already, the Chinese public is demanding more accountability from their local leaders in managing risks from extreme weather. In July 2012, a heavy rainstorm hit Beijing (the worst in 60 years) that caused massive flooding in the city and killed some 70 people. Many Beijingers blamed the municipal government for not upgrading the city's woefully outdated storm drain network, which has not been upgraded in some parts of the city since the network was first designed by Soviet engineers in the 1950s. Waterlogged streets, flooding in the subway tunnels, and severe traffic disruptions have become a common occurrence during summer storms. In the face of this discontent, the city's mayor and vice mayor resigned.

149 The following retelling draws from Tony Saich, *Governance and Politics of China*, 2nd ed. (Palgrave Macmillan, New York, 2004).

150 These estimates follow an adjusted human capital approach, which is used here because it translates most directly into a measure of GDP loss (for that reason, spending on treatment at hospitals and other health costs are also not included). This approach tends to underestimate the "true" value of health damages, which is not completely captured by foregone wages. See World Bank and PRC SEPA, *Cost of Pollution in China.*

151 Authors' calculations based on World Bank and PRC SEPA, *Cost of Pollution in China*; and M. Shi and G. Ma, *The Real Price of China's Economic Growth—An Empirical Study of Genuine Savings* (中国经济增长的资源环境代价) (China Sciences Press, Beijing, 2009). Firms have been able to compensate for such losses by investing in other productivity-enhancing technologies (e.g., more-efficient machines or better fertilizers), but they may not be able to do so indefinitely. For example, since 1980, crop yields in China have increased an impressive 56 percent thanks to new seed varieties, cropping techniques, and agrochemicals. Yet, for every 1 percent increase in yields, the use of industrial chemical fertilizers has increased 4 percent, leading to a decline in natural fertility, reduced numbers of wild pollinators such as bees, and the eutrophication of downstream water bodies. See PRC Ministry of Environmental Protection, and Chinese Academy of Engineering (PRC MEP and CAE), *Macro-Strategy for China's Environment: Strategy for Protection of China's Environmental Factors* (中国环境宏观战略研究：环境要素保护战略卷), Volumes 1 and 2 (China Environmental Sciences Press, Beijing, 2011).

152 Maximo Torero, "Food Prices: Riding the Rollercoaster," in *2011 Global Food Policy Report* (International Food Policy Research Institute, Washington, D.C., 2012): 15–24.

153 World Bank, "Double Jeopardy: Responding to High Food and Fuel Prices," Report for G8 Hokkaido-Toyako Summit, Japan (July 2008); World Bank, "Rising Food and Fuel Prices: Addressing the Risks to Future Generations" (Human Development Network and Poverty Reduction and Economic Management Network Report, World Bank, Washington, D.C., 2008).

154 Food and Agriculture Organization of the United Nations (FAO), "World Food Situation: FAO Food Price Index" (Sept. 6, 2012), www.fao.org/worldfoodsituation/wfs-home/foodpricesindex/en/.

155 Organization for Economic Cooperation and Development (OECD), "Rising Food Prices: Causes and Consequences" (2008), www.oecd.org/trade/agriculturaltrade/40847088.pdf; World Bank, "Double Jeopardy"; World Bank, "Rising Food and Fuel Prices: Addressing the Risks to Future Generations" (Human Development Network and Poverty Reduction and Economic Management Network Report, World Bank, Washington, D.C., 2008); Torero, "Food Prices: Riding the Rollercoaster."

156 Movements in world oil prices have begun to track more closely with the Chinese market. However, at present, the U.S. economy still has a much larger influence on prices in oil markets. See S. K. Roache, "China's Impact on World Commodity Markets," IMF Working Paper WP/12/115 (International Monetary Fund, Washington, D.C., 2012), www.imf.org/external/pubs/ft/wp/2012/wp12115.pdf; César Calderón, "Trade, Specialization, and Cycle Synchronization: Explaining Output Comovement between Latin America, China, and India," in *China's and India's Challenge to Latin America: Opportunity or Threat?*, edited by Daniel Lederman, Marcelo Olarreaga, and Guillermo E. Perry (World Bank, Washington, D.C., 2009).

157 Liming Ye and Eric Van Ranst, "Production Scenarios and the Effect of Soil Degradation on Long-term Food Security in China," *Global Environmental Change* 19 (2009): 464–81.

158 For example, declines and year-on-year variability in maize production are expected to increase. See NARCC, *Second National Assessment Report.* According to economists at the International Food Policy Research Institute, declines in yields for both rain-fed and irrigated crops as a result of increasing water stress in grain-producing regions are expected to cause the prices of wheat and rice to increase by 24–24 and 18–20 percent, respectively (relative to a world absent of climate change). In these situations, improved trade flows, greater investment in nutrition and education, and better social safety nets will be critical to dampening the effects of droughts, floods, and other weather disasters on the world's poor and preventing large increases in the number of malnourished children. See Gerald C. Nelson et al., *Food Security, Farming, and Climate Change to 2050: Scenarios, Results, Policy Options*, IFPRI Research Monograph Series (International Food Policy Research Institute, Washington, D.C., 2010).

159 Luc Christiansen, "The Role of Agriculture in a Modernizing Society—Food, Farms and Fields in China 2030," in *Green Development in China* (Development Research Center, World Bank, Washington, D.C., forthcoming).

160 Joachim von Braun and Getaw Tadesse, "Global Food Price Volatility and Spikes: An Overview of Costs, Causes, and Solutions," ZEF-Discussion Papers on Development Policy No. 161 (2012), http://ssrn.com/abstract=1992470.

161 Paul Stares, "Overview," in *Managing Instability on China's Periphery* (Council on Foreign Relations Center for Preventive Action, 2011), www.cfr.org/thinktank/cpa/asia_security.html.

162 Stares, "Overview."

163 Environmental News Service (ENS), "China's Illegal Wildlife Trade in Tigers, Turtles, Timber" (March 17, 2010), www.ens-newswire.com/ens/mar2010/2010-03-17-02.html; Environmental News Service (ENS), "US, China Cooperate to Fight Climate Change, Illegal Fishing" (May 16, 2011), www.ens-newswire.com/ens/may2011/2011-05-16-02.html; Shuai Tang and Weiming Song, "Analysis of Status and Trends in China's Timber Imports" (我国原木进口现状及面临的形势分析), *Forestry Economics* (林业经济) 5 (2012): 34–69; Matthias Dieter, "Analysis of Trade of Illegally Harvested Timber: Accounting for Trade via Third Party Countries," *Forest Policy and Economics* 11 (2009): 600–607; Ruhong Li, J. Buongiorno, J. A. Turner, S. Zhu, and J. Prestemon, "Long-term Effects of Eliminating Illegal Logging on the World Forest Industries, Trade, and Inventory," *Forest Policy and Economics* 10 (2008): 480–90.

164 Joshua Kurlantzick, "Myanmar: Sources of Instability and Potential for U.S.-China Cooperation," in *Managing Instability on China's Periphery* (Council on Foreign Relations Center for Preventive Action, 2011), www.cfr.org/thinktank/cpa/asia_security.html; Katherine Morton, "China and Environmental Security in the Age of Consequences," *Asia-Pacific Review* 15, no. 2 (2008): 52–67; Illegal-Logging.info, "Myanmar (Burma)," site managed by Chatham House and financed by UK Department for International Development, www.illegal-logging.info/approach.php?a_id=80.

165 Jiaman Jin, Ren Peng, Zhu Rong, and Kong Linghong, "China's 'Go Out' Strategy and Corporate Environmental and Social Responsibility" (中国'走出去'战略与企业环境社会责任), in *China Sustainable Development Report 2012: China's Sustainable Development in the Shifting Global Context* (2012中国可持续发展战略报告——全球视野下的中国可持续发展) (Chinese Academy of Sciences Sustainable Development Research Group (中国科学院可持续发展战略研究组 2012): 159–78; Grace Mang, Testimony before U.S.-China Economic and Security Review Commission, *China's Global Quest for Resources and Implications for the United States* (Jan. 26, 2012), www.uscc.gov/hearings/2012hearings/written_testimonies/hr12_01_26.php.

166 Chellaney, *Water: Asia's Next Battleground.*
167 In fact, China has not entered into water-sharing agreements with any of the downstream riparian states. See Brahma Chellaney, "Asia's Worsening Water Crisis," *Survival: Global Politics and Strategy* 54, no. 2 (2012): 143–56.
168 NARCC, *Second National Assessment Report*; Xuejie Gao, Shi Ying, and Filippo Giori, "A High Resolution Simulation of Climate Change over China" (中国区域气候变化的一个高分辨率数值模拟), *Science China, Series D: Earth Sciences* (中国科学D版：地球科学) 54, no. 3 (2010), doi:10.1007/s11430-010-4035-7; Gao et al., "Climate Change in China"; Gao et al., "RegCM3 High Resolution."
169 See M. Erikkson, XuJianchu, A.B. Shrestha, R.A. Vaidya, S. Nepal, and K. Sandström, *The Changing Himalayas: Impact of Climate Change on Water Resources and Livelihoods in the Greater Himalayas* (International Centre for Integrated Mountain Development, Kathmandu, 2009); National Assessment Report on Climate Change, Editorial Committee (NARCC), *National Assessment Report on Climate Change* (气候变化国家评估报告) (Sciences Press, Beijing, 2007).
170 Of course, it is difficult to say whether these peoples will retain their traditional lifestyles, which are already in flux as a result of dams, railroads, mines, factories, tourism, and government policies. Since the 1960s, for example, China has pursued a policy of settling nomadic herders on the Tibetan Plateau. The government claims to have "settled" 50–80 percent of the nomads already. There are about 2.25 million nomads today. See Watts, *When a Billion Chinese Jump*; PRC Central Government, "Resettlement of 40,000 Nomadic Tibetan Households during 11th Five Year Plan" ('十一五'共完成西藏4万多户游牧民定居工程建设) (Nov. 29, 2010), www.gov.cn/jrzg/2010-11/29/content_1755860.htm; PRC Central Government, "Wen Jiabao Leads State Council Standing Committee Meeting in Discussion of Passing the National Plan for the Development of Strategic Emerging Industries during Twelfth Five Year Plan and the Twelfth Five Year Plan for National Nomad Settlement" (温家宝主持召开国务院常务会议讨论通过《"十二五"国家战略性新兴产业发展规划》和《全国游牧民定居工程建设"十二五"规划) (May 30, 2012), www.gov.cn/zxft/ft231/content_2187981.htm; "China's Tibetan Nomads," Radio Netherlands Worldwide; C.G. Brown, S.A. Waldron, and J.W. Longworth, *Sustainable Development in Western China: Managing People, Livestock, and Grasslands in Pastoral Areas* (Cheltenham and Camberley, Edward Elgar, United Kingdom, 2008).
171 For a discussion of the potential security concerns of "climate refugees" moving across China's southern and western borders, see Lewis, "Climate Change and Security"; J. Podesta and P. Ogden, "Security Implications of Climate Scenario 1," in *The Age of Consequences: The Foreign Policy and National Security Implications of Global Climate Change*, edited by K.M. Campbell, J. Gulledge, J.R. McNeill, et al. (Center for Strategic & International Studies and Center for a New American Security Report, 2007): 55–69, http://csis.org/files/media/csis/pubs/071105_ageofconsequences.pdf. The complex relationship between existing social and economic vulnerability and the displacement or migration of peoples because of extreme weather events linked to climate change and other environmental pressures are discussed in Inter-Governmental Panel on Climate Change (IPCC), *Managing the Risks of Extreme Events and Disasters to Advance Climate Change Adaptation*, Special Report of Working Groups I and II of the IPCC, edited by C.B. Field, V. Barros, T.F. Stocker, et al. (Cambridge University Press, Cambridge, UK, 2012).
172 Asian Development Bank (ADB), "Mekong Leaders Endorse Biodiversity Conservation Corridors Initiative" (July 5, 2005), www.adb.org/news/mekong-leaders-endorse-bio

diversity-conservation-corridors-initiative; Xia Li, "China's Participation in Greater Mekong Subregion Environmental Cooperation" (中国参与的湄公河次区域环境合作), *Around Southeast Asia* (东南亚纵横) no. 6 (2008): 29–32.

173 E.C. Economy, Testimony before U.S.-China Economic and Security Review Commission, *China's Global Quest for Resources and Implications for the United States* (Jan. 26, 2012), www.uscc.gov/hearings/2012hearings/written_testimonies/hr12_01_26.php; Mekong River Commission (MRC), "Mekong River Commission and China Boost Water Data Exchange," Press Release (Aug. 30, 2013), www.mrcmekong.org/news-and-events/news/mekong-river-commission-and-china-boost-water-data-exchange/.

174 Katherine Morton, "Climate Change and Security at the Third Pole," *Survival: Global Politics and Strategy* 53, no. 1 (2011): 121–32.

175 Robert D. Kaplan, "The Coming Anarchy," *Atlantic* (Feb. 1994), www.theatlantic.com/magazine/archive/1994/02/the-coming-anarchy/304670/.

176 Much of this debate has centered on whether Chinese trade and investment are hurting the growth of manufacturing in other developing countries and perpetuating a reliance on natural resource exports, with particular attention to the countries in Latin America and Africa. See, for example, Kevin P. Gallagher and Roberto Porzecanski, *The Dragon in the Room: China and the Future of Latin American Industrialization* (Stanford University Press, Stanford, CA, 2010); Rhys Jenkins and Alexandre de Freitas Barbosa, "Fear for Manufacturing? China and the Future of Industry in Brazil and Latin America," *China Quarterly* 209 (March 2012): 59–81; Javier Santiso (ed.), *The Visible Hand of China in Latin America* (Organization for Economic Cooperation and Development, Paris, 2007); Daniel Lederman, Marcelo Olarreaga, and Guillermo E. Perry (eds.), *China's and India's Challenge to Latin America: Opportunity or Threat?* (World Bank, Washington, D.C., 2009); World Bank, "Latin America and the Caribbean's Long-Term Growth: Made in China?" Report by the Office of the Chief Economist for Latin American and the Caribbean (World Bank, Washington, D.C., 2011), http://siteresources.worldbank.org/LACEXT/Resources/Annual_Meetings_Report_LCRCE_English_Sep17F2.pdf; Richard Schiere, Léonce Ndikumana, and Peter Walkenhorst (eds.), *China and Africa: An Emerging Partnership for Development?* (African Development Bank Group, Tunis, Tunisia, 2011); Erik Myersson, Gerard Padrói Miguel, and Nancy Qian, "The Rise of China and the Natural Resource Curse in Africa," Programme Research Paper (Economic Organization and Public Policy, London School of Economics, London, UK, 2008), http://personal.lse.ac.uk/padro/meyersonpadroqian_20080407_all.pdf; Thierry Ogier, "OECD Attacks China-Africa Trade 'Myths,'" *Emerging Markets* (June 7, 2011), www.emergingmarkets.org/Article/2844091/OECD-attacks-China-Africa-trade-myths.html.

177 Export values are expressed in nominal terms, from UNCTAD, International Trade data. Data on foreign direct investment reported in Schiere, Ndikumana, and Walkenhorst (eds.), *China and Africa*.

178 Schiere, Ndikumana, and Walkenhorst (eds.), *China and Africa*; Martyn Davies, "How China Is Influencing Africa's Development," Background paper for *Perspectives on Global Development 2010: Shifting Wealth* (Organization for Economic Cooperation and Development, Paris, 2010), www.oecd.org/dataoecd/34/39/45068325.pdf; World Bank, "Infrastructure Financing Gap Endangers Development Goals" (April 23, 2009), http://web.worldbank.org/WBSITE/EXTERNAL/NEWS/0,,contentMDK:22154463~pagePK:64257043~piPK:437376~theSitePK:4607,00.html.

179 Vivien Foster, William Butterfield, Chuan Chen, and Nataliya Pushak, "Building Bridges: China's Growing Role as Infrastructure Financier for Africa," *Infrastructure Trends and Policy Options* no. 5 (Public-Private Infrastructure Advisory Facility, World Bank, Washington, D.C., 2008), http://siteresources.worldbank.org/INTAFRICA/Resources/Building_Bridges_Master_Version_wo-Embg_with_cover.pdf.
180 See Serge Michel and Michel Beuret, *China Safari: On the Trail of Beijing's Expansion in Africa* (Nation Books, New York, 2009).
181 Chris Buckley, "China's Leader Tries to Calm African Fears of His Country's Economic Power," *New York Times* (March 25, 2013), www.nytimes.com/2013/03/26/world/asia/chinese-leader-xi-jinping-offers-africa-assurance-and-aid.html.
182 United Nations Conference on Trade and Development (UNCTAD), "International Trade Data, Merchandise Trade," http://unctadstat.unctad.org/.
183 Myersson, Padrói Miguel, and Qian, "The Rise of China."
184 Surveys of local employment by Chinese firms in Africa exhibit significant variability. In some countries, Chinese firms tend to employ more Chinese workers than locals (especially in post-conflict settings) and in others the opposite is true. Cited in Bendicte Vibe Christensen, "China in Africa: A Macroeconomic Perspective," Center for Global Development Working Paper No. 230 (2010): 15, www.cgdev.org/content/publications/detail/1424567/; Ruben Gonzalez-Vicente, "China's Engagement in South America and Africa's Extractive Sectors: New Perspectives for Resource Curse Theories," *Pacific Review* 21, no. 1 (2011): 65–87.
185 Myersson, Padrói Miguel, and Qian, "The Rise of China."
186 These examples from Gabon, Sierra Leone, Sudan, and Zambia are drawn from Jin et al., "China's 'Go Out' Strategy"; Peter Bosshard, "China's Environmental Footprint in Africa," Working Papers in African Studies 01–08, School of Advanced International Studies (SAIS), Johns Hopkins University (2008), www.sais-jhu.edu/academics/regional-studies/africa/pdf/BosshardWorkingPaper.pdf; and Appendix V in Barbara Kotschwar, Theodore H. Moran, and Julia Muir, "Chinese Investment in Latin American Resources: The Good, the Bad, and the Ugly," Peterson Institute for International Economics Working Paper 12–3 (2012),www.piie.com/publications/wp/wp12-3.pdf.
187 Oxfam, "An Introduction to China's OFDI Legal System" (中国境外投资法律体系概论), Report produced for Oxfam Hong Kong, PRC (Jan. 11, 2012), www.oxfam.org.cn/Resources/reports/An_Introduction_to_China%27s_OFDI_Legal_System_eng.pdf (English), or www.oxfam.org.cn/Resources/reports/An_Introduction_to_China%27s_OFDI_Legal_System_chi.pdf (Chinese); Organization for Economic Cooperation and Development (OECD), "China: Encouraging Responsible Business Conduct," *OECD Investment Policy Review* (2008), www.oecd.org/investment/investmentfordevelopment/41792733.pdf; Schiere, Ndikumana, and Walkenhorst (eds.), *China and Africa*.
188 Equator Principles website, www.equator-principles.com/.
189 Haotong Wang, "Keeping an Eye on China's Bankers," *Chinadialogue* (May 14, 2012), www.chinadialogue.net/article/show/single/en/4922-Keeping-an-eye-on-China-s-bankers.
190 Mang, Testimony before U.S.-China Economic and Security Review Commission.
191 PRC Ministry of Commerce and Ministry of Environmental Protection (MOFCOM and MEP), "Notification of the Ministry of Commerce and the Ministry of

Environmental Protection on Issuing the Guidelines for Environmental Protection in Foreign Investment and Cooperation," *Shang He Han* no. 74 (Feb. 18, 2013), http://english.mofcom.gov.cn/article/policyrelease/bbb/201303/20130300043226.shtml; Denise Leung and Yingzhen Zhao, "Environmental and Social Policies in Overseas Investments: Progress and Challenges for China," Issue Brief (World Resources Institute, Washington, D.C., 2013), www.wri.org/sites/default/files/pdf/environmental_and_social_policies_in_overseas_investments_china.pdf; Jin et al., "China's 'Go Out' Strategy"; Oxfam, "An Introduction to China's OFDI Legal System."

192 Gallagher and Porzecanski, *The Dragon in the Room*; Rhys Jenkins, "China and Brazil: Economic Impacts of a Growing Relationship," *Journal of Current Chinese Affairs* 41, no. 1 (2012): 21–47; Caroline Freund and Çağlar Özden, "The Effect of China's Exports on Latin American Trade with the World," in *China's and India's Challenge to Latin America: Opportunity or Threat?,* edited by Daniel Lederman, Marcelo Olarreaga, and Guillermo E. Perry (World Bank, Washington, D.C., 2009): 179–217; Ron Sandrey and Hannah Edinger, "China's Manufacturing and Industrialization in Africa," in *China and Africa: An Emerging Partnership for Development?,* edited by Richard Schiere, Léonce Ndikumana, and Peter Walkenhorst (African Development Bank Group, Tunis, Tunisia, 2011): 51–71.

193 Based on reference case (New Policies) scenario projections by IEA for CO_2 emissions from energy from International Energy Agency (IEA), *World Energy Outlook 2013* (IEA, OECD, Paris, 2013); and medium-fertility population projections by United Nations, Department of Economic and Social Affairs, Population Division (UNDESA), *World Urbanization Prospects: The 2012 Revision* (2012), POP/DB/WPP/Rev.2012/POP/F01-1.

194 Watts, *When a Billion Chinese Jump.*

195 U.S. Department of Defense, *Quadrennial Defense Review Report* (Office of the Secretary of Defense, Washington, D.C., 2010), www.defense.gov/qdr/qdr%20as%20of%2029jan10%201600.PDF.

196 Food and Agriculture Organization of the United Nations (FAO), "Review of the State of World Marine Fishery Resources," FAO Fisheries and Aquaculture Technical Paper No. 569 (2011), www.fao.org/docrep/015/i2389e/i2389e00.htm.

197 Sarika Cullis-Suzuki and Daniel Pauly, "Marine Protected Area Costs as 'Beneficial' Fisheries Subsidies: A Global Evaluation," *Coastal Management* 38, no. 2 (2010): 113–21.

198 Tabitha Grace Mallory, "China's Distant Water Fishing Industry: Evolving Policies and Implications," *Marine Policy* (2012), http://dx.doi.org/10.1016/j.marpol.2012.05.024.

199 Mallory, "China's Distant Water Fishing Industry."

200 Tony J. Pitcher, Daniela Kalikoski, Ganapahiraju Pramod, and Katherine Short, "Safe Conduct? Twelve Years Fishing Under the UN Code," Report (World Wildlife Fund, Washington, D.C., 2008), http://wwf.panda.org/about_our_earth/blue_planet/publications/?uNewsID=154581.

201 E.C. Economy, "The Impact of International Regimes on Chinese Foreign Policy-Making: Broadening Perspectives and Policies . . . But Only to a Point," in *The Making of Chinese Foreign and Security Policy in the Era of Reform, 1978-2000*, edited by David Lampton (Stanford University Press, Stanford, CA, 2001): 230–53.

202 Lieberthal and Wang, "Addressing U.S.-China Strategic Distrust"; Economy and Segal, "The G-2 Mirage," page 14.

203 Ian Fergusson and Bruce Vaughn, "The Trans-Pacific Partnership Agreement," Congressional Research Service Report R40502 (2011): 5, www.fas.org/sgp/crs/row/R40502.pdf.

204 This is despite the fact that TPP was initiated in 2005 by Brunei, Chile, New Zealand, and Singapore. The United States did not announce its intent to join TPP until 2009. See Jin Yuan Wen, "The Trans-Pacific Partnership and China's Corresponding Strategies," Freeman Briefing Report (Center for Strategic & International Studies, 2012), http://csis.org/files/publication/120620_Freeman_Brief.pdf.

205 Authors' calculations using data from the UNCTAD stat database (United Nations Conference on Trade and Development (UNCTAD), UNCTAD stat database, http://unctad.org/en/Pages/Statistics.aspx).

206 Aaditya Mattoo and Arvind Subramanian, "China and the World Trading System," World Bank Policy Research Working Paper 5897 (World Bank, Washington, D.C., 2011), www-wds.worldbank.org/servlet/WDSContentServer/WDSP/IB/2011/12/05/000158349_20111205135456/Rendered/PDF/WPS5897.pdf.

207 Peter Petri and Michael Plummer, "The Trans-Pacific Partnership and Asia-Pacific Integration: Policy Implications," Policy Brief PB12–16 (Peterson Institute for International Economics, 2012), http://xxx.iie.com/publications/pb/pb12-16.pdf; Evelyn Davadason, of the University of Malaya, has also found that Chinese exports would benefit from China's inclusion in the TPP. See Evelyn Davadason, "The Trans-Pacific Partnership (TPP): The Chinese Perspective," SSRN Working Paper (2012), http://ssrn.com/abstract=2101839.

208 Fergusson and Vaughn, "The Trans-Pacific Partnership Agreement." Involving China in the TPP will likely generate controversy, as did including Vietnam, and trade officials may face stiff opposition from industry groups within the United States in getting the agreement approved by Congress—that is, if China, the United States, and others are able to reach an agreement. By bringing China into the talks, concerns over intellectual property rights, state-owned enterprises, and government subsidies may become a sticking point. Still, despite these obstacles, the potential gains from bringing China into the fold of the TPP framework and a regional economic architecture consistent with U.S. standards are well worth it.

209 Mattoo and Subramanian, "China and the World Trading System." Professor Carolyn Evans makes a similar argument, writing, "Despite the difficulties involved in reaching an agreement involving so many countries, the WTO's Doha Round deserves continued focus and effort. While countries have completed many bilateral and regional agreements, a broad multilateral agreement offers the possibility of additional, unique benefits." See Carolyn Evans, "Bilateralism, Multilateralism, and Trade Rules," Federal Reserve Bank of San Francisco Economic Letter (Jan. 9, 2012), www.frbsf.org/publications/economics/letter/2012/el2012-01.html.

210 Federal and state subsidies for consumption of fossil fuels in the United States are estimated at $5.3 billion. See International Energy Agency (IEA), *World Energy Outlook 2010* (IEA, OECD, Paris, 2010).

211 See Juliet Eilperin, "G20 Leaders Agree to Phase Out Fossil Fuel Subsidies," *Washington Post* (Sept. 25, 2009), www.washingtonpost.com/wp-dyn/content/article/2009/09/25/AR2009092502453.html.

212 Production subsidies estimated by IISD and cited by IEA, "Fossil-Fuel Subsidies in APEC."

213 IEA projection cited by Ernst & Young, *Renewable Energy Country Attractiveness Indices*, no. 31 (Nov. 2011): 3, www.ey.com/Publication/vwLUAssets/Renewable_energy_country_attractiveness_indices_-_Issue_31/$FILE/EY_RECAI_issue_31.pdf.

214 To its credit, the Obama administration's budget for 2013 calls for oil and gas subsidies to be reduced by $55.9 billion. Reported in Ernst and Young, *Renewable Energy Country Attractiveness Indices*, no. 33 (May 2012), www.ey.com/Publication/vwLUAssets/Renewable_energy_country_attractiveness_indices_-_Issue_33/$FILE/EY_RECAI_issue_33.pdf.

215 J. Xu et al., "China's Ecological Rehabilitation: Unprecedented Efforts, Dramatic Impacts, and Requisite Policies," *Ecological Economics* 57, no. 4 (2006): 595–607.

216 Kristen Nowell, "Wildlife Crime Scorecard: Assessing Compliance with and Enforcement of CITES Commitments for Tigers, Rhinos, and Elephants," Report (World Wildlife Fund, Washington, D.C., 2012), http://awsassets.panda.org/downloads/wwf_wildlife_crime_scorecard_report.pdf.

217 World Wildlife Fund (WWF), "Countries Get Failing Grades on Illegal Wildlife Trade Enforcement—WWF Analysis," Press Release (World Wildlife Fund, Washington, D.C., July 23, 2012), www.worldwildlife.org/who/media/press/2012/WWFPresitem28315.html.

218 Bloomberg New Energy Finance, "Joined at the Hip: The US-China Clean Energy Relationship," White Paper (May 17, 2010), http://bnef.com/PressReleases/view/116.

219 Linden Ellis, Devin Kleinfield-Hayes, and Jennifer L. Turner, "Chinese Investment in Clean Energy," *China Business Review* (April-June 2012), https://www.chinabusinessreview.com/public/1204/ellis.html.

220 China Greentech Initiative, *China Greentech Report 2012*; American Council on Renewable Energy and Chinese Renewable Energy Industries Association (ACORE and CREIA), "US-China Quarterly Market Review" (2011), www.acore.org/wp-content/uploads/2011/12/ACORE_QMR-fall2011_FNLhi.pdf.

221 Solar Energy Industries Association (SEIA), "U.S. Solar Energy Trade Assessment" (2011), www.seia.org/research-resources/us-solar-energy-trade-assessment-2011. The positive trade balance was reversed in 2011, but this was because of a number of factors. First, there was a severe glut of production capacity in China, which caused a significant decline in unit prices for PV models and a frantic rush to clear inventory. See Melanie Hart, "Shining a Light on U.S.-China Clean Energy Cooperation" (Center for American Progress, 2012), www.americanprogress.org/issues/china/report/2012/02/09/11030/shining-a-light-on-u-s-china-clean-energy-cooperation/. Second, anticipatory fears that a ruling by the U.S. Department of Commerce in late 2011 or early 2012 would impose new tariffs on PV modules from China caused a frantic surge in orders, with imports from Suntech, the world's largest solar PV manufacturer, spiking by 76 percent in November and imports from another Chinese manufacturer, Trina Solar, jumping by 209 percent in early December compared with the previous year. There were also reports of companies stockpiling panels. See Andrew Burger, "Chinese Solar Panel Exports." Third, bankruptcies by a handful of U.S. solar manufacturers blunted growth in U.S. exports. See China Greentech Initiative, *China Greentech Report 2012*.

222 Based on a survey of jobs in the solar industry by The Solar Foundation. See The Solar Foundation, "National Solar Jobs Census 2010: A Review of the U.S. Solar Workforce" (2010), www.thesolarfoundation.org/sites/thesolarfoundation.org/files/Final%20TSF%20National%20Solar%20Jobs%20Census%202010%20Web%20Version.pdf; WRI, "Clean Tech's Rise, Part II."

223 Edward Steinfeld, *Playing Our Game: Why China's Rise Doesn't Threaten the West* (Oxford University Press, Oxford, UK, 2010).
224 Lieberthal and Wang, "Addressing U.S.-China Strategic Distrust."
225 U.S. Bureau of Economic Analysis, "Direct Investment and Multinational Companies: Comprehensive Data" (U.S. Bureau of Economic Analysis, Department of Commerce), www.bea.gov/international/direct_investment_multinational_companies_comprehensive_data.htm.
226 Lieberthal and Wang, "Addressing U.S.-China Strategic Distrust."
227 PRC Central Government, "Chen Deming Attends Third Meeting of U.S.-China CEO and Former Senior Officials' Dialogue" (陈德铭出席第三轮中美工商领袖和前高官对话会) (July 20, 2012), www.gov.cn/gzdt/2012-07/20/content_2188338.htm; U.S. Chamber of Commerce, "Chamber Convenes U.S.-China CEO Dialogue to Expand Bilateral Commerce," Press Release (July 18, 2012), www.uschamber.com/press/releases/2012/july/chamber-convenes-us-china-ceo-dialogue-expand-bilateral-commerce.
228 Ting Xu, "Destination Unknown: Investment in China's 'Go Out' Policy," *Jamestown Foundation China Brief* 11, no. 17 (2011), www.jamestown.org/single/?no_cache=1&tx_ttnews[tt_news]=38413&tx_ttnews[backPid]=517.
229 Economist Intelligence Unit, "Evaluating a Potential US-China Bilateral Investment Treaty: Background, Context and Implications," Report to the US-China Economic and Security Review Commission (March 30, 2010), www.uscc.gov/researchpapers/2010/EIU_Report_on_US-China_BIT—FINAL_14_April_2010.pdf.
230 U.S. Department of State, "United States Concludes Review of Model Bilateral Investment Treaty," Press Release (April 20, 2012), www.state.gov/r/pa/prs/ps/2012/04/188198.htm.
231 U.S. Treasury Department and Federal Reserve Board, "Major Foreign Holders."
232 For a review of the important role of government support in the energy innovation process and a comparison of how the United States, Brazil, Russia, India, Mexico, China, and South Africa stack up against one another, see Kelly Sims Gallagher, Laura Diaz Anadon, Ruud Kempener, and Charlie Wilson, "Trends in Investments in Global Energy Research, Development, and Demonstration," *WIREs: Climate Change* 2, no. 3 (2011): 373–96.
233 Construction of the GreenGen plant is being led by Huaneng, with significant financing from the Chinese government. The first phase of the GreenGen plant came online in early 2012, making it the world's largest gasified-coal power generator and one of the most efficient. The Edwardsport plant was being built by Duke Energy and was expected to become commercially operational in late 2012 or early 2013. U.S.-China Clean Energy Research Center (CERC), "Joint Work Plan for Research on Clean Coal Including Carbon Capture and Storage" (Jan. 18, 2011), www.us-china-cerc.org/Advanced_Coal_Technology.html; Jeff Tollefson and Richard Van Noorden, "Slow Progress to Cleaner Coal," *Nature* 484, no. 793 (2012), www.nature.com/news/slow-progress-to-cleaner-coal-1.10411; Peter Fairley, "Cleaner Coal's Last Stand," *IEEE Spectrum* (2012), http://spectrum.ieee.org/energy/fossil-fuels/cleaner-coals-last-stand/; Angel Hsu, "Updates from Tianjin: Progress on the GreenGen IGCC Project," *China FAQs Blog* (Oct. 8, 2010), www.chinafaqs.org/blog-posts/updates-tianjin-progress-greengen-igcc-project; Duke Energy, "Edwardsport Integrated Gasification Combined Cycle (IGCC) Station," www.duke-energy.com/about-us/igcc.asp.
234 WRI, "Clean Tech's Rise, Part I."
235 Gallagher et al., "Trends in Investments."

236 Mattoo and Subramanian, "China and the World Trading System."
237 World Bank and Development Research Center, *China 2030.*
238 Andrews-Speed, *The Institutions of Energy Governance in China*; *Economy and Nation Weekly* (财经国家周刊), "The Vicissitudes of China's Ministry of Energy" (能源部沉浮录: 建国60年能源主管部门三立三撤), Sina.com.cn (July 16, 2012), http://finance.sina.com.cn/china/20120716/225212580668.shtml.
239 Erica Downs, "China's 'New' Energy Administration," *China Business Review* (Nov.-Dec. 2008), www.brookings.edu/research/articles/2008/11/china-energy-downs; Downs, "Pursuing Policy—and Profit."
240 Downs, "China's 'New' Energy Administration."
241 Shisheng Yang and Xiao Lin, "The Next Stage of Reform: Create a Ministry of Energy" (改革下一步:成立能源部), *China Times* (华夏时报) (April 20, 2012), www.chinatimes.cc/yaowen/hongguan/2012-04-20/30139.shtml; *Economy and Nation Weekly*, "The Vicissitudes of China's Ministry of Energy."
242 Lewis, "The State of U.S.-China Relations."
243 U.S. Trade Representative (USTR), Memorandum of Understanding between the Government of the United States of America and the Government of the People's Republic of China on Combatting Illegal Logging and Associated Trade (USTR, Department of Commerce, Washington, D.C., and Beijing, April/May 2008), www.ustr.gov/sites/default/files/US-China%20MOU%20to%20Combat%20Illegal%20Logging_0.pdf.
244 U.S. and Chinese officials agreed at the Third Strategic and Economic Dialogue in 2011 to develop a framework plan for cooperation between NOAA and China's State Oceanic Administration for 2011–2015. See ENS, "US, China Cooperate to Fight Climate Change, Illegal Fishing."

5

COASTAL EAST AFRICA

Ambassador Mark Green

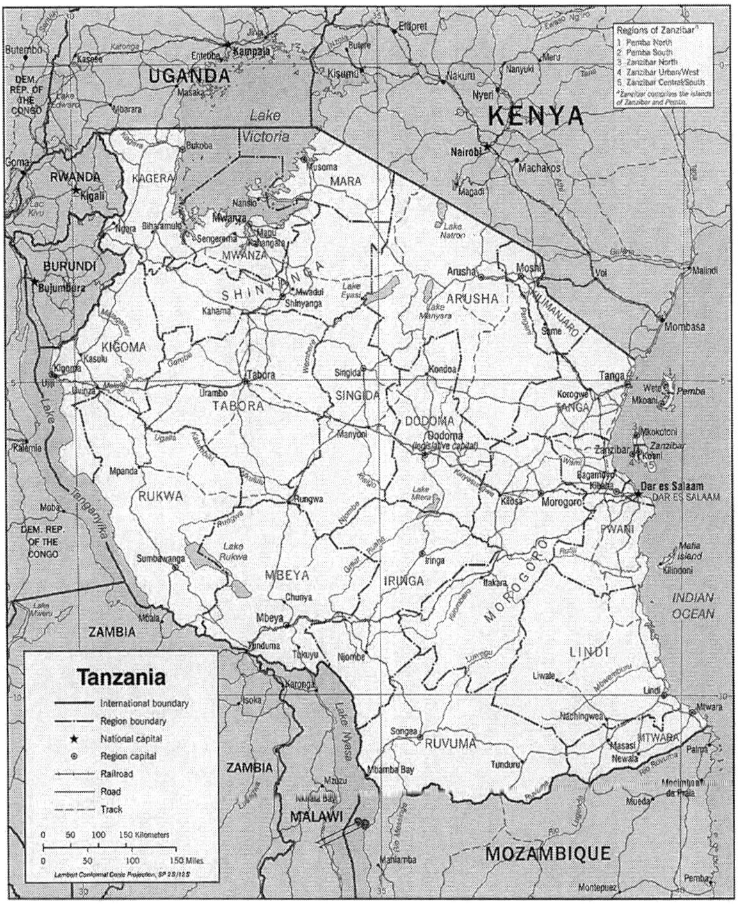

I began my work in development as a volunteer teacher in Kenya in the late 1980s. During our teaching days, my wife and I traveled on a shoestring budget throughout Kenya, Tanzania, Burundi, Rwanda, Malawi, and Uganda. We admired the raw beauty of the region and enjoyed the legendary hospitality of its people. Twenty years later, we returned to East Africa when I had the honor of serving as the U.S. ambassador to Tanzania. Since my diplomatic service ended, I have been back to the region numerous times for organizations such as Malaria No More, the Initiative for Global Development, and the World Wildlife Fund.

For many people, East Africa *is* Africa. From the majestic mountains such as Kilimanjaro and Meru to the sweeping Serengeti plains, from the timeless streets and alleyways of Stone Town in Zanzibar to the dense forests of Gombe Stream National Park with its colony of chimpanzees, East Africa captures so much of the continent's beauty and charm. For many decades, visitors, from legendary explorers to Peace Corps volunteers, have journeyed here to experience some of the area's unique treasures.

In recent years, the region has also played a pivotal role in U.S. foreign policy. Since the deadly terrorist bombings of 1998 in Nairobi and Dar es Salaam, the United States has joined democratic leaders in the region to take on the ravages of poverty, hunger, and disease. In fact, nearly every modern development initiative of the United States is at work in the region—the President's Emergency Plan for AIDS Relief (PEPFAR), the Millennium Challenge Corporation (MCC), the President's Malaria Initiative, Feed the Future (FTF), and the new Power Africa initiative, just to name a few. Political leaders in Washington, D.C., have also joined the region's security leaders in building the capacity to fight the challenges of piracy, narcotics, humanitarian crises, and terrorism.

This chapter will explore the view that economic well-being, social stability, and national security have to be built on a foundation of environmental sustainability in the three main countries of coastal East Africa—Kenya, Tanzania, and Mozambique. It will provide illustrations and evidence that the products and services that are made possible by the unique biodiversity of this ecoregion must be safeguarded and conserved. Otherwise, the communities and countries of the region will not achieve stability, security, or prosperity in the long run.

Looking forward, the management and protection of the region's precious natural resources are becoming increasingly important parts of the U.S. partnership with democratic leaders in East Africa. In addition to the predictable resource challenges that often accompany rapid economic growth, the governments of the region also face daunting challenges in the emergence of piracy, overfishing, wildlife poaching, and deforestation. East Africa's wisest leaders recognize that these new threats, left unchecked, could destroy the area's unique features and limit its potential. Oftentimes, leaders lack the resources and capacity to turn back these threats effectively. The United States can make a difference. As a focal point for U.S. foreign assistance programs and a key ally in the region, Tanzania is a logical starting point for assessing the U.S. relationship with the countries of coastal East Africa.

U.S. Relations with Tanzania

Stretching over 364,945 square miles, Tanzania is not only the largest country in area of coastal East Africa but also a veritable biodiversity hotspot because of its plains and coastal forests and the mountains of the Eastern Afromontane.[1] The Tanzanian plains of Serengeti National Park host the largest terrestrial wildlife migration in the world, with 2 million wildebeests and hundreds of thousands of gazelles and zebras annually migrating through the park. Tanzania contains the highest point in Africa, Mount Kilimanjaro, and is bordered by three of the largest lakes on the continent: Lake Victoria (the world's second-largest freshwater lake) in the north, Lake Tanganyika (the world's second deepest) in the west, and Lake Malawi in the southwest.[2] Tanzania's eastern border stretches along 500 miles of coastline bordering the shrimp- and tuna-rich waters of the western Indian Ocean. Home to 15 national parks and seven UNESCO World Heritage sites, Tanzania possesses a rich tapestry of ecosystems that contribute to the reputation of coastal East Africa as one of the most resource-rich areas on the continent.

The United States established diplomatic relations with Tanzania in 1961. In recent years, the United States and Tanzania have developed a deep partnership. The United States remains committed to Tanzania's development, as demonstrated through major foreign assistance investments in areas such as economic development, food security, and health. The MCC operates its largest Compact program in Tanzania, having invested approximately $700 million in roads, energy, water, and other development efforts over the past five years.[3] Tanzania is currently in the process of pursuing a second MCC Compact. In addition, Tanzania is among the greatest beneficiaries of the PEPFAR, which was created by President George W. Bush in 2003 to stem the tide of the global AIDS epidemic. Over the past decade, PEPFAR has been continually committed to supporting Tanzania's leadership role in Africa's fight against HIV/AIDS; through PEPFAR support in 2011, 289,000 Tanzanians received antiretroviral treatments, more than 1,227,700 HIV-positive individuals received care and support, and an estimated 17,386 infant HIV infections were averted.[4] Another Bush administration initiative, the President's Malaria Initiative, has been operating in Tanzania since 2005. Tanzania is also a focus country for several of President Obama's signature development initiatives: FTF, the Partnership for Growth, the Global Health Initiative, and the Global Climate Change Initiative. Tanzania is also included in the new Power Africa initiative that President Obama announced during his trip to Africa in July 2013.

In recent years, the United States and Tanzania have significantly strengthened their military relations. Ties between the U.S. and Tanzanian militaries have expanded and deepened to include capacity building and training in coastal water surveillance, international peacekeeping, humanitarian projects, and civil military operations.[5] Since its establishment in 2007, the United States Africa Command (U.S. AFRICOM) has been a leading partner in U.S.-Tanzanian health initiatives. In 2010, the U.S. Department of Defense and the Tanzania People's Defence Force cohosted the International Military HIV/AIDS Conference in Tanzania. In March 2011, U.S. AFRICOM partnered with the U.S. Agency for International Development's (USAID) Pandemic Response Program to lead a disaster response exercise with the Tanzanian government.[6] The exercise helped strengthen Tanzania's capacity to plan for national and regional pandemics.

The U.S. military also works closely with its Tanzanian counterparts to strengthen maritime security. Under the U.S. Navy's maritime security cooperation program, Africa Partnership Station, the U.S. military works with members of the Tanzanian People's Defence Force, the local police, and port security officials to bolster regional maritime security in the areas of counter-piracy, illicit trafficking, and energy and resource security.[7] Furthermore, military cooperation does not stop at the bilateral level. Multilateral security cooperation is critical to the region's peace and security. Tanzanian forces frequently contribute to the United Nations' and African Union's regional peace and security operations. Most recently, Tanzania contributed approximately 800 soldiers toward an African Union operation to combat the rebel military group M23 in the Democratic Republic of Congo.[8] U.S. AFRICOM has been a key supporter of these types of African-led regional stability missions. In early 2013, U.S. AFRICOM cohosted a conference with the Tanzanian government that brought together seven African countries. The conference provided a forum for participants to voice their unique perspectives and build on partnerships to strengthen the collective effort to combat shared security threats.[9]

In addition, the United States and Tanzania are partners through a number of international organizations to promote priority development initiatives. The World Bank currently finances approximately 25 such initiatives in Tanzania, ranging from improving food security to expanding transportation infrastructure. Indicative of the region's biodiversity, Tanzania is one of the top recipients of the World Bank's biodiversity support and has received more than $60 million in the past 10 years.[10] Tanzania is also currently the largest beneficiary of the African Development Bank's (AfDB) concessionary funding. With an investment portfolio of more than $2 billion in Tanzania, the AfDB is predominantly engaged in the development of Tanzania's water and sanitation sectors.[11] The East African Development Bank (EADB) is actively engaged in infrastructure development of the region. The EADB recently increased Tanzanian transportation investment in the East African Road Network, a project to support cross-border economic development in the region.[12]

Over the past decade, a significant increase in economic ties and U.S. investment in Tanzania has further strengthened the growing U.S.-Tanzanian partnership. The United States signed Trade and Investment Framework Agreements with the East African Community in 2008 and with the Common Market for eastern and southern Africa in 2001; Tanzania is a member of both of these regional organizations. U.S. goods exports to Tanzania in 2011 were $258 million, up 57.7 percent from 2010, and up 474.7 percent from 2000.[13] In 2013, Tanzania is eligible for the African Growth and Opportunity Act, as well as textile and apparel benefits to further aid U.S.-Tanzania two-way trade and economic integration.

U.S. Relations with the Greater Coastal East Africa Region

Leaders inside and outside the region are beginning to recognize that if Africa is going to continue to rise in economic and strategic importance, its resources need to be effectively conserved and cultivated. There is a growing recognition that friends such as the United States can help bolster these efforts by supporting partnerships and initiatives that strengthen the political will and capacity of regional governments to make the difficult decisions that are often necessary for long-term conservation.

Tanzania is a major focus in numerous presidential initiatives. Several of these and other U.S. development programs are also present in Kenya and Mozambique. In 2011, USAID spent more than $296.4 million in humanitarian assistance in Kenya, $215.5 million in Tanzania, and $114.6 million in Mozambique.[14] USAID is working with Kenyans for Kenya to advance democracy and the rule of law, increase access to and improve the quality of health and education services, and modernize and grow the economy so that more can share in Kenya's wealth.[15] In Mozambique, USAID's current Country Assistance Strategy provides support to strengthen democratic governance, improve the competitiveness of key economic sectors, improve health, expand opportunities for education and training, improve agriculture and food security, and begin to respond to climate change.[16] Since 2002, U.S. economic relations with the coastal East Africa region have increased significantly. While U.S. exports to Tanzania have increased more than 300 percent in the past 10 years,[17] exports to Kenya are up approximately 200 percent and to Mozambique more than 400 percent.[18]

Over the past decade, the United States has increasingly seen the coastal East Africa region as a valuable strategic partner, in part because of its potential links to Islamic terrorism, Chinese resource interests, strategic minerals (e.g., tantalum), and offshore oil and gas development, as well as the potential for future conflicts or humanitarian disasters to which the United States would likely be compelled to respond. The strengthening movement toward greater strategic importance of Africa culminated with the 2006 U.S. National Security Strategy, which identified Africa as "a high priority" and "recogniz(ing) that our security depends on partnering with Africans to strengthen fragile and failing states and bring ungoverned areas under the control of effective democracies."[19] The February 2007 announcement of the creation of the U.S. AFRICOM further reflected a shift in perception of the strategic importance of Africa in world affairs.

Until now, however, U.S. strategic interests have not been based on the usual reasons, such as ensuring access to large mineral or hydrocarbon resources. In fact, trade between the United States and any of these countries is small compared with U.S. trade with Europe, Asia, and South Africa. U.S. interests in the region have been related to global health issues (e.g., HIV/AIDS, malaria), humanitarian assistance (e.g., refugees from conflicts, floods, and other natural disasters), and scientific and conservation concerns. Accordingly, at the most basic and direct level, to allow the unsustainable extraction of resources to continue in this region is categorically impeding and directly limiting the efficacy of current U.S. development programs in the region.

One area that will increasingly affect the stability and prosperity of the coastal East Africa region is natural resource and environmental management issues. The lack of defense for protected areas, unsustainable energy, poverty, and population growth are the drivers of natural resource exploitation and unsustainable economic development. Moreover, overfishing, deforestation, and illicit wildlife trafficking represent some of the most pressing obstacles to sustainable economic growth and development, improved political governance, and regional security.

Natural Resource Challenges for the Environment of Coastal East Africa

The three countries of coastal East Africa combined contain Africa's largest intact wilderness and account for 4,600 kilometers of biodiverse coastline.[20] While we focus in this chapter on the main environmental challenges faced by Tanzania, the greater coastal East Africa region confronts numerous similar environmental and natural resource issues that have potentially far-reaching implications for the region's governance, security, and human development. The similar ecosystems and resources of the three countries have effectively expanded country-level problems to regional issues in many cases.

Protected Areas

Each of the countries of coastal East Africa has a national system of protected areas. In Kenya, approximately 12 percent of the national land and marine territory falls into one of the eight categories of protected areas, including 23 terrestrial and 4 marine national parks, 26 terrestrial and 6 marine national reserves, and 4 national sanctuaries.[21] Tanzania protects more than 25 percent of its land area, including 12 national parks, 540 forest reserves, 28 game reserves, 38 game-controlled areas, and the Ngorongoro Conservation Area.[22] In Mozambique, a process of protected-area restoration started in 1995 has resulted in an increase in the percentage of total land covered by protected areas from about 11 percent in 1995 to about 25 percent in 2012.[23]

Although between 12 and 25 percent of the national territories of the countries of coastal East Africa are nominally in protected areas, these protected areas are not necessarily well or permanently protected. Tanzania provides a number of recent examples. The government of Tanzania is considering a proposal for a new dam at Stiegler's Gorge on the Rufiji River within the Selous Game Reserve. Also under consideration is a proposed uranium mine at the southern edge of the Selous Game Reserve, in an area that conservation organizations think of as the "Selous-Niassa Wildlife Corridor" for transboundary wildlife movement between Tanzania and Mozambique. The Tanzanian government has lobbied the UNESCO World Heritage Committee to change the boundaries of the game reserve to allow the Mkuju River uranium development project to go forward. An environmental impact assessment of the proposed mine has not been conducted.

The Tanzanian government also plans significant irrigation development in the Kilombero Valley, a designated Wetland of International Importance under the Ramsar Convention. The irrigation development is part of the government's proposed economic development in the Southern Agricultural Growth Corridor.

The Tanzanian government had been considering plans to pave the current two-lane highway across Serengeti National Park to make it more suitable for long-distance trucks and other traffic. The government was also considering connecting Lake Victoria to coastal ports and fencing the road to prevent vehicle-wildlife collisions. After protests by international conservation organizations and donors, the government announced that, for the time being, the road will remain gravel and be managed mainly for tourism and administrative purposes. An alternative route for a major trade highway that would run to the south of the park is being considered.

Another proposal under consideration is soda ash mining at Lake Natron, one of Tanzania's saline Rift Valley Lakes and a Ramsar wetland. Lake Natron is the most important breeding site for lesser flamingos in the world. East Africa has 1.5–2.5 million pink flamingos (three-quarters of the global population), and most them are hatched at Lake Natron.

Energy

Discussions of energy in coastal East Africa, as everywhere, have to distinguish between different types and uses of energy. In Tanzania, wood fuels provide 70 percent of the energy used in cooking; in urban areas, charcoal is the single largest source of household energy.[24] In fact, the charcoal sector is estimated to contribute around $650 million per year to employment, rural livelihoods, and the wider economy, providing income to several hundred thousand people in urban and rural areas.[25] In Mozambique, fuelwood and charcoal account "for approximately 83% of the total energy consumed," according to the National Directorate of Energy.[26] Although wood and other biomass fuels are potentially sustainable sources of renewable, "clean" energy, the forests are not being managed to sustain this energy supply. Some interventions could support the use of biomass fuels as a source of renewable energy for low-emissions development, including improved forest management, better enforcement of charcoal production and transport regulations, more efficient cookstoves and charcoal kilns, and development of fuelwood plantations.[27]

Hydroelectricity is the dominant source of electricity in all three countries, although it should be noted that electricity is not available to most households and electric use is very low compared with developed countries. In Kenya, hydropower supplies 44 percent of the electricity; in Tanzania, 61 percent; and in Mozambique, 99 percent (because of the Cahora Bassa Dam on the Zambezi River).[28] This dependence on hydropower suggests the importance of managing the water and the mountain watersheds that provide this energy source. In Tanzania, agricultural production of crops such as maize, cassava, and millet accounts for more than one-quarter of gross domestic product (GDP), provides 85 percent of exports, and employs more than 80 percent of the workforce.[29] With an economy that depends so heavily on a healthy agricultural sector, water flow integrity is vital. Dependence on hydropower foreshadows difficult trade-offs, as electricity demand rises, between other uses of water for agriculture, domestic uses, and environmental flows that maintain valuable ecosystems, such as the mangroves and the offshore fisheries they support.

Poverty

Kenya and Mozambique share Tanzania's rich natural resource base; they also face similar rates of poverty. The three countries have some of the highest rates of poverty in the world. All are low-income countries. According to the World Bank's World Development Indicator statistics for 2011, Kenya's gross national income (GNI) per capita was $820 and the country ranked 182 of 213 countries. Tanzania's GNI per capita was $540 (ranking 196/213) and Mozambique's GNI per capita was $460 (ranking 203/213). By comparison, GNI per capita in the United States was $48,620 (ranking 17/213).[30]

Population Growth

All three countries of coastal East Africa have rapid population growth. Health programs for water, basic health, sanitation, immunization, and HIV/AIDS and malaria prevention have decreased death rates, but fertility rates have not declined proportionately. The latest figures show that the rate of natural increase in Kenya is 2.7 percent per year, leading to a doubling-time estimate for the population, currently around 43 million, of 26 years. For Tanzania, the rate of natural increase is 3 percent; therefore, the population of about 48 million is expected to double in 23 years, by 2036. For Mozambique, the current population of about 24 million will double by around 2038, given its population growth rate of 2.8 percent per year.[31] Any opportunity to hasten the demographic transition toward lower fertility rates through improvements in girls' education, increased economic opportunities for women, maternal and child health, nutrition, family planning services, and improved water supply and sanitation will have the indirect benefit of reducing some of the pressures on the ecosystems and species on which the societies depend.

The human population is not distributed evenly in East Africa because of climatic and geographic factors that affect food production and water availability. Average population densities range from 30 persons per square kilometer in Mozambique to 52 per square kilometer in Tanzania to 73 per square kilometer in Kenya. Large areas of each of these countries are arid and semiarid lands not suitable to farming (although appropriate for pastoralism). In Kenya, for example, more than 80 percent of the country is arid and semiarid. Distinct rainy and dry seasons occur, and as is usual for equatorial countries, total precipitation can vary widely from year to year and droughts are common. Rain-fed agriculture generally requires about 450 millimeters of rainfall per year, so most of Kenya is not suitable for crop production without irrigation. Croplands and the associated agro-ecosystems cover about 19 percent of the country. In Kenya, the most densely populated areas are in western Kenya around Lake Victoria, the Western Highlands south of Mount Kenya and west of Nairobi, and the southern coast around Mombasa. In Tanzania, the densest populations are on the shores of Lake Victoria, in northern Tanzania around Mount Meru and Mount Kilimanjaro, on the islands of Pemba and Zanzibar, and on the coast near Dar es Salaam. In Mozambique, the northern provinces of Cabo Delgado and Nampula have 40 percent of the national population, distributed relatively evenly from the coast inland.

Although it is sometimes stated that population growth is a threat to the environment and biodiversity, this claim is not technically correct. Population is only one factor that influences environmental impact. A person's environmental "footprint" is also affected by one's level of resource consumption (or affluence) and the types of technologies one uses to support one's food, water, shelter, energy, and other needs. This relationship has been described since the 1970s by the formula I = PAT, where environmental impact (I) is seen to be affected by population (P), affluence (A), and technology (T).[32] However, population growth often acts as a root cause or driver underlying other social, political, and economic causes of direct threats to biodiversity and the biophysical environment. If it is not addressed and the population is not ultimately stabilized, actions necessary to address the social, political, and economic causes of threats to biodiversity will be all the more difficult to carry out. Population growth, combined with real development needs and aspirations, puts additional pressure on already scarce natural resources.

Overfishing

A critical component of Tanzania's rich natural resources are the fisheries that lie within the coastal waters of the Indian Ocean. More than 70 percent of Indian Ocean tuna—worth $2 billion to $3 billion per year—is caught in the coastal East Africa region.[33] Over the past 10 years, the demand for these fish, increasingly fueled by European and Asian markets, has resulted in trade that is not only unsustainable but also illegal in many instances. Unsustainable and illegal harvesting practices not only result in significant revenue loss for the country but also degrade the subsistence resources that support the poorest communities. Tanzania's 800 kilometers of exclusive economic zone (EEZ) coastline and the country's massive freshwater lakes provide great economic potential as both inland and marine fisheries. Yet the recent overfishing in European and other regional fisheries has led to an increase in foreign commercial fleets off the coast of Tanzania. These fleets generally operate through fisheries partnership agreements or joint ventures, while the local fishing industries and coastal communities reap few if any of the benefits. Moreover, the Tanzanian management authorities often lack the capacity to regulate small-scale fishing enterprises, which are believed to account for more than 40 percent of the total catch not currently reflected in the government's official statistics.[34] This type of inadequate data can lead to foreign commercial operations being over-licensed for harvest in the coastal waters.

Unregulated and illegal fishing have significantly affected the region. Current estimates suggest that Tanzania loses $200 million in revenue collection each year because of unregulated or illegal fishing.[35] These fishing operations inflict further damage on the ocean environment through wasteful and destructive fishing techniques, such as dynamite fishing and shrimp trawling. Dynamite fishing is particularly wasteful because each blast can kill thousands of marine organisms with as little as 3 percent of the killed organisms being harvested. In addition, dynamite-fishing techniques destroy coral and spoil the breeding grounds of fish populations and the potential profits coral tours generate for the coastal tourism sector.

Accounting for roughly 1.5 percent of GDP, Tanzania's fishing industry contributes minimally to the country's national economy.[36] Yet it is vitally important in coastal village communities where fishing is the primary food source. The vast potential of the Tanzanian fisheries sector is underperforming because of loose regulations coupled with unsustainable rates of extraction. Recent community-level efforts to educate coastal Tanzanians on sustainable fishing practices have been successful. Awareness of sustainable fishing management has increasingly prompted community-driven regulations whereby local fishing communities organize beach patrols and other associations to ensure best practices among the larger coastal population. The growing awareness of the importance of sustainable fishing practices has created opportunities to further develop the economic sector by shifting the country's mind-set from small-scale subsistence fishing toward fishing as an industrial-scale economic enterprise. Director General of the Tanzanian Fisheries Research Institute Dr. Benjamin Ngatunga is leading these efforts by developing commercial-scale fishing facilities and increasing technological skills to develop the fishing sector in a sustainable system.[37]

Over the past decade, overfishing in Mozambique and Kenya has proliferated too. Mozambique's shrimp fishery, once one of the world's largest, is now overfished and in decline. The Food and Agriculture Organization of the United Nations estimated that small-scale fishers, who caught 84,065 tons of fish for the domestic market in 2000, would need to catch 171,040 tons to meet the local demand of the growing population in 2025.[38] But, similar to the increase in foreign fleets operating in Tanzania, an influx of foreign demand is depleting fish stocks and destabilizing the thousands of Mozambicans who rely on small-scale fishing as a critical food source and income generator.

A 2007 report by the Institute for Security Studies estimated that illegal, unreported, and unregulated fishing in Africa is a $1 billion-a-year industry with illegal fishing in Mozambique alone estimated at $38 million.[39] The United States and South Africa have recently supported Mozambique's efforts to combat illegal fishing by donating navy patrol vessels to assist in patrolling Mozambique's 2,700-kilometer coastline. Kenya, as well, is negatively affected by overfishing of its coastal waters. Nearly 60,000 fishers live along the coastline of Kenya, and another 600,000 Kenyans are involved in the fishing industry through fish processing and trade.[40] As such, fisheries play an important role in the region's economic growth and poverty reduction plans. The current unsustainable extraction by foreign and domestic fleets threatens the livelihood of hundreds of thousands of citizens that reside in coastal communities.

Continuing unsustainable fishing practices threatens to increase the already high rates of poverty in these communities. Increased regional poverty has the potential, in turn, to affect the security of the greater region. The threat to regional fishing communities' way of life is directly related to the increase in crime as local communities take more desperate and even illegal measures to ensure their livelihoods. Over the past decade, links between overfishing and security have been well documented. Abdirahman Mohamed Farole, the former president of Somalia's Puntland government, suggested that it was the "violation of Somali waters by foreign fleets, which triggered a reaction of armed resistance by Somali fishermen."[41]

As overfishing depletes resources for the coastal population that relies heavily on small-scale fishing, it simultaneously reduces the stock of predatory fish in the marine environment. The loss of predatory fish has been shown to trigger collapse of marine ecosystems because of subsequent proliferation of organisms such as sea urchins, which significantly damage reef structures.[42] With coral reefs running nearly 240 square miles along the Kenyan coastline, the country has increasingly come to count on revenue from diving excursions and reef tours.[43] Destruction of these revenue-generating reefs has negative effects on Kenya's tourism industry. The lack of efficient rules and regulations to limit the amount of fishing to a sustainable level is in part responsible for the problem of overfishing. Another factor is that the countries of coastal East Africa lack the capacity to enforce existing regulations to combat illegal fishing. The current rate of overfishing threatens the region's long-term food security and the livelihoods of coastal residents. And it ultimately limits the region's economic and human development.

Moreover, the effects of illegal fishing and piracy have global implications that threaten U.S. security and trade interests. In recent years, the high level of piracy off the coast of Somalia has restricted U.S. aid deliveries and increased their cost. The danger of piracy affects U.S. and global insurance premiums for shipping operations and can force shippers to take longer, more expensive routes to avoid pirates. In 2008, insurance premiums for the Gulf of Aden increased tenfold.[44] An increase in insurance premiums risks increasing the costs of manufactured goods and oil from Asia and the Middle East. The alternative scenario may require shipping operations to avoid the Gulf of Aden and the Suez Canal and instead divert transport around the Cape of Good Hope. Moreover, piracy ransom funds have recently been linked to international terrorist organizations such as the U.S. terror-listed Al-Shabaab in Somalia.[45]

Deforestation

Currently, more than 20 million people live in and along the coastal forests of East Africa. Coastal East Africans rely heavily on the region's rainforests and grasslands for their food and freshwater supply. Yet, all three countries suffer from poorly regulated and even illegal timber extraction. Poorly regulated investment in commercial agriculture destroys large swaths of the forests that are essential for long-term watershed protection and soil erosion prevention. Tanzania's 129,000 square miles of forests and woodlands have increasingly come under the threat of overharvesting of timber and illegal commercial logging. Between 1990 and 2005, Tanzania lost 37.4 percent of its forests and woodland habitats.[46] Currently, Tanzanian forests are being cleared at a rate of 400,000 hectares (nearly 1 million acres) per year, the third-highest deforestation rate in Africa.[47] With the recent upswing in demand from Asia, spurred by China's rapidly expanding middle class, poorly regulated timber extraction has led to deforestation in areas critical to Tanzania's water supply. Conditions are similar in Kenya and Mozambique.

The region is endemically prone to some of the highest levels of food and water insecurity in the world, and the current unsustainable agricultural practices threaten to destabilize the already high-risk coastal East Africa region. In Tanzania, the United Nations World Food Programme estimates that more than 40 percent of the population lives in chronic food-deficit areas.[48] Despite progress made in recent years, the three countries depend very heavily on subsistence agriculture for food and livelihoods.[49] In Kenya, 75 percent of the labor force is engaged in agriculture, while in Tanzania the figure is 80 percent, and in Mozambique it is 81 percent.[50] Small farmers in East Africa are also highly dependent on ecosystem products, such as wood for cooking and construction, fish and shellfish, and wild plant foods and medicines.

Deforestation threatens to negate the strides that have been made to improve agricultural productivity and combat the region's chronic food insecurity issues. Current models suggest that increased agricultural growth combined with improved regional markets has the potential to lift 107 million Africans out of poverty.[51] The FTF model alone is set to reduce poverty by 6.1 million in Kenya.[52] Similarly, Mozambique—a country with some of Africa's poorest and most undernourished people—is currently cultivating only 10 percent of its arable land, making it uniquely situated to benefit from U.S. government agricultural initiatives.[53] The U.S. government, including FTF, has been working in concert with the governments of the countries of coastal East Africa and regional economic communities, such as the East African Community, to invest in inputs and techniques to improve agricultural productivity, expand markets and infrastructure to increase trade, and support African leadership and capacity building. Yet poor management and lack of clear land and resource ownership and rights leave large swaths of land inadequately protected from forest extraction. These issues threaten the natural resource base on which agriculture depends. With economic development and poverty alleviation so highly dependent on agricultural growth, sustainable forest extraction and agricultural production practices are emerging as a central component of the larger food security initiatives.

The risk of water scarcity, an already growing concern of climate predictions and population growth, is often exacerbated when forest-protected watersheds are exposed and topsoil is lost or penetrated. Without vegetation to moderate heavy rainfall, the topsoil, which develops under forested conditions, is directly exposed to rainfall that increases rates of erosion. Without topsoil absorbing and slowly releasing the precipitation to surface water and groundwater, the adjacent soil is more susceptible to erosion. As this cycle progresses and the region is not reforested at a sustainable level, the rate of erosion will continue to increase over the entire watershed. Consequently, the soil's natural cleansing effect as a groundwater filter will be lost. The far-reaching implication of watershed destabilization is a threat to the water supply of local communities and the urban centers that receive a substantial portion of their water supply from underground aquifers.

Moreover, because agriculture uses 70 percent of the world's freshwater supply, threats to forest-protected watersheds pose a direct threat to agricultural productivity.[54] In 2012, the United Nations Environment Programme (UNEP) found that the economic cost of deforestation caused by watershed disruption in Kenya far exceeds the gains from logging. With Kenya's five main watersheds providing more than 75 percent of the country's renewable surface water resources annually, a threat to these forests endangers Kenya's water flow during dry periods.[55] A joint study released in 2012 by UNEP and the Kenya Forest Service found that deforestation deprived Kenya's economy of "5.8 billion shillings ($68 million) in 2010 and 6.6 billion shillings in 2009, far outstripping the roughly 1.3 billion shillings injected from forestry and logging each year."[56]

In sum, the current rate of timber extraction from the coastal East Africa region is poised to exacerbate the region's food and water security issues. Moreover, illegal timber extraction further encumbers regional development by restricting the aggregate royalties (duties and taxes) the coastal East African governments would receive from legal timber exports. Illegal timber extraction also affects the global market; it depresses the price of timber worldwide, which ultimately is a disadvantage for law-abiding logging companies.

Illicit Wildlife Poaching

The effects of illicit poaching and trafficking of Tanzanian wildlife is another problem that impedes the country's development efforts. Tanzania is home to one of the world's largest herds of elephants, an estimated 70,000 to 80,000 elephants, accounting for nearly a quarter of all African elephants.[57] In recent years, there has been a massive influx of poachers into the country. Whether serving as a shipping transfer point or directly taken from the country's parks, in 2009–2011 Tanzania was the world's leading trafficker of illegal ivory.[58] The demand for such wildlife products is strongly linked to the East Asian market, where these illicit products are highly prized for their perceived medicinal value and social status symbolism. Consequently, the recent upsurge in illicit wildlife trafficking has also been closely linked to increases in consumer purchasing power in China, the primary market.[59]

Illegal killing of wildlife threatens many species already on the brink of extinction. It also poses a direct and severe economic threat to the country and to local communities that are heavily dependent on wildlife-based tourist revenues. Significant efforts have been made to expand Tanzania's tourism sector over the past decade. Between 2005 and 2010, Tanzanian President Jakaya Kikwete pushed to establish tourism as Tanzania's leading economic sector. The highly successful initiative increased tourism revenues from $823.5 million in 2005 to $1.19 billion in 2010.[60] Yet, the recent growth of Tanzania's tourism sector runs the risk of being reversed if the illicit harvesting of wildlife continues. For Kenya, a country with a $5 billion wildlife-based tourism industry, such severe poaching has the potential to significantly harm its economic security. Mozambique is underdeveloped relative to Tanzania's and Kenya's wildlife tourism sectors. However, a recent effort supported by the Mozambican government, nonprofit organizations, and private safari companies has been underway to develop Mozambique's tourism sector. Yet the current rate of wildlife poaching threatens to interrupt the development of this highly profitable sector.

The recent upsurge in illicit wildlife trafficking is another factor threatening to destabilize coastal East Africa's security and development. Wildlife crime networks employ sophisticated technology and organizational techniques to obtain ivory and other wildlife products. While the countries of coastal East Africa recognize the necessity to protect their wildlife for purposes of conservation, as well as economic growth, their customs and the capacity of law enforcement limit the current efforts to halt poaching and wildlife trafficking. Corruption among wildlife rangers is also becoming a serious impediment to combating poaching. Encouraged by soaring compensation that is significantly outpacing wildlife rangers' salaries, corruption is increasingly becoming systematic. At times it creates a sense of powerlessness among those of the Tanzanian population who largely appreciate the value and importance of conserving the animals. In 2012, the top officials at Tanzania's Wildlife Department were fired for taking bribes and even arranging for 116 live animals to be loaded onto a jet bound for Qatar.[61]

While wildlife trafficking has the direct impact of decreasing revenue from the region's wildlife tourism industry, it also compromises the greater development, governance, and security of the region. Kenya, sharing the vast Serengeti with Tanzania, is at a critical point with wildlife crime networks infiltrating its farthest reaches to obtain ivory. The scale of the illegal wildlife trade problem was demonstrated in early 2013 when "a gang of heavily armed poachers entered Tsavo National Park, Kenya, and slaughtered eleven elephants."[62] The government of Kenya recognizes the potential impact of illicit wildlife trafficking and has made substantial strides to combat the issue in recent years. However, the country's limited resources and enforcement capabilities restrict its ability to deter the often highly skilled and organized criminal networks involved in illicit wildlife trafficking. Heavily armed poachers are frequently the most formidable force in the region, undermining or supplanting legitimate government authority. To counter these organized criminal networks, greater collaboration is needed at the transnational level. A similar situation exists in Mozambique, where ports are frequently used as transit stops for large-scale shipments of elephant tusks and rhino horns en route to international markets in Asia. The enormous magnitude of the illicit trafficking rings calls attention to the need for a collaborative effort between the Mozambican government and the international community to combat the problem.

Currently, the value of the illicit wildlife trafficking industry is estimated to be between \$7.8 billion and \$10 billion.[63] As such, it is now the fifth-largest illicit transnational activity worldwide, even outranking small arms trade.[64] According to a report from CITES, the Convention on International Trade in Endangered Species, elephant poaching levels are the worst in a decade and recorded ivory seizures are at their highest levels since 1989. In 2011 alone, 38.8 tons—representing more than 4,000 elephants—of ivory was seized worldwide, the highest year on record for elephant poaching.[65] With the upsurge in Asian demand, the trade has become highly lucrative for criminal organizations and rebel groups who see the illicit trafficking of wildlife as a highly profitable enterprise. In many instances, the criminal groups trafficking wildlife are connected to other illegal trade networks and often use the same techniques and smuggling routes to move drugs and guns. Wildlife trafficking often thrives in places with weak governance and monitoring capacity. Ultimately, because of its often violent nature, wildlife trafficking will hinder further capacity building in the region by eroding the rule of law, undermining confidence in the state, and ultimately deterring investment and obstructing growth.

Through its links with other forms of organized crime, illicit wildlife trafficking also threatens coastal East Africa's transnational security, as many of these groups use the revenue collected from poaching to finance rebel groups and other destabilizing operations. In July 2012, Interpol called attention to the effects of wildlife trafficking and suggested that the organized criminal networks most associated with wildlife trafficking "are responsible for the corruption of officials, fraud, money laundering and violence, causing social unrest and undermining the rule of law and confidence in government institutions."[66] Recently, illicit wildlife trafficking has been even more widely linked to terrorist groups. Two al-Qaeda affiliate terrorist groups—Jama'atul Mujahideen Bangladesh and Harkat-ul-Jihad-al-Islami—have been reported to be raising funds for their operations through illegal poaching of ivory, tiger pelts, and rhino horns.[67] Terrorist networks are not only funding their activities through illicit wildlife trafficking but also generally profiting from the destabilization of the coastal East Africa region. The 1998 embassy bombings in Kenya and Tanzania attest to the concern about terrorist networks capitalizing on weak governance and law enforcement to attack U.S. allies and interests in the region.

Recommendations

The coastal East Africa region is endowed with some of the most biodiverse ecosystems in the world. This natural resource base, if properly protected, could contribute significantly toward the greater economic growth and development of the region. However, if overfishing, deforestation, and illicit wildlife trafficking go unaddressed, they may contribute to destabilization of the region through negative effects on economic growth and development, as well as by impeding improvements to governance and security. As highlighted in this chapter, more often than not the region's environmental issues overwhelm the capacity of local authorities and, too frequently, involve rebel groups and transnational crime rings. If the misuse and degradation of resources is not addressed, it threatens to undermine development efforts and the rule of law in these countries. Economic well-being, social stability, and national security have to be built on a foundation of environmental sustainability.

Over the past decade, increased U.S. involvement in the region not only through extensive development assistance but also through expanding military cooperation and commerce has created a strong basis for cooperation. Increased involvement of these countries in regional platforms and international agreements also offers potential for addressing region-wide natural resource degradation.

Tackling the environmental issues of overfishing, deforestation, and illicit wildlife trafficking will require a collaborative effort at the bilateral and multilateral levels to improve monitoring and data availability, incorporation of natural resource sustainability into development efforts, and enforcement of regulations to control illegal and unsustainable use. The following paragraphs discuss some potentially fruitful ways in which the U.S. government can use foreign policy to address these needs.

Combating Illegal Natural Resource Trade

To ensure that fisheries, forests, and wildlife resources can continue to support the economies of coastal East Africa, it is essential to combat illegal harvesting and trade. Given the complexity of these sectors, and the widespread nature of illegal resource appropriation and trade, it will be useful to draw on the full range of U.S. government agencies, including not only the Department of State and USAID but also the Departments of Justice, Interior, and Defense, with the support of the White House in a whole-of-government effort to address these problems.

First, on-the-ground enforcement should be strengthened. Support for existing monitoring and enforcement programs could greatly facilitate local efforts. In the case of fisheries, FISH-i Africa, a regional initiative to improve monitoring and information sharing to combat fisheries crimes in southeast Africa, includes the three countries discussed in this chapter. Mozambique and Tanzania are also members of the Southern African Development Community, which supports a Monitoring Control and Surveillance Coordination Center to address illegal fishing. Beyond these regional organizations, the United States should support the implementation of relevant international agreements, such as the Port State Measures agreement, which aims to prevent illegally caught fish from entering international markets, and the CITES agreement regulating trade in wildlife.

Given the heavy involvement of sophisticated criminal organizations and rebel groups in the trade of illegal natural resource products, it will be critical to break up these organizations and interrupt the flow of illegal products at major transit points. The United States currently works with the governments of coastal East Africa through the Africa Partnership Station (under U.S. AFRICOM) to monitor and combat illegal fishing, but further action is needed. Augmented international security cooperation agreements and appropriate training and equipment could assist the countries of coastal East Africa in dealing with maritime security issues that both hamper regional development and pose a global security threat.

Finally, much of the illegal trade in wildlife products is driven by East Asian markets. The problem is unlikely to be reduced unless some serious efforts are made to curb demand in destination countries, through both consumer education and law enforcement.

Trade and Investment for Sustainability

As commerce continues to grow between the United States and the countries of East Africa, incentives to U.S. business through the Overseas Private Investment Corporation and the U.S. Export-Import Bank could support investments in sustainable agriculture and food production that would boost food security and limit environmental degradation. The African Growth and Opportunity Act, expected to be renewed in 2015, offers trade preferences to African countries and could provide a regional umbrella for promotion of sustainability through trade. Cooperation in areas such as clean energy and agricultural productivity could help provide a stronger platform for development in these countries.

Sustainable Development

Improving conditions for economic growth and development in the coastal East Africa region will require an improved capacity for governance in each of the countries, particularly in the forestry, fisheries, and wildlife sectors. Capacity building and design of appropriate regulations, monitoring, and enforcement programs can be supported by USAID, the MCC, and the Global Environmental Facility (GEF). For wildlife, strengthening of Wildlife Management Authorities in the region, particularly to reduce corruption and improve monitoring and enforcement, will be essential. While efforts to protect the forests of coastal East Africa have increased, capacity building and support for reforestation and forest management are needed to reverse current trends, and basic data on the region's forests is needed to plan for sustainable forest management. For the fisheries sector, management rules should be established, and enforced, within the countries' EEZs. Principles should be established governing resource access agreements that will prevent overfishing, degradation, and local impoverishment. At the regional level, the Regional Fisheries Management Organizations, such as the Indian Ocean Tuna Commission, can also play a critical role.

While regional and national efforts are important, experience shows that effective resource management for sustainability is often best supported by devolving authority to the local level. Community-based natural resource management organizations for forests, fisheries, and wildlife or tourism are well positioned to ensure sustainable use, particularly when provided with technical support to implement best practices. Regulatory and technical support for the development and empowerment of these local organizations will need to be a key component of sustainable development efforts.

Mainstreaming Natural Resource Management

The U.S. government is already heavily invested in health and development initiatives in coastal East Africa. Despite their successes, these programs have not effectively addressed the problems of resource degradation that threaten long-term stability. Mainstreaming natural resource management along with climate-smart approaches, through appropriate benchmarks for the major U.S. development initiatives, could significantly increase the effectiveness of those investments and reduce threats to resources and stability. Ongoing initiatives for which natural resource management is central include FTF, Power Africa, and the Global Climate Change Initiative, among others.

Strengthening Regional Initiatives

A number of regional organizations in Africa, including the New Partnership for Africa's Development, Common Market for Eastern and Southern Africa, and the African Union, are supporting transformative agendas for agriculture, fisheries, forestry, and poverty. These regional organizations are growing in importance and capacity. The U.S. government could boost their efforts to address region-wide problems, such as the illegal wildlife trade, through greater engagement with these regional cooperation platforms.

Notes

1 Julian Lee, George Ledec, and Claudia Sobrevilla, "Toward Africa's Green Future" (working paper, World Bank, Washington, D.C., 2012), 6.
2 Central Intelligence Agency of the United States (CIA), *The World Factbook,* https://www.cia.gov/library/publications/the-world-factbook/geos/tz.html.
3 Millennium Challenge Corporation (MCC), "Tanzania," www.mcc.gov/pages/countries/overview/tanzania.
4 The United States President's Emergency Plan for AIDS Relief, "Partnership to Fight HIV/AIDS in Tanzania," www.pepfar.gov/countries/tanzania/index.htm.
5 U.S. Department of State, "U.S. Relations with Tanzania," Fact Sheet (Jan. 30, 2014), www.state.gov/r/pa/ei/bgn/2843.htm.
6 Maggie Menzies, "Exercise Participants in Tanzania Practice Disaster Response," United States Africa Command (March 9, 2011), www.africom.mil/NEWSROOM/Article/8064/exercise-participants-in-tanzania-practice-disaste.
7 Joe Keily, "Swift Hosts Environmental Workshop in Tanzania," United States Africa Command (July 3, 2012), www.africom.mil/NEWSROOM/Article/9060/swift-hosts-environmental-workshop-in-tanzania.
8 Juakali Kambale, "Tanzania to Deploy Troops to DRC Soon, Says AU Top Official," *East African* (Jan. 5, 2013), www.theeastafrican.co.ke/news/Tanzania-to-deploy-troops-to-DRC-soon-says-AU-top-official-/-/2558/1658336/-/rc9d49/-/index.html.
9 "East African Security Forces Host Inaugural Special Operations Conference," United States Africa Command (Feb. 11, 2013), www.africom.mil/Newsroom/Article/10311/east-african-security-forces-host-inaugural-specia.
10 Lee et al., "Toward Africa's Green Future," 15.
11 African Development Bank, "Water Supply & Sanitation," www.afdb.org/en/topics-and-sectors/sectors/water-supply-sanitation/projects-activities/activities-in-tanzania/.
12 Deodatus Balile, "African Development Bank Funds Road Infrastructure in Tanzania," *Sabahi* (Nov. 19, 2012), http://sabahionline.com/en_GB/articles/hoa/articles/features/2012/11/19/feature-02.

13 Office of the United States Trade Representative, "Tanzania," www.ustr.gov/countries-regions/africa/east-africa/tanzania.
14 U.S. Agency for International Development (USAID), "Dollars to Results," http://results.usaid.gov/kenya.
15 USAID-Kenya (2013). Accessed July 2013. www.usaid.gov/kenya.
16 USAID-Mozambique (Feb. 2014). Country Development Cooperation Strategy www.usaid.gov/sites/default/files/documents/1860/Mozambique%20CDCS%202014-2018%20FINAL%20PUBLIC%20VERSION.pdf.
17 U.S. Department of Commerce, "Trade in Goods with Tanzania," www.census.gov/foreign-trade/balance/c7830.html.
18 U.S. Department of Commerce, "Trade in Goods with Kenya," www.census.gov/foreign-trade/balance/c7790.html; U.S. Department of Commerce, "Trade in Goods with Mozambique," www.census.gov/foreign-trade/balance/c7870.html.
19 Lauren Ploch, *Africa Command: U.S. Strategic Interests and the Role of the U.S. Military in Africa*, CRS Report 7-5700 (Washington, D.C.: Library of Congress, Congressional Research Service, July 22, 2011), 14.
20 World Wildlife Fund (WWF), "Coastal East Africa," http://worldwildlife.org/places/coastal-east-africa.
21 USAID-Kenya (2011). Country Development Cooperation Strategy.
22 USAID-Tanzania (2012). Country Development Cooperation Strategy.
23 USAID-Mozambique (2012). Country Development Cooperation Strategy.
24 A. Eberhard et al. (2008). "Underpowered: The State of the Power Sector in Sub-Saharan Africa," Africa Infrastructure Country Diagnostic Background Paper, 6.
25 World Bank (2009).
26 USAID-Mozambique (2012).
27 Eberhard (2008).
28 CIA, *The World Factbook* (2013).
29 CIA, *The World Factbook* (2013).
30 World Bank (2013). *World Development Indicators.* Washington: World Bank.
31 Population Reference Bureau (2012). *World Population Data Sheet.* http://www.prb.org/Publications/Datasheets/2012/world-population-data-sheet.aspx.
32 Paul R. Erlich and John P. Holdren (1971). "Impact of Population Growth," *Science* 171 (3977): 1212-1217.
33 WWF, "Coastal East Africa."
34 WWF, "Coastal East Africa."
35 allAfrica, "Tanzania: State Loses Billions in Illegal Fishing," http://allafrica.com/stories/201301300084.html.
36 The Fish Site, "The Paradox of Tanzania's Fishing Industry," www.thefishsite.com/fishnews/17718/the-paradox-of-tanzanias-fishing-industry.
37 The Fish Site, "The Paradox of Tanzania's Fishing Industry."
38 IRIN (Integrated Regional Information Networks), "Mozambique: Commercial Over-fishing Threatens Coastal Livelihoods" (United Nations Office for the Coordination of Humanitarian Affairs, 2008).
39 IRIN, "Mozambique."
40 International Monetary Fund, "Kenya: Poverty Reduction Strategy Paper" (strategy paper, International Monetary Fund, Washington, D.C., 2010), 64.
41 John Vidal, "Will Overfishing by Foreigners Drive Senegalese Fisherman to Piracy?" *Guardian* (April 3, 2012).

42 "Coral Reef Study Traces Indirect Effects of Overfishing," *Science Daily* (Feb. 27, 2012), www.sciencedaily.com/releases/2012/02/120227132835.htm.
43 "Kenya Coral Reefs," LetsGoKenya.com, www.letsgokenya.com/kenya-coral-reefs.
44 Roger Middleton, "Piracy in Somalia: Threatening Global Trade, Feeding Local Wars" (briefing paper, Chatham House, 2008), 1.
45 Middleton, "Piracy in Somalia," 9.
46 Mongabay. Accessed March 30, 2013. http://rainforests.mongabay.com/deforestation/2000/Tanzania.htm.
47 Feed the Future (FTF), "Tanzania FY 2011–2015 Multi-Year Strategy" (U.S. Government Document, approved Feb. 22, 2011), 12, www.feedthefuture.gov/sites/default/files/country/strategies/files/TanzaniaFTFMulti-YearStrategy.pdf.
48 World Food Programme, "United Republic of Tanzania," www.wfp.org/countries/tanzania-united-republic.
49 FTF, "Tanzania FY 2011–2015 Multi-Year Strategy"; International Fund for Agricultural Development, "Enabling Poor Rural People to Overcome Poverty in Kenya" (2012), 1, www.ifad.org/operations/projects/regions/pf/factsheets/kenya.pdf; Public Radio International, "Farmers in Mozambique Trying to Adapt Farming to Climate Change" (Jan. 29, 2012), www.pri.org/stories/science/environment/farmers-in-mozambique-trying-to-adapt-farming-to-climate-change-8173.html.
50 CIA, *The World Factbook* (2013).
51 FTF, "East Africa FY 2011–2015 Multi-Year Strategy" (U.S. Government Document, approved April 8, 2011), 9, www.feedthefuture.gov/sites/default/files/country/strategies/files/EastAfricaFTFMulti-YearStrategy.pdf.
52 FTF, "East Africa FY2010 Implementation Plan" (Feed the Future, U.S. Government, 2010), 8, www.feedthefuture.gov/sites/default/files/country/strategies/files/FTF_2010_Implementation_Plan_East_Africa.pdf.
53 FTF, "Mozambique FY 2011–2015 Multi-Year Strategy" (U.S. Government Document, approved June 30, 2011), 4, www.feedthefuture.gov/sites/default/files/country/strategies/files/Mozambique%20FTF%20Multi-Year%20Strategy_Public_FINAL.pdf.
54 Office of the Director of National Intelligence (ODNI), "ODNI Releases Global Water Security ICA" Press Release (ODNI, U.S. Government, 2012), www.dni.gov/index.php/newsroom/press-releases/96-press-releases-2012/529-odni-releases-global-water-security-ica.
55 UN News Centre, "Cost of Deforestation in Kenya Far Exceeds Gains from Forestry and Logging," United Nations (Nov. 5, 2012), www.un.org/apps/news/story.asp?NewsID=43417#.U7RWw_ldWSo.
56 UN News Centre, "Cost of Deforestation in Kenya."
57 John Burnett, "Poachers Decimate Tanzania's Elephant Herds," NPR (Oct. 25, 2012), www.npr.org/2012/10/25/163563426/poachers-decimate-tanzanias-elephant-herds.
58 Burnett, "Poachers Decimate Tanzania's Elephant Herds."
59 WWF, *Fighting Illicit Wildlife Trafficking* (WWF Report, A Consultation with Governments Conducted by Dalberg, 2012), 13, http://awsassets.panda.org/downloads/wwffightingillicitwildlifetrafficking_lr.pdf.
60 Apolinari Tairo, "Tourism Leads as Tanzania's Key Economic Sector," *eTN Global Travel Industry News* (July 18, 2010), www.eturbonews.com/17316/tourism-leads-tanzania-s-key-economic-sector.
61 Oliver Milman, "Ranger Corruption 'Impeding Global Fight against Poaching,'" *Guardian* (March 27, 2013).

62 WWF, "Killing Elephants Threatens Kenya's Economic Security" (Feb. 26, 2013), http://wwf.panda.org/?207683.

63 United States Senate Committee on Foreign Relations, "Ivory and Insecurity: The Global Implications of Poaching in Africa" (May 24, 2012), 11, www.foreign.senate.gov/imo/media/doc/Tom_Cardamone_Testimony.pdf.

64 United States Senate Committee on Foreign Relations, "Ivory and Insecurity," 11.

65 Jeffrey Gettleman, "Elephants Dying in Epic Frenzy as Ivory Fuels Wars and Profits," *New York Times* (Sep. 3, 2012).

66 WWF, "Killing Elephants," 19.

67 Ann Hollingshead, "Poaching and Its Consequences for Development and Security," Financial Transparency Coalition, Transparency International (Aug. 1, 2012), www.financialtransparency.org/2012/08/01/poaching-and-its-consequences-for-development-and-security/.

6

CONGO'S ENVIRONMENTAL CATCH-22

Theodore Trefon

The Democratic Republic of the Congo (DRC) is a country of contrast and diversity. Dense tropical forest covers roughly half of the territory, and savannah covers the other half. Ecologically and culturally, the lush green mountains in the eastern part of the country are worlds away from the narrow Atlantic coast in the western part and the southern copper belt area. There are also striking imbalances with respect to population density and demographic distribution. The daily lives of rural people are much different from those of the city dwellers of Kinshasa, Lubumbashi, Kisangani, and Goma because of disproportionate access to infrastructure, administration, basic services, and entertainment. Although the traditional versus modern cleavage is becoming increasingly obscure, it still influences how people live in the present and perceive their future. The gap between political, economic, and military elites and ordinary citizens is vast, although their destinies are entwined.

Once named Zaire, Congo is located in the heart of central Africa, and with its 905,355 square miles of land, Congo is the size of the United States east of the Mississippi. Congo borders eight countries—more than any other African nation—and straddles the Equator. Its population is estimated at 70 million inhabitants composed of up to 350 ethnic groups. Ethnicity is a powerful force on the political landscape. The rural-urban population ratio is approximately 65:35, but as with the number of people, no one really knows for sure because the last census dates to 1984. Urban growth in Congo is taking place in the absence of urban planning and has negative social and environmental impacts. Urban populations devastate the forest hinterlands in the inexorable search for housing space, agricultural land, fuelwood, and building materials.

A Country That Fascinates and Disturbs

For most Americans, Congo conjures up images of Joseph Conrad's *Heart of Darkness,* the Ali-Foreman Rumble in the Jungle, a flamboyant dictator in a leopard-skin cap, and more recently, Hillary Clinton's condemnation of rape in the Kivus. U.S.-Congo relations are, however, far deeper and punctuated by a series of events that are part of American culture and history. American Ambassador Henry Shelton Sanford helped King Leopold II appropriate the Congo at the Berlin Conference that partitioned Africa in 1885.[1] Henry Morton Stanley, the Welsh-born American reporter, was King Leopold's agent in the Congo. Mark Twain was a pioneering activist who condemned Congo Free State atrocities in the damning book *King Leopold's Soliloquy.*[2] During World War II, the United States and the Belgian government in exile worked hand in hand in the effort against the Axis alliance. The uranium that was used for the Manhattan Project to make the atomic bombs that devastated Hiroshima and Nagasaki hailed from Shinkolobwe in Congo's mineral-rich Katanga Province. Joseph Désiré Mobutu was a pure American creation, put in place during the heydays of Cold War paranoia.[3] The U.S. government, informed by Ambassador William Swing, was decisively supportive of Joseph Kabila when his father was assassinated in 2001. Swing headed the United Nations peacekeeping mission in Congo after retiring from the U.S. Department of State. Congolese remember him with fondness for his mastery of Lingala and his vintage Cadillac. The rich and famous of America have expressed concern too. Billionaire media tycoon Ted Turner gives money for wildlife protection. Film star Ben Affleck set up the Eastern Congo Initiative and talks about it on Capitol Hill. Cindy McCain, the wife of Republican Senator John McCain, has been an outspoken activist to protect women in the DRC.

The DRC is a country of paradox that fascinates and disturbs. It is a rich country whose people live in poverty. Is the Congo too rich to fail? Is it too big to manage? For some, it is perpetually on the verge of collapse. For others, a long-overdue rendezvous with prosperity is just around the corner. Despite the country's potential to be "the Brazil of Africa," a history of corruption and poor leadership has led to state failure, which has in turn sabotaged good governance of the natural resource sectors. International partners have been actively involved in preparing Congo's economic future since 2001. The World Bank's position—endorsed by other major protagonists, such as the United States, the European Commission, and Belgium—is that stability in post-conflict DRC will largely be contingent on improved management of the country's outstanding renewable and nonrenewable natural resources.[4]

However, a vicious circle is firmly in place. Poor natural resource management handicaps efforts to rebuild the state, and because the state is weak, it cannot regain authority over its natural capital. This vicious circle also contributes to the endurance of the DRC's security vacuum. This situation justifies the catch-22 title of this chapter, which uses a political economy framework to analyze the relations between governance and natural resource management.

The political economy framework is useful here because improved governance will not take place in a poverty-reduction vacuum. Governance and state-building initiatives need to be embedded in improved natural resource management. This may appear as a chicken-and-egg debate because some could argue that governance needs to be improved before private-sector investment and economic development can take place. Others contend that economic growth first will facilitate social awareness, stronger political institutions, and civic responsibility. Without trying to resolve this debate, policy makers should carefully track trends in the agriculture, forestry, mining, hydroelectric, and oil sectors and make policy links between these sectors. For example, it is impossible to have a sound forestry policy without improving agriculture or energy provision. Given Congo's abundant natural resources, all governance-strengthening strategies have to be pegged to these sectors.

Development Indicators and the Informal Economy

According to the United Nations' latest Human Development Report, Congo's Human Development Index ranks 186 of 187 countries surveyed, nearly rock bottom.[5] The World Bank's *Doing Business 2013* report indicates that Congo's score was worse than the year before: 181 of 185.[6] Congo today is one of the worst places in the world to be a woman. Another World Bank report deplores that "critical institutional reforms are lagging, and elements of political culture and general capacity issues create a downside risk for the economy."[7] Other barometers tell tragically similar stories. In the diamond-rich city of Mbuji-Mayi (approximately 2 million inhabitants), the number of people connected to public water plummeted between 2002 and 2012, going from 18,000 to 3,000. Nationwide, less than 9 percent of the people have access to electricity. Food security is another problem. The DRC is unable to meet its citizens' nutritional requirements. Most Congolese are vulnerable to food availability, its affordability, and stability of access. Despite fascinating anecdotes of the legendary Congolese joie de vivre, this is real poverty. The narrowing of the gap between very rich and dirt poor, which is visible in other African countries, does not seem to be taking place in Congo, aside from sparse evidence in the large cities.

Most economic activity in DRC takes place outside the official economy. Informal economic activities (such as charcoal production, bushmeat hunting, and artisanal mining) have negative effects on the environment. These activities are unrecorded and, to varying degrees, illegal or illegitimate because they circumvent administrative controls and taxation. They include small-scale street vending, large-scale trading and manufacturing, cross-border smuggling, and schemes intended to avoid payment of taxes on legal production. Bargaining, embezzling, smuggling, hustling, pilfering, featherbedding, and collusion also characterize the informal economy.[8] These activities enable people to survive but not to develop.

The magnitude of the informal economy far exceeds official recorded economic activity. A convincing indicator of the imbalance between the formal economy and the informal is the national budget, which amounted to less than $8 billion for 2013, a slight increase over the 2012 budget. Eight billion dollars is insignificant given the country's size, resources, and population. This proves how little the central government really controls. Internal revenues (mainly from customs duties and corporate taxation) come to nearly $5 billion. Contributions from international donors are $3 billion. For reasons of comparison, the annual operating budget of Boston University is $1.6 billion.

Contemporary History

The origins of the crisis in Congo's political economy take root in the patrimonial system put in place by King Leopold II. The Congo was his personal property from 1885 until 1908 when it became a Belgian colony. Colonial rule was paternalistic. Congolese were considered as children that needed to be civilized and educated. The trinity of missionary endeavors, commercial enterprise, and an intrusive administration structured the colonial vision.

Independence was poorly planned, and a crisis overlapped with the post colonial transition in Congo. Joseph Mobutu came to power in a coup in 1965 in the wake of this crisis, which included the secession of Katanga. Mobutu proved to be a ruthless dictator who also exploited the Congo as if it were his personal property. Because of Cold War politics, the West supported him unconditionally. Mobutu outlived his strategic usefulness when the Soviet Union disintegrated and was forced to accept democratic transition in the early 1990s. The Mobutu dictatorship coincided with Laurent-Désiré Kabila's capture of power.

One million Tutsis and moderate Hutus were massacred in Rwanda in 1994, and then 1.2 million refugees poured into the Kivus, including 100,000 Interahamwe (Hutu militias from Rwanda and Burundi).[9] Mass movements of refugees and internally displaced persons had significantly negative effects on the environment in terms of food production, energy, water management, sanitation, and waste management. In late 1996, Banyamulenge (members of the Tutsi community indigenous to South Kivu), supported by Rwanda, started a rebellion. This facilitated the creation of the Alliance of Democratic Forces for the Liberation of Congo in 1996. In May 1997, Laurent-Désiré Kabila captured Kinshasa and proclaimed himself the country's new leader. This liberation war was supported by Rwanda and Uganda, but Kabila broke ties with these allies in May 1998 and organized new power networks based on his ethnic group, the Baluba. This led to the formation of the pro-Tutsi Rally for Congolese Democracy. Kabila terminated debt repayment, putting the country off track in terms of its international financial commitments. The circumstances of Laurent-Désiré Kabila's assassination in January 2001 are not clear, but it is likely that Angola was involved because of Kabila's support of National Union for the Total Independence of Angola rebel forces.

Joseph Kabila was appointed president after the assassination of Laurent-Désiré Kabila and was elected president in 2006. Upon assuming the presidency, he broke with his predecessor's economic policies and rapidly sought the support of Belgium, France, the United States, and the Bretton Woods institutions. Many Congolese, especially those in the diaspora, believe that Laurent-Désiré Kabila was not Joseph Kabila's biological father but his stepfather. Opponents and many diaspora Congolese refer to Joseph Kabila as Hyppolite Kanambe. They say he is a native Rwandan with a fake Congolese identity, a former taxi driver in Tanzania, and Paul Kagame's "Trojan Horse." Is this rumor or fact? The truth or falsehood of these beliefs is less important than the perceptions that people have of their "Father of the Nation."

Elections

Holding presidential and legislative elections in 2006 was a major political accomplishment that followed other important peace-building efforts. Kabila scored 58 percent in the 2006 elections, ahead of former warlord Jean-Pierre

Bemba (42 percent).[10] Under the aegis of international partners who invested heavily in legitimizing Joseph Kabila, the security and political context improved slightly. This led the way to a series of ambitious institutional reforms. The new institutional framework is widely believed to be theoretically sound, but implementation remains a major challenge. Voting created false hopes. Electoral promises have not been transformed into concrete results, which helps explain why fewer people registered to vote in the 2011 elections compared with 2006.[11] People expect very little from the state; they expect much more from other social groups, such as the church, women's groups, and the diaspora.

The electoral process that was initiated in 2006 legitimized poor leadership. President Kabila used his first five-year term of elected office to consolidate power. His position as incumbent, plus the money generated by selling off state assets at bargain prices, enabled him to dominate the campaign landscape.[12] Candidate Kabila had disproportionate access to government media, and he used state planes, jeeps, and helicopters while on the campaign trail. The security forces under his control systematically obstructed opposition candidates from campaigning, notably veteran political opposition leader Étienne Tshisekedi.[13]

Presidential and legislative elections took place again in November 2011. They were immediately followed by claims of manipulation, fraud, and human rights violations. Congolese and international observers found proof of numerous irregularities in the electoral process. The country remains divided between those who believe Kabila's reelection to be legitimate and those who do not. Tshisekedi refuted the results, proclaiming that he was "the people's choice." Officially, Kabila won with 49 percent of the votes. Nevertheless, the truth will never be known because the ballots and reports on the results were lost or destroyed. Chaos in the electoral process led to a loss of local and international credibility and significant social frustration. President Kabila consequently remains in a position of marginalization and vulnerability. A year after the elections, the government had made minor progress in addressing some macroeconomic priorities but had failed to bring peace to the country or improve social conditions for ordinary people.

Political Culture and Identity

State crisis is anchored in a shattered social, political, and cultural landscape. Cultural factors determine where individuals fit in the complex web of social networks and hierarchies. Cultural factors also have direct and indirect impacts on how political systems evolve. The cultural context helps account for poor governance and lethargic human development. Culture is not necessarily the dominant explanation, but it is a factor that contributes to the challenges inherent in inducing political and institutional change. Although the cultural environment is always evolving, there are some historically embedded patterns. Some are positive, such as the fabulous sense of Congolese agency and creativity and the multiple ramifications of solidarity networks. Others are clearly negative and detrimental to democratic governance, including the absence of transparency, extreme secrecy, disinformation, and propaganda.

The DRC is a diverse society but one with a strong sense of national identity. It is multiethnic, multilingual, and multidenominational. About 80 percent of Congolese are Christian, half of whom are Roman Catholic. From an anthropological perspective, Congo is the thing and its opposite. The sentiment of being Congolese is vibrant, although people complain about government and leadership. Mobutu's "authenticity" discourses and wars of aggression contributed to the emergence of a Congolese sense of belonging. Music, sports, fashion, and religion contribute to the consolidation of a transethnic national conscience. This emotion has been translated into words by a French political geographer: "The map of Congo is stamped in peoples' minds."[14]

Territory

State crisis and the problems related to Congo's large, diverse, and fragmented territory are intimately interconnected. Improved land-use planning, territorial integration, and state building are interdependent preconditions for development. The rehabilitation of the country's woefully dilapidated infrastructure is a major priority. Although the concept of statehood is necessarily contingent on people who adhere to the sentiment of belonging, it is equally dependent on a coherent, unifying transportation network that provides mobility for traders, civil servants, political authorities, security forces, and ordinary people. This, however, is wishful thinking for the time being. Dugout canoes and bicycles are the principal means of transportation in much of rural Congo in the twenty-first century.

Without a unifying road-rail-river network, there can be no state building, development, or security. Without transportation, there can be no public administration and no sentiment of national unity. But ecological constraints bedevil infrastructure rehabilitation and development. Dense, humid forest and swampland cover the vast central basin, limiting the movement of goods and people. This sparsely populated equatorial enclave of approximately 1 million square kilometers, inhabited by slash-and-burn farmers and indigenous peoples, deprives the country of a geographic and political centrality. The forest underbelly separates the country more than it unites it, explaining the emergence of extraverted dynamics. The eastern provinces, for example, are more connected to Rwanda, Burundi, Tanzania, and Uganda than they are to other areas of the DRC. At the complete opposite end of the territory, Kinshasa and the Atlantic coast are distant concepts.

Congo's international partners have been involved in the transportation challenge for years, supporting numerous projects and programs. The European Commission's *Programme d'appui à la rehabilitation*, the World Bank and United Kingdom's Pro-Routes Project, and China's roads-for-minerals barter deal are some examples. Despite these initiatives, which are handicapped by corruption, inefficiency, and mismanagement, funding remains insufficient. The amounts required to rehabilitate and develop road infrastructure alone (exclusive of rail and port infrastructure) would absorb more than half the national budget. "To rebuild the country . . . the DRC needs to spend \$5.3 billion a year over the next decade. . . . Of this total, as much as \$1.1 billion a year needs to be devoted to maintenance alone."[15]

Decentralization is another important element in the complicated mosaic of land-use planning and natural resource management. Although the 2005 constitution called for a territorial reorganization from 11 to 26 provinces, the process is on hold. Decentralization is a complicated political process that requires the commitment and involvement of the central government and the provincial authorities. It cannot take place in a democratic vacuum. Congo does not have the means or the political will to decentralize. From the Kinshasa perspective, decentralization is antithetical to President Kabila's efforts to consolidate power. At the provincial level, administrative staff, infrastructure, and material resources are insufficient to deal with the responsibilities of decentralization. In addition to these political and institutional challenges, resolving the financial technicalities of decentralization has proven particularly difficult for the Congolese government. Discussions are at a stalemate over tax collection and revenue distribution.

Natural Resources: Assets, Management, and Predation

Congo is a land of plenty with the resources the world craves. These include mineral and forest resources, agricultural land, oil, and hydroelectric potential. Congolese authorities, with the support of international partners, have been trying to reform the management of these sectors for the past decade, subscribing to the discourse that "environmental management should become an instrument in the post-war recovery toolbox."[16] But the results have been poor. Conflicts over resources, corruption, and mismanagement persist. Patrimonialism is the term most often used to account for this situation. Patrimonialism refers to the way individuals and groups—national and foreign—appropriate resources for private interests to the detriment of the common good.

Forests of Wealth and Mystery

The Congo Basin is home to the world's second-largest contiguous tropical rainforest after the Amazon. Sustainable management of Congo's outstanding forest biodiversity is consequently a priority for local populations and a challenge for the international community. Congo matters to the United States because of Congo's tropical forests, which are vital in the fight against global climate change. Forest conservation can also help alleviate poverty, contribute to macroeconomic development, and protect biodiversity. Congo's forests could well be home to the plants, roots, or barks, yet to be discovered, that will save lives through new medicines. These forests are geostrategic because they affect relations with Congo's neighbors and regional partners. Congolese authorities could gain considerable international recognition by appropriating the fight to save their forests, just as the authorities stand to lose credibility by not doing enough. The U.S. government has devoted funding and diplomacy to the struggle to save the forests of the Congo Basin. This work should be pursued, but it needs to be governed by the principle that improved forest management is more of a political, social, and cultural problem than a technical challenge.

Congo has been described as a "geological scandal" because of its amazing mineral wealth. It is unequivocally a "biodiversity scandal" too. Its complex patchwork of ecosystems, based on an intricate balance between forest and water, is home to 47 percent of Africa's dense, humid tropical forest. Congo has 1.3 million hectares of dense tropical forests, mangroves, and savannahs. Snow caps the Rwenzori Mountains in eastern Congo. These forest mosaics are full of life, wealth, and mystery. Congo has 1,000 types of birds, 500 types of mammals, 100 types of primates, and endemic species such as the "make love not peace" bonobo and the elegant okapi, which resembles a cross between a zebra and a giraffe.

The country's rural populations depend on forests for food, traditional medicines, building materials, and fuelwood. Forests are culturally important for initiation rituals, ancestor worship, and burial. Approximately 35 million Congolese depend on these resources for their daily needs. Nevertheless, they do not always engage in environmentally sustainable practices. Forests, rivers, and even national parks are exploited as sources of quickly earned cash.

Deforestation rates in Congo are relatively low for the time being, at around 0.3 percent nationally, although with high regional variability.[17] The deforestation rates are constant with a strong cumulative effect. Agriculture is the primary driver of deforestation; urbanization and charcoal production are lesser causes. American, European, and international institutions recognize the significance of the Congo Basin forest in the struggle to deal with global climate change. The U.S. Central African Regional Program for the Environment is a major player. Congo is a key regional actor, strongly committed to the Congo Basin Forest Partnership (CBFP). The CBFP is a voluntary multistakeholder initiative contributing to the implementation of an intergovernmental plan that brings together the 10 member states of the Central African Forests Commission (COMIFAC), donors, international organizations, nongovernmental organizations (NGOs), scientific institutions, and representatives from the private sector. The CBFP works in close relationship with COMIFAC, the regional body in charge of forests and environmental policy, with the objective to promote conservation and sustainable management of the Congo Basin's forest ecosystems. The government has ceded part of its sovereignty over forest management. Funding, program design, and important decisions emanate more from international experts than from Congolese authorities.

The World Bank took an active role in the preparation of a new forestry code in 2002, believing the forestry sector could help kick-start the economy. The code lays the foundation for sustainable, socially and environmentally responsible management. Today, however, industrial logging provides less than 1 percent of official state revenues, so there is tremendous potential for growth in the sector. Although there are about 60 companies registered with the Department of Forest Resources in the Environment Ministry, only around 20 are operational. This discrepancy can be accounted for by the numerous macroeconomic constraints on the sector. Freight and transport costs are exorbitant because of poor road, port, and rail infrastructure. Operating costs are high, and insecurity is a disincentive to investors that makes economies of scale unattainable. The tax system is arbitrary and unpredictable, and loggers complain that they have to replace the state with respect to provision of social services and development of infrastructure. As in other sectors, investment security is a constant worry.

Worldwide, and Congo is no exception, a large percentage of timber harvesting for both local use and commercial export is carried out by illegal loggers. This is a serious environmental and security threat. "Illegal logging is linked to armed conflicts and exploitation and can indirectly contribute to the occurrence of other crimes such as trade in endangered species, corruption, money laundering and organised crime."[18] As a response to this growing problem, President George W. Bush signed the President's Initiative Against Illegal Logging.[19] The European Commission set up Forest Law Enforcement, Governance, and Trade. These initiatives provide a number of measures to exclude illegal timber from U.S. and European markets, improve the supply of legal timber, and increase the demand for sustainably harvested wood products. They work with other control mechanisms, such as the Forest Stewardship Council. These initiatives are laudable, but they are threatened by other large importers, such as China, that are neither inclined nor bound to respect the principles of these initiatives.

Congo cannot boast of many real, post-conflict, state-building success stories. Nature conservation, however, is an emerging exception. International environmental NGOs, such as the World Wildlife Fund, Conservation International, the World Conservation Society, the Bonobo Conservation Initiative, and the Dian Fossey Gorilla Fund International, in close partnership with the Congolese Institute for Nature Conservation, are actively involved in developing and maintaining a network of protected areas. Their achievements in terms of conservation, stakeholder partnerships, generation of funding, and promotion of the forest heritage of the DRC are significant. The Congolese government has pledged to allocate up to 15 percent of national territory as protected areas. As peace and security come to Congo, so will ecotourism, another potential growth sector. Popular awareness of the value of the forest is a positive trend. The way Kinshasa's residents decry trucks carrying timber through the city for export is an indicator. They know that it takes just one hour for a man with a chainsaw to cut down a tree that grew for 300 years.

Payment for environmental services, sometimes called payment for ecosystem services, is one of Congo's potentially most profitable growth sectors. The complicated name denotes a rather simple concept. If the international community wants countries such as Congo, Brazil, Bolivia, and Indonesia to save their forests, then the international community will have to pay. Global climate change results from many factors, including deforestation. Experts say deforestation contributes to around 20 percent of all global climate change.[20] Congo has the forest resources the world needs to mitigate global warming; therefore, high-level international bodies, such as the Intergovernmental Panel on Climate Change, are actively involved in securing compensation funding. In 2008, the United Kingdom and Norwegian governments put up £100 million for the newly created Congo Basin Forest Fund. The Programme Policy Board of the United Nations Collaborative Programme on Reducing Emissions from Deforestation and Forest Degradation in Developing Countries (UN-REDD), for example, approved US$4.7 million for the DRC in March 2010. If Congo agrees to transform logging concessions (which contribute to state revenues in the form of logging surface taxes and taxes on the amount of timber exported to the world market) into conservation concessions, there is going to be a cost. The strategy is that Congo's international partners would help assume the costs of forest conservation.

UN-REDD is one of the compensation mechanisms being tested in the DRC today. Congo was the first country in the Congo Basin to benefit from UN-REDD financing through the World Bank's Forest Carbon Partnership Facility. Concretely, pilot studies and projects are underway to diminish the drivers of deforestation and forest degradation by compensating the stakeholders that rely on forests for their livelihoods. Some of these pilot studies, which are defined in Congo's "REDD Readiness Plan," focus on improved agricultural strategies, design and distribution of improved cooking stoves, plantation forests, and land-use planning.

Blue Gold

The DRC has a vast network of rivers and lakes that provide sustenance, transportation, and irrigation for farmland. Congo's rivers and forests are vital regulators of rainfall cycles that in turn influence climate patterns. Half of Africa's water resources are in the DRC. Images of the majestic Congo River, which is 2,900 miles long, immediately come to mind. This is the mighty power source for the Inga Dam complex, which has more potential than China's Three Gorges Dam.[21] The Inga Dam complex could light up all of Africa. But Inga is hobbled. The two existing dams operate at low output because of lack of maintenance (a political and economic choice) and heavy silting (an ecological problem). Donors and investors (including Westinghouse and General Electric) have plans to develop the site, but as for many other national priorities in Congo, "discussions are ongoing." Without the commitment of high-energy-consumption industries, the prospects of moving ahead are remote.[22] The production capacity of Inga and dams on other rivers is woefully behind demand. Only nine percent of Congolese have access to electricity. This is a direct cause of deforestation, especially around Congo's rapidly expanding urban areas, which are another environmental threat. Because people have no electricity for cooking, they rely on charcoal. Without electricity, there is no refrigeration, which is another challenge for food availability in tropical climates.

Agriculture and Food Security

Congo is endowed with abundant arable land. There is plenty of rain and sunshine. The country's agricultural potential is significant, but people are hungry. The average Congolese's dietary energy supply is approximately 1,600 kilocalories per day,[23] which is far below the 2,500 kilocalories per day recommended by the Food and Agriculture Organization of the United Nations. About 40 percent of children are malnourished, and 20 percent of children suffer from severely retarded growth. Cassava, plantains, corn, rice, beans, and groundnuts are Congo's principal crops. Food production is carried out mainly by small-scale farmers engaged in slash-and-burn subsistence agriculture, which explains why agriculture is the main driver of deforestation. As use of inputs such as fertilizers and improved seeds is rare and fertility is low over much of the territory, productivity is poor. Intercropping of several food crops is supplemented by fruit growing and small-animal production. Many international NGOs and government agencies are involved in helping rural populations intensify their farming techniques and marketing strategies.

Commercial agriculture and the livestock sector collapsed in the 1970s following a series of nationalizations. Congo was a major exporter of industrial palm oil during the colonial period, for example, but palm oil production today has become an artisanal activity. Subsistence food production declined in the 1990s to below population growth levels because of war, population displacement, migration into the small-scale informal mining sector, and transportation problems. The gap between population growth (around three percent annually) and growth in food production (around two percent annually) led to an increase in imports and ongoing food insecurity for most households. Urban and peri-urban gardening plays a vital role for survival of the urban poor, but poor waste management is a source of vegetable contamination. The government passed a new agricultural code in 2011 aimed at modernizing the sector. At the same time, however, the Ministry of Finance reduced import taxes on imported foodstuffs.[24] This type of incoherence reveals the government's lack of development vision. Nonetheless, the agricultural code was also motivated to avoid the potential threats of land grabbing. This is not a major problem in the DRC today, but given emerging pressure for palm oil plantations and biofuel production, it is an important trend to monitor. China's Zhongxing Telecommunication Equipment and India's Siva Group have secured purchases of agricultural land and have plans to exploit it for palm oil.[25]

Mineral Resources and Mining

Mining in Congo is a multifaceted activity that has ramifications for the macro-financial situation of the country, social issues, security concerns, and the environment. Congo is the world's largest producer of cobalt ore and a major producer of copper and industrial diamonds. The country has cadmium, cassiterite, gold, silver, tantalum, tin, zinc, and uranium. These are some of the country's 1,100 mineral substances.[26] Metals such as coltan—which is used in cell phones, laptop computers, and iPads—are mined illegally in the eastern provinces and continue to fund conflict. Congo's subsoil is inextricably linked to the "global greed for gadgets."[27]

Numerous paradoxes typify the mineral sector. One striking example is that vast underground reserves are underexploited because of insufficient investment in infrastructure and extraction. Popular voice translates this into a commonly heard expression: "Our bed should be of gold and diamonds, but we are just sleeping on straw mats." Another tragic inconsistency is that mineral wealth benefits a small cluster of political and military elites but hardly contributes to national development. Mining is carried out by formal industrial actors and artisanal, small-scale, informal diggers working with sifters, picks, and shovels. Between 1.8 million and two million people who earn around a dollar a day are involved in informal mining. Given the nature of family structures, this means that up to 12 million people depend on artisanal digging.[28]

The United Nations Environment Programme identified landscape degradation, water and air pollution, and radioactive contamination as environmental problems emerging from large-scale industrial mining. Mercury contamination (mercury is used in gold mining), human health hazards, forest and biodiversity degradation, and human rights abuses (such as child labor) are some of the negative consequences of small-scale mining.[29] Prostitution is another common social problem in the small-scale mining business. The DRC simply does not have the means to carry out adequate social and environmental impact assessments, especially in the informal mining sector.

There is a direct link between state crisis in Congo and the collapse of Gécamines (the major state-owned mining company). During the colonial period and into the early 1980s, Gécamines (along with its sister mining companies such as Miba, Sominki, and Okimo) produced a significant percentage of Congo's wealth. Katangese used to refer to Gécamines as their mother and father. In addition to work and salaries, it provided them with housing, health care, education, and food from company stores. Its collapse in the late 1980s turned the Katangese into orphans. At the end of the Mobutu dictatorship, artisanal mining, mainly for diamonds, replaced the revenues earned from copper and cobalt whose extraction, processing, transportation, and commercialization required a functioning state apparatus and industrial support system. Artisanal mining is more conducive to the kind of patrimonial control desired by the mafia-type networks that thrive in Congo. These networks control access to mining sites, the workforce, production, and commercialization.[30]

Laurent-Désiré Kabila needed to constitute a war chest as he marched to power in 1997. He did so by signing dubious mining contracts with foreign investors, some more or less respectable, others clearly rogue. Zimbabwean investors were well represented in the new deals. For example, Billy Rautenbach, a white Zimbabwean businessman with close ties to President Mugabe, was appointed boss of Gécamines in November 1998. Ten years ago, a Belgian expert commented that the mining sector, which was once completely dominated by the monolithic colonial state system, became highly globalized during the Laurent-Désiré Kabila presidency.[31] Since he made this observation, the sector has globalized increasingly rapidly as international partners from multiple countries have become involved.

The lack of transparency in the concession award process, in addition to the disproportional benefits attributed to investors compared with the Congolese state and Congolese workers, inspired the World Bank to help design Congo's new mining law, just as it did for forestry. The undertaking was politically sensitive because mining is a high-stakes business controlled by politically well-connected clans that operate according to their own nontransparent rules. The mining code, signed into law in 2002, aimed at improving governance and thus increasing stimulus for international investment. It was accompanied by the drafting of a series of bylaws and the setting up of some specialized committees and departments within the Ministry of Mining.[32] Environmental protection is one of its clearly stated objectives.[33] The code mirrors World Bank policy, which is based on the idea that economic growth can be achieved by attracting and facilitating foreign investors. The strategy met with only limited success because by 2008 the mining sector had generated only $92 million.[34]

Another initiative to improve mining governance was the mining review that was launched in 2007. It was motivated by the need to clarify the concessions signed by Laurent-Désiré Kabila. Sixty-one mining licenses were reviewed, 43 contracts were approved, and 17 contracts were rejected in 2009. China, Lundin, First Quantum Minerals, and Katanga Mining Ltd. were major players. Freeport McMoRan invested approximately $700 million, but its contract was canceled because of what was considered to be excessive benefits (a compensation deal was eventually struck). This is clearly not the kind of message Congo should be sending to multinationals who claim to respect the principles of due diligence. Israeli businessman Dan Gertler is a big player and close Kabila ally. Chinese, North Korean, Pakistani, Indian, and Lebanese traders are involved in uranium trading of ore exploited by artisanal diggers (whose urine samples reveal high concentrations of uranium). There have been reports that Lebanese

Hezbollah groups are associated with uranium exports to Iran. The U.S. Department of the Treasury has sanctioned a Lebanese businessman active in Congo who is allegedly a Hezbollah financier.[35]

Well-respected international NGOs—such as Global Witness, Enough, and the Eastern Congo Initiative—have lobbied strongly to make the government and the general public aware of the link between conflict minerals and violence in the Kivus. The United States signed into law the Dodd-Frank Act, which requires American companies to prove that the minerals they are buying from various supply chains are not fueling violence and bloodshed in Congo. Advocates say Dodd-Frank will help end violence in the region by depriving militia of the profits they earn from conflict minerals. Skeptics criticize the act, claiming it will drive out investors, which will threaten the livelihoods of miners and their families. This makes up-to-date information and monitoring of the actors involved in artisanal mining, trade, commodity chains, transport, and protection a prerequisite for meaningful policy design for the Kivus.[36] Like many other reform initiatives in Congo, setting up normative frameworks is one thing, but implementation and enforcement are another.[37]

A serious concern for the U.S. government relates to access to mineral substances and the problem of "disruptive fluctuations."[38] This is probably a relatively minor risk in Congo, however, because throughout the country's troubled past, the supply of minerals has not been significantly disrupted. Corruption and political influences in the mining sector can lead to illegitimate nationalization (Mobutu nationalized the copper and cobalt giant in the 1960s) and contract manipulation (Canada's First Quantum saw a major mining contract nullified in 2009). In some cases, artisanal diggers have replaced industrial extraction, testifying to the resiliency of markets and producers. Fifteen years ago, most experts thought that Congo's large-scale copper industry would never recover. Chinese investment rapidly changed that false impression. These examples tend to reveal the shifting redistribution of profits more than strategies to disrupt markets.

Although Congo does indeed have strategic minerals, these substances can be found elsewhere. Production of coltan in Congo appears to be far less than often indicated. Some media sources and NGOs refer to 70 percent of world reserves, but credible geological sources place it at between 15 percent and 20 percent. A far greater danger is Congo's minerals—such as uranium—getting into the wrong hands, such as Iran or the Lebanese Hezbollah. The United States and regulatory agencies such as the International Atomic Energy Agency appear unable to control the mafia-type trade networks involved in extracting uranium from cobalt ore.

Black Gold

Congo has oil too. Oil is the number one tax earner for the state and the third most important export earner after cobalt and copper but ahead of diamonds.[39] Oil production was 8.6 million barrels in 2010.[40] The French company Perenco is currently the DRC's only oil producer and operates in Bas-Congo near Muanda and off the Atlantic coast. Other companies have been awarded oil blocks but are not pumping. Shady deals have been reported about obscure British Virgin Islands companies Caprikat Ltd. and Foxwhelp Ltd. being awarded blocks in 2010 by presidential decree.[41]

In addition to the oil fields in Bas-Congo and offshore, there are known reserves in the east along the border with Uganda and around Lake Tanganyika. There is speculation that the central basin may also have important reserves (Texaco and Exxon were already exploring the central basin in the 1970s), but exploration has been inconclusive. As the United States pursues its policy of reducing imports from the Middle East, favoring African sources, Congo's central basin could prove profitable.

Can oil help Congo develop? There is potential for new sources of revenues for the government, and there is the possibility of using oil to improve electricity availability, which would have the positive spin-off of reducing deforestation. However, experts tend to think that oil will not help.[42] The challenges and disadvantages outweigh the benefits. The country does not have an official oil policy or a regulatory framework.[43] The governance deficit described for the other natural resource sectors applies here too. There are absolutely no safeguards or mediating strategies to ensure that new revenues would benefit ordinary people.

At the geopolitical level, oil politics could embitter the already difficult relations Congo has with Uganda and Angola. Because Congolese politics is based in part on the economic weight of the provinces (notably that of Katanga and Bas-Congo), new oil revenues could disrupt the balance of power between provinces and political clans. Oil reserves in the east overlap with the conflict-torn Kivus. Conflict oil could well become the new conflict mineral with all of the accompanying social and environmental problems. On the environmental front, oil would certainly be a calamity. The government's handling of oil exploration rights in the emblematic Virunga National Park has been very poor, and the government seems to be ready to sacrifice rare mountain gorillas for oil money.

Obstacles to Natural Resource Management

Poor governance is the main obstacle to natural resource management in Congo. State institutions are unable to take sovereign control over resources and territory. Elites—in the spirit of patrimonial politics—are disinclined to govern resources democratically because they derive benefits from the status quo of cleverly designed disorder. This explains why no realistic environmental master plan exists. Predation by neighbors exacerbates these challenges.

Fragile Administrations

The weakness of public administrations is part of the environmental catch-22.[44] Natural resource management requires managers. But Congo does not have a qualified, dynamic, honest, hard-working cadre of civil servants who are decently paid, respected by service users, and motivated to take charge of the natural resource sectors for sustainable development. The Congolese public administration is ambiguous and arbitrary. Administrative procedures are conditioned by the mood, availability, and personal expectations and needs of civil servants who thrive on the ambiguity of their work environment. Depending on the context, they may adopt a formal discourse (strictly adhering to rules and regulations) just as they may opt for an informal approach (inventing or "interpreting" rules). This is not surprising considering that mid-level civil servants earn salaries of less than $100 a month. From a strictly formal perspective, the administration is based on legal instruments that define state-society relations and specify rights and responsibilities. In practice, "negotiation" is the word that best characterizes transactions between service users and service providers.

Bribery and deal making are commonplace in public and private business transactions despite legislation. Corruption and predation go hand in hand and represent one of the commonalities in Congolese history from Leopold II to Joseph Kabila. Underpaid primary school teachers force their pupils to buy snacks from their wives according to the same logic that Kabila's close advisors levy heavy commissions before signing major commercial deals with foreign partners for mining concessions, oil exploration rights, or arms sales. Honor is important on the social and cultural landscape, but many Congolese say honor is not enough to feed the family. This helps explain corrupt practices at all levels of society and government.

Parliament has likewise proven ineffective in contributing to improved natural resource management. In a strong presidential system such as that of Congo, where power is controlled by the top, Members of Parliament (MPs) do not have much weight in influencing policy. The executive branch of government is still vulnerable and is in the phase of consolidating power; therefore, it is not strong enough to share power with other agencies such as the judiciary, the Parliament, and civil society. Parliament is not a meaningful political force because the president has curtailed its powers. Although the Parliament is awarded operating funds from the national budget and money for investigations is theoretically available, accessing it requires political approval. When the Parliament has tried to carry out oversight activities, it has met strong political resistance, including physically intimidating MPs and withholding of their salaries.[45] The large majority of the MPs elected in 2011 are not experienced in the business of parliamentary procedures. They lack professionalism and staff and can barely provide for their own operational needs. There is also a serious deficit in communication between the Parliament and the general public. The fact that the official Internet site of the DRC Parliament is dead is a telling indicator of this communication problem. This situation of parliamentary powerlessness is a handicap to sustainable environmental management.

Environmental Civil Society

Environmental civil society is slowly developing in Congo. A few environmental NGOs exist and carry out important awareness, watchdog, and conservation work.[46] A good example of this type of work is the pressure that NGOs have put on foreign oil companies that are exploring for oil in the Virunga National Park.[47] But civil society in Congo, in general, and environmental civil society, in particular, remain fragile and powerless. Civil society does not have the necessary popular support, financial means, or professionalism to play the role of a vibrant political force that is able to combat vested interests that operate to the detriment of the environment. There are no outstanding Congolese environmental civil society champions.

Congolese civil society is still largely dominated by the government because, first, there is strong pressure from the government and, second, there is considerable overlap between government elites who double as civil society activists. Congo remains one of those countries with "governmental nongovernmental organizations." Another problem is the relative artificialness of Congolese civil society. It is boosted financially, conceptually, and ideologically by international NGOs. This support makes it difficult to establish how embedded the NGOs really are in local communities and how these communities appropriate their message and work.

Sovereignty and Dependency

The role of international support for Congolese environmental management needs to be applauded and encouraged. Post-conflict countries rarely have the means or political will to prioritize the natural resource sectors given other pressing priorities. In Congo's case, foreign advice (ranging from large institutions, such as the World Bank, to a small Belgian NGO) has been crucial in creating links between poverty reduction, macroeconomic development, and good governance, on the one hand, and natural resource management, on the other hand.

The reverse side, however, is that international partners undermine appropriation and state building by acting on behalf of or replacing the state. This perpetuates dependency and exonerates the relevant Congolese technical, administrative, and political authorities from their responsibilities. Congolese sovereignty is consequently weakened. To whom do these resources belong? Local communities, provincial governments, the national government, and Congo's regional neighbors, as well as public and private international partners, all have competing stakes over the resources. The environmental risk here relates to the paradox whereby Congo has tremendous resources but lacks the capacity to manage them. Capacity-building initiatives exist but are insufficient.

Land-Use Planning

Congo suffers from a conceptual deficit with respect to land-use planning. There is no national map that clearly attributes activities to space. The most flagrant confusion is the overlap of mining and logging concessions with protected areas. Congo has a land law and an environment law, but these legal instruments are too theoretical and too new to produce improved management. There is an absence of strategic links because it is impossible to design a viable agriculture policy without considering forestry priorities or conservation issues. Forestry and energy policies are intimately related. Mining and food production are largely incompatible. Although an inter-sector approach is necessary, striking a balance between stakeholders, vested interests, and policy makers remains an overwhelming challenge.

Part of the problem relates to the juxtaposition of two contradictory land tenure frameworks.[48] According to the government, land belongs to the state. The 1966 Bakajika land law enabled the state to claim ownership of land and award agricultural, forest, and mining concessions. The other logic is the one maintained by the people, particularly rural communities. They consider themselves to be the real landowners based on ancestral rights. The people perceive themselves as the guardians of the land and its resources, guaranteeing the continuity between their ancestors and future generations. The potential for conflict throughout the country results from this hybrid system, which is also a disincentive for investors. The ambiguity that surrounds procedures exacerbates this situation. Because there is no clearly defined set of rules, whoever has the slightest form of power or authority exploits it to maximize gain or personal advantage.

The Resource Curse

The obstacles to natural resource management described above clearly fall into the poor governance category. But Congo is also a victim. It is victim to the predation of its neighbors and suffers from what is known as the resource curse. This refers to the paradox that countries with an abundance of natural resources tend to have less economic growth and worse development outcomes than countries with fewer natural resources. Although scarcity of natural resources can breed conflict, in Congo abundant resources have led to and perpetuate conflict and contribute to underdevelopment.

Congo's geostrategic position in the heart of central Africa is more of a liability than an asset. Its adherence to regional groupings has not paid diplomatic or peace dividends.[49] The country's relations with most of its immediate neighbors are poor. This handicaps Congo's development, jeopardizes its security, and undermines environmental management. The pillaging of Congo's natural resources is a reality documented by a United Nations group of experts.[50] Disputes over oil revenues and offshore oil exploitation blocks continue to embitter relations between Kinshasa and Angola and between Kinshasa and Uganda. There were also disputes over diamond fields in the south in Congo's Bandundu Province and Lunda Norte in Angola. On the eastern front, things could not be worse. Rwanda, the "mosquito," unabashedly plunders the "elephant's" gold, diamonds, coltan, and other minerals. Paul Kagame's support of rebel groups in the Kivus is a well-known secret. Congolese timber and minerals are illegally exported to Uganda. Credible sources reveal that Ugandan President Museveni armed rival ethnic groups in the northeast Congo. His strategy was deliberately to perpetuate a situation of conflict to facilitate the illegal export of Congo's natural wealth.[51] The South Sudanese military has joined Uganda in slaughtering elephants in Congo's Garamba National Park and exporting ivory mainly to China.[52]

Congo Matters

Although they have crippling social and economic implications for the Congolese people, patrimonialism, predation, and poor natural resource management have relatively limited effect on vital American interests. This conclusion does not aim to make strategic or operational recommendations. However, it does seek to draw attention to certain crucial policy considerations. American policy makers should be sensitive, most notably to the diplomatic and security aspects of U.S. foreign policy. Congo may be rock bottom today, but this nation will emerge. Therefore, there is an urgent need for policy makers to monitor closely the nature of change and opportunities.

Crisis in the Great Lakes region is an ongoing social tragedy that is unacceptable in the twenty-first century. Crisis in Congo should be seen as a diplomatic embarrassment to Washington, the self-proclaimed champion of human rights and rule of law. U.S. Secretaries of State Madeleine Albright and then Hillary Clinton have articulated forceful critiques of the human rights conditions in eastern Congo and notably the horrible trauma experienced by women, in part because rape is a deliberately orchestrated political strategy. In the second half of 2012, U.S. Assistant Secretary of State for African Affairs Johnnie Carson shuttled back and forth between Washington and the Great Lakes region, attempting to mediate between Kinshasa, Kigala, and the M23 rebellion. He was also outspoken in his criticism of the DRC government's inability to deal with the root causes of the rebellion.

There has also been U.S. military involvement in the region. The United States participated in the reform of the DRC security sector by training a light infantry battalion through the Special Operations Command component of the U.S. Africa Command. U.S. military personnel and contractors hired by the

U.S. Department of State implemented the training. The Kinshasa government sent this battalion to Goma to fight the M23 rebels, but it proved ineffective. The United States sent special forces to root out Kony and fight the Lord's Resistance Army, but again with little to show in terms of results.

Trade diplomacy does not count much in U.S.-DRC relations. Oil is the main U.S. import from the DRC, and pharmaceuticals and poultry are the top-ranking American exports. India and China are rapidly replacing Europe and the United States as Congo's key trade partners. Already a very minor trading partner for the United States, Congo lost trade advantages in 2010 because President Barack Obama stripped the DRC of its status as a beneficiary of the African Growth and Opportunity Act.

American aid delivery systems to the DRC, like those of other like-minded partners, are also poor. The assessment of a former deputy administrator of the U.S. Agency for International Development is damning: "We are pretty sure the $1.6 billion in aid the United States has provided Democratic Republic of Congo since 1960 has failed to produce lasting positive development results, mainly because of the political context of corruption, incapacity, and conflict."[53]

These very poor results testify to the challenges facing the DRC and its partners. The poor results are also related to some weaknesses in U.S. capabilities. Most importantly, the United States has little capacity to influence the direction of Congolese affairs. The globalized Congo of today is not the bipolar Zaire of Mobutu Sese Seko. Because Congo has the natural resources the world needs, Congolese authorities do not have to acquiesce to Western opinions about good governance. The engagement of newer partners with no-strings-attached business agendas, such as China, South Africa, Brazil, and South Korea, further diminishes Western leverage over Kabila and his entourage. The kinds of diplomatic pressures that were effective in the past are increasingly difficult to implement today as Congo's contribution to the global market is shifting.

Other challenges to U.S. diplomatic capacities relate to Congo's inadequate expertise. There is a lack of human resources with in-depth country understanding, cultural sensitivity, and relevant language skills. Celebrities and well-intentioned NGOs without sufficient policy expertise increasingly influence U.S. government official policy. One side effect of this is viewing Congo through a Rwanda lens. Washington appears to confuse Congo with the Kivus. Similarly, Africa is often imagined as a country, not a continent of multiple realities with divergent risks and opportunities.

Notes

1 Adam Hochschild, *King Leopold's Ghost: A Story of Greed, Terror and Heroism in Colonial Africa* (Houghton Mifflin, Boston and New York, 1998): 76–82.

2 Mark Twain, *King Leopold's Soliloquy: A Defense of His Congo Rule,* 2nd ed. (P.R. Warren Co., Boston, 1905).

3 Georges Nzongola-Ntalaja, "United States Policy toward Zaire," in *African Crisis Areas and US Foreign Policy,* edited by Gerald Bender, James Colemean, and Richard Sklar (UCLA Press, Los Angeles, 1985); Larry Devlin, *Chief of Station, Congo* (Public Affairs, New York, 2007).

4 Jean A.P. Clément, "The Democratic Republic of the Congo: Lessons and Challenges for a Country Emerging from War," in *Postconflict Economics in Sub-Saharan Africa: Lessons from the Democratic Republic of the Congo,* edited by J. A. P. Clément (International Monetary Fund, Washington, D.C., 2004).

5 United Nations Development Programme (UNDP), *Human Development Report 2013: The Rise of the South: Human Progress in a Diverse World* (UNDP, New York, 2013).

6 World Bank, *Doing Business 2013* (World Bank, Washington, D.C., 2013).

7 Johannes Herderschee, Kai-Alexander Kaiser, and Daniel Mukoko Samba, *Resilience of an African Giant: Boosting Growth and Development in the Democratic Republic of Congo* (World Bank, Washington, D.C., 2012): 21–22.

8 Anastase Nzeza Bilakila, "The Kinshasa Bargain," in *Re-inventing Order in the Congo: How People Respond to State Failure in Kinshasa,* edited by Theodore Trefon (Zed Books, London, 2004).

9 Gérard Prunier, *From Genocide to Continental War: The 'Congolese' Conflict and Crisis of Contemporary Africa* (Hurst, London, 2009).

10 Jean-Pierre Bemba is now sitting in an International Criminal Court prison cell in The Hague, charged with war crimes.

11 Economist Intelligence Unit, *Country Report: Democratic Republic of Congo* (Economist Intelligence Unit, London, 2011): 15.

12 Eric Joyce, chair of the United Kingdom Parliament's Great Lakes of Africa Group, documented a $5.5 billion loss to the Congolese people through questionable mining deals with British Virgin Island "shell" companies. It is widely believed that several of these companies are connected to Israeli businessman and Kabila crony Dan Gertler. See http://ericjoyce.co.uk/wp-content/uploads/2011/11/summary-5–5m-losses-to-congolese-people-through-questionable-mining-deals.pdf.

13 Georges Nzongola-Ntalaja, "Congo's Violent Election Countdown Reflects Rejection of Regime," *Guardian Poverty Matters Blog* (Nov. 22, 2011), www.guardian.co.uk/global-development/poverty-matters/2011/nov/22/congo-violent-election-countdown.

14 R. Pourtier, "L'Etat et le territoire: Contraintes et defies de la reconstruction," in *Réforme au congo (RDC): Attentes et Désillusions,* edited by T. Trefon (Musée royal de l'Arique central/L'Harmatan, Tervuren/Paris, 2009): 35.

15 International Bank for Reconstruction and Development (IBRD; World Bank), "The Democratic Republic of Congo's Infrastructure: A Continental Perspective" (IBRD/World Bank, Washington, D.C., 2010): 1.

16 Richard Milburn, "Mainstreaming the Environment into Postwar Recovery: The Case for 'Ecological Development,'" *International Affairs* 88, no. 5 (2012): 1099.

17 United Nations Environment Programme (UNEP), "Forestry and Deforestation in Bas-Congo," UNEP, http://postconflict.unep.ch/congo/en/content/forestry-and-deforestation-bas-congo.

18 Lieslot Bisschop, "Out of the Woods: The Illegal Trade in Tropical Timber and a European Trade Hub," *Global Crime* (2012): 2, DOI:10.1080/17440572.2012.701836.

19 The White House, "President Bush's Initiative Against Illegal Logging" (White House, Washington, D.C., Feb. 14, 2002), http://georgewbush-whitehouse.archives.gov/infocus/illegal-logging/.

20 Romain Pirard, "Reducing Emissions from Deforestation and Degradation in Non Annex 1 Countries" (The Climate Group, Institut du Développement Durable et des Relations Internationales, 2008), www.theclimategroup.org/_assets/files/reducing-emissions-from-deforestation.pdf.
21 François Misser, *La Saga d'Inga* (Les Cahiers de l'Institut Africain/L'Harmattan, Tervuren/Paris, 2013).
22 The Australian aluminum giant BHP Billiton expressed interest in developing an aluminum production facility in the Inga zone but did not go ahead with the project even though negotiations were rather advanced. See www.bbc.co.uk/news/world-africa-17056918.
23 François Misser, "Democratic Republic of Congo: Starving in the Land of Plenty," *Africa in Fact,* no. 6 (2012): 10–12.
24 Theodore Trefon, "Land Grabbing, Sovereignty and a New Agriculture Law," *Congo Masquerade* (Feb. 13, 2012), http://congomasquerade.blogspot.com/2012/02/land-grabbing-sovereignty-and-new.html.
25 Grain, "Who's behind the Land Grabs? A Look at Some of the People Pursuing or Supporting Large Farmland Grabs around the World" (Grain, Barcelona, 2012), www.grain.org/attachments/2606/download.
26 Banque Mondiale, *République démocratique du Congo: La bonne gouvernance dans le secteur minier comme facteur de croissance* (Banque Mondiale, Kinshasa, 2008): 15.
27 Jeffrey W. Mantz, "Improvisational Economies: Coltan Production in the Eastern Congo," *Social Anthropology* 19, no. 1 (2008): 37.
28 United Nations Environment Programme (UNEP), "The Democratic Republic of the Congo: Post-conflict Environment Assessment Synthesis for Policy Makers" (UNEP, Nairobi, 2011): 32.
29 UNEP, "The Democratic Republic of the Congo."
30 Marie Mazalto, "RD Congo: de la réforme du secteur minier celle de l'état," in *Réforme au Congo: Attentes et désillusions,* edited by Theodore Trefon (Les Cahiers de l'Institut Africain/L'Harmattan, Tervuren/Paris, 2009).
31 Erik Kennes, "Footnotes to the Mining Sector," *Review of African Political Economy* 29, no. 93–94 (2002): 601–607.
32 Mazalto, "RD Congo."
33 Didier Mopiti Ilanga, Paulin Mbalanda Kisoka, Gérard Mosolo Esemola, and Gaby Kabwe Kayombo, *Analyse de la législation environnementale et sociale du secteur minier en RDC* (Avocats Verts/WWF, Kinshasa, 2010).
34 Carole Vaporean, "We Would Rather Grow Internally Than Pay a Premium for Outside Assets—Freeport," Mineweb (*Reuters*) (Feb. 26, 2010), www.mineweb.com/mineweb/view/mineweb/en/page36?oid=99695&sn=Detail.
35 Dino Mahtani, "Exclusive: Congo under Scrutiny over Hezbollah Business Links," *Reuters* (2012), www.reuters.com/article/2012/03/16/us-congo-democratic-hezbollah-idUSBRE82F0TT20120316.
36 Jeroen Cuvelier (ed.), *The Complexity of Resource Governance in a Context of State Fragility: The Case of Eastern DRC* (International Alert/IPIS, London/Antwerp, 2010).
37 Theodore Trefon, *Congo Masquerade: The Political Culture of Aid Inefficiency and Reform Failure* (Zed Books, London, 2011).
38 Committee on Critical Mineral Impacts on the U.S. Economy, Committee on Earth Resources, and National Research Council, *Minerals, Critical Minerals, and the U.S. Economy* (National Academies Press, Washington, D.C., 2008).

39 Banque Centrale du Congo, *Rapport annuel 2010* (Banque Centrale du Congo, Kinshasa, 2011): 127.
40 Banque Centrale du Congo, *Rapport annuel 2010.*
41 Global Witness, *Rigged? The Scramble for Africa's Oil, Gas and Minerals* (Global Witness, London, 2012): 29.
42 Joshua F. Keating, "Joshua Keating: 10 Stories You Missed in 2012," *Foreign Policy* (Dec. 3, 2012), www.twincities.com/ci_22100357/joshua-keating-10-stories-you-missed-2012.
43 www.crisisgroup.org/.
44 Theodore Trefon, "Administrative Obstacles to Reform in the Democratic Republic of Congo," *International Review of Administrative Sciences* 76, no. 4 (2010): 702–22.
45 Dizolele Mvemba Phezo, "The Mirage of Democracy in the DRC," *Journal of Democracy* 21, no. 3 (2010): 143–57.
46 A few examples are Avocats Verts at www.accessinitiative.org/partner/advocats-verts and Océan at http://newsmotion.org/es/feed-story/1%E2%80%99ong-ocean-et-la-protection-de-1%E2%80%99environnement-en-province-orientale.
47 World Wildlife Fund Global (WWF Global), "WWF Calls on SOCO to Get Out of Virunga National Park," *WWF Global* (Oct. 3, 2012), http://wwf.panda.org/wwf_news/?206343/WWF-calls-on-SOCO-to-get-out-of-Virunga-National-Park.
48 Theodore Trefon, "Urban-Rural Straddling: Conceptualizing the Peri-urban in Central Africa," *Journal of Developing Societies* 27, no. 3–4 (2011): 421–43.
49 Some of these are the Southern Africa Development Community, the Economic Community of the Great Lakes Countries, and the Central Africa Forests Commission.
50 United Nations Panel of Inquiry, "Final Report of the Panel of Experts on the Illegal Exploitation of Natural Resources and Other Forms of Wealth of the Democratic Republic of the Congo" (United Nations, New York, 2009).
51 Marie-France Cros, "La culpabililité du Congolais Mathieu Ngudjolo n'a pas été prouvée. Mais . . ." *La Libre Belgique* 19 (Dec. 2012).
52 Jeffrey Gettleman, "Elephants Dying in Epic Frenzy as Ivory Fuels Wars and Profits," *New York Times* (Sept. 3, 2012), www.nytimes.com/2012/09/04/world/africa/africas-elephants-are-being-slaughtered-in-poaching-frenzy.html?pagewanted=all.
53 Carol Lancaster, "How Smart Are Aid Donors? The Case of the United States," in *Smart Aid for African Development,* edited by R. Joseph and A. Gillies (Lynne Rienner, Boulder, 2009): 33.

7

MODERN INDIA

Rich Verma

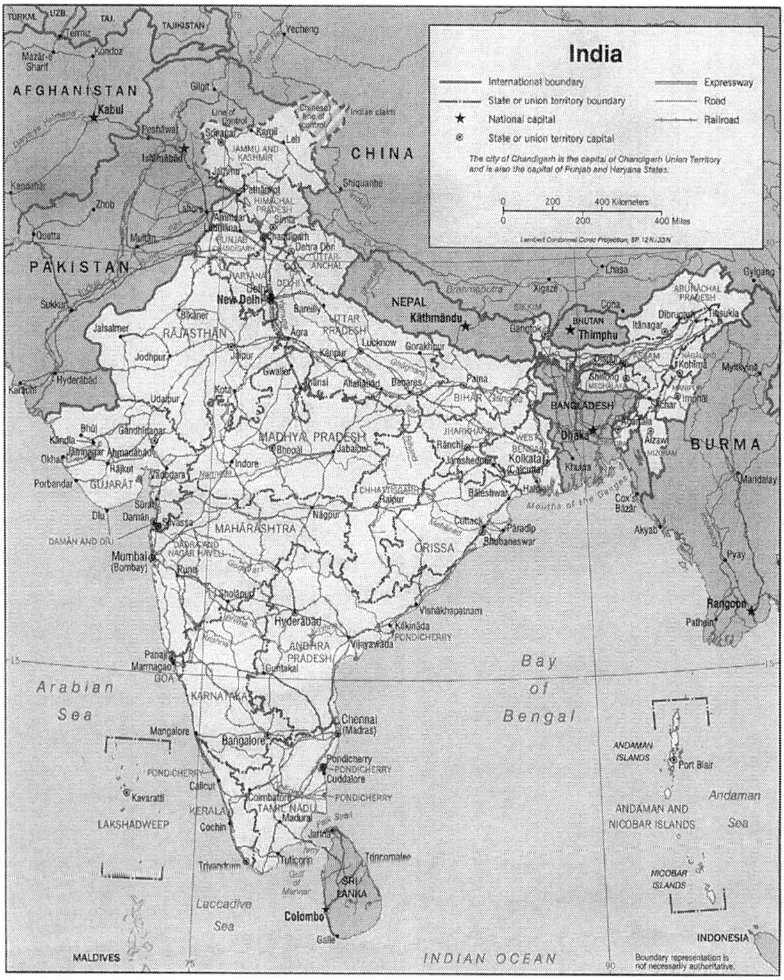

Modern India is a land of incredible contradictions. India's economy has grown rapidly and holds the promise for enormous expansion, yet poverty still ravages much of the country. India led the world in the creation of new millionaires last year,[1] but it also leads in the number of the world's poor, with some 900 million people living on less than $2 a day.[2] It is the world's largest and arguably most vibrant democracy, yet it is plagued by political paralysis and corruption. It has vast coal and gas reserves, but still imports most of its energy.[3] It enjoys significant agricultural diversity and is the world's largest exporter of rice,[4] but hundreds of millions of Indians still go hungry each day.[5] India sits at the foot of the Himalayas and borders some of the world's largest glaciers, yet much of the country cannot access clean water.[6] India seeks global influence and respect on the world stage, but it often remains unwilling to flex its military, economic, or diplomatic power abroad, as it maintains a decades-long inward-looking foreign policy. And while it remains relatively secure and peaceful, forces from outside and now inside India threaten the country's tranquility and stability with increasing frequency.[7] This is modern India—complex, confounding, and contradictory in so many ways.

Despite its challenges, India is poised to be a global power for decades to come. By 2025, it will be the world's most populous country, with an estimated 1.4 billion people.[8] It is the fourth-largest world economy, and despite some recent slowing, 7 percent annual economic growth is expected to continue for many years.[9] India is making the necessary investments that come with a greater global role. India intends to spend $1 trillion on its infrastructure in the next five years,[10] and it will continue to be the world's largest importer of defense goods for the foreseeable future.[11] It produces more movies than any other country,[12] it is home to a large number of the world's most successful and innovative technology companies, and it will soon overtake the United States in the global share of university graduates.[13]

Those are powerful statistics that point to India's promise and potential. But there is one category of concerns that are growing more severe by the day and risk upending India's rise as a world power—and that is India's environmental challenges. The challenges relate, somewhat predictably, to a country on a rapid rise but without the resources or infrastructure to manage the environment effectively. The complexity and severity of India's environmental concerns cannot be overstated. They span such a wide range of issues and confront India on so many levels. India has been ravaged by the effects of climate change; too much of India's air is polluted, and too much of its water is unclean. Rapid urbanization has put added pressure on the country's cities, power generation, and basic infrastructure, such as sanitation. Deforestation, drought, biodiversity challenges, poor governance, and a myriad of other concerns have exacerbated already severe environmental challenges.

Historically, the United States played only a small and outsider's role in working with the Indians on environmental matters. The environment was never at the forefront of U.S. foreign policy toward India. But that position has changed over the past decade, particularly over the past four years. There are several reasons for this change.

First, in an increasingly complex world of emerging threats, shifting alliances, and economic crises, the United States needs friends and allies more than ever, especially those that share its values. As two strong constitutional democracies, India and the United States need each other to prosper economically and to be secure strategically. Both countries now rather freely accept that conclusion. The Indians are open to U.S. engagement, counsel, technical assistance, and financing on a broad array of topics where they may have resisted partnership in years past.

Second, the United States has dropped its "hyphenization" policy in South Asia. For decades, the United States implemented a foreign policy with India-Pakistan that was supposed to be balanced, with economic assistance, trade, and strategic cooperation designed to maintain stability and ensure that the United States did not unwittingly shift the balance of power for one country over the other. The drop of the hyphen was long overdue, as it limited the American ability to build strong and independent relationships with each country based on its interests and needs on the ground. The United States is now free to develop foreign policies with Pakistan and India that are neither identical nor balanced, which has led to a more diverse agenda with each nation, including on the environment.

Third, India's environmental issues are increasingly being viewed by policy makers as having a strategic impact, with national security, regional, and international implications. For example, the shortage of water has sparked an increase in regional tensions. Rising temperatures and drought conditions have driven millions into Indian cities, putting added strain on the infrastructure and the political system. The health and development challenges stemming from India's pollution are well documented and are increasingly believed to be a drag on India's economic growth. Taken together, these are concerns that can no longer be characterized as "soft" or "second tier" issues. Rather, the magnitude of these problems, as well as the tendency to view them through a strategic lens, has elevated their status and their urgency. The environment is becoming a "hard power" issue. Obviously, the United States can do more and, as this chapter indicates, it should take advantage of the important openings in the bilateral dialogue and the broader relationship to ensure the environment becomes a core pillar of U.S. foreign policy toward India for years to come.

The United States and India—Evolution

The U.S.-India relationship has seen its ups and downs over the past several decades. During the Cold War, India was a leader of the so-called nonaligned movement. As such, it formed no security alliance with Western or Eastern powers. It was independent and proud to remain so, even if such independence proved costly to India's economic prosperity.[14] India relied on indigenous manufacturing and production and grew much of its own food. It did have a defense procurement relationship with the Soviet Union, which served as a point of friction with U.S. officials.[15] India was a relatively new democracy, and there were monumental challenges to tackle within its own borders and with its neighbors. Therefore, India adopted an inward and insular international orientation, much of which still remains in place today. It did not aspire to be a global player or become consumed in other nations' ambitions or problems. This approach left India somewhat isolated, which, again, suited its desire to be independent.

This posture had consequences for the U.S.-India relationship. It meant that there was a generally friendly but distant connection between the two countries for roughly the first 50 years of India's post-independence existence. The United States traded very little with India, and India's markets remained largely closed to U.S. investors. The governments were cordial, if not somewhat distrustful. Tensions did peak at times, mostly with regard to nuclear proliferation. As mentioned above, U.S. foreign policy toward India was driven largely in terms of achieving a strategic balance of power between Pakistan and India. This counterbalancing and the years of an "Indo-Pak" foreign policy helped ensure that cooperation between the United States and India on a range of areas, including the environment and development, never reached its full potential.

Meanwhile, people-to-people relationships continued to grow and deepen while government-to-government cooperation between the United States and India faltered. Indian immigrants were welcomed into the United States in the tens of thousands between 1950 and 1990. Many stayed permanently, eventually becoming the country's most educated and prosperous ethnic group.[16] The number of Indian Americans now stands at some 3 million strong. It is an important bloc and one that still wields considerable influence over the path of U.S.-India relations.

The Clinton and Bush Administrations

Most experts now believe it was President Clinton who achieved the first actual breakthrough in modern U.S.-India relations. He not only undertook a highly successful trip to India, but his administration also put together a package of economic, diplomatic, and security initiatives to try to move past the decades-long stalemate in the relationship.[17] Tensions remained, largely over nuclear proliferation, but the opening was real. President George W. Bush built on the Clinton administration's progress, with a particular focus on security and strategic issues. The Bush administration framed the relationship through a Strategic Partnership Agreement and launched a specific initiative to improve defense cooperation.[18] The Bush administration also moved forward with the U.S.-India Civil Nuclear Accord.

The U.S.-India nuclear agreement opened the Indian market to the U.S. nuclear industry and gave India access to much-needed nuclear fuel, parts, and technology.[19] India had been a nuclear weapon state since 1974, but its civilian nuclear industry struggled. With each country giving its approval to the deal by early 2007, the agreement was formally concluded. It was as big as anything the two countries had ever accomplished together. In 2005 when the Civil Nuclear Accord was signed, less than 1 percent of India was powered by nuclear energy. That number has grown over the past 10 years, and the Indians would like to produce more nuclear energy, although there are domestic political challenges in expanding nuclear sourcing post-Fukushima. Although the agreement was controversial, it was the first significant cooperation between the United States and India on the question of energy.[20] The Indian American community was essential in ensuring passage of the civil-nuclear agreement, as the community worked both sides of Capitol Hill in a highly organized and unprecedented manner. As discussed toward the conclusion of this chapter, the diaspora, especially younger Indian Americans who may be more inclined to support environmental causes, can play an important role in raising the importance of the environment in the bilateral relationship.

The Obama Administration and India

Early in its first term, the Obama administration put significant emphasis on the relationship between the United States and India. The Obama administration launched the first-ever Strategic Dialogue with India, and it promised a broad and deep relationship on a range of fronts, including trade, defense, and infrastructure development. It was no mere coincidence that President Obama's first state dinner was held in honor of India's Prime Minister Singh.

Skeptics of the partnership suggest that the U.S.-India alliance has failed to live up to the hype and that the Indians have been neither a reliable nor a trustworthy partner. The skeptics cite the failure to enact civil nuclear liability limitations for U.S. industry and the rejection of the U.S. bid for the multi-billion-dollar Indian advanced fighter contract.[21] They point to India's continued importation of Iranian oil and India's silence on many pressing human rights issues. They note that the two nations have made little progress toward a comprehensive trade agreement and, in fact, many now view India as an adversary in international trade negotiations. The same can be said for international climate negotiations, where India has proven to be a highly independent, if not obstinate, player in the climate debate.[22]

Slow and Steady Progress

However, the skeptics have failed to take note of the steady and deliberate progress made on many fronts in the U.S.-India relationship, including on energy and environmental matters. Although there have been few large and notable achievements, there have been plenty of smaller but still important developments. As some India watchers say, there will be few home runs in this relationship, but there will be plenty of singles. For example, over the past 10 years, India has purchased some $10 billion in U.S. defense equipment. That number is expected to climb steadily in the coming years, as India will be the world's largest defense importer. Intelligence cooperation and joint defense training are at an all-time high.

On trade and investment, through a series of recent economic reforms, the Indian government has begun to open India's markets to U.S. investors. Two-way trade between the United States and India now stands at $100 billion. That is a tenfold increase over 10 years. Once a destination for outsourcing, Indian companies now invest billions in the United States in information technologies and manufacturing. Indian companies have created some 50,000 jobs in the United States. There is even talk that a bilateral investment treaty is in the works, which, if successfully negotiated, would set the stage for a free trade agreement.

On matters of foreign policy, the once nonaligned India is beginning to align more closely and more often with the United States. India has reduced its petroleum imports from Iran. India has supported United Nations Security Council Resolutions on Iran and Libya, opening the way for sanctions against Tehran and military action against Kaddafi. India has supported the American transition out of Afghanistan by taking a lead role in training Afghan security forces. And India has stepped in to provide aid to the new Burmese government. For its part, the Obama administration has promised a reform of the arcane U.S. export control system that has denied India the most sensitive military hardware for decades;[23] President Obama explicitly said he supported India's bid to join the Security Council as a permanent member;[24] and Secretary Clinton launched the first-of-its-kind Strategic Dialogue with India, covering a wide range of defense and economic issues.[25]

To be sure, there are still major obstacles and differences in the relationship, and there will be for years to come. But over the past four years in particular, the two nations have found areas where they can make progress. President Obama and Prime Minister Singh have developed a close relationship. More broadly, there has developed a systematic and routine quality to the way the two bureaucracies work together. Thousands of diplomats, development professionals, military officials, and other civilian experts of all kinds engage in the largely behind-the-scenes work of statecraft, making the necessary links that can pull two nations together. This is in addition to the millions of people-to-people relationships that have brought the countries closer and have delivered significant benefits for each country. Again, although policy differences certainly remain, the two nations now work together more closely, on a sustained basis, than at any time in the past.

Making the Move into Environmental and Energy Cooperation

This slow and steady progress has opened the door to new initiatives in a range of areas, including on the environment, homeland defense, education, and agriculture.[26] With regard to energy and the environment, a number of joint initiatives have been launched on clean energy, low-carbon growth, climate, and a range of related topics. The U.S.-India Partnership to Advance Clean Energy (PACE) is the overarching initiative that ties together U.S.-India cooperation on clean energy research and deployment.[27] The United States and India are also collaborating with the energy and environment ministers of the world's major economies as part of the Clean Energy Ministerial to promote policies and programs that encourage low-carbon energy production and consumption.[28] Never before have the United States and India worked on the diversity and multitude of energy and environmental issues as they do now.

Bringing the environment into the mainstream of U.S.-India bilateral issues is gaining significant traction. Take, for example, the recent remarks of Deputy Secretary of State Bill Burns, who many view as the administration's point person on India, when asked about the importance of the environment in the U.S.-India partnership: "This is one of the areas of our relationship as you look out over the next few years that deserves our greatest attention and where there is the greatest potential." He went on to say that with regard to energy, climate, and environmental issues, there is "a great deal more we can do to deepen cooperation that serves our shared interests."[29]

India faces a range of complex and potentially catastrophic environmental challenges, as discussed in more detail below. The consequences for not partnering with India to see its way through this crisis could be staggering, not only for India, but also for the region and beyond, as well as for the United States. Thankfully, U.S. and Indian policy makers have recognized this fact and are beginning to move in the direction recommended by Secretary Burns. It is because of the countries' shared interests and the potential risks of inaction that the United States and India have begun to forge this common undertaking together. Understanding India's risk factors is key for knowing whether the policy makers are in fact moving in the right direction. The risks and challenges to India are set out in more detail below.

India's Challenges

Water and Climate Change

India faces many severe environmental challenges, and perhaps top among them are challenges related to water, including water shortages, inadequate access to clean water, and regional instability caused by the decreasing availability of water.

According to India's Institute for Defence Studies and Analyses (IDSA), India will be water stressed by 2025 and water scarce by 2050.[30] The World Bank estimates that India's per capita water supply has dropped substantially since 1947, when it stood at 5,000 cubic meters per year, to 1997, when it dropped to 2,025 cubic meters annually.[31] By 2025, that figure is projected to drop to 1,500 cubic meters annually per person, which falls well within the definition of "water stress."[32]

India's water shortages stem from a variety of factors, but overuse for agricultural purposes may be one of the largest problems. Indian farmers tend to produce crops that are heavily reliant on large amounts of water, such as wheat and rice. There has been little attempt to diversify away from such crops. In addition, the cost of water to the farmers is either artificially low because of subsidies or mostly free. There is no economic deterrent for overuse, because the cost of water is largely not a factor. Another problem is that, in general, power from diesel generators is used to irrigate the crops. The diesel fuel, like the water itself, is highly subsidized by the government for the farming community. It is not uncommon for diesel generators to run through the night, pumping water into the fields long after it may actually be required. The effects have been devastating. Water tables in India, particularly in the north, are at an all-time low. The water tables will take decades to be restored to adequate levels, if at all.

Climate change has also had a significant impact on water availability, as well as heat waves, drought, severe storms, and flooding caused by increasing temperatures.[33] Hundreds of millions of Indians are affected by climate-sensitive factors. India has faced a general warming trend, with northern India facing the brunt of the higher temperatures. Receding glaciers have dried up riverbeds in northern India that are supposed to supply hundreds of downstream villages with sufficient water.[34] Glaciers have been receding at an average rate of 10 to 15 meters per year. While the melting snow generates a short-term surge in water levels, and even flooding in the nearest downstream villages, it creates shortages and diminished flow farther downstream. In addition, the once predictable Indian monsoon has become unpredictable and subject to more irregular rainfall patterns. In fact, the average number of hours of precipitation has fallen, but the frequency of torrential outbursts has increased.[35] The slight increase in average total rainfall has been caused by these more extreme rains that ravage the land and population but do little to benefit agriculture.[36]

The National Intelligence Council (NIC), the think tank for the U.S. intelligence community, warns that if India's climate change issues continue to worsen, the country may face mass migration within India and from India's neighbors, particularly Bangladesh.[37] The NIC further warns of humanitarian crises, state failures, and increased tensions with Pakistan, China, and Bangladesh.[38]

Finding clean water is also a major obstacle for large segments of India's rural and urban populations. Too many of India's rivers and much of the groundwater is contaminated from industrial sources and inadequate sanitation. Some estimates suggest that more than 600 million people are without access to toilets.[39] According to the World Health Organization (WHO), some 21 percent of communicable diseases in India are water related.[40] Diarrhea-related illnesses brought on by unclean water afflict millions and are still the leading cause of death for children under age five.[41] In addition, because the water tables are so depleted, those who get their water from wells must dig deeper, where there are greater contaminants, particularly from arsenic and fluoride.[42] Inadequate infrastructure, including insufficient wastewater treatment facilities, has compounded the already severe water-quality issues. India's expected population growth over the next decade will also further stress and complicate the ability to find clean water for millions of people.

Energy Scarcity and Sustainable Development

India faces a difficult and interrelated set of development, energy, and economic problems. First, the country must find a way to deal with the severe energy shortages. Second, it must continue to grow the economy at nearly 8 percent per year for the next two decades if it hopes to lift some 400 million people out of poverty. And, third, India must find a way to reduce its reliance on traditional carbon-based sources of energy in order to decrease carbon dioxide (CO_2) emissions and begin to make a dent in the climate change problems. Many would argue that these are inconsistent goals that cannot simultaneously be pursued and achieved. How can a nation alleviate poverty while at the same time protect the environment? This is perhaps India's greatest national challenge.

India faces a severe energy shortage. About 300 million Indians are without access to electricity.[43] India fell 50 percent short of its planned megawattage capacity upgrades over the past five years. The shortage became abundantly clear during the summer of 2012, when some 600 million Indians, or nearly 10 percent of Earth's population, were thrown into darkness. India relies on coal for about 70 percent of its power supply; it had hoped to produce 660 million tons of coal this past year, but it is likely to fall nearly 140 million tons short because of new regulations, delays in granting licenses, and other problems related to exploration and distribution.[44] The World Bank concluded that the shortage of electric power is the largest barrier to job growth in India.[45]

In addition to the coal shortages, India must import most of its oil. Yet, at the same time, it has had to decrease its petroleum imports from Iran in order to avoid being the target of U.S. sanctions. Therefore, coal and oil must be imported at fairly high prices. India will be the world's largest importer of coal by 2020.[46] There are significant shortages of natural gas, as well as domestic infrastructure limitations.[47] The state utilities are in financial trouble because they have been paying for costly energy imports, but they can rarely pass on these costs because energy is grossly underpriced to the Indian consumers.

On its current trajectory, India will remain highly dependent on imports and subject to the volatility, market disruptions, and geopolitical risks inherent in the global energy markets. Domestically, most experts assess that India's energy production needs must quadruple over the next 20 years to expand access and reliability while powering India's growing economy. At the same time, with India's current energy mix, CO_2 emissions will increase from 1.2 billion tons annually to 4.5 billion tons per year by 2032, further exacerbating the risk factors associated with climate change.[48]

Achieving sustainable development in India, thus, is a paradox requiring new technologies, new ways of living, and new policy initiatives. It is also why clean energy has been such a focus of the U.S.-India bilateral engagements in recent years. Moving away from carbon-based, more traditional forms of energy usage in India will certainly be a struggle for years to come for India's population and economy. Seventy-five percent of rural India is still reliant on traditional sources of energy, such as firewood for cooking fuel. Some 33 percent rely on kerosene. India's planned infrastructure investments, especially those in transportation, may actually further complicate matters.[49] For example, growth in rail, highway, and air transport will connect millions more Indians, but these will also generally be carbon-intensive endeavors. Growth will also likely put more people in automobiles. Currently, India has eight cars for every 1,000 people; by 2050, it is expected to have more than 380 cars for every 1,000 people.[50] Today, transportation accounts for around 10 percent of India's total CO_2 emissions; that number is expected to double in the next 20 to 30 years. Agriculture, too, will require new technologies and approaches, as some 60 percent of Indians depend on agriculture for their livelihoods and 20 percent of India's CO_2 emissions stem from farming-related activities.[51]

Renewables will clearly be an important part of the solution, particularly wind, solar, and even hydroelectric. India has the fifth-largest wind capacity in the world.[52] India's National Solar Mission, which was launched in 2009, is designed to deploy solar power in phases to larger parts of the country, with a goal of generating some 20,000 megawatts of solar power by 2022.[53] Natural gas will also continue to be vitally important. But renewables are still costly compared with India's heavily subsidized traditional power sources. And the transmission and distribution of renewable energy will continue to require significant investments over the next two decades. Many of the technologies that will be required to turn India's power sources more green are still being developed and deployed. And India itself is investing less than 1 percent in research and development in these areas, which, given the current threat, is unlikely to be adequate.

Urbanization

Rural populations are expected to continue their migration into Indian cities. India already has some 45 cities with a million people or more. Some 30 percent of the total population lives in cities, and over the next 20 years, some 200 million more citizens will flock from rural to urban settings.[54] The migration has been fueled by a complex yet interrelated set of environmental and economic factors. Many of those moving have been affected by climate change and the increasingly high temperatures and water shortages. Agricultural production has suffered, driving food prices higher and forcing people into the cities, looking for a new source of income. Others are moving to find better economic opportunity, social justice, and political standing—something a city is more likely to offer than an Indian rural environment. Transportation and modern communications have also facilitated the move from country to city, as people can better link up with those who have migrated and learn about opportunities for lodging or work that may be available.

Indian cities are not currently equipped to handle the scope of mass urbanization taking place. Poor land and title registration processes and sporadic enforcement against squatting have led to a proliferation of shantytowns and cardboard villages on the outskirts of major metropolitan areas. These areas are largely unregulated. There is little sanitation, clean water, or clean energy sources in these areas, which serves to exacerbate the already difficult health situation among the urban poor. This is part of the reason India intends to commit some $1 trillion in new infrastructure spending over the next five years. If this urbanization trend continues, without corresponding investment in city infrastructure (e.g., water treatment, modern transportation networks, and deployment of clean energy technologies), Indian cities will face a serious crisis. The crisis will be fueled in part by environmental challenges, and if the crisis is left untended, environmental conditions will be even worse. The effects of urbanization are also likely to spill into politics as socioeconomic conditions worsen for both the poor and the urban elites. The government is likely to bear the brunt of such frustrations, but even worse, the country could experience some instability as the various economic, social, and political tensions within Indian urban centers boil over.

Impact on U.S. Interests

India's environmental problems, if left unchecked, will undoubtedly have regional implications, but there will also be direct consequences for the United States. The United States increasingly relies on India to provide stability across South Asia and the Indian Ocean. The United States and India face common threats from international terrorism, which has prompted unprecedented intelligence sharing, joint military exercises, and homeland security cooperation. The United States needs a strong, secure, and democratic India to prosper in Asia. India's prosperity is, in fact, fundamental to the success of the American strategic rebalance in Asia that was announced by President Obama in November 2011.[55] Beyond Asia, the United States would welcome a stronger partnership with India internationally to stand up for human rights, to help maintain the global commons, and to deter other threats from state and non-state actors that may arise.

But an India riven with environmental disasters is going to face staggering internal challenges, including political instability and possible civil unrest. India's neighbors, particularly in Pakistan and Bangladesh, are expected to face similar difficulties, and increased tensions would be expected along shared borders where competition over resources would likely intensify. Moreover, climate change and water shortages will force thousands from their homes, most likely into Indian urban centers, as they search for clean water, food, personal security, and economic opportunities. This migration will occur within India and across India's borders as well. Tensions across the region will rise as more and more citizens confront the environmental calamity head on.

Should this be the scenario that arises, India will have no choice but to focus on its internal domestic affairs. It will not be able to become the strategic partner on which so many in the United States are counting. But even more consequential for the United States, India could become highly destabilized and set off shock waves of instability across South Asia. This could require the United States to come in with economic or material support to assist India. It could even require some form of security assistance, if the United States is asked for such help from India. The bottom line is that an India plagued by internal instabilities would upend the American security framework for South Asia and even East Asia. It would eviscerate the potential for a true strategic partnership; it would require a complete reassessment of policy and possibly significant U.S. assistance, both financial and military, to help ameliorate the impacts of India's severe environmental degradation.

A significant slowdown in India's economic growth could be expected should the environmental problems continue to grow. Already, India has experienced a slowdown from the growth rate of 8 percent or more it has enjoyed for many years. The consequences of an Indian slowdown or even negative growth would be dire for much of India's population but particularly for the very poor, who count on Indian growth to escape the harshest elements of poverty's wrath. The continued worsening of environmental conditions would also likely drive up the prices of food and energy inputs. The corresponding drain on government accounts to cope with the price increases would impact India's ability to make investments in critical industries, infrastructure, health, and education, weakening India's global economic position and hampering its ability to trade with Western partners, such as the United States. And a truly severe financial crisis in India could spark a wider contagion across Asia and lead to destabilized global financial markets. In short, it is in the wider interest to ensure that India's environmental challenges do not spill over to create these kinds of massive security and economic consequences. These are not India's problems alone. Given the risks to the United States, it should come as no surprise that environmental matters are increasingly coming to the forefront of the bilateral agenda.

The following section details some of the key programs that have been launched, notes some of the lead agencies, and explains how the U.S. government has organized to engage with India on the environment. These issues, starting with the U.S.-India Strategic Dialogue, are discussed further below.

The U.S. Approach

In the summer of 2009, U.S. and Indian leaders formalized work in five key areas as part of the first-ever U.S.-India Strategic Dialogue. The concept was to institutionalize a range of government-to-government contacts, set benchmarks for progress, and ensure that both sides would meet and talk regularly. The five pillars of the Strategic Dialogue are as follows:

- Strategic Cooperation
- Energy and Climate Change
- Education and Development
- Economics, Trade, and Agriculture
- Science and Technology, Health, and Innovation

The first area, Strategic Cooperation, is meant to further progress on security-related issues, specifically on nonproliferation, military cooperation, and counterterrorism. The Education and Development pillar has been designed to enhance cooperation between the United States and India across the spectrum of education, with particular focus on higher education, as well as women's empowerment. The Economics, Trade, and Agriculture pillar focuses on addressing business-to-business challenges, including limitations on foreign direct investment and regulatory burdens, with the Agriculture component built on food security. The Science and Technology, Health, and Innovation pillar is intended to explore new areas for cooperation in leading technologies and addressing global health challenges. The Strategic Dialogue and its five pillars have spawned some 16 different subgroups and sub-dialogues on issues from university cooperation to women's empowerment.

An important facet of the Strategic Dialogue is the wide range of participation from the private sector, think tanks, and nongovernmental organizations that has been sought and encouraged by government officials. This has helped the Strategic Dialogue generate enthusiasm and buy-in from a broad cross section of key actors who care about the relationship but who see it and experience it from different vantage points. In short, the Strategic Dialogue is not simply the same old meetings of government bureaucrats. The meetings, agendas, and corresponding benchmarks are driven by an important convergence of public and private actors. Where there was once a shortage of institutionalized and regular contacts between the two nations, there is now a plethora of forums established and issues covered within the Strategic Dialogue that draw a wide range of participants from key sectors.

The Energy and Climate Change pillar has been particularly important. It was built on progress achieved by the George W. Bush administration, but for the first time this particular basket of issues has become formalized and organized across the two governments.[56] It also marks the first time climate change has been elevated to a prominent place on the bilateral agenda. On the U.S. side, the work on this initiative takes place principally across four agencies: the U.S. Department of State, the U.S. Agency for International Development (USAID), the U.S. Department of Energy (DOE), and the U.S. Environmental Protection Agency (EPA).

PACE has served as an anchor program within the Energy and Climate Change pillar. For the past two and a half years, PACE has drawn resources from both the government and private sectors to improve energy access and promote low-carbon growth.[57] PACE has two main parts: (1) the research component known as PACE-R and (2) a deployment component called PACE-D. DOE leads the research plank, while USAID manages the deployment component. As part of PACE-R, the U.S. and Indian governments announced the creation of a Joint Clean Energy Research and Development Center (JCERDC) to improve energy access and promote low-carbon growth. The center will involve more than 95 government, private, and university organizations in this $125 million effort over five years. DOE's Office of Policy and International Affairs and the Indo-U.S. Science and Technology Forum serve as the secretariat for the JCERDC. The research focus areas include improving building efficiency, expanding solar energy opportunities, and experimenting with advanced biofuels.

PACE-D was launched in 2010 pursuant to a bilateral agreement between India's Ministry of Power, the Ministry of New and Renewable Energy, and USAID. PACE-D aims to bring to the marketplace clean, reliable, and affordable technologies that facilitate clean energy solutions and improved energy efficiency. PACE-D also provides technical assistance to Indian state and local governments and seeks to spur private investment and engage the private sector in the deployment of clean energy technologies.

Providing access to capital and risk insurance is another critical component of PACE. For example, the Overseas Private Investment Corporation (OPIC) established a $350 million private equity fund to invest in Indian hydro, biomass, wind, and solar power projects. This builds on the establishment of the $300 million South Asia Clean Energy Fund, most of which will end up in Indian-backed projects, as well as the $520 million in financing and insurance that OPIC intends to commit to Indian solar projects. The Export-Import Bank has also financed some $75 million in solar projects and is reportedly considering another $500 million to support India's infrastructure needs related to solar energy. Many of the financing activities are coordinated at the Clean Energy Finance Center located at the American Center in New Delhi, which brings interagency experts from across the U.S. government to help facilitate and oversee some $1.7 billion in public and private funds that have been committed to clean energy projects.

Beyond the PACE set of activities, there are other important initiatives underway. USAID's South Asia Regional Initiative for Energy (SARI/Energy), which has been in existence since 2000, promotes energy security by bringing together experts from a number of different South Asian countries, sharing best practices, and facilitating cross-border solutions to the region's energy challenges.[58] The Clean Cookstoves initiative in India builds on the United Nations' global commitment to put clean and efficient stoves and cooking fuels in 100 million homes by 2020. In the summer of 2012, in Chennai, India, U.S. Secretary of State Clinton announced partnerships with two major Indian industrial organizations to promote clean cookstoves across India. According to the WHO, unsafe exposure to cookstoves that rely on solid fuels, such as wood or dung, causes nearly 500,000 women and children in India to die prematurely each year and accounts for about half of India's black carbon inventory.

These initiatives, although important, are not the sum total of the efforts taking place between the United States and India on energy, the environment, and climate change. There is a wide range of technical discussions and scientific and educational exchanges that occur with regularity, as well as joint government, university, and private-sector initiatives. For instance, the U.S. DOE and the Indian Department of Atomic Energy have agreed to conduct joint research on nuclear energy reliability and safety. Similarly, the EPA and its Indian partners have been working together on pilot programs in the areas of drinking water quality, air-quality management, governance, and the transboundary flow of electronic waste into India.[59] These are just two examples of the many contacts taking place.

There is, thus, no shortage of recent action on the U.S.-India energy and environment front. The question is whether this is the right kind, scope, and level of activity, given both the importance of the relationship and the severity of the environmental challenges confronting India. Experts and policy makers alike should be asking whether the U.S.-India energy, climate, and environmental programs are adequately structured, funded, and staffed. Do they address the right kinds of problems, and are they likely to lead to sustainable solutions? Can and should the United States as a nation do more? This is the right time to be asking these important questions and exploring what more can be done.

Recommendations

This section provides a number of recommendations for moving the U.S.-India environmental agenda forward and elevating the issues within the U.S. foreign policy framework.

Building on the Clean Energy and Climate Initiatives

The PACE program is one example of how the U.S. government can mobilize behind an important cutting-edge initiative. PACE is structured creatively, with multiple agencies, private-public partnerships, a commitment to science, and a leveraging of discoveries through innovative financing mechanisms. This is exactly the kind of work that can and should be replicated. But it is also still a rather small part of the overall effort with regard to U.S. engagement with India. The United States and India could further advance cooperation on climate and clean energy.

First, as detailed in a Center for American Progress paper on India by Andrew Light and Arpita Bhattacharyya, the United States and India should develop a joint platform for open innovation in clean energy.[60] Open innovation involves using new strategies to link disparate research and thinkers through virtual collaboration platforms, innovation prizes, and intellectual property rights strategies. The authors demonstrate how clean energy could use the same model that information and communication sectors used in the development of the Internet, computer operating systems, hardware, and software. These strategies can be powerful tools in accelerating the adoption of clean energy technologies.[61]

Second, a recent Council on Foreign Relations/Aspen Institute India report recommends a number of steps for the United States and India to engage on climate and clean energy cooperation, which take into account the need to grow India's economy and support India's poor while attempting to put a dent in greenhouse gas emissions. The recommendations include providing greater support to India's attempts to combat deforestation through the United Nations Collaborative Programme on Reducing Emissions from Deforestation and Forest Degradation, funding a joint U.S.-India innovation center to "provide clean energy services to the poor focused on creating a bottom-up framework for accommodating the local needs and conditions of Indian citizens," and collaborating with India to pressure international organizations and forums to place a greater focus on finance for climate change.[62]

Seeking Common Ground on Climate Change

The impacts of climate change are becoming clearer by the day. There has been a steady increase in global temperatures, the buildup of greenhouse gases is at the highest level in a half-million years, and 9 of the 10 hottest years on record have occurred since 2000.[63] Nearly 55 percent of global fossil fuel emissions come from the developing world, led by China and India. But for too long, developed and developing countries have taken different and oftentimes contradictory approaches to combatting climate change. Thankfully, the line between the developed and developing is being eliminated. This has occurred over the course of negotiations at climate conferences from Copenhagen to Durban and beyond. It was scientifically and politically impossible to make much progress in the effort to combat global warming without the leading economies, both developed and developing, coming together. With the United States and India now on the same side of the ledger, with similar obligations and responsibilities, it will be up to the parties to prove that they can work together and achieve real change.

Although the United Nations' framework for combatting climate change is important, it should not be the only forum for the United States and India to make meaningful headway. For example, there has been solid progress in smaller but powerful forums, such as the G-20 and the Major Economies Forum on Energy and Climate. These are important endeavors, and the United States and India should continue to play a leading role and not wait for a breakthrough within the United Nations System. India and the United States should also designate high-level officials to meet regularly, outside the forums noted here, to explore what common positions could be advanced at the next multilateral negotiating round. At a minimum, the effort will help build and instill much-needed trust and confidence on both sides.

Renewing Focus on Water Security

Regrettably, water has not yet gotten the attention it deserves within the list of policy initiatives with India. It is time for water security to be elevated to a top-tier issue, bringing in all the expertise across the U.S. and Indian governments, as has been done on clean energy. As noted here, India faces water shortages, severe water pollution, and regional disturbances over water rights and flow. The potential for instability is real, as are the more immediate impacts on development, health, farming, and the economy. In addition, the United States may want to consider launching a regional dialogue on water security. The United States has the expertise, relationships, and standing to bring together all the countries in the region to help facilitate broader regional discussions on water that are so essential, as this issue really knows no particular boundary.

Broadening the Security Lens to Include the Environment

It is also time for the United States to recognize more formally the strategic threats posed by India's environmental issues. The environmental trends in water, pollution, urbanization, greenhouse gases, and the like, if left unchecked, will be a crisis for India, for the region, and for India's allies, including the United States. This is not mere hyperbole. The NIC's report on climate change effects in India is the kind of analytical work that helps make this case. The U.S. Department of Defense, the intelligence community, and the U.S. State Department should convene a working group, either as an extension of the current defense dialogue or as a stand-alone group, to begin constructing a framework for responding to these potential environmental threats and how they might be mitigated. The U.S. group should engage with its Indian counterparts to introduce the environment and its related issues as a core national security matter to be added to the bilateral security agenda.

The National Security Council should also consider reestablishing a senior director position to focus on environmental security in order to bring these issues in India, South Asia, and elsewhere into the interagency decision-making and deliberation process. Covering India's and the region's environmental challenges through a security lens in the U.S. National Security Strategy document, which outlines the main threats and challenges to the United States and how it intends to respond, would also give the issue newfound importance. In addition, in its Quadrennial Defense Review, the Pentagon's coverage of South Asia should note the environmental security challenges emanating from India and South Asia more broadly. This, too, would encourage defense planners and other professionals across the interagency to begin to deal with these issues in a more focused manner. In its Quadrennial Diplomacy and Development Review, the State Department should elevate the region's environmental challenges and how it has reorganized to deal with these pressing challenges.

Creating a Second Green Revolution

India's first Green Revolution helped transform Indian agriculture; facilitated new crops, irrigation, and fertilization techniques; and turned India into a breadbasket for South Asia and beyond. But it also resulted in severe environmental damage, including the overuse of fertile land, the depletion of water tables, and an overreliance on low-price power. India's prime minister has advocated for a second Green Revolution, one to be focused on a diversification away from water-intensive crops, on sustainable growth, and on efficient land and power usage.[64] U.S. technical experts are well suited to help India foster this second revolution. U.S. officials should consider consolidating university, think tank, and private industry experts to collaborate with Indian officials on the set of topics that would help India achieve this worthwhile goal. Much of this expertise resides in farms and towns across America, and it would be a welcome initiative to try to channel the U.S. expertise in a way that the Indians would value. U.S. experts could also help Indian cities with improving building and appliance efficiency, for example, which is desperately needed, given the massive construction boom occurring in Indian urban centers. This kind of initiative would also help build people-to-people contacts in an area where there are only modest contacts today.

Renewing Focus on Governance

Part of India's environmental challenges stem from problems in governance, including corruption, inadequate monitoring of industry actors, difficult regulatory burdens for new entrants into the energy sector, and problems of coordination and authority between the central government and the states. In addition, India's central government currently divides responsibility for the environment among more than a dozen federal ministries, further complicating the ability to move forward in a unified way. Ultimately, the issue of governance is for the Indians to solve and they likely would not welcome American intrusion into their internal political processes. But what the United States can offer is greater collaboration with U.S. agencies, technical consultations on governance, and even exchanges of government bureaucrats to share information and foster better working relationships. The United States engages in such exchanges and close collaboration with other nations; it should do the same with India. The consultations could include technical discussions on permitting and regulatory approvals, the division of responsibilities between U.S. states and Washington, and how the United States takes enforcement actions. The United States could also learn a great deal from Indian officials as well, particularly with regard to India's establishment of so-called green courts, which have been formed to give citizens the ability to bring civil claims against polluters for environmental harm.[65]

Consolidating the Whole-of-Government Approach

The Obama administration's Strategic Dialogue with India has served as an important institutionalizing mechanism to regularize, broaden, and deepen engagements between the bureaucracies. Where these engagements were once sporadic and haphazard, they are now regular and planned. There are more than 20 sub-dialogues ongoing at any particular time. This is a welcome and challenging development. It is obviously beneficial to have the breadth and depth of the ongoing conversation with India, but it has become challenging to prioritize the issues, mobilize the attention and resources of the government, and focus on the most pressing needs. With so many issues on the agenda, it can become a struggle to elevate an issue, such as the environment, to near the top of the list; it also becomes a struggle to remain coordinated and to consult fully with interagency partners. The U.S. government should, therefore, consider designating one agency and one official to lead the way on the environment and energy dialogue. This does not mean that the other agencies would be of lesser importance, but it does mean that there would be a central point of contact, a point at which to measure progress and funnel requests for communication and coordination. The Department of State's assistant secretary for oceans, the international environment, and scientific affairs would be a natural candidate to serve in such a lead and organizing role.

Putting Money Behind the Programs

Despite the breadth of the Strategic Dialogue and its subcomponents, including on energy, the actual amount of budget authority and appropriated dollars flowing to these programs is small. Because the programs involve multiple agencies, with money allocated from general and not India-specific pots, it is difficult to track the actual amount spent. Regardless of the actual figure, it pales in comparison with the seriousness of the issue. The money committed by the multilateral investment banks, such as the Export-Import Bank and OPIC, has been significant, but again, federally appropriated U.S. money has not kept pace. U.S. officials may want to consider establishing a separate budget element for funding programs related to India and the environment. The U.S. chief of mission in India would be instrumental in establishing the need, identifying a specific budget request across the agencies, and pushing that request through the interagency for consideration. The current process is far different, with each agency coming up with independent, not integrated, budget forecasts for India, which results in a rather scattered and, ultimately, inadequate appropriations stream to tackle these issues in the urgent and professional way that is required.

Linking the Legislatures—Using the Environment as a Bridge

The U.S. Congress and the Indian Parliament are remarkably disconnected bodies. Their members do not interact with any frequency, they rarely visit each other's institutions, they have few opportunities to work together, and as a result they have grown disconnected over the years. As a result, small disagreements can become large problems, such as on nuclear energy, export controls, Iran, and trade and economic sanctions. But there is goodwill in both legislatures and interest in building a stronger relationship. The leadership in both bodies should consider establishing an inter-parliamentary dialogue or exchange on the foreign policy and security implications of the U.S.-India relationship on energy, climate, and the environment. The United States currently has a number of parliamentary exchanges with other countries but none with India. This would be another important way to further connect the countries, but at a different level, with an important group of policy makers who can actually effect change. It would also be a relatively easy way to build trust and tear down misconceptions, and it will have spillover benefits across the bilateral agenda.

Improving Investment Opportunities in Infrastructure

India claims it intends to commit some $1 trillion to infrastructure over the next five years to help build modern and efficient sanitation, transportation, power generation systems, and new cities. These are vital investments. But this is $1 trillion that the Indian government has acknowledged it does not have. India has encouraged U.S. contractors, engineers, and scientists interested in working with India on its infrastructure needs to seek public-private financing options and contracting opportunities at both the national and state levels, across some 28 states in India. The result has been to produce a scattershot approach that has deterred outside investment, expertise, and collaboration from coming into India, as most of the risk and regulatory burden has been shifted to non-Indian companies and professionals. If India is serious about rehabilitating its infrastructure, it has to be equally as serious in attracting the best help. That will require the United States and India working together to ease the point of entry for U.S. and other Western firms looking to support India's needs. India should develop a single agency of responsibility; a consolidated list of needs, financing, and insurance consistent with internationally recognized standards; and a streamlined approach for contracting and regulatory approvals that does not require companies to traverse all 28 states. The United States should make this a priority in its bilateral relationship with India, either as part of the Strategic Dialogue or independent of it. In either case, helping to facilitate these investments and technical know-how will have important benefits for India's environment.

Channeling the Diaspora

The Indian American diaspora has grown in power and influence in recent years. There are a number of Indian American governors and congressional, state, and local officials in the United States, as well as senior officials within the Obama administration. Moreover, private citizens, some 3 million Indian Americans, are a potent political bloc. They are not uniform, by any means, in terms of party affiliation or in terms of issue set. But they are, generally speaking, committed to a stronger U.S.-India relationship, and they are interested in supporting efforts that advance that goal. Indian Americans have proven their effectiveness along those lines in the past, and the U.S. government should look for ways to involve them in these new sets of challenges related to the environment. Marshaling their involvement or support behind one or two important programs—asking for their expertise and involvement—would generate interest and enthusiasm that could help maintain the environment's place atop the foreign policy agenda in both Washington, D.C., and Delhi. Speaking to the diaspora groups and looking for ways to include them should be a priority for U.S. officials, and it would help diversify the agenda for the Indian American population, which for so long has been focused on security and matters related to immigration.

Energizing the Youth

It would also be important to involve and inform the younger populations of both countries on the environmental challenges the two countries are attempting to solve collaboratively. The evidence already points to the environment as a top issue for today's younger populations. They do not have to be convinced of its gravity and importance as an issue. Today's younger generations also have a better understanding of the interconnectedness of the planet and how challenges, such as greenhouse gases emitted in the United States and India, will impact their collective futures. Finding ways to move the Strategic Dialogue, for example, beyond the bureaucrats and into the universities, high schools, and social media platforms would give greater voice and support to the environment as a top-tier foreign policy issue for years to come. The support of the youth is needed now and well into the future.

Conclusion

There is no shortage of steps that can be taken with regard to sharpening U.S. foreign policy to ensure the environment becomes even more of a priority in the coming years. The U.S.-India relationship is too important, and the costs of inaction are too high. India is a global player. Its influence and reach will likely grow stronger over the coming decade. India's partnership with the United States is vital for both countries in achieving shared economic prosperity and strategic security. As Vice President Biden once said, "My dream is that in 2020, the two closest nations in the world will be India and the United States. If that occurs, the world will be safer."[66]

But modern India is changing, and the world around it is changing rapidly as well. U.S. policy must adapt too. Elevating the environment in the bilateral relationship between India and the United States would signal that the two countries can change how they do business and that they are capable of seeing the world as it is today and not how it was in years past. India's environmental issues reach into many other areas, including energy, development, climate, food security, health, economic productivity, and geostrategic security. The Obama administration should be credited for elevating many of these issues. Now is the time to make the environment a core pillar of the U.S.-India relationship for years to come. The threats are significant, but so are the opportunities to make real and lasting change.

Notes

1 Daniel Tencer, "Countries with the Most Millionaires," *Huffington Post Canada* (June 12, 2012), www.huffingtonpost.ca/2012/06/12/countries-with-most-millionaires_n_1590824.html#slide=1087643.
2 Population Reference Bureau, "World Population Data Sheet" (Population Reference Bureau, 2011), www.prb.org/pdf11/2011population-data-sheet_eng.pdf.
3 U.S. Energy Information Administration (U.S. EIA), "India" (U.S. EIA, Nov. 21, 2011), www.eia.gov/emeu/cabs/india/full.html and www.eia.gov/countries/country-data.cfm?fips=IN.
4 Nathan Childs, "Rice Outlook" (U.S. Department of Agriculture, Oct. 12, 2012), www.ers.usda.gov/media/928481/rcs-12j.pdf.
5 See the World Food Program Report on India at www.wfp.org/countries/india.
6 Institute for Defence Studies and Analyses (IDSA), *Water Security for India: The External Dynamics* (IDSA, New Delhi, India, 2010).
7 Michael Kugelman, "Looking In, Looking Out: Surveying India's Internal and External Security Challenges," in *India's Contemporary Security Challenges,* edited by Michael Kugelman (Woodrow Wilson Center, Washington, D.C., 2011).

8 India is currently the second most populous country. It will overtake China by the year 2025. See U.S. Census Bureau, "International Data Base" (International Programs, U.S. Census Bureau, Aug. 28, 2012), www.census.gov/population/international/data/idb/region.php.

9 Government of India, "Union Budget and Economic Survey" (National Information Centre, Government of India, 2013), http://indiabudget.nic.in/es2011–12/echap-14.pdf.

10 Brianna Panzica, "India's $1 Trillion Plan," *Energy and Capital* (June 12, 2012), www.energyandcapital.com/articles/indias-1-trillion-plan/2246.

11 Over the past five years, India accounted for 10 percent of the world's arms imports. In that same period, India increased by 38 percent its share of major weapons imports. See *BBC News India,* "India behind 24% Jump in World Arms Trade," *BBC News India* (March 19, 2012), www.bbc.co.uk/news/world-asia-india-17433630.

12 Internet Movie Database, "Films Produced by Country" (Internet Movie Database, 2003), www.nationmaster.com/graph/med_fil_pro-media-films-produced.

13 India currently produces 11 percent of the world's college graduates. Soon it will be 12 percent and overtake the share of the United States. See Elise Young, "Global Education Shifts," *Inside Higher Ed* (July 12, 2012), www.insidehighered.com/news/2012/07/12/china-and-india-producing-larger-share-global-college-graduates.

14 The so-called "Hindu rate of growth" during the Cold War remained relatively flat at 3.5 percent, while other Asian powers grew in excess of 10 percent. See "Redefining the Hindu Rate of Growth," *Financial Express* (April 12, 2004), www.financialexpress.com/news/redefining-the-hindu-rate-of-growth/104268/.

15 Pavel Aksenov, "Russia-India Arms Deal Backed by Historic Ties," *BBC News Europe* (Dec. 21, 2010), www.bbc.co.uk/news/world-europe-12053004.

16 "The Rise of Asian Americans," Pew Research (June 19, 2012), www.pewsocialtrends.org/2012/06/19/the-rise-of-asian-americans/.

17 Lloyd I. Rudolph and Susanne Hoeber, "The Making of U.S. Foreign Policy for South Asia: Offshore Balancing in Historical Perspective," *Perspectives Economic and Political Weekly* (Feb. 25, 2006), http://political-science.uchicago.edu/faculty/rudolphs/us-asia.pdf.

18 The White House, "Joint Statement between President George W. Bush and Prime Minister Manmohan Singh" (July 18, 2005), http://georgewbush-whitehouse.archives.gov/news/releases/2005/07/20050718–6.html.

19 U.S. Department of State, "U.S.–India: Civil Nuclear Cooperation" (U.S. Department of State), www.state.gov/p/sca/c17361.htm.

20 India has been a nuclear weapon state since 1974, but the country's civilian nuclear industry has struggled. With each country giving its approval to the deal in late 2006 in the United States and in early 2007 in India, the agreement was formally concluded.

21 There have been significant problems in fulfilling the promise of the original deal. The Indians have failed to limit non-Indian suppliers of nuclear parts and fuels as is generally done under international protocols, which has resulted in U.S. companies being left on the sidelines. See "India Yet to Address Concerns on Civil Nuclear Liability Law," *Economic Times* (Sept. 27, 2012), http://articles.economictimes.indiatimes.com/2012–09–27/news/34127609_1_civil-nuclear-liability-concerns-of-american-companies-convention-on-supplementary-compensation.

22 Lisa Lerer, "President Obama's Dramatic Climate Meet," *Politico* (Dec. 18, 2009), www.politico.com/news/stories/1209/30801.html.

23 The Deputy Secretary of Defense, Ash Carter, was appointed by Secretary of Defense Panetta to review and reform the rules and regulations governing defense trade with

India in order to jump-start greater two-way defense cooperation and investment between the two countries. For Ash Carter's speech in India, see U.S. Department of Defense, "Remarks by Deputy Secretary of Defense Carter to the Confederation of Indian Industry, New Delhi, India" (U.S. Department of Defense, July 23, 2012), www.defense.gov/transcripts/transcript.aspx?transcriptid=5084.

24 In his visit to India in November 2010, President Obama announced U.S. support for India's bid to become a permanent member of the United Nations Security Council. See Scott Wilson and Emily Wax, "Obama Endorses India for U.N. Security Council Seat," *Washington Post* (Nov. 8, 2010), www.washingtonpost.com/wp-dyn/content/article/2010/11/08/AR2010110807129.html.

25 The U.S.–India Strategic Dialogue was announced in July 2009. See U.S. Department of State, "U.S.–India Strategic Dialogue" (U.S. Department of State, 2013), www.state.gov/p/sca/ci/in/strategicdialgue/index.htm.

26 U.S. Department of State, "U.S.–India Strategic Dialogue."

27 U.S. Department of Energy (U.S. DOE) and U.S. Department of State, U.S. Agency for International Development (USAID), U.S. Trade and Development Agency (USTDA), U.S. Department of Commerce, Overseas Private Investment Corporation (OPIC), and Export-Import Bank (EX-IM), "U.S.–India Partnership to Advance Clean Energy (PACE): A Progress Report" (U.S. DOE, 2012), http://energy.gov/sites/prod/files/PACEProgressReport_Final.pdf.

28 For additional details on the Clean Energy Ministerial, see www.cleanenergyministerial.org/.

29 Center for American Progress (CAP), "The United States and India: A Vital Partnership in a Changing World: A Conversation with the Deputy of State" (Oct. 26, 2012), www.americanprogress.org/events/2012/10/18/42027/the-united-states-and-india-a-vital-partnership-in-a-changing-world/.

30 Water stress generally indicates water availability between 1,000 and 1,700 cubic meters per person per year, while water scarcity means water availability between 500 and 1,000 cubic meters per person per year. See IDSA, *Water Security for India: The External Dynamics* (IDSA, New Delhi, India, 2010).

31 IDSA, *Water Security for India,*15.

32 IDSA, *Water Security for India,*15.

33 National Intelligence Council (NIC), "India: The Impact of Climate Change to 2030, Geopolitical Implications," Conference Report (NIC, Washington, D.C., 2009): 7.

34 Nitin Pai, "Climate Change and National Security: Preparing India for New Conflict Scenarios," *Indian National Interest Policy Brief* No. 1 (April 2008), http://nationalinterest.in/wp-content/uploads/2008/04/inipolicybrief-no1-climatechangeandnationalsecurity-nitinpai-april2008.pdf.

35 Shankar Jha, "The Politics of Climate Change in India," in *Green Dragons: The Politics of Climate Change in Asia,* edited by Michael J. Green, Charles W. Freeman III, and Amy E. Searight (Center for Strategic and International Studies, Washington, D.C., 2010): 48.

36 Jha, "The Politics of Climate Change in India."

37 Jha, "The Politics of Climate Change in India."

38 Jha, "The Politics of Climate Change in India."

39 Samir Saran, "Responding to Change: Searching for a Path through the Climate Haze," *Chevening Fellowships—Economics of Climate Change: A Global Perspective* (University of Cambridge, 2010).

40 Justin DeNormandie and Janette Sunita, "Combating Diarrhoeal Disease in India through Safe Drinking Water" (Media Centre, World Health Organization, 2002), www.who.int/mediacentre/multimedia/2002/ind_sanitation/en/index.html.
41 DeNormandie and Sunita, "Combating Diarrhoeal Disease in India."
42 Sara Sidner and Harmeet Shah Singh, "Indian Communities Face Daily Struggle for Clean Water," CNN (July 16, 2012), www.cnn.com/2012/07/12/world/asia/india-clean-water-struggle/index.html.
43 Samir Saran and Vivan Sharan, "Identity and Energy Access in India—Setting Contexts for Rio+20," *Energy Security Insights Journal* (June 2012), http://weekendmacro.blogspot.com/2012/06/identity-and-energy-access-in-india.html.
44 Some mining officials suggest it can take about seven years to get environmental and forest approvals to start mining in India. See Rama Lakshmi, "India's Coal Shortage Spurs Larger Debate," *Washington Post* (Sept. 11, 2011), http://articles.washingtonpost.com/2011–09–11/world/35276456_1_coal-shortage-coal-mines-coal-minister.
45 Lakshmi, "India's Coal Shortage."
46 Simon Denyer and Rama Lakshmi, "Satisfying India's Thirst for Power Could Be Nation's Biggest Challenge," *Washington Post* (Aug. 22, 2012), www.washingtonpost.com/world/asia_pacific/satisfying-indias-thirst-for-power-could-be-nations-biggest-challenge/2012/08/22/65f6c6d2-e21c-11e1-98e7-89d659f9c106_story.html.
47 Charles K. Ebinger and Govinda Avasarala, "Emerging Power Crisis," *Foreign Policy* (Aug. 1, 2012), www.foreignpolicy.com/articles/2012/08/01/emerging_power_crisis.
48 Rajan Gupta, Harihar Shankar, and Sunjoy Joshi, "Development, Energy Security, and Climate Security—India's Converging Goals," Center for Nonlinear Studies, http://cnls.lanl.gov/~rajan/Gupta_orf_writeup_v9.pdf.
49 Saran, "Responding to Change."
50 Saran, "Responding to Change."
51 National Intelligence Council, "India," 8.
52 Saran, "Responding to Change."
53 Shruti Chakraborty, "India's Solar Mission on Track, But Needs More Props," *Wall Street Journal* (May 31, 2011), http://online.wsj.com/article/SB10001424052702303745304576356740170323036.html.
54 Chakraborty, "India's Solar Mission on Track."
55 Elisabeth Bumiller, "Words and Deeds Show Focus of the American Military on Asia," *New York Times* (Nov. 10,2012), www.nytimes.com/2012/11/11/world/asia/us-militarys-new-focus-on-asia-becomes-clearer.html.
56 The United States and India launched the first Energy Dialogue in 2005. Projects were aimed at finding mutually beneficial initiatives that complemented Indian and U.S. development, security, and economic interests.
57 Remarks of Ambassador Nancy Powell at the launch of PACE-D on July 31, 2012, in New Delhi, India.
58 For additional details regarding SARI/Energy, go to www.sari-energy.org/.
59 Go to www.epa.gov/oia/regions/Asia/india/index.html#priorities for a detailed description of EPA's activities in India.
60 www.americanprogress.org/issues/green/news/2010/09/22/8353/united-states-joins-alliance-to-promote-clean-cooking-in-developing-countries/.
61 See Richard Verma and Caroline Wadhams, "Deepening the U.S.–India Partnership" (Center for American Progress, Oct. 26, 2012), www.americanprogress.org/issues/security/news/2012/10/26/43080/deepening-the-u-s-india-partnership/.

62 Council on Foreign Relations–Aspen Institute India (CRF-Aspen Institute India), *The United States and India: A Shared Strategic Future,* A CFR-Aspen Institute India Joint Study Group Report (CFR-Aspen Institute India, 2011): 35, www.cfr.org/india/united-states-india-shared-strategic-future/p25740.

63 Remarks by Todd D. Stern, U.S. Special Envoy for Climate Change, "International Cooperation on Climate Change—the Path Forward," Dartmouth College, Aug. 2, 2012.

64 "India Needs Another Green Revolution, Says Manmohan Singh," *Hindu* (July 16, 2011), www.thehindu.com/sci-tech/article2233318.ece.

65 Aastha Kukreti, "Go Green India: The Future Deciding Green Courts," *Delhi Greens Blog* (Oct. 20, 2010), http://delhigreens.com/2010/10/20/go-green-india-the-future-deciding-green-courts/.

66 www.freerepublic.com/focus/news/1747167/posts?page=56.

8

MEXICO

Water Scarcity and the Border

Pamela Stedman-Edwards

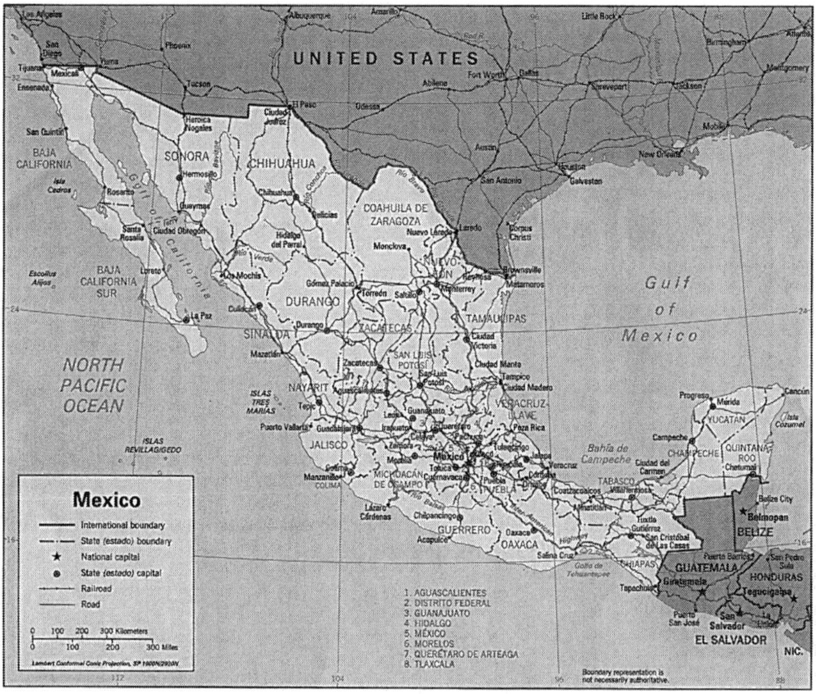

Mexico's development has long been interwoven with the economics and policies of the United States. Along the almost 2,000-mile border, economic change, population growth, government policies, and natural resource use on the U.S. and Mexican sides affect communities on both sides. The close linkages are evidenced by the 15 sister-city pairs along the border, the nearly 1 million border crossings made every day, and the $367 billion in annual cross-border trade.[1] Given the extensive economic and cultural ties between the United States and Mexico, the diplomatic and security relationship between the countries is broad and includes many areas of cooperation. Along the border, not only the federal governments but also state, municipal, and other local governments, as well as numerous civil society organizations, work together on cross-border issues. Although the U.S. public may see the border as dominated by problems of illegal immigration, potential terrorism, and violence, in fact the critical regional problems faced by both countries are similar: rapid population growth, poverty, insufficient infrastructure, and a challenging natural environment. Northern Mexico and the Southwest of the United States are semiarid and arid regions, defined by the Sonoran Desert and the Chihuahuan Desert. Of all the issues that arise along the border, allocation of water is one of the most critical and one that is likely to remain problematic for many years.

This chapter will explore how water scarcity has led both to conflict and to U.S. and Mexican efforts to work together to find solutions. Looking at the region's two major rivers, the Colorado River and the Rio Grande, it explores the history of water use and allocation in the region, the centrality of water to regional development, and the treaties and agreements that have governed international water allocations. Although these solutions have functioned so far, the threat posed by climate change and growing populations in the region and the failure to address the overuse of groundwater may require new approaches and greater efforts to conserve and share water resources. Whether this will be feasible depends in part on the place that border relations take in the broader U.S. relationship with Mexico. Cross-border ties are strong, but the border remains a political and economic boundary that creates substantial differences. Success in managing this difficult international problem could provide a useful model not only for the United States but also for other countries of the world that share scarce water resources.

Mexico and the United States

The border between the United States and Mexico is unusual in that the two countries have substantially different levels of economic development. Mexican gross domestic product (GDP) per capita is less than one-third of U.S. GDP per capita. For many years, this disparity has driven heavy out-migration from Mexico to the United States. Within Mexico, too, there is a large gap between rich and poor. Nevertheless, standards of living are improving in Mexico. Economic growth has created a rapidly expanding urban middle class. Poverty rates in Mexico have fallen substantially from more than 50 percent in 2002 to 40 percent today.[2] Once heavily dependent on subsistence and small-scale agriculture, Mexican employment in agriculture now accounts for only 15 percent of the workforce and 5 percent of GDP. However, despite a number of agricultural support programs, poverty and economic disparities remain particularly problematic in rural areas and remittances from migrants to the United States continue to account for a large share of rural income.

Mexico is heavily dependent on its exports to the United States, with overall trade with the United States reaching $500 billion in 2011 and accounting for one-third of Mexico's GDP. For the U.S. economy, exports to Mexico are also quite important. Mexico is the second-largest market for U.S. exports after Canada, and looking at imports and exports combined, Mexico is the third-largest trading partner of the United States. Eighty percent of Mexico's agricultural exports, almost $16 billion, go to the United States; the United States exports about $18 billion in agricultural products to Mexico. Not surprisingly, Mexican economic growth was severely set back by the recent economic crisis in the United States, with a 6.1 percent decline in GDP in 2009, much greater than any other Latin American country. Mexico is now diversifying away from its dependence on the U.S. market by expanding exports throughout the hemisphere and to Asia; this diversification may lessen the impact of the next economic shock. On the whole, the Mexican economy is considered robust. Much of the 2009 loss was recouped in 2010, with exports to the United States reaching a new record high and growth in 2011 and 2012 close to four percent, thanks to a booming business sector.[3]

Other changes are also reshaping Mexico and its relationship with the United States. Politically the country has become much more open in recent decades, despite the long history of control by the Institutional Revolutionary Party and the ongoing battle against corruption and organized crime. The government has implemented some effective social welfare and infrastructure programs, and increased transparency has been lauded.[4] Population growth has slowed dramatically, with fertility falling from 7.2 children per household in the 1960s to two per household in 2010.[5] Migration of Mexicans to the United States fell to its lowest level in 60 years in 2010. By one estimate, the number of Mexican immigrants in the United States fell below 100,000 in 2010, compared with an average of 525,000 annually during 2000–2004.[6] Nevertheless, immigrant labor is still of great importance in the United States; as of 2009, there were an estimated 7.8 million unauthorized immigrant workers. Despite the extensive economic ties between the United States and Mexico and high levels of cooperation on many issues of mutual interest, all of which are dependent on an open border, the relationship, at least in the eyes of the U.S. public, has been dominated by the need to secure the border.

The Border Region

The border region, considered as 100 miles on either side of the border, is now home to some 14 million people[7] and may reach 20 million by the year 2020.[8] Urbanization has occurred rapidly on both sides, with the population of the 10 border states (six in Mexico and four in the United States)[9] up from 33 million in 1960 to some 90 million in 2010.[10] In the six Mexican states alone, the population grew from 5.5 million to almost 20 million in this time frame, in large part because of the expansion of industrial employment.[11] Much of the growth on the U.S. side has been directly associated with the growth on the Mexican side, as well as new jobs in defense, high-tech industries, construction, agribusiness, and tourism and the growth of retirement communities.

Poverty is a problem on both sides of the border. On the U.S. side, apart from the city of San Diego, about 23 percent of the population is living below the poverty line, with the median household income for the region at about two-thirds the national average.[12] Almost 70 percent of the population is Hispanic, and 90 percent of the population is urban. However, the 1.3 million rural residents play a key role in agriculture, energy development, and natural resource management. The small rural communities, both on and off tribal lands, are among the poorest and most in need of clean water and other infrastructure.[13] *Colonias*—slums that have arisen along the U.S. side of the border, as well as the Mexican side—often lack basic services, including drinking water, waste collection, and electricity. Substantial investments have been made through a number of government programs, but problems persist.[14]

The population on the Mexican side is privileged by Mexican standards because of the relatively high wages and high levels of employment in the region. As the gateway to the United States, the region has consistently attracted jobs and workers and urban areas have grown much faster than on the U.S. side. However, infrastructure, including clean drinking water supplies, wastewater treatment, and solid waste collection, is strained by the growing population.[15] In Ciudad Juárez, for example, although about 98 percent of the population is hooked up to the tap water system, only 80 percent have a sewage hookup.[16] Similar to the U.S. side, about 90 percent of the population is urban.[17] Access to clean water and sewerage is much lower in rural areas. In fact, the indigenous populations in Sonora and Baja are among the country's poorest and most isolated populations.[18] Nevertheless, the situation has improved greatly in the post-North American Free Trade Agreement (NAFTA) period and infrastructure in the border region is now better than in many other parts of Mexico.

Two rivers are central to life in the border region. The Colorado River reaches the Gulf of California through a wide delta between Baja California and Sonora after flowing 1,400 miles from its headwaters in Wyoming; the river forms about 17 miles of the border between Arizona and Mexico. The Colorado River provides the only dependable water supply for some 244,000 square miles, although it is only about 3 percent of the size of the Mississippi River.[19] The Rio Grande (known as the Rio Bravo in Mexico) is the country's fifth-longest river, arising in the Colorado Rockies and flowing through New Mexico before forming about 1,000 miles of the U.S.-Mexico border to the Gulf of Mexico. The Rio Grande watershed drains about one-tenth of the United States and two-fifths of Mexico.[20] Although the Rio Grande never flows into Mexico, 78 percent of its watershed, including two major tributaries—Rio Conchos and Rio Salado—is on the Mexican side. Both the Colorado River and the Rio Grande have been dramatically altered by a series of dams, reservoirs, and hundreds of miles of aqueducts and canals built over the course of the past century. This infrastructure has allowed for the expansion of agriculture and urban areas on both sides. However, the water of the two rivers is now being used almost to the maximum extent possible and the region is drawing heavily on its groundwater reserves. Information about the region's aquifers is sketchy, in part because they are difficult to measure in terms of geographic extent, volume, flow, and renewability. Even estimates of the number of transboundary aquifers vary, from 8 to 20.[21]

Mexico on the whole is an arid country. Of its freshwater withdrawals, 17 percent are for domestic use, 6 percent for industrial use, and 77 percent for agriculture. Comparable figures for the United States, reflecting the very different shape of the economy and water availability, are 13 percent for domestic use, 46 percent for industrial use, and 41 percent for agriculture.[22] Land under irrigation in Mexico nearly doubled between 1960 and 2000, with much of the increase provided by groundwater. About 25 percent of Mexican agricultural land is irrigated compared with 12 percent in the United States. This is by way of saying that the dilemmas of water use that Mexico faces in the border region are in fact widespread throughout the country. In the border region, little agriculture is possible on either side without irrigation and most water withdrawals are for agriculture.

Exploiting the Rivers

Demand for water in the region has risen substantially over the past century, beginning with the arrival of the railroads in the 1880s and construction of the first major irrigation systems and infrastructure projects after 1900.[23] The first canals taking water from the Colorado River to California's Imperial Valley, some 60 miles away, were built early in the twentieth century.[24] In the U.S. Southwest, an increase in irrigated agriculture in the 1930s, supported by the construction of the Hoover Dam, the Imperial Dam, and the world's largest irrigation canal, known as the All-American Canal, led to the first complaints by the Mexicans that water flows from the Colorado River were being compromised. On the Rio Grande, the Elephant Butte Dam, constructed around 1915, dramatically reshaped the flow of that river, drawing off most of the water for El Paso and

Ciudad Juárez. On both sides of the border, agricultural use of water expanded in the 1950s, primarily by large commercial farms employing migrant labor.[25] The Glen Canyon Dam, constructed in the 1960s, added a second giant reservoir for the Colorado River. The various reservoirs, including Lake Mead and Lake Powell, have capacity for about four times the Colorado River's annual flow, meaning that, in theory, water reserves can be used to even out flows between dry and wet years. However, use of both rivers largely proceeds as if all years were wet years.[26]

In Mexico, industrial and urban use of water first began to expand in the 1960s as a result of the U.S. Bracero Program (1951–1964), which attracted more workers to the border than could be accommodated by the temporary visa program. When the program was canceled, many of the workers remained in the border area and unemployment rose above 40 percent. To provide employment and promote industrialization, Mexico established what came to be known as the *maquiladora* program. In essence, this program provided major tax breaks to assembly companies that set up factories along the border. These industries expanded slowly through the next decades, increasing the population of the region and contributing substantially to water pollution.[27]

In 1994, when the United States, Canada, and Mexico signed NAFTA, among various consequences for the border region was a boom in the *maquiladora* industries. Some 500,000 new jobs were created, and exports to the United States rose dramatically.[28] In addition to expansion of industrial exports, agricultural exports to the United States have risen by about 9 percent per year since 1994. NAFTA has been effective in supporting economic growth in Mexico and may be credited with reducing immigration pressures. However, it has increased environmental pressures in the border area, because of industrial pollution and agricultural use of water and because of rapid urban growth without proper water and sewerage infrastructure.

The water of both the major rivers is almost entirely spoken for. The Colorado River serves about 30 million people, providing water to the U.S. cities of Phoenix, Tucson, Las Vegas, Los Angeles, and San Diego, as well as irrigating 500,000 hectares in Imperial County in California and areas upstream. On the Mexican side, the Colorado River serves much of Baja California, including Mexicali and the Mexicali Valley, Tijuana, and Tecate.[29] These cities are still growing rapidly. Phoenix, for example, is one of the fastest-growing urban areas in the United States, despite its location in the Sonoran Desert. As early as 1956, the flow of water into the Colorado River Delta began to stop in some summer months as a result of extraction. The Rio Grande river basin now serves about 9 million people.[30] Over the past 10 years, population has grown about 15 percent on the U.S. side but has come close to doubling on the Mexican side of the Rio Grande.[31] Most of the river's upstream flow is removed at Elephant Butte Dam and Caballo Dam in New Mexico to supply El Paso and the nearby farms.[32] Between El Paso–Ciudad Juárez and Presidio–Ojinaga, where the Rio

Conchos enters the Rio Grande, it slows to little more than a trickle and may dry up completely in the summer months.

Despite the growth of urban areas, agriculture remains by far the largest user of water along the border.[33] More than 70 percent of the water withdrawn from the Colorado River[34] and at least 80 percent of the water withdrawn from the Rio Grande is used for agriculture.[35] Agriculture in the region tends to be high-value, water-intensive crops supported by farm subsidies in the United States and Mexico. As of 2003, the Colorado River was being used to irrigate 1.1 million hectares,[36] accounting for 15 percent of U.S. crops.[37] The Mexicali Valley initially largely produced cotton in the 1950s and 1960s; more recently, production has expanded to include wheat and vegetables for export. On the U.S. side, the Imperial Valley produces hay, which supports a large dairy industry, sheep, and a range of vegetables. In the Rio Grande Valley, three water-intensive perennials are widely grown—alfalfa, pecans, and sugarcane—as well as cotton.[38] By 2003, the Rio Grande was being used to irrigate 2.7 million hectares of cropland. Agriculture is a highly consumptive use of water, meaning that little returns to the source after use for irrigation and livestock or loss to evaporation from reservoirs and inefficient irrigation systems.[39] According to some estimates, only 40 percent of the water extracted for irrigation in the region actually reaches the crops and there is an estimated loss to evaporation from just the Elephant Butte reservoir of 245,000 acre-feet annually.[40]

Mexico's clean water now comes largely from groundwater pumping, causing potentially irreversible degradation of the aquifers. In the border region, groundwater accounts for about one-third of Mexico's water for agriculture, half the water for industry, and two-thirds the water for domestic use. Heavy use of groundwater resources is common on the U.S. side too, particularly in Texas. For some border communities, aquifers are the only source of water for hundreds of miles.[41] Twenty-five counties on the U.S. side of the border get more than 40 percent of their water from groundwater sources.[42] El Paso, Las Cruces, and Ciudad Juárez draw municipal water from the aquifer that underlies the region, the Hueco Bolson. Ciudad Juárez depends entirely on this aquifer; El Paso relies on it for about half of its municipal water. By some estimates, the aquifer will run dry by 2023.[43] Residents of El Paso use about twice as much water per capita as residents of Ciudad Juárez; in fact, many residences on the Mexican side are not connected to the public water system,[44] which leaves little scope for conservation on that side. Yet, the border population—on both sides—is expected to continue to grow.

Governance

In Mexico, water is part of the national patrimony and is governed by the National Water Law. Conagua, the National Water Commission created in 1989, is responsible for administering water-use permits and supporting infrastructure investments. The 1990s saw extensive decentralization of environmental governance, including the privatization and decentralized management of municipal water supply and sewerage systems, transfer of irrigation districts to management by water users, and shrinking of the federal government's water bureaucracy. More recently, changes in the National Water Law have aimed to strengthen watershed management principles and structures and increase public participation in water resource decisions.[45] River basin councils (*Consejos de Cuenca*), which include representatives of federal, state, and local government, as well as water users and nongovernmental organizations (NGOs), have been created in at least 26 river basins. However, Conagua retains the final decision-making power. Under the Mexican system, the needs of urban users are to be met first. A recent constitutional amendment provides that every person is entitled to affordable, accessible, and safe water for domestic use. Apart from municipal use, the government has allocated water primarily to agriculture. Expanding industries have had to purchase water rights from farmers. Conagua can legally limit the taking of groundwater but has generally not taken steps to manage this resource.

On the U.S. side, the institutional framework has always been much more decentralized. Water is treated as property, which can be owned by individuals, rather than as part of the national patrimony. The states, not the federal government, control water rights, and even within the border region states there is a great variety of legal regimes governing the allocation of water rights.[46] States set water-quality standards, which are subject to review by the U.S. Environmental Protection Agency (EPA), and can develop large-scale water projects.[47] However, individuals' use rights do not depend on state allocation of those rights but rather on who established first use, in most cases. A number of Native American tribes in the region have rights to the water on their land, but water settlements with the U.S. government have not been fully worked out.[48] Jurisdiction over groundwater is fragmented, as it is for surface water. State laws and regulations vary and do not necessarily correspond with laws on surface water, despite the fact that these water sources are often closely interlinked. States have begun to share water data, but there is no federal body superintending either surface water or groundwater issues.

Because water is a state issue, interstate "compacts" are used to ensure water deliveries. The allocation of the Colorado River's flow within the United States depends on compacts among the seven states through which the river passes. The first Colorado River Compact dates from 1922 and allocates water between the upper and lower basins. The Boulder Canyon Project Act (1928) apportioned the lower basin waters among Arizona, California, and Nevada.[49] Division of the waters of the Rio Grande among Colorado, New Mexico, and Texas is governed by a compact agreed on in 1938. The New Mexico–Texas Water Commission, established to address disputes in the El Paso–Las Cruces area, and the Pecos River Compact Commission, which oversees this tributary of the Rio Grande in Texas and New Mexico, are also relevant to the region. On top of this already complex set of institutions are layered various irrigation districts, municipalities and municipal water suppliers, and Native American rights.

Only the U.S. federal government can enter into international agreements on transboundary water, meaning that the states cannot negotiate this issue directly with Mexico. However, the federal government must first negotiate an agreement with the states, through the complex of local and state institutions. Despite the difficulty of working through this network of water rights, the United States and Mexico have negotiated several important agreements. Many of these have been hammered out in response to regional tensions over the past century.

Treaties and Negotiations

Tensions over water use and allocation have a long history in the borderlands, dating as far back as the Mexican-American War (1846–1848), when the United States appropriated the headwaters of the Colorado River along with much of what is now the U.S. Southwest as far as the Rio Grande. Over the years, several major treaties and a number of minor agreements have shaped water rights in the region. Negotiation of these agreements has been closely intertwined with the construction of hydraulic infrastructure and urban and agricultural expansion.

The need for cross-border agreements and infrastructure arose as soon as the region began to develop. In 1906, after the United States expanded irrigation in the San Luis Valley and flows of the Rio Grande available to Mexico declined, the two countries signed a treaty governing water allocation for El Paso and Ciudad Juárez, for water to be stored behind the Elephant Butte dam in New Mexico. A 1933 treaty supported the straightening of the Rio Grande through El Paso, essentially confining the river to a concrete channel for a long stretch. The project stabilized the border and provided flood control for the El Paso–Juárez Valley,[50] but it also shortened the river by 85 miles.

The most comprehensive treaty was signed in 1944, following major investments in dams, reservoirs, and canals on the U.S. side in the 1930s. This U.S.-Mexico Water Treaty established allocation of the waters of the lower Rio Grande and the Colorado and Tijuana Rivers.[51] It is still the primary international accord governing water allocation in the region, forming the core of a collection of compacts, federal laws, court decisions and decrees, contracts, and regulating guidelines, known collectively as the Law of the River, which guides U.S. domestic and international water allocation.[52] Under the terms of the treaty, Mexico is guaranteed an annual quantity of 1.5 million acre-feet of the Colorado River flow and the United States is guaranteed one-third of the Rio Grande flow (350,000 acre-feet) from the six Mexican tributaries of that river. Calculations of the flow are based on five-year periods, allowing the countries to make up shortfalls from drought years in wetter years. Only in the case of "extraordinary drought" can Mexico or the United States deliver less over the five-year cycle; the shortfall must be made up in the next cycle.

The treaty also established the International Boundary and Water Commission (IBWC) and its Mexican counterpart, the Comisión Internacional de Limites y Aguas (CILA). The IBWC/CILA supports treaty implementation and serves as a negotiating body over interpretation and implementation. The joint commission is responsible for determination of national ownership of the waters of boundary rivers. It is also responsible for maintaining infrastructure and water quality, monitoring and salinity control, and carrying out relevant studies and planning efforts. The IBWC has played a central role in managing the U.S.-Mexico water relationship; it is the primary institution for addressing conflict over water in the region.

Over the years, hundreds of "Minutes" have been agreed to between the two countries, primarily under the aegis of the IBWC/CILA; the Minutes serve essentially as addendums to the 1944 treaty. The Minutes, because they are not officially amendments to the treaty but rather "interpretations" of the treaty, do not require congressional ratification and are thus relatively easily approved. The Minutes have given the treaty a large degree of flexibility, serving not only to clarify matters addressed by the treaty but also to expand its reach to new areas of concern, including water quality, environmental protection, and groundwater use.

Tensions and Conflicts

A number of events have led to serious tensions over water use along the border; some of these are clearly linked to shortfalls in the treaty and others to changing water use. In the 1950s, as water extraction increased in the United States for irrigation, one of the largest projects, the Wellton-Mohawk Irrigation and Drainage District in Arizona, began pumping saline water back into the Colorado River in order to make up some of the 1.5 million acre-feet owed to Mexico. Mexico objected that the poor water quality was affecting production in the Mexicali Valley, making a formal allegation in 1961 that the United States was violating the 1944 treaty. However, the treaty did not expressly deal with questions of water quality. Resolution of the problem took more than 10 years. Mexico considered taking the issue to the International Court of Justice or an ad hoc international tribunal; however, both sides agreed that a prompt and practical solution would be preferable. Pending a solution, through much of the 1960s, the United States used selective pumping of the Wellton-Mohawk drainage wells to reduce salinity and released an additional 50,000 acre-feet annually of stored water to meet the Mexican entitlement.[53] Mexico began a crash program of groundwater development in the border region to make up for the losses.[54] In the end, it took a call for action at the presidential level, with the IBWC providing the forum for negotiations, to reach an agreement. The resulting Minute 242, agreed to in 1973, guarantees Mexico water of the same quality, on average, as that being used in the United States. To meet this standard, the United States built the Yuma desalinization plant in Arizona,[55] the largest in the

United States, as well as a lined drain to carry waste directly to the Gulf of California.[56] The United States also agreed to help Mexico obtain financing for improvements and rehabilitation of the Mexicali Valley water infrastructure.

More recently, California decided to line a large portion of the All-American Canal. Lining the earthen canal with concrete was expected to save 67,000 acre-feet per year of water that was being lost to seepage, enough to support 500,000 people in San Diego. The canal lining was the centerpiece of a federally mandated seven-state agreement for sharing the Colorado River water on the U.S. side, made necessary by increased upstream withdrawals.[57]

Mexico objected on the grounds that the seepage from the canal had been replenishing the underground water on the Mexican side, creating a critical water source for farms in the Mexicali Valley. The government of Mexico lodged a formal complaint with the IBWC in 2006, demanding that the United States collaborate on an environmental assessment of the canal-lining project; the city of Calexico, along with a Mexicali business organization, filed for an emergency injunction, pending an appeal against the United States and the Imperial Irrigation District.[58] The court issued the injunction, but subsequently the U.S. Congress passed legislation waiving environmental requirements and ordering the secretary of the interior to proceed. Lining of the canal was completed in 2009. The United States essentially ignored the Mexican objection, asserting that the United States was only claiming its legal water rights,[59] leaving the Mexicans to believe that proper diplomatic channels and protocol were ignored and creating an antagonism that made subsequent cooperation more difficult.[60]

On issues where the United States has faced the loss of its own water resources, it has been more willing to cooperate with Mexico. The United States has made investments in water treatment to prevent Tijuana's sewage from reaching California. Substantial investments have been made in water conservation and municipal water supply on the Mexican side to ensure clean water supplies on the U.S. side. And more recently, the two countries have been discussing the construction of a desalinization plant on the Mexican side that could free up for the United States some of the Colorado River flow now used by Mexico. It seems unlikely, however, that Mexico will accept any curtailment of its allotment.[61]

Several periods of drought over the past two decades have also raised tensions. In the 1990s, a prolonged drought led to a large Mexican water debt—water owed to the United States by Mexico under the terms of the 1944 treaty[62]—to the tune of 733,000 acre-feet.[62,63] This became a major economic and political issue on the U.S. side, because agriculture was severely affected in Texas, and resentment of the Mexicans for "withholding" the water grew. A group of Rio Grande Valley irrigators and farmers sued Mexico under NAFTA, seeking $500 million for crop loss and damages they blamed on Mexico's failure to comply with the treaty.[64] Dissatisfaction ran high in part because this was not the first time that Mexico had failed to meet its water delivery obligations and because of the perception that the Mexicans were taking the water they needed first before delivering on their commitment to the United States,[65] allegedly forcing farmers in Texas out of business while Mexican agricultural produce flowed into Texas. The Texas commissioner of agriculture attributed a souring of the U.S.-Mexico relationship to the water debt issues, and Texan and federal officials pushed the Bush administration to make the water debt a priority.[66] The U.S. Congress even passed an "accusatory" resolution calling on Mexico to repay its debt.[67]

A breakthrough came in 2002, once again when the problem was taken to the presidential level.[68] Under Minutes 307 and 308, Mexico agreed to pay down its water debt and the United States agreed to help Mexico with water conservation infrastructure in the Rio Conchos headwaters.[69] Mexico did not concede its diplomatic position, that is, it did not concede the U.S. right to demand the water; nevertheless, Mexican farmers felt they were giving away their water to Texas.[70] This incident highlighted two lacunae in the treaty: it does not define what constitutes "extraordinary drought," and it does not define what should be done when drought extends for periods beyond the five-year cycle. The situation was ameliorated when increased precipitation largely replenished the region's reservoirs, allowing Mexico to pay off its water debt in 2005. At that point, the United States and Mexico announced their intention to formalize procedures for operations under drought and to meet annually to review basin conditions, develop water delivery plans, and work cooperatively on drought management.

Notably missing from the treaty agreements to date are groundwater issues. Part of the difficulty is the fact that groundwater resources are hidden from view and fewer data are available about aquifers and their replenishment than about aboveground sources. Nevertheless, many transboundary aquifers are the cause of dispute, with 18 or more at issue along the border.[71] There is currently no mechanism for divvying up groundwater that crosses the border.[72] The Hueco Bolson is one of the most pressing cases. Water rights differ between Texas, New Mexico, and Chihuahua. To date, cross-border discussions have led to no solutions.[73] Minute 242 limits some groundwater withdrawals on both sides of the border and commits both countries to consult the other regarding any future development of groundwater. However, it addresses salinity, not the broader issues of groundwater quantity or quality; as the only Minute that addresses groundwater, it has not led to any serious restrictions on groundwater use.[74]

Cooperation and Collaboration

Treaties and negotiations have been critical to the U.S.-Mexico relationship along the border. At the same time, a broad range of cooperative investments and programs has shaped the use of water and the U.S.-Mexico relationship. A host of U.S. government programs, some of which function on both sides of the border, addresses regional water, poverty, and environmental issues.[75] The

1983 Agreement for the Protection and Improvement of the Environment in the Border Area, known as the La Paz Agreement, is the foundation of many of these cooperative efforts.[76] Its current incarnation, Border 2020, includes among its goals improving water quality, maintaining water infrastructure sustainability, and reducing exposure to contaminated water. Border 2020 emphasizes "regional, bottom-up approaches for decision making, priority setting and project implementation to address the environmental and public health problems in the border region,"[77] encouraging meaningful participation from communities and local stakeholders and strengthening tribal, state, federal, and international partnerships.

Substantial cooperative efforts and bilateral investments have also resulted from NAFTA. NAFTA does not address the question of bulk water or trade in water. However, because environmental issues came to the forefront in the debate over free trade in the United States, a side agreement on the environment was signed along with the main treaty. The side agreement requires enforcement of national environmental standards and promotes cooperation. In addition, the North American Development Bank (NADB) and the Border Environment Cooperation Commission (BECC) were created to address environmental infrastructure issues in the border region. Funded initially with $450 million (with equal shares from the United States and Mexico), the NADB is authorized to (a) finance projects that will prevent, control, or reduce environmental pollutants or contaminants; (b) improve drinking water supply; (c) protect flora and fauna so as to protect human health; (d) promote sustainable development; and (e) contribute to a higher quality of life, through loans to both public- and private-sector borrowers in the United States or Mexico. To date, the NADB has financed $1.3 billion in environmental infrastructure projects through loans and EPA-funded Border Environment Infrastructure Fund (BEIF) grants.[78] Among other things, the NADB has supported construction of municipal drinking water infrastructure and improvement of Mexico's irrigation systems, with some of the resulting water savings going to the United States.[79]

In 2010, a strong earthquake damaged many of the irrigation canals in the Mexicali Valley. New forms of cooperation have emerged, enshrined in several recent Minutes, to help Mexico restore its irrigation system and, at the same time, introduce water conservation measures that will have benefits for both countries. This cooperation stands in sharp contrast to the brouhaha over the lining of the All-American Canal and the accumulation of water debt.

Moving Toward River Basin Management

After the All-American Canal and the water debt confrontations, border relations took a stronger turn toward collaboration and the debates over water use are evolving in a new direction. For most of the past century, the strategy for dealing with water scarcity, on both sides of the border, was to build more infrastructure. More recently, some observers have seen a shift away from the traditional view of the border rivers as spaces to be engineered, toward a river basin-based approach.[80]

Two issues have gained increasing salience in recent negotiations that provide evidence of this new vision of the river basins.[81] One is requirements for environmental flows to restore healthy habitats; the other is the push for public participation in watershed management.[82] Environmentalists, including both local and national NGOs, have been working during the past decade to persuade governments on both sides of the border to find a way to allocate some of the river flow for ecological functions. In 2010, in a trial case, Minute 316 authorized advocacy groups for the Colorado River Delta to use the Wellton-Mohawk bypass drain at Yuma to send 10,000 acre-feet to the Santa Clara Slough, a wetland about 50 miles south of the border.[83] Likewise, the importance of public participation in decision making is gaining ground in the context of a new emphasis on river basin management. The BECC has encouraged the formation of river basin committees on the Mexican side. On the U.S. side, state-mandated regional planning groups are moving ahead in Texas. Local-level cross-border cooperation has grown with Mexican decentralization, although there are significant differences in the institutional capacities of local water management agencies on the two sides of the border.[84] Both El Paso–Ciudad Juárez and San Diego–Tijuana have developed binational working practices, with community participation.[85]

These trends bore fruit in late 2012 when Minute 319 was signed, with approval from a wide range of stakeholders on both sides of the border. Minute 319 makes a number of innovative changes to the way transboundary water is managed.[86] First, it allows Mexico to defer delivery of a portion of its Colorado River allotment not only while it makes repairs to the earthquake-damaged infrastructure but also when conservation measures or new water sources allow it to reduce the use of Colorado River water, effectively "banking" its water on the U.S. side of the border. This provision can be expected to increase the incentives for conservation measures on the Mexican side. Second, and perhaps of greater import, Minute 319 makes provision for reductions in delivery of water, on both sides of the border, when reservoir levels drop below certain pre-agreed levels. In return for this concession from Mexico, the Minute offers Mexico additional deliveries of water (above the 1.5 million acre-feet) when reservoir levels are high. Third, for the first time in the history of the treaty, provision is made for environmental flows, ensuring that conservation projects will generate water for the Colorado River and Delta ecosystems.

Environmental Problems

The shift to river basin management and greater emphasis on sustainability reflects a growing recognition that the approach to water use and allocation over the past decades has become increasingly unsustainable. Not only is more water allocated than is actually available, but also the overuse is leading to water-quality problems that reduce productivity. This is true not only for the Rio Grande and the Colorado River but also for the region's aquifers, about which much less is known and for which there are few governance mechanisms. Existing problems will only grow worse as climate change makes rainfall more irregular and the region becomes more arid.

Water Quantity

The Colorado River Compact, negotiated in the 1920s, and the subsequent Treaty of 1944 were based on river observations made in the 1900s, which we now know was "the greatest and longest high flow period of the last five centuries."[87] Assuming that the Colorado River has an annual flow of almost 20 million acre-feet,[88] the treaties shared out 16.5 million acre-feet. However, with a return to more normal precipitation patterns, the flow has been consistently lower, averaging about 13 million acre-feet since 1922. From 1999 to 2003, average flow was only 7 million acre-feet.[89] The Colorado River Delta used to form one of the world's largest desert estuaries, an oasis of 7,800 square kilometers. Today, the delta is 5 percent of its original size and highly saline, and much of the region's biodiversity has disappeared.[90] Even in normal decades, the Colorado River does not have enough water to meet the agreed-on allocations. Likewise, in the Rio Grande, most of the water is being withdrawn; much of the river channel is being invaded by salt cedar or clogged by water hyacinth.[91]

The region suffers from chronic drought problems, with the current period of drought far from the worst over the past couple of millennia.[92] In fact, it bears saying that drought is perhaps the normal condition, with years of "sufficient" rainfall unusual. A recent government study of the Colorado River Basin that looks at water supply and demand over the next 50 years projects "imbalances" throughout the Colorado River Basin, with the average imbalance projected as greater than 3.2 million acre-feet per year by 2060; in other words, demand will far exceed water availability.[93] The largest increase in demand is expected to come from municipal and industrial uses. In the face of this evidence, discussions have begun to focus on overall reductions in allocations. For example, in 2007, the United States secretary of the interior adopted guidelines for reducing allocations if Lake Mead reaches critically low levels;[94] Minute 319 includes Mexico in a similar arrangement. Nevertheless, water quantity will always be an issue.

Water Quality

Water-quality problems are a natural outcome of the overuse of this scarce resource, aggravated by inadequate or improper management of human, agricultural, and industrial waste.[95] Salinity, which results as irrigation water seeps through the mineral-rich soils and returns to surface water along with dissolved minerals, is a problem throughout the region.[96] Despite the interventions of Minute 242, salinity is on the rise.[97] In both river basins, soil salinization is already affecting agricultural production. Much of the water that is used for irrigation is extracted and returned to the system several times. Each time, it carries a heavier load of minerals. Irrigation systems have "become a vast system for collecting and distributing salt. Each year about 10 million tons of salt enter the system, but virtually none reaches the ocean."[98] Despite this problem, since the mid-1970s there have been important shifts in the crops grown in the border region irrigated by the Colorado River, notably from low-value, salt-tolerant crops to higher-value, less-salt-tolerant plants, leading to losses.[99] Along the Rio Grande, farming is declining because of the loss of water quantity and quality. The Delicias Irrigation District, for example, the largest on the Rio Conchos, was a rich cotton-growing area in the 1960s and 1970s; today, many farmers there are growing low-value alfalfa, and some receive no irrigation water.[100]

Beyond the problem of salinity, current problems with water quality also include runoff of pesticides, fertilizers, and herbicides; industrial discharges; and untreated residential effluents. In addition to problems for farming, human and industrial waste have raised disease levels above national averages on both sides of the border.[101] Perhaps most important, inadequately treated wastewater that is discharged into streams and river systems eventually enters the groundwater system, which is largely unregulated.[102]

Groundwater

Data on aquifers is largely insufficient; nevertheless, it is clear that groundwater is being withdrawn faster than the aquifers can recharge and that, as a result of urban and agricultural runoff and falling water levels, groundwater is increasingly contaminated and brackish. On the Mexican side, studies suggest that of 96 identified aquifers, 21 are already being overexploited.[103] In the Colorado River Basin, where aquifers depend on recharge from the river, estimates a decade ago already put extraction at 4 percent over replenishment rates.[104] Hueco Bolson is perhaps the most urgent case, but it is certainly not the only transboundary aquifer being drawn on unsustainably from both sides. The Mimbres aquifer joins Columbus, New Mexico, and Palomas, Chihuahua. Lakes in the region disappeared as long ago as the 1960s, and the water table has dropped by as much as 140 feet since the introduction of electric pumps for irrigation.[105] Evidence of the rising local concern about water availability is found in the fact that El Paso has been buying up properties from local farmers in order to control the underground water resources.[106] El Paso has taken other steps to ensure its municipal water supply, including increased use of surface water, which may simply reduce the recharge rate of the aquifer.[107]

Contamination of groundwater is increasingly a problem. The city of El Paso has been running a desalinization plant for several years to treat water extracted from the Hueco Bolson. In Tijuana, wastewater contamination of the aquifer has led to the closing of numerous wells because of high levels of dissolved solids, nitrates, and coliforms.[108]

Along the Texas border, shale gas development is expanding rapidly. About 1,000 drilling permits were issued for the Eagle Ford Shale in 2010, 2,826 in 2011, and 1,452 from January to April 2012. The amount of water used by the new fracking industry is small compared with agricultural and municipal use, but local impacts on aquifers and surface water can be significant. Little is known yet about the effects of fracking on aquifers, and the U.S. Geological Survey does not have an extensive groundwater monitoring network near the Mexican border in Texas.[109]

Climate Change

Climate change is predicted to take a heavy toll on the border region. Recent warming in the U.S. Southwest has been the most rapid in the nation, driving a decline in the snowpack and river flow. The average temperature has already increased by 1.5°F over the 1960–1979 baseline and is expected to rise by 4°F to 10°F by 2100.[110] Although there is some debate about how the water cycle in the region will change, almost certainly it will be substantially drier.[111] Rising temperatures, even without a drought, decrease surface water, increase evapotranspiration, and decrease soil humidity.[112] Already, rising temperatures have aggravated the impacts of the current drought.[113] Paradoxically, with more precipitation falling as rain rather than snow, flood-like conditions will be more common.[114] Evidence is strong that change is already occurring. For example, as of spring 2012, less than 50 percent of the average snowpack was left from 1981 in the Sangre de Cristo Mountains, which form the headwaters of the Rio Grande.[115]

Increasing temperatures, reduced water flows, drought, increased wildfires, and invasive species will transform the landscape, posing a major threat to agriculture and ranching in the region, as well as creating water and energy problems for urban areas. The region's biodiversity and protected areas will be affected too, as environmental flows dwindle. Some of the region's iconic landscapes are likely to be affected, such as the saguaro cactus of the Sonoran Desert. The effects on the economy will be numerous and will go beyond the problem of reduced water availability for agriculture. Long-lasting heat waves will increase the demand for energy use, which is often highly water consumptive. Specialty crops that require cool winter temperatures (apricots, almonds, figs, kiwis, olives, and walnuts, among others) will suffer. Estimates for California's agricultural losses range up to 40 percent.[116] Mexico will be particularly hard hit by the losses in agriculture; an estimated 48 percent of all land in Mexico is vulnerable to the impacts of climate change, especially in the north.[117] These effects of climate change will clearly increase competition for water as it becomes increasingly scarce.[118]

Looking to the Future

Addressing the growing pressures on this evaporating resource will be complex. To date, the complicated system of laws, treaties, compacts, and institutions has sufficed, in large part because of the willingness of the two countries to cooperate on technical and financial issues. This political cooperation has been put to the test on a number of occasions but has always forestalled major conflict. The flexibility of the system has allowed it to address new situations, but the challenges ahead will require broader and faster responses.

Effective solutions to water scarcity will have to include technical, financial, and institutional components. Technically, much can be done to reduce water use and reduce the amount of water lost from the system. Overall, regional experience with conservation and efficiency measures has been positive, with many municipalities already using less water for a larger population, and there has been rapid expansion of the use of treated wastewater in recent years.[119] Lining of canals and drip irrigation can further reduce water loss from agricultural systems. However, as we have seen with the case of the lining of the All-American Canal, these water savings may be a water loss for another producer or for the environmental flow. Desalinization may offer some promise for the future. Financing has been available for infrastructure projects through a variety of government programs, particularly for urban water infrastructure in recent years. Some of the projects, such as the current assistance with the Mexicali post-earthquake reconstruction, are paid back in water savings. Mexico has recently announced a plan to invest $83 billion in water projects over the next 20 years, which will include strategies for cleanup of basins and rivers, as well as universal water and sanitation coverage.[120]

However, funding has diminished in recent years for international programs, such as the BECC and the BEIF. Funds administered through the NADB decreased from about $100 million for 1995–1997 to about $10 million for 2008–2013.[121] To give an idea of the unmet demand, BECC-NADB applications totaled $800 million last year; $10 million was funded.[122] With the growing population and aging infrastructure, the amount of investment in the region will need to increase substantially. The existing institutions will need not only more funding but also a broader mandate to address regional water scarcity. To ensure that investments address the region's water problems in a comprehensive way, river basin institutions will need to take the lead.

River Basin Institutions

The shortcoming of all these programs has been the piecemeal approach, generally focused on infrastructure projects, which does not see the river basins and their aquifers as an integral natural system. Technical and financial solutions will have to be coupled with institutional solutions that ensure equity in water allocation and address urban growth and the changing climate. This will require effective, efficient, and participatory institutions. There is a push in this direction, as discussed above, with greater emphasis being put on river basin management and planning, including looking at environmental flows and integrating a wide range of stakeholders in the decision-making process. Minute 319 is strong evidence that this approach is having some positive impacts. And river basin-focused solutions are being considered and discussed by the relevant U.S. government agencies, as is evidenced by two recent reports discussed here.[123]

In late 2012, the Bureau of Reclamation of the U.S. Department of the Interior released a study of the pressures on the Colorado River. The study looks at a range of proposals to work with basin stakeholders to find solutions, in essence laying the groundwork for a basin-based approach. On the release of the study, Secretary of Interior Salazar stated,

> There is no silver bullet to solve the imbalance between the demand for water and the supply in the Colorado River Basin over the next 50 years—rather it is going to take diligent planning and collaboration from all stakeholders to identify and move forward with practical solutions.[124]

Another recently released report, the 15th Good Neighbor Environmental Board (GNEB) Report to the President,[125] focuses on the status of water resources in the border region.[126] Prior GNEB reports have emphasized the need for river basin approaches.[127] In this edition, recommendations call for increased collaboration and coordination, proposing that the U.S. federal government convene groups including the government of Mexico, stakeholders in Mexican border states, tribal and local governments, and citizens to solve problems with the binational water bodies. It calls on (a) the U.S. federal government to enhance binational watershed planning and increase institutional support and technical assistance for local planning efforts in smaller watersheds; (b) the U.S. Department of the Interior, the U.S. Department of Agriculture, the IBWC, and the EPA to continue their cooperative binational approach to watershed level management; and (c) the U.S. federal natural resource agencies and the IBWC to begin to incorporate environmental flows into plans for the region.

Experts are divided as to whether the existing institutions will have the flexibility to deal with the growing regional pressures. Some analysts and administrators believe that the existing compacts and international treaties will have to be renegotiated in the context of climate change and increasing pressures on water supplies. Pombo and Wright, for example, recommend revamping the 1944 treaty to deal with a "potentially explosive scenario," warning that the 1944 treaty may "fall short of what is needed to guide policymakers through the process of reevaluating and reallocating water rights among all the dependent states."[128] They suggest that an incremental approach, rather than a drastic overhaul, will suffice; local actions will be fundamental to finding "new, creative ways to cooperate." However, in the event of serious impacts from climate change, the United States is likely to meet its own needs first, leaving Mexico high and dry. A 2003 report prepared for the Department of Defense predicts that, in the case of catastrophic climate change, the United States will turn inward, committing any resources to its own population and creating friction with Mexico.[129] Likewise, the U.S. Global Change Research Program warns that "competing demands from treaty rights, rapid development, and changes in agriculture in the region, exacerbated by years of drought and climate change, have the potential to spark significant conflict over an already over-allocated and dwindling resource."[130] However, given that the existing complex arrangements have worked so far, the IBWC, the GNEB, and other government agencies hold to the belief that the Law of the River and these institutions will be flexible enough to face increased variability in climate and continued economic growth through continuing incremental change.

Groundwater

Certainly, the existing framework and functional international institutions have facilitated the process of addressing surface problems. Groundwater, however, stands out glaringly as a critical transboundary water issue for which a system of regulation and institutions for dispute settlement has not been established. Any blueprint for the future of the region must include not only better information gathering about the extent and sustainability of its aquifers but also the inclusion of groundwater in water management institutions both domestically and internationally. If the depletion of the aquifers that serve the region's rapidly expanding cities is not addressed preemptively, it will be much thornier to address when a crisis arises.[131]

Several developments suggest that a move toward a groundwater agreement may be possible.[132] A web of institutions already exists—the IBWC, the BECC, and departments or ministries of environment and internal affairs—which could all be involved,[133] and NAFTA-based initiatives have led to sharing of information across the border. The GNEB has called for efforts to address transboundary aquifers, specifically for strengthening of government institutions, research efforts, and treaty instruments.[134] The BECC has drawn attention to water issues and the need to achieve sustainable solutions. It has fostered a more collaborative approach among border institutions and, by pushing the limits of the IBWC mandate, has brought other institutions into the debate over sustainability.[135] The tri-national Commission for Environmental Cooperation has also contributed to a new emphasis on sustainable development in the border region and lends its support to the development of multinational environmental agreements.[136] Minutes 242 and 319, among others, have acknowledged the need for a comprehensive groundwater agreement[137] and have broadened the binational regime to include environmental and water-quality issues, both clearly linked with groundwater management. The IBWC and CILA adopted a cooperative process in 2009 to implement a transboundary aquifers assessment program.[138] However, because there has been little political support and ongoing disagreements among the state governments on the U.S. side, little has been accomplished.[139]

Recommendations as to how to proceed toward an international agreement on groundwater focus on an incremental and procedural approach.[140] Tackling the problem aquifer by aquifer and prioritizing settlement of the most tractable disputes are proposed as effective ways to start. Focusing on procedure, for example, information sharing, will allow for the development of transboundary institutions before addressing substantive issues of water allocation that raise sovereignty issues.[141] In terms of considering a more comprehensive agreement, it is important to note that groundwater agreements are largely unprecedented. However, there are a number of international dialogues and some advances in international law that could provide a good starting point for developing such an agreement.[142,143] It is worth noting that most advances in the current set of institutions have come in response to tensions or conflict in the region.

Making Critical Development Decisions

Climate change may put extraordinary pressures on the resources of the region. As water scarcity worsens, critical decisions will need to be made not only about ongoing development in the region, such as limiting population growth, but also about scaling back existing human activities. The growth of urban areas has required the most dramatic expansion of water use in recent years, but agriculture remains by far the largest consumer in the region. Increasing drought will lead to declines in water quantity and quality, while human activities, including urban life, agriculture, industry, and fracking, will continue to overdraw these resources. When technological and financial solutions are not enough, cutbacks will need to be made in agricultural production and possibly industrial production as well.

Substantial adjustments will need to be made in crop production and irrigation. Given that farmers on the U.S. and Mexican sides of the border are each other's greatest competitors, these decisions will almost inevitably lead to disputes.[144] Any cutbacks will be socially disruptive and will have serious effects not only on the region's economy but also on the larger U.S. and Mexican economies. Reductions in the region's agricultural output could have serious impacts on food markets in the United States and Mexico at a time when production may be declining in other regions. Will the existing institutions have the authority and the flexibility to take on these difficult tasks? The sheer complexity of the institutional matrix on the U.S. side of the border has routinely meant that addressing conflicts over water allocation takes years, even decades, as evidenced by the slow response to salinization problems in the 1960s or the long process of allocating water for environmental flows. The international institutions, while having shown flexibility and a capacity to expand their orbit, have not addressed one of the fundamental transboundary water issues, namely aquifers, at all. To understand whether these regional solutions—technical, financial, and institutional—will be effective, it is important to understand the place of water conflicts in the U.S. relationship with Mexico.

Water, the Border, and the U.S.-Mexico Relationship

The U.S. relationship with Mexico always plays a central role in U.S. foreign policy, given the importance of Mexico to the U.S. economy and the extent to which problems in Mexico can spill over into the United States. Although many of the conflicts and agreements over water along the border have a decidedly local cast, the ways in which the two countries approach these problems are tied to broader foreign policy positions. It must be remembered, of course, that much of this territory once belonged to Mexico and was obtained by the United States either through the Treaty of Guadalupe Hidalgo (1848) or the Gadsden Purchase (1853). This history is reflected in the cultural characteristics of the region and the long-standing expectation of injustice in their dealings with the United States on the part of many Mexicans. The large disparities between the two countries give the United States greater leverage in almost any confrontation or negotiation.

Development on the U.S. side of the border over the past century has time and again increased the competition for resources in the region. For example, the Mexican Revolution (1910–1920) stalled development on the Mexican side, while U.S. states created ever more extensive irrigation systems. After the revolution, the Mexican government saw irrigation expansion in the northern states as a way to secure the rather tenuous border, as well as providing a basis for water claims in any treaty negotiations.[145] In the 1930s, just as agriculture was taking off in the region and major investments in infrastructure were beginning, President Franklin Roosevelt instituted the Good Neighbor Policy. This policy originated in the concern of the United States with developments in Europe and the need to secure allies, or at least neutrality, in its own hemisphere.[146] The Treaty of 1944, which reflected this policy of maintaining a positive relationship with Mexico, was made possible by the federal government, including the U.S. Department of State, which took the lead in bringing the basin states together, most notably overcoming the opposition of California to restrictions on its water use.[147] Nevertheless, Mexico did not get all it asked of the treaty; 1.5 million acre-feet was only half what it asked for. Years later, when the thorny issue of the lining of the All-American Canal first arose, Mexico was concerned about keeping NAFTA negotiations on track and avoided making waves about the canal,[148] so the United States was able to ignore Mexico's concerns. Water remains one of the more intractable disputes between the United States and Mexico and a potential source of friction.[149]

Today, the relationship with Mexico has shifted, becoming both more collaborative and more controversial at the same time.[150] While cooperation is broad, the United States is highly concerned with Mexico's place in the wars on terrorism and drugs, as well as the immigration question. Domestically, these are the issues that draw public attention in the United States. U.S. concerns have led to significant investments in border security, beginning with the shift to greater reliance on infrastructure under the Clinton administration, followed by an unprecedented buildup since September 11, 2001. The U.S. Border Patrol now has more than 21,000 agents in the region, a 518 percent increase since the early 1990s, in addition to large investments in fencing and technology such as sensors.[151] Concerns about terrorists, unrealized in the case of the Mexican border, have been confounded with efforts to "seal the border." Despite the fact that unauthorized immigration is now way down from its peak, preventing illegal border crossings remains a U.S. priority.[152]

The border security issue is not isolated from other policy areas; security measures have slowed economic integration and had divisive impacts on border communities. For example, although large investments have been made to prevent illegal crossings, little has been done to upgrade the existing ports of entry to facilitate the legal flow of goods or people.[153] In terms of water management, unilateral border security measures make it more difficult to address and discuss water and sustainability issues on a regional basis.[154] Nevertheless, from the perspective of addressing regional issues, it is important to understand that security issues—immigration, guns, drugs, and terrorism—are not problems that arise at the border. These problems have their roots in other regions of Mexico and the United States; they are the products of economic disparities, governance, and public safety issues.[155] But the border has been the place where the United States has confronted these problems. Pushing these issues away from the border, by dealing with them where they originate, could do much to facilitate cooperation and collaboration on actual border issues, including water use. Mexico's new president indeed seems to be shifting the focus away from the persistent problems of violence and the drug trade and trying to refocus Mexico's attention on trade, poverty, and education, areas that can highlight the positive aspects of the Mexico-U.S. relationship.[156]

Addressing the water issues along the border is critical for improving development opportunities and reducing international tensions in the region. Working jointly on water issues provides a means to strengthen the United States' positive relationship with Mexico. The extensive consultation, cooperation, and collaboration entailed by joint water management in the border region can provide a very positive context for dealing with other issues between the United States and Mexico. The reverse is also true: engendering a more positive relationship by emphasizing the extent of cooperation and commerce between the two countries will create better conditions for dealing with tensions and even crises created by water scarcity. Probably the best tools to reduce violence and illegal immigration and promote development are economic growth and improving the rule of law for Mexico. However, working together to maintain and develop effective infrastructure and institutions for dealing with worsening water scarcity can provide an important element of a positive relationship.

Global Possibilities

The relevance of developing an effective and adaptable model for water allocation and management goes beyond the Mexican border. Globally, freshwater scarcity is likely to be one of the most destabilizing impacts of climate change.[157] A 2012 National Intelligence Council Report concludes that it is critical to be proactive in the face of coming water scarcities.[158] The report finds that global demand for water will be up by 40 percent by 2030, which, combined with climate change–related declines in precipitation in some already arid areas, will leave much of the world's population in water-scarce regions.[159] Water stress is projected to be a serious issue in the fragile states of Africa and the Middle East by 2030, with China and India also vulnerable. Complicating this increasing scarcity is the fact that some 200 major river basins are shared by more than two countries and an estimated 40 percent of the world's population lives in or near one of these basins.[160] The report concludes that many countries will not be able to avoid food and water shortages without massive help. Such scarcity will certainly harm the economic performance of some major U.S. trading partners; it may even lead to state failure in the worst cases.[161] Models and leadership for effective transboundary water management will be critical for preventing or ameliorating these problems.

Reducing the risks created by water scarcity around the world will require major investments not only in technology and knowledge building but also in the more challenging process of institution building. Institutions, most prominently international treaties and river basin committees that are resilient in the face of changing conditions, can be particularly useful for managing and defusing disputes. A recent review of 276 international river basins finds that 24, mainly in north and sub-Saharan Africa, have a high potential for conflict, given the impending scarcity of water and the lack of resilient institutions.[162] By 2050, with the accumulating effects of climate change, more than 60 river basins will be at risk. The attributes of resilient river basin institutions therefore need to be well understood, and efforts need to be made to promote their establishment in at-risk basins. The United States has already made some efforts toward addressing the need for better water management globally.

The U.S. Water Partnership, which was launched by the U.S. Department of State in 2012, is a public-private partnership that aims to mobilize U.S. expertise and resources to address water challenges in developing countries.[163] Given the centrality of good water management to development and security, establishing effective institutions should be a priority in U.S. dealings with many countries, including Mexico. The institutions along the U.S.-Mexico border have many of the characteristics of resiliency, which include flexibility, capacity to deal with variability, conflict-resolution mechanisms, and river basin organizations,[164] although there are improvements to be made in terms of treating the river basins as whole ecosystems, including groundwater, rather than the property of states, municipalities, or land owners. The U.S.-Mexico situation could serve as a technological, financial, and institutional model of how to govern scarce international resources, but management of these resources will need to evolve and adapt to changing economic and climate conditions.

Notes

1 Bureau of Transportation Statistics (U.S. BTS), Research and Innovative Technology Division, www.rita.dot.gov/bts/data_and_statistics/intermodal_transportation_database.html.
2 Center for Strategic and International Studies (CSIS), "A New Narrative for Mexico," *Hemisphere Insider* 1, no. 4 (2011): 1–2.
3 CSIS, "A New Narrative for Mexico."
4 CSIS, "A New Narrative for Mexico."
5 CSIS, "A New Narrative for Mexico."
6 Pew Hispanic Center, cited in CSIS, "A New Narrative for Mexico."
7 Good Neighbor Environmental Board (GNEB), *The Environmental, Economic and Health Status of Water Resources in the U.S.-Mexico Border Region,* 15th Report of the Good Neighbor Environmental Board to the President and Congress of the United States (Dec. 2012).
8 G. Eckstein, "Buried Treasure or Buried Hope? The Status of U.S.-Mexico Transboundary Aquifers under International Law," *International Community Law Review* 13: (2011): 273–90.
9 California, Arizona, New Mexico, and Texas on the U.S. side; Baja California, Sonora, Chihuahua, Coahuila, Nuevo Leon, and Tamaulipas on the Mexican side.
10 GNEB, *Environmental, Economic and Health Status.*
11 GNEB, *Environmental, Economic and Health Status.*
12 S. Lauer, "U.S.-Mexico Border Infrastructure: Meeting Current Needs with an Eye to Future Challenges," Colorado River Project River Report, Water Education Foundation (Winter 2008–2009): 1-11.
13 GNEB, *Environmental, Economic and Health Status.*
14 GNEB, *Environmental, Economic and Health Status.*
15 Lauer, "U.S.-Mexico Border Infrastructure."
16 R. Sáenz and K. Manges Douglas, "Environmental Issues on the Mexico-U.S. Border: An Introduction," *Southern Rural Sociology* 24, no. 1 (2009): 1–6.
17 U.S. Environmental Protection Agency and Mexican Secretariat of Environment and Natural Resources (U.S. EPA and SEMARNAT), *Border 2012: U.S.-Mexico Environmental Program, State of the Border Region Indicators Report 2010* (U.S. EPA and SEMARNAT, 2010).
18 U.S. Environmental Protection Agency (U.S. EPA), "Region 9," accessed Feb. 2, 2013, www.epa.gov/aboutepa/region9.html.
19 O.A. Pombo and R. Wright, "Water Perspective in the Western U.S.-Mexico Border: Future Conflict?" in *SCERP Monograph Series No. 16,* edited by Erik Lee and Paul Ganster (San Diego, CA: Southwest Consortium for Environmental Research and Policy, San Diego University Press, 2012): 187-199.

20 F. Pearce, *When the Rivers Run Dry: Water—The Defining Crisis of the Twenty-first Century* (Beacon Press, Boston, 2006).
21 Eckstein, "Buried Treasure or Buried Hope?"
22 Commission for Environmental Cooperation (CEC), "The North American Mosaic: An Overview of Key Environmental Issues" (2008), www.cec.org/files/PDF//Mosaic-2008_en.pdf.
23 International Boundary and Water Commission (IBWC), www.ibwc.state.gov/.
24 Pearce, *When the Rivers Run Dry.*
25 C. Walsh, "Aguas Broncas: The Regional Political Ecology of Water Conflict in the Mexico-U.S. Borderlands," *Journal of Political Ecology* 11 (2004): 43–58.
26 Pearce, *When the Rivers Run Dry.*
27 Pearce, *When the Rivers Run Dry.*
28 Lauer, "U.S.-Mexico Border Infrastructure."
29 Massachusetts Institute of Technology (MIT), "Mission 2012: Clean Water" (2012), http://web.mit.edu/12.000/www/m2012/finalwebsite/problem/international.shtml#mexico.
30 Pearce, *When the Rivers Run Dry.*
31 IBWC, www.ibwc.state.gov/.
32 Pearce, *When the Rivers Run Dry.*
33 A. Wolf and J. Newton, "Case Study of Transboundary Dispute Resolution: U.S./Mexico Shared Aquifers" (Program in Water Conflict Management and Transformation, Institute for Water and Watersheds, Oregon State University, 2013), accessed Feb. 2, 2013, www.transboundarywaters.orst.edu/research/case_studies/US_Mexico_Aquifer_New.htm.
34 M. Cohen, *Municipal Deliveries of Colorado River Basin Water* (Pacific Institute, Oakland, CA, 2011).
35 Pearce, *When the Rivers Run Dry;* Sáenz and Douglas, "Environmental Issues."
36 IBWC, www.ibwc.state.gov/.
37 *Colorado River Day,* http://coloradoriverday.com/common-sense-solutions/.
38 Environmental Defense Fund and Woodrow Wilson Center (EDF and WWC), "Agricultural Production Trends and the Future of the Trans-boundary Rio Grande/Rio Bravo Basin," Conference Proceedings (Sept. 2004); Pearce, *When the Rivers Run Dry.*
39 CEC, "The North American Mosaic."
40 Pearce, *When the Rivers Run Dry.*
41 Eckstein, "Buried Treasure or Buried Hope?"
42 V. Sánchez-Mungía, "The U.S. Mexico Border: Conflict and Cooperation in Water Management," *International Journal of Water Resources Development* 27, no. 3 (2011): 577–93.
43 H. Ingram, "Transboundary Groundwater on the U.S.-Mexico Border: Is the Glass Half Full, Half Empty, or Even on the Table?" *Natural Resources Journal* 40 (2000): 185–88; Pearce, *When the Rivers Run Dry.*
44 O. Chávez, "Mining of Internationally Shared Aquifers: The El Paso–Juárez Case," *Natural Resources Journal* 40 (2000): 238–60.
45 M. Wilder and P. Romero Lankao, "Paradoxes of Decentralization: Water Reform and Social Implications in Mexico," *World Development* 34, no. 11 (2006): 1977–95.
46 For an explanation of the various regimes, see Eckstein, "Buried Treasure or Buried Hope?"; B. Hume, "Water in the U.S.-Mexico Border Area," *Natural Resources Journal* 40 (2000): 189–97; S. Mumme, O. Ibanez, and S. Till, "Multi-level Governance of Water on the U.S.-Mexico Border," *Regions and Cohesion* 2, no. 2 (2012): 6–29.

47 GNEB, *Environmental, Economic and Health Status.*
48 U.S. Global Change Research Program (U.S. GCRP), *Global Climate Change Impacts in the U.S.* (Cambridge University Press, Cambridge, 2009), www.globalchange.gov/usimpacts.
49 GNEB, *Environmental, Economic and Health Status.*
50 IBWC, www.ibwc.state.gov/.
51 Officially, the Treaty for the Utilization of the Waters of the Colorado and Tijuana Rivers and of the Rio Grande.
52 GNEB, *Environmental, Economic and Health Status.*
53 Wolf and Newton, "Case Study of Transboundary Dispute Resolution."
54 Wolf and Newton, "Case Study of Transboundary Dispute Resolution."
55 This desalinization plant has never been used because of the high cost of operation (Pearce, *When the Rivers Run Dry*).
56 Wolf and Newton, "Case Study of Transboundary Dispute Resolution."
57 Lauer, "U.S.-Mexico Border Infrastructure."
58 Lauer, "U.S.-Mexico Border Infrastructure."
59 S. Dibble, "U.S., Mexico Boost Collaboration on Colorado River," *San Diego Union-Tribune* (Feb. 6, 2011), www.utsandiego.com/news/2011/feb/06/us-mexico-boosting-collaboration-colorado-river.
60 Lauer, "U.S.-Mexico Border Infrastructure."
61 E. Spagat, "Mexico's Newest Export to the U.S. May Be Water," *Boston Globe* (Oct. 15, 2011), www.boston.com/news/nation/articles/2011/10/15/mexicos_newest_export_to_us_may_be_water/.
62 "Mexico, U.S. Reach Agreement on Water Debt," *U.S. Water News Online* (March 2005), www.uswaternews.com/archives/arcglobal/5mexiu.s.3.html.
63 Between 1992 and 2002, the water level in the two largest reservoirs on the Mexican side, Amistad Reservoir and Falcon Reservoir, fell to 30 percent of capacity (Sánchez-Mungía, "The U.S. Mexico Border").
64 "Mexico, U.S. Reach Agreement," *U.S. Water News Online.*
65 J. Aguilar, "Texas Mexico Water Dispute Could Reemerge," *Texas Tribune* (March 19, 2010); Commission for Environmental Cooperation (CEC), "The North American Mosaic: An Overview of Key Environmental Issues" (2008), www.cec.org/files/PDF//Mosaic-2008_en.pdf; "Mexico, U.S. Reach Agreement," *U.S. Water News Online.*
66 "Mexico, U.S. Reach Agreement," *U.S. Water News Online.*
67 Mumme et al., "Multi-level Governance of Water."
68 Sánchez-Mungía, "The U.S. Mexico Border."
69 Wilder and Romero Lankao, "Paradoxes of Decentralization."
70 Pearce, *When the Rivers Run Dry.*
71 S. Mumme, "Minute 242 and Beyond: Challenges and Opportunities for Managing Transboundary Groundwater on the U.S.-Mexico Border," *Natural Resources Journal* 40 (2000): 341–77.
72 Hume, "Water in the U.S.-Mexico Border Area."
73 Mumme, "Minute 242 and Beyond."
74 Wolf and Newton, "Case Study of Transboundary Dispute Resolution."
75 These include not only the North American Development Bank, Border Environment Cooperation Commission, and Business and Economic Inequality Forum, but also other EPA programs, such as the Tribal Border Infrastructure Program, U.S. Department of Agriculture, U.S. Department of Housing and Urban Development, U.S. Department of Health and Human Services, and U.S. Bureau of Reclamation,

which have invested substantially in modernization of infrastructure (GNEB, *Environmental, Economic and Health Status*).

76 The La Paz Agreement has been implemented through the Integrated Border Plan (1992–1994), Border XXI (1996–2000), and Border 2012 (2003–2012), which focused on water quality (GNEB, *Environmental, Economic and Health Status*).

77 U.S. EPA, "Region 9."

78 GNEB, *Environmental, Economic and Health Status.*

79 The EPA's BEIF provides grant funding exclusively for implementation of high-priority municipal drinking water and wastewater infrastructure projects within 100 kilometers of the border. It has been particularly important in providing affordable financing for projects in Mexico (GNEB, *Environmental, Economic and Health Status*).

80 J. Donahue and I. Klaver, "Sharing Water Internationally, Past, Present and Future—Mexico and the United States," *Southern Rural Sociology* 24, no. 1 (2009): 7-20.

81 Donahue and Klaver, "Sharing Water Internationally."

82 Environmental flows are the water flows, defined in terms of quantity, quality, and timing, required to sustain freshwater and estuarine ecosystems and the human livelihoods and well-being that depend on them (GNEB, *Environmental, Economic and Health Status*).

83 Mumme et al., "Multi-level Governance of Water."

84 Sánchez-Mungía, "The U.S. Mexico Border."

85 Sánchez-Mungía, "The U.S. Mexico Border."

86 International Boundary and Water Commission (IBWC), "Commission Signs Colorado River Agreement," Press Release (Nov. 20, 2012). Accessed Jan. 15, 2014. www.ibwc.state.gov/.

87 U.S. GCRP, *Global Climate Change Impacts.*

88 GNEB, *Environmental, Economic and Health Status.*

89 Pearce, *When the Rivers Run Dry.*

90 CEC, "The North American Mosaic."

91 Pearce, *When the Rivers Run Dry;* CEC, "The North American Mosaic."

92 U.S. GCRP, *Global Climate Change Impacts.*

93 U.S. Department of the Interior, "Secretary Salazar Releases Colorado River Basin Study Projecting Major Imbalances in Water Supply and Demand," Press Release (Bureau of Reclamation, U.S. Department of the Interior, Dec. 12, 2012).

94 GNEB, *Environmental, Economic and Health Status.*

95 GNEB, *Environmental, Economic and Health Status.*

96 CEC, "The North American Mosaic."

97 MIT, "Mission 2012: Clean Water."

98 Pearce, *When the Rivers Run Dry,* 198.

99 MIT, "Mission 2012: Clean Water."

100 Pearce, *When the Rivers Run Dry.*

101 Pearce, *When the Rivers Run Dry.*

102 GNEB, *Environmental, Economic and Health Status.*

103 Sánchez-Mungía, "The U.S. Mexico Border."

104 S. Mumme and N. Pineda, "Administracíon del Agua en la Frontera México-Estados Unidos: Retos de Mandato para las Instituciones Binacionales," in *Seguridad, Agua y Desarrollo: El Futuro de la Frontera México-Estados Unidos,* edited by A. Alfonso, L. Cortez, S. Whiteford, and M. Chávez Márquez (Colegio de la Frontera, Tijuana, 2005).

105 Hume, "Water in the U.S.-Mexico Border Area."

106 Pearce, *When the Rivers Run Dry.*

107 Pearce, *When the Rivers Run Dry.*
108 Sánchez-Mungía, "The U.S. Mexico Border."
109 GNEB, *Environmental, Economic and Health Status.*
110 U.S. GCRP, *Global Climate Change Impacts.*
111 U.S. GCRP, *Global Climate Change Impacts.*
112 World Bank, *Mexico Country Note: Climate Change Aspects in Agriculture* (World Bank, Washington, D.C., 2009).
113 U.S. GCRP, *Global Climate Change Impacts.*
114 Pombo and Wright, "Water Perspective."
115 GNEB, *Environmental, Economic and Health Status.*
116 U.S. GCRP, *Global Climate Change Impacts.*
117 World Bank, *Mexico Country Note.*
118 GNEB, *Environmental, Economic and Health Status;* U.S. GCRP, *Global Climate Change Impacts.*
119 P. Gleick, "Roadmap for Sustainable Water Resources in Southwestern North America," *Proceedings of the National Academy of Sciences* 107, no. 50 (2010): 21300–21305.
120 http://dsiaplicaciones.semarnat.gob.mx/sdp2009/index.php?option=com_content&view=article&id=3162:mexico-to-invest-83-bn-in-water-projects&catid=53:prensa-internacional&Itemid=117.
121 GNEB, *Environmental, Economic and Health Status.*
122 GNEB, *Environmental, Economic and Health Status.*
123 U.S. Department of the Interior, "Secretary Salazar"; GNEB, *Environmental, Economic and Health Status.*
124 U.S. Department of the Interior, "Secretary Salazar."
125 The Good Neighbor Environmental Board is an independent federal advisory committee that develops recommendations to the President. It includes representatives from federal departments and agencies; state, local, and tribal governments in the border region; community development; and academic, health, environmental, and other NGOs, with the U.S. EPA taking responsibility for managing activities.
126 GNEB, *Environmental, Economic and Health Status.*
127 Specifically, the reports have called for watershed-based analysis and management and the development of a binational water database as the baseline for a cross-border water planning process. The current report reiterates these recommendations.
128 Pombo and Wright, "Water Perspective," 195–96.
129 P. Schwartz and D. Randall, "An Abrupt Climate Change Scenario and Its Implications for United States National Security," Report prepared for the U.S. Department of Defense (2003), www.climate.org/PDF/clim_change_scenario.pdf.
130 U.S. GCRP, *Global Climate Change Impacts,* 131.
131 A. Hardberger, "What Lies Beneath: Determining the Necessity of International Groundwater Policy along the United States-Mexico Border and a Roadmap to an Agreement," *Texas Tech Law Review* 35 (2004): 1211–57; Eckstein, "Buried Treasure or Buried Hope?"
132 Mumme, "Minute 242 and Beyond."
133 Ingram, "Transboundary Groundwater."
134 GNEB, *Environmental, Economic and Health Status.*
135 Mumme, "Minute 242 and Beyond."
136 Mumme, "Minute 242 and Beyond."
137 Mumme, "Minute 242 and Beyond."
138 Eckstein, "Buried Treasure or Buried Hope?"

139 Mumme, "Advancing Binational Cooperation in the Transboundary Aquifer Management on the U.S.-Mexico Border." Paper presented at Groundwater in the West Conference (2004).
140 Mumme, "Minute 242 and Beyond"; Hume, "Water in the U.S.-Mexico Border Area"; Eckstein, "Buried Treasure or Buried Hope?"
141 Eckstein, "Buried Treasure or Buried Hope?"
142 Mumme, "Minute 242 and Beyond"; Hardberger, "What Lies Beneath."
143 Mumme ("Minute 242 and Beyond") and Hardberger ("What Lies Beneath") point to the work of the United Nations Committee on International Water Resources Law, including the Helsinki Guidance Rules and the Seoul Rules (1986), state laws, oil and gas laws, the recent United Nations Convention on the Law of the Non-Navigational Uses of International Watercourses, and the Bellagio Draft Treaty on Transboundary Groundwater.
144 Wolf and Newton, "Case Study of Transboundary Dispute Resolution."
145 Walsh, "Aguas Broncas."
146 Donahue and Klaver, "Sharing Water Internationally."
147 Donahue and Klaver, "Sharing Water Internationally."
148 Hume, "Water in the U.S.-Mexico Border Area."
149 Mumme, "Minute 242 and Beyond."
150 E. Olson and E. Lee, "The State of Security in the U.S.-Mexico Border Region," Working Paper Series on the State of the Border (Border Research Partnership, Woodrow Wilson Center, 2012).
151 Olson and Lee, "The State of Security."
152 Olson and Lee, "The State of Security."
153 Olson and Lee, "The State of Security."
154 Sáenz and Douglas, "Environmental Issues."
155 Olson and Lee, "The State of Security."
156 N. Miroff, "A Quieter Drug War in Mexico, But No Less Deadly," *Washington Post* (Feb. 1, 2013).
157 L. DeStefano et al., "Climate Change and the Institutional Resilience of International River Basins," *Journal of Peace Research* 49, no. 1 (2012): 193–209.
158 See also Office of the Director of National Intelligence, "Global Water Scarcity: Intelligence Community Assessment," ICA 2012–08 (Office of the Director of National Intelligence, Government of the United States, 2012).
159 These will include the Middle East, North Africa, West-Central Asia, southern Europe, and the U.S. Southwest.
160 National Intelligence Council, *Global Trends 2030: Alternative Worlds* (Office of the Director of National Intelligence, Government of the United States, 2012), www.dni.gov/nic/globaltrends.
161 Office of the Director of National Intelligence, "Global Water Scarcity."
162 DeStefano et al., "Climate Change and the Institutional Resilience."
163 World Wildlife Fund is one of the partners in this program.
164 DeStefano et al., "Climate Change and the Institutional Resilience."

9

PAKISTAN'S ECOLOGICAL PRECIPICE

An Opportunity for Redefining Security

Saleem H. Ali and Shuja Nawaz

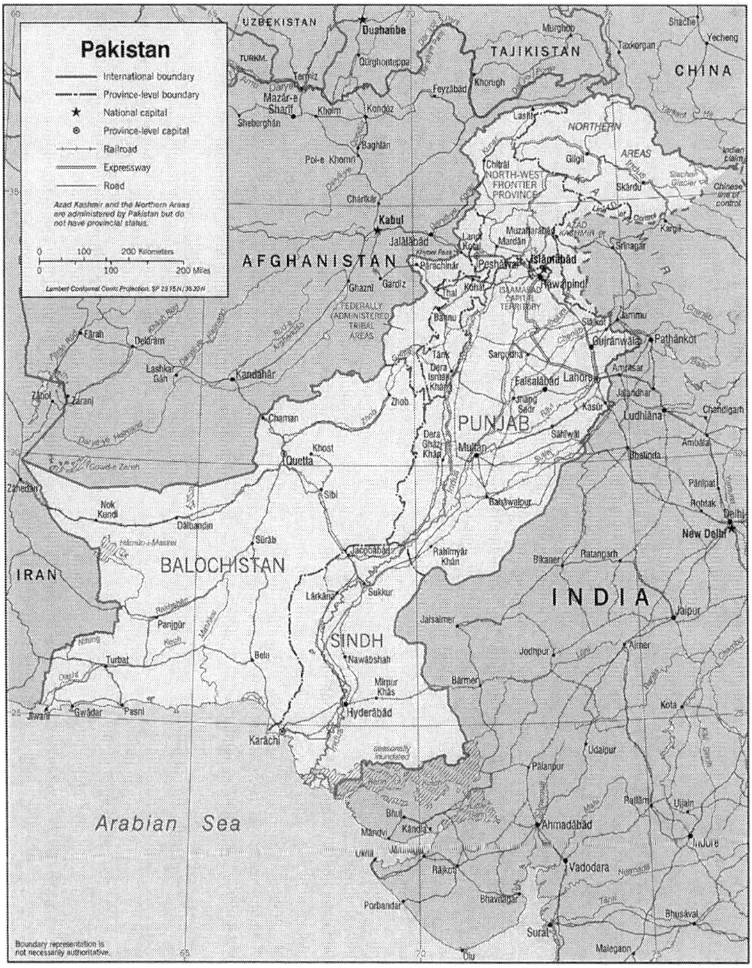

Pakistan remains a land of missed opportunities. A fledgling democratic system is emerging from relatively free and fair elections. Yet, old-style party politics is still struggling to protect incumbents even as some 190 brand-new members of the National Assembly, who came on board in May 2013, have begun the process of carving a new system from the country's benighted politics. The surprisingly large majority for the Pakistan Muslim League-Nawaz (PML-N) group of Prime Minister Nawaz Sharif defied all predictions, even within his own party. Pakistan faces an uncertain future as it searches for stability and growth. The list of challenges facing the country, which has leveraged its geo-strategic location ever since its painful birth in 1947 from the partition of British India, is long and growing. A burgeoning population, a huge energy crisis, declining environmental conditions, water stress, poor governance arising from a fractured system of governance, and external and internal threats have led to a pall of fear and suspicion. Pakistan fears hegemony from a growing India to the east and faces a potential disaster in the wake of the end of the coalition-led war in Afghanistan if that country descends into chaotic civil war. Pakistan also faces a massive internal insurgency in its western border region and growing militancy in the hinterlands.

Pakistan has paid a heavy price for the latest war in Afghanistan, which helped spawn the internal militancy and insurgency that threaten the unstable state. Pakistan has a weak and imbalanced political system and a failing economy. The civil-military divide remains wide, and unless the country's politicians manage to transition smoothly from one civilian government to another without unleashing further conflict and violence inside the country, Pakistan could well tumble into a self-destructive downward spiral. Standing in this path of disaster are the PML-N and its new allies in the provinces. With its home base in the Punjab, the PML-N will try to take advantage of the all-important Punjab economy and the National Assembly to restore growth to Pakistan's economy.

Against this backdrop, the question of a sustainable environmental policy and program is a difficult one for the government of Pakistan to tackle, because of factors that are within its control and external factors, such as climate change, over which it has little control. The effects of climate change are especially significant for Pakistan because of its dependence on rainfall for its agriculture-based economy. Some key elements of the climatic changes confronting Pakistan are as follows:[1]

- Increase in temperature—Pakistan is in the heat-surplus zone.
- High pressure on land and other natural resources has already led to severe degradation; additional pressure from climate change will be difficult to withstand and will exacerbate the problem.
- Potential increase in crop yields may occur, but this may be offset by water shortages, excessive heat, and shorter growing seasons.

- There is potential for increases in insects, pests, and diseases.
- Impacts on water include overflooding in the summer, acute water shortages in the winter, and reduction in the storage capacity of existing water reservoirs.

In addition, Pakistan faces the threat of retreating glaciers that feed its rivers and irrigate its plains. Most of the glaciers in northern Pakistan are retreating, which has been causing increased flooding in the Indus and Kabul Rivers. The government of Pakistan's own analysis predicts that the projected decline in precipitation will make Pakistan extremely food insecure, particularly if glacial reserves shrink in the next 45 years.[2]

However, it is the underlying political and economic instability that remains a clear and ever-present danger to the state. Despite the passage of many new laws by the democratic government of the Pakistan People's Party, including the reapportioning of the state's revenues under the National Finance Commission Award and the devolution of power from the center to the provinces, the polity remains weak and unable to implement change. There are many pressing reasons and crises that militate in favor of Pakistan righting its security and governance arrangements before the country can preserve the environment. Time is not on the country's side.

This chapter examines the overwhelming political and economic forces at play that hinder Pakistan's ability to address social and environmental challenges, despite a vibrant civil society and growing environmental activism. The international community can use engagement on environmental policy as a means to help stabilize the country's resource access problems and thereby provide a more efficient path toward reaching regional security. Water and food availability are inextricably linked to environmental conservation in Pakistan and hence are necessary for the country's development. Although conventional security measures, such as military operations against terrorists, may still be necessary, public support for such activities in Pakistan would grow if there were palpable progress on development indicators, particularly addressing underlying environmental problems.

The chapter lays out the case for why the United States and other international donors should recognize the salience of strengthening resource security, particularly in the areas of water, food, and energy, in order to gain conventional security in Pakistan.

On the Roller Coaster with Uncle Sam

To ensure its security within the tough neighborhood that it inhabits, since its independence Pakistan has sought to make alliances that would allow it to counter the potential threat from the much larger India. Pakistan went to the United States with a request for $2 billion in aid soon after independence but was rebuffed. Yet, Pakistan found its way into the good books of the United States by signing up for the anti-Soviet alliance, first via the Baghdad Pact and then via the Central Treaty Organization. A willing Uncle Sam was prepared to look the other way as Pakistan strengthened its defenses against India with U.S. aid. In the event, Pakistan did not have to prove its capacity to resist the Soviets until 1979 when the Soviet Union invaded Afghanistan. But Pakistan's regular army was never part of the guerrilla war that the United States and others helped the Pashtun Mujahideen wage against the Soviet invaders in the 1980s. That role fell to the Inter-Services Intelligence, which ran a parallel military operation based in the Western Borderlands of Pakistan and created an infrastructure to provide training and military hardware to the Afghan freedom fighters of the 1980s; the same infrastructure of militant Madrassas and training sites now appears to be fueling the internal insurgency and providing safe haven to the Afghan Taliban.

The Soviet invasion of Afghanistan also led to a reprise of U.S. behavior toward Pakistan: whenever the United States needed Pakistan as part of a global or regional strategy, the United States was willing to accept a relationship with Pakistan's military dictators and pour in massive amounts of military and economic aid that helped strengthen the hold of the military rulers over Pakistan's polity. Conversely, this weakened the civilian structures and made them incapable of ruling effectively when military rulers were toppled by popular unrest. Field Marshall Ayub Khan (1958–1969), General Yahya Khan (1969–1971), General Muhammad Zia ul-Haq (1977–1988), and General Pervez Musharraf (1999–2009) benefited from this U.S. policy.

General Zia and General Musharraf were initially ostracized by the United States, but circumstances in the neighborhood forced a change in U.S. behavior toward them. The attacks by al-Qaeda from bases in Afghanistan led to the invasion of Afghanistan by the United States and coalition forces in October 2001. General Musharraf was put in the front line by President George W. Bush with the warning that "either you are with us, or against us." General Musharraf chose an alliance, repudiated recognition of the Taliban government of Afghanistan, and provided the United States passage over Pakistan's territory by land and air to attack Afghanistan. From that point onward, Pakistan remained a partner in a war that many Pakistanis, including its military, saw as an American war. Perhaps Pakistan was an unhappy and unwilling partner over time, but it was wedded to a relationship with the United States that has become ragged and the cause of much tension.

The nature of that hasty alliance continues to plague the relationship between Pakistan and the United States and will be another cause of unhappiness as the coalition begins its withdrawal from Afghanistan. Other than the initial list of seven items that were demanded from Pakistan by the United States soon after September 11, 2001, the agreements between the two countries were not put down on paper. The rights, expectations, and obligations of the alliance between the two "partners" were left to interpretation and misinterpretation by both sides. Although regular military relations could have been easily put down in writing, the role of the covert programs run by the U.S. Central Intelligence Agency, especially the emerging use of drone technology, made it difficult for the United States to agree to written agreements. Pakistan reportedly sought such agreements but was rebuffed. As a result, the government and military of Pakistan continued to maintain the charade that they opposed drone attacks inside their territory. The United States refused to publicly acknowledge the existence of the drone warfare program. The people of Pakistan resented drone attacks and, fueled by their leaders' public denunciation of these attacks, a huge groundswell of anti-American sentiment was created that persists to this day and will likely persist beyond the North Atlantic Treaty Organization's (NATO) withdrawal from Afghanistan.

The lack of a clearly defined objective of the United States and NATO forces in Afghanistan and of U.S. policy toward Pakistan has compounded the difficulties that have emerged in U.S.-Pakistan relations since 2001. From the removal of al-Qaeda in Afghanistan, the relationship has morphed into a loosely defined nation-building effort, something with which the United States and NATO have had little experience in recent decades. One of the continuous sources of unhappiness with Pakistan was the Coalition Support Fund (CSF) payment to Pakistan to cover the costs of moving coalition forces to the western border in order to support the war in Afghanistan. This was the first time since 1947 that regular Pakistani troops entered the Federally Administered Tribal Areas (FATA). This "invasion" and a Pakistan army operation against militant Islamists in the capital Islamabad's Red Mosque created a huge backlash among the tribes that inhabited FATA. The backlash led to the birth in 2006 of Tehreek-i-Taliban Pakistan, which began a growing insurgency against the state of Pakistan. Pakistan lost more than 31,000 lives in the ensuing militancy inside the country, including more than 3,000 military personnel.

This war within the state reduced the ability and willingness of Pakistan's military to devote full attention to sealing the border with Afghanistan and preventing the Afghan Taliban from using Pakistan's territory in FATA and Balochistan as a sanctuary. Pakistan's inability to control the Afghan Taliban fueled U.S. anger, especially on Capitol Hill, where aid to Pakistan was seen as a quid pro quo for Pakistan to move against the Afghan Taliban. Over time, reimbursements under the CSF facility became a source of debate, as the U.S. government rejected many claims of expenditures as bogus. Repayment arrears mounted, adding to the ire on Pakistan's side. It became clear that the CSF was a bad idea, yet neither side chose to end it and replace it with an agreed military aid program with rights and obligations duly spelled out. At the time of the inception of the CSF, Pakistan apparently did not pay much attention to the mechanism nor did the government expect a protracted war in Afghanistan. General Musharraf's rush to agreement on the aid program hurt the country's relations with the United States.

The Military-Civilian Standoff

External pressures and events have proven central in shaping the domestic military-civil relationship in Pakistan. The latest war in Afghanistan, coupled with poor policy making and governance inside Pakistan, first under the military government of General Musharraf and then under the weak civilian coalition led by the Pakistan Peoples' Party of President Zardari, reduced the state's ability to protect its citizens and provide the economic and social conditions for societal well-being. When the Pakistan Taliban took over parts of Malakand and Swat in 2009, the army was blamed for doing too little to oust them. With public anger mounting, the army's public approval plummeted and finally prompted the army to move against the Taliban to clear the region. In the wake of the U.S. raid on Abbottabad on May 2, 2011, that killed Osama bin Laden, the internal power balance shifted against the military as a result of public anger at the inability of the armed forces to protect Pakistan's frontiers and resist U.S. pressure on both economic and political fronts. The U.S. raid put the army back at the center of a growing discussion inside the country about the role and efficacy of the army. Was the army complicit in the raid? Or was it simply unable to detect and deter the incursion? The stature of the army was seriously challenged. Although the Pakistani security state is under increasing stress due to external and internal factors, the state is not likely to collapse in the near term. Nonetheless, it remains vulnerable to both internal and external shocks that could destabilize the governance regime and force a shift of power back in favor of the military unless civilian groups remain united and are supported by the judiciary.

In the past five-plus years, the army, under its chief, General Ashfaq Parvez Kayani, has attempted to rebuild its professionalism and capacity to fight. Both had been compromised under the long autocratic rule of General Pervez Musharraf. Indeed, the army had penetrated the ranks of the civilian bureaucracy, taking over education and training institutions and running certain ministries, especially those dealing with defense matters. General Kayani ordered all army officers serving in government either to resign from the military or to return to it. Today, the defense ministry is still largely run by retired military officers. So the reality has not been altered much. And the economic interests of the military, which include a wide range of industries and sectors, including banking, real estate, and transport, remain a powerful incentive for the military to influence national decision making. On top of that, Pakistan's sharply declining economy under a divided and inept civilian government threatens to reduce the size of the economic pie. This would also reduce the army's share of spending, which has been estimated to run as high as 40 percent of the budget, along with debt-servicing accounts for most of the national expenditures.

Setting Priorities

It is said that a budget represents the values of a government and society. In Pakistan, a steady decline of civilian structures from 1947 onward, the ascendance of feudal and predatory political systems, the decline of the civil service as a brake on the excesses of venal government officials, and the rise of the security state all have contributed to setting budget priorities. Poor governance has been rampant. As a result, an examination of the budget shows a massive share of expenditures going toward debt servicing and defense. Not much goes toward saving or preserving the environment. Pakistan has been ranked sixtieth in terms of percentage of the population with access to safe drinking water.[3]

In the combined current and development expenditures for the financial year 2011–2012, Environmental Protection was the lowest item in terms of costs, coming in at PKR 599 million of a total current budget of PKR 2,631,911 million.[4] Defense Affairs and Services came in at PKR 510,179 million. For 2012–2013, the environment's share of current expenditures, entirely devoted to wastewater management, was PKR 736 million, still the lowest item in the list, while defense spending had risen to PKR 545,386 million.[5] Interestingly, the subsidy to just one military-owned and operated fertilizer company in 2012 alone was PKR 3,400 million,[6] while the remission of loans to the Agricultural Development Bank of Pakistan (Zarai Taraqiati Bank Limited) was PKR 1,000 million. The only identifiable environment-related expenditures visible in the Public Sector Development Programme (PSDP) budget of PKR 206,563 million for 2012–2013 were PKR 135 million for the Ministry of Climate Change. The variances in the expenditure items for the environment and the most-favored sectors of Pakistan's polity are staggering.

There is also a clear preference for nuclear energy versus other sources of power, which might not necessarily be the most ecologically or economically efficient. Pakistan's 44 percent increase for atomic energy in its 2012–2013 budget contrasts with a massive drop in funds for crop research and scientific research. Compared with $1.43 million for the newly formed Ministry of Climate Change, $416 million of the budget was allocated to atomic energy development. Although nuclear energy can be presented as a low-carbon energy source, carbon emissions are hardly a major issue for Pakistan. Rather, adaptation to impending climatic threats caused by extant factors should be a priority alongside better research and development in this arena. Pakistan's science, technology, and innovation policy, approved by Parliament in September 2011, had sought 2 percent of the country's gross domestic product (GDP) to be spent on science sectors by 2020 against the 0.59 percent being spent in the current budget.[7]

On paper, Pakistan's government and civil servants recognize the importance of the environment and the sustainable development challenges they face. Their diagnoses are also accurate. The Planning Commission has taken the lead to identify the issues and present answers to them. The National Task Force on Climate Change presented its recommendations in the 2011–2012 Annual Plan. The Planning Commission's assessment of environmental challenges is sharp and very much on target:

> Pakistan is faced with serious challenges of degradation and pollution of land, water, and air. Industrial pollution, though not too high at the moment, is unchecked and may get worse unless economic activity is underpinned with sustainable development. Air pollution is endemic because of a surge in automobiles, insufficient emission standards, and absence of effective enforcement. All major cities of Pakistan face haphazard, unplanned expansion leading to increase in pollution. This unchecked growth has led to creation of slum areas around city peripheries and low-lying areas. Elsewhere, mining, erosion, and deforestation are major causes of land degradation. All this is compounded by relentless urbanization, continuous industrialization, changing consumption patterns, and climate change.[8]

The review of past performance under the PSDP for 2010–2011 does not make for encouraging reading:

> There were around 40 projects under implementation through Ministry of Environment, Special Initiatives, Water & Power, Defense, Finance, KA&NA and Interior Division. The focus areas included capacity building, clean drinking water, biodiversity, air pollution control, and watershed management. It is further noted that PSDP's allocation for the Environment Sector for the fiscal year 2010–2011 was Rs 2,500 million, which was a sharp reduction from the previous year (Rs 3,500 million). Besides, due to the financial crunch, releases were inadvertently deferred, which severely slowed down the realization of progress. Overall, the implementation remained weak mainly because of unavailability of required funds. The major initiatives/reforms undertaken were:
>
> - Implementation of National Environment, National Sanitation, and National Drinking Water Policies were pursued.
> - Planning Commission's Task Force on Climate Change completed its report, delivering its guidelines for improving climate change adaptation and mitigation measures.
> - Climate change policy has been finalized awaiting approval.
> - Core groups on environment and climate change are regularly meeting for environmental integration in development planning.[9]

Much of the report on the environment by the Planning Commission was a restatement of goals and objectives, ending with a statement that the provinces would henceforth be expected to take over the Forestry Sector Development Programme through their annual development programs "to continue the effort for sustainable development." The decentralization of the Ministry of Environment functions to the provinces has passed the buck on these matters to provincial administrations whose abilities and resources vary considerably and, in general, that are ill-equipped to handle even the most basic development planning and environmentally sustainable development efforts. Meanwhile, the Ministry of Disaster Management took over some of the functions related to the environment at the federal level, but the ministry's ability to plan for environmental protection is limited compared with the provinces, even if the ministry had the resources. As the government's own assessment proclaimed,

> Due to the limited resources at its disposal, government efforts alone are not sufficient to address challenges resulting from climate change. A much larger participation and support from other stakeholders including industry, civil society, and the public at large as well as the donors is needed to effectively respond to climate issues.[10]

Water resources are at the heart of these challenges. At times, water can act as a conduit for fostering cooperative mechanisms, as exemplified by agreements involving hostile states, such as the Indus Water Treaty between India and Pakistan. Although the treaty withstood three wars between India and Pakistan, it was not able to play any role in averting armed conflict. Internally, the dispute resolution system of the treaty, which was negotiated with financial and institutional support from the World Bank, has withstood many security challenges, but it has not led to broader regional conflict resolution. This is largely because the institutions that deal with water and environmental resources are purposely divorced from national security strategies. More recently, water resources have been used as a means of reinforcing existing suspicions between hostile parties. After the Mumbai attacks of November 2008, Pakistan's military commentators began to focus on India's violations of the Indus Water Treaty, suggesting that water resources were a latent cause of the perpetuation of the Kashmir conflict. Although such causality is plausible with the limited distribution of resources even within countries, the underlying factors that lead to lack of trust and violations of agreements are usually extant factors such as ethnic rivalries, inequalities, and a lack of institutional arrangements for monitoring and enforcement of allocation regimes. As such, consideration of institutional responses to the transboundary resource allocation of water is essential for ensuring long-term security in unstable geopolitical areas.

As the World Bank's study on the environmental challenges of accelerated growth in Pakistan states, the costs of inaction remain very high. Conservative estimates presented in the report suggest that environmental degradation costs the country at least 6 percent of GDP, or about PKR 365 billion per year, and these costs fall disproportionately on the poor. The most significant causes of environmental damage identified and estimated in the report are

- illness and premature mortality caused by indoor and outdoor air pollution (almost 50 percent of the total damage costs);
- diarrheal diseases and typhoid caused by inadequate water supply, sanitation, and hygiene (about 30 percent of the total); and
- reduced agricultural productivity caused by soil degradation (about 20 percent of the total).

Despite these dire indicators, the report also noted,

> Pakistan has a commendable record of efforts to promote conservation and longer-term sustainability, from the National Conservation Strategy of 1992 through to the adoption of a National Environment Policy (NEP) in 2005. Implementation of these initiatives remains a challenge, however. Whether judged in terms of regional performance or environmental stress factors, there is significant scope to better ensure the sustainability of Pakistan's economic growth.[11]

In early 2013, the country announced a National Climate Change Strategy that sets forth 120 recommendations for action. The goal of the policy, according to Ministry of Environment Director General Javed Ali Khan, is to "ensure that climate change is mainstreamed in the economically and socially vulnerable sectors of the country."[12]

In the final analysis, however, formal government policy and statements can be realized only if the national security apparatus recognizes the connection between environmental scarcity and national stability. Today, Pakistan's climate change policy exemplifies this fact. The civilian government that inherited power from the military government of General Pervez Musharraf continues on the path to identifying the challenges and suggesting changes but without the ability to devote more resources to the effort or to provide the security and political stability that the country needs, these remain largely pious hopes. The international community can provide many opportunities for such a realization to take root within the armed forces of Pakistan, but so far most opportunities for ecological learning have been missed. U.S. involvement in Pakistan during the first four years of the Obama administration was largely driven by the conventional security imperative. As Dr. Vali Nasr, a preeminent South Asia advisor to the Obama administration, noted, the engagement with Pakistan was

> predictably narrow in scope and all terrorism-focused. . . . For every dollar we gave Pakistan in aid, we gave $20 to Afghanistan. That money did not go

very far; it was like pouring water into sand. . . . The 2009 Kerry-Lugar-Berman legislation earmarked $7.5 billion in aid to Pakistan over five years—the first long-term civilian aid package. It was no Marshall Plan.[13]

The Imperative of Righting the Economy

The role of the military against the insurgency and as an ally of the coalition forces in Afghanistan allowed the military to extend its power domestically during the regime of President Pervez Musharraf, as was the case during earlier extended periods of military rule. The military remains racked by fear about a growing India to the east and a militarily strengthened Afghanistan, allied with India, to the west. It has good reason to worry about India's growing presence: a recent National Intelligence Council Global Trends 2030 report points to the Indian economy growing to 16 times the size of Pakistan's economy by 2030, more than doubling the difference in the sizes of the two economies. And, although in late 2012 there was movement to repair Pakistan's relationship with the United States by reviving working groups to deal with common issues, Pakistan remains uncertain, nay suspicious, about this relationship.

Pakistan would have to seek another way, beyond military parity, to create equilibrium with India. Economic growth could be the key element in seeking a balance with India. For example, recent work on this topic by Mohsin Khan (senior fellow at the Atlantic Council) indicates that Pakistan could benefit enormously by opening up trade with India. Simply restoring trade between the two countries to the level of 1947 would potentially increase volume from around $2 billion a year to as much as $100 billion, with income effects that would increase per capita income substantially. And the potential for expanding trade and pipelines to Iran and central Asia would provide the added bonus of transit fees for Pakistan. The United States now has a strategic relationship with both countries in the subcontinent for the first time in history. A U.S. bank shot via India could help improve relations with Pakistan and the situation in Afghanistan. But India is resistant to direct third-party involvement. Therefore, private-sector and behind-the-scenes activity by U.S. negotiators would be the key to improving Indo-Pakistan relations.

But Pakistan's economy is under severe stress. Its instability will increase over time, as the United States and coalition forces begin withdrawing, and may be exacerbated as reduced economic aid to both Afghanistan and Pakistan follows the military disengagement. This may end up repeating the roller-coaster behavior of U.S. aid to Pakistan.[14] Pakistan risks losing CSFs of more than $1 billion a year that have helped tide the country over a number of economic crises. Its foreign exchange reserves are falling, and the CSF monies remain a valuable safety net for its economy for the time being, but not for long. By fast-tracking payments to Pakistan under this program, the United States has helped stave off a financial train wreck for Pakistan. But the question remains whether Pakistan can stabilize its economy and put it back on the path to growth without becoming dependent yet again on external aid.

Economically, the country faces a difficult future. The International Monetary Fund's (IMF) report of November 2012 painted a bleak picture:

> Pakistan's economy faces many challenges. Deep-seated structural problems and weak macroeconomic policies have continued to sap the economy's vigor. Real GDP growth over the past four years has averaged only about 3 percent annually, and is projected to be about 3 1/4 percent in 2012/13, insufficient to achieve significant improvement in living standards and to absorb the rising labor force. A key structural impediment to growth is the problems in the energy sector, which have resulted in widespread and unpredictable power outages. Headline inflation has decelerated recently, but is likely to return to low double digits by the end of 2012/13. The external position has weakened substantially, as export growth turned negative in 2011/12 while imports grew. The financial account has also deteriorated, reflecting weak financial inflows and debt repayments. This has led to a decline in the State Bank of Pakistan's (SBP) foreign exchange reserves to less than $10 billion in October 2012, below adequate levels.
>
> The fiscal deficit (excluding grants) reached 8 1/2 percent of GDP in 2011/12, well above the original budget target of 4 percent, reflecting both revenue and expenditure slippages, including higher subsidies mainly to clear arrears in the power sector. The 2012/13 budget targets a deficit of 4.7 percent of GDP, but on current policies the deficit would likely be closer to 6 1/2 percent of GDP.[15]

A year earlier, the State Bank of Pakistan had cast an equally gloomy picture in its 2011 report:

> Pakistan's economy managed to grow by 2.4 percent in FY11, despite devastating floods in the early part of the fiscal year. One-fifth of the country's agricultural heartland was inundated, which interrupted production processes and disrupted the subsequent supply of both labor and capital. It is estimated that 6.6 million of Pakistan's labor force was out of work for 2 to 3 months, and capital stock worth $2.6 billion (1.2 percent of GDP) was lost. . . .
>
> However, the 2010 floods cannot mask the structural deficiencies in Pakistan's economy. For simplicity, we would identify four interrelated issues that need urgent policy attention to break out of Pakistan's current stagflation. First and foremost is the fiscal problem, specifically increasing tax revenues; then is the spillover of fiscal slippages on domestic debt and the crowding out of the private sector; then, the acute shortage of power; and finally, the external sector.[16]

Successive governments in Pakistan have failed to improve the fiscal situation. Pakistan's tax-to-GDP ratio remains abysmal at below 9 percent, compared with India's 17 percent. Pakistan's growth rate has also plummeted from the highs of the recent past. Its 2.4 percent growth compares with Bangladesh's 6.3 percent and India's estimated 7.8 percent in 2011. Inflation has been officially hovering around 15 percent and may well rise in years to come, largely because of lack of governance.

As the State Bank of Pakistan concluded, "A cross-country comparison shows that institutional weakness at all levels of government; the judiciary; civil services; law enforcement; regulatory bodies; and agencies for oversight and accountability, are directly responsible for poor economic growth."[17]

These are some of the obstacles that Prime Minister Sharif's government will face as it tries to tackle economic and environmental issues in short order and reopen the doors to assistance from the IMF and other aid agencies.

Greening the Regional Divide

Much of the foreign policy discourse within the United States ties Pakistan inextricably to Afghanistan—hence the title of the special envoy for "Afghanistan and Pakistan" and the favored acronym "AfPak." Yet this conflation is defined by a perceived security threat rather than ecological or historical underpinnings. Afghanistan and Pakistan started off on the wrong foot, and this has affected their relations from 1947 to date. Pakistan's application for membership to the United Nations was opposed by Afghanistan because Afghanistan did not recognize the Durand Line, the boundary that the British Empire had created in 1893 between British India and Afghanistan and that Pakistan had inherited. Afghanistan followed up with a demand for Pushtunistan, or the Land of the Pushtuns, incorporating all Pushtun tribal territory inside Pakistan into a single entity, comprising its own Pushtun heartland and that of Pakistan. Afghanistan also played host to independence-minded Pushtun leaders, including Khan Ghaffar Ahmed Khan, the leader of the Red Shirt movement in British India. Pakistan has also felt that the refuge it gave to more than 3 million Afghan refugees during the Cold War invasion of the country by the Soviets was underappreciated by the international community and by Afghans themselves. In turn, Afghans feel that since that period, Pakistan has interfered too profoundly in Afghanistan's own governance trajectory. The mistrust is thus acute on both sides. With this historic backdrop, the United States needs to be particularly cautious in trying to define its policy in binary terms that might be perceived as a zero-sum game between these two countries that have historical mistrust for each other.

Instead of focusing on AfPak, the United States should have a more ecologically and historically appropriate approach. For example, the riparian systems that traverse South Asia need more effective and efficient regional management systems, which could provide a more resilient approach to security. In particular, the international community should invest far more resources in strengthening existing organizations dedicated to environmental cooperation.

Regional cooperation in South Asia is a relatively recent phenomenon. While East Asia was busy working on free trade zones through organizations such as the Association of Southeast Asian Nations, much of South Asia was embroiled in conflicts. As with other parts of the world, the Cold War created a polarization that prevented regional cooperation. India, the dominant power, was focused on developing the Non-Aligned Movement as an antidote to Cold War allegiances. It was not until 1980 that the idea of establishing a separate organization focused on South Asian cooperation was moved forward. The preconditions for establishing the South Asian Association for Regional Cooperation (SAARC) were confining in terms of what could be achieved but similar to those of several other organizations for regional cooperation conceived at the time. Five key principles define all SAARC activities:[18]

- Respect for sovereignty, territorial integrity, political equality, and independence of all member states
- Noninterference in internal matters
- Cooperation for mutual benefit
- All decisions to be taken unanimously and need a quorum of all eight members
- All bilateral issues to be kept aside and only multilateral (involving many countries) issues to be discussed without being prejudiced by bilateral issues

SAARC was formally established as a permanent organization in 1985, with a secretariat hosted in Kathmandu, Nepal. Its seven original members—Bangladesh, Bhutan, India, Maldives, Nepal, Pakistan, and Sri Lanka—agreed to admit Afghanistan as an eighth member in 2007.[19] The addition was particularly significant because SAARC could thereby act as a forum for India and Pakistan to negotiate their strategic influence over Afghanistan's development path. In Pakistan, there has been recurring suspicion about ulterior motives for India's high level of development aid to Afghanistan. Allowing for a transparent exchange on regional development investment in Afghanistan could be an effective means of assuaging some of this mistrust. At the same time, there has been movement by Pakistan and India to establish their own spheres of influence, heading west and east, respectively, for regional partners.

The Bay of Bengal Initiative for Multi-Sectoral Technical and Economic Cooperation (BIMSTEC) was formed partly as a response to the perceived inefficacy of SAARC because of the repeated deadlocks between India and Pakistan. The BIMSTEC agreement also includes Burma and Thailand, with which India has strong trade ties. Energy and some environmental areas of cooperation, such as fisheries, are proposed subjects of activity in addition to a broader trade and infrastructure cooperation agenda. However, there has been modest progress on ecological cooperation, although the Asian Development Bank has engaged with BIMSTEC to support infrastructure linkages, particularly in the transport sector, whereby environmental planning criteria may be more directly incorporated.

On the western frontier, the Economic Cooperation Organization (ECO) has a specific directorate pertaining to minerals, energy, and the environment. This organization was established in the same year as SAARC (1985) by Iran, Pakistan, and Turkey. ECO's goals are to promote economic, cultural, and technical cooperation. With the dissolution of the Soviet Union, several central Asian states joined ECO, and the organization now comprises 10 member states. All members are Muslim-majority states, and 6 of the 10 are landlocked. ECO is a forum for Afghanistan and Pakistan to have more-direct communication facilitated by central Asian partners and is considered a counterweight to the dominance of India in communications within SAARC. However, Iran's involvement in the organization and the fact that its secretariat is based in Tehran make it difficult to gain much interest from international donors despite some important proposed initiatives related to regional ecotourism and energy infrastructure collaboration.[20]

One possible connection that could be made between ECO and SAARC was suggested by Pakistan's then Prime Minister Yousuf Raza Gillani at the SAARC summit in 2011. The suggestion involved the road link between Tajikistan and Pakistan to connect South Asian markets to SAARC countries.[21] This broader vision would also tie in with the "New Silk Road" initiative that then U.S. Secretary of State Hillary Clinton announced at a regional meeting in Chennai in 2011. The goals of the Silk Road vision were elaborated by U.S. Department of State official Geoffrey Pyatt in an official policy speech at a conference in Tokyo in June 2012. He noted that, in addition to the expansion of merchandise flow, the vision involves cooperation "through energy, water, transport, and infrastructure—which includes roads, bridges, electrical transmission grids, railways and pipelines—*to connect* goods, services, and people."[22]

However, to make such a Silk Road work better and with far greater consequence, these initiatives will inevitably need the assistance of China, which has established its own regional grouping that overlaps with the central Asian members of ECO. The Shanghai Cooperation Organization (SCO) was established as a means of strengthening China's partnership with Russia in the region. The SCO also has environmental and energy cooperation dimensions that could have a bearing on South Asian regional cooperation.[23] Among SAARC countries, India, Pakistan, and Afghanistan join Iran and Mongolia as "observers" within the SCO. Pakistan has been actively lobbying for full SCO membership, and in November 2011, the Russian government indicated it would officially support Pakistan's full membership despite concerns from India. The SCO has the potential of becoming a much more consequential partner in areas of energy and transport cooperation as the northern Asian states seek access to the lucrative high-demographic-growth markets of South Asia.

Despite the growth of these regional organizations, the potential for SAARC to play a role in multilateral ecological cooperation remains strongest. Within the ecological arena, SAARC has a program of work on environment and energy that includes the aims of establishing a specific Convention on Environmental Cooperation, which was reaffirmed in the Thimphu Statement on Climate Change (2010). Among SAARC's lesser-known accomplishments is the establishment of the South Asian University in New Delhi,[24] where students from all member countries study together under one institutional umbrella. The university held its first classes in 2010, just five years after the idea was introduced at the SAARC summit in Dhaka, initially offering master's degree programs in computer applications and development economics. At the 2011 SAARC summit, Indian Prime Minister Manmohan Singh announced that India would increase the number of SAARC Silver Jubilee Scholarships at the university from 50 to 100 (75 at the master's level and 25 at the doctoral level).

The persistent acrimony and nuclear rivalry between India and Pakistan have often hampered substantive progress on regional cooperation. Yet, SAARC is evolving into a forum that links civil society and governments in the region through common denominators such as education, the environment, and human rights. At the 2011 summit, "People's SAARC,"[25] a parallel initiative to the official SAARC established in 1996 as a means of providing policy evaluation to local governments, provided a "memorandum" with detailed practical "demands" concerning the rights of fishermen in regional waters, migratory populations, and communities affected by climatic changes and disasters.

In his formal remarks at the SAARC summit in 2011, the Indian Prime Minister also stated unequivocally that "India has a special responsibility that flows from the geography of our region and the state of our economy and market."[26] Environmental cooperation was highlighted specifically in the context of the India Endowment for Climate Change, which will provide 10 scholarships per year to citizens of SAARC member states for postgraduate and doctoral studies in forestry courses at the Forest Research Institute in Dehradun, India.

South Asian diplomacy has taken on a broad range of technocratic initiatives that are achieving more success in comparison with relatively scant progress on territorial disputes. Despite the general stagnation of diplomacy in South Asia, particularly since the Mumbai attacks of 2009, there are some signs of progress that should be used to promote a clear agenda for sustainable cooperation. In September 2012, the Pakistan-India Joint Commission (originally established in 1983)[27] was revived after a seven-year hiatus. It identified eight avenues of mutually beneficial cooperation in agriculture, education, environment, health, information, information technology and telecommunications, science and technology, and tourism. Some of the working groups within the commission focused on agriculture, the environment, and science. Noted in particular was the need to train scientists in crop improvement through the use of biotechnology, quarantine-related matters, livestock and dairy development, high-efficiency irrigation systems, and rainwater harvesting. The working group on the environment agreed to cooperate on climate change, renewable energy, environmental protection, energy conservation, clean development mechanisms, biodiversity, sustainable forest conservation, and solid waste management. The commission's revival is the most promising sign that some long-term cooperation around ecological issues may indeed be possible and could have a much larger impact on conflict resolution. Supporting such regional efforts that broaden the definition of security in both topical and geographical terms is far more likely to be successful for achieving peace and improving American relations with South Asian countries.

Pakistan and the United States: A New Security Pact

An erstwhile ally of the United States, Pakistani dictator General Zia ul-Haq once famously told his ambassador to the United States, "Being a friend of the United States is like living on the banks of a great river. Every four years it changes course and you are either left flooded or high and dry!"[28] At its heart, the U.S.-Pakistan alliance has remained a transactional relationship. Attempts to make it a consistent, longer-term relationship, based on economic and political ties, have foundered on lack of mutual understanding of shared aims in the region. Pakistan has continued to see Afghanistan solely through the Pushtun prism, leading to U.S. suspicions that Pakistan has been playing both sides against each other: aiding and abetting the U.S. allies, on the one hand, while maintaining ties with the Afghan Taliban who were fighting the allies, on the other hand. Pakistan has also had a wary eye toward the east, on India, fearing that India might seek to weaken and divide Pakistan by direct or indirect means. Even the relatively generous five-year U.S. aid program under the Kerry-Lugar-Berman bill, which provided $7 billion over the period and had prospects of being extended for another five years, ran into trouble in Pakistan. The U.S. Congress chose to impose conditions on the aid program that the powerful Pakistan military found galling. Then the actual aid flow remained a trickle, largely because of the inability of the U.S. Agency for International Development (USAID) to come up with systems to identify and assist worthy projects, the lack of the capacity of Pakistani counterparts to manage the flow of aid, and massive floods in Pakistan in 2010 that led to the halt and redesign of the aid program.

Pakistan's vulnerability to climate change and environmental stresses is now well recognized at the domestic level, and there is a vibrant civil society sector focusing public attention on climate issues. For example, one of the largest country offices for the International Union for Conservation of Nature is in Karachi, and the Worldwide Fund for Nature in Lahore is among the most well resourced of the South Asian offices of the organization. This has partly been due to the support offered to environmental organizations by industrialists such as Syed Babar Ali. Numerous retired army officials serve on environmental organization boards within Pakistan. Yet, such organizations are still dependent on donor investments and need cooperation from the government for implementing policies. Although environmental issues and nonconventional security matters might not seem to be a priority at the governmental level, they impact the daily lives of Pakistanis, particularly in the areas of water, food, and energy availability. Thus, if the United States or other international donors can make a palpable difference in these sectors, they will undoubtedly make it easier for the government to justify alliances on conventional security matters.

For example, renewable energy sources in terms of small-scale hydropower, solar, and wind should still be given importance for rural electrification despite their limitations in meeting large-scale demand. There are some tentative positive cases that the United States should consider in this regard, and it should help to expand and empower such networks. The USAID-funded South Asia Regional Initiative for Energy (SARI/Energy) is an important effort in this regard. The mandate of SARI/Energy is to "promote technical and institutional frameworks for regional energy planning and infrastructure investment involving cross-border trade in energy."[29] This is a bold effort with the potential for considerable impact in fostering broader linkages between water and power. However, USAID has been limited in its ability to encourage more direct cooperation between Pakistan and India, given the lack of political will on the part of the U.S. administration to make such leveraging a priority.

Such inertia will need to change if the full potential of ecological cooperation is to be realized. U.S. government agencies should consider a more "naturalized" approach to defense engagement, as well as diplomacy, recognizing that natural resources are an essential threshold metric in determining the stabilization of societies. Water and energy are the most basic limiting factors in development. U.S. security engagement in South Asia should consider providing protection to natural resources and allowing for the enhancement of water and energy infrastructure in more ecologically and economically efficient ways. Directly related to water and energy stabilization is food security, which constitutes the most palpable indicator of poverty alleviation. The use of hard power to protect and nurture such natural resources and energy infrastructure is likely to stabilize regions while also improving the chances that citizen diplomacy from the U.S. government will gain traction.

In summary, a gradual shift from bilateralism to multilateralism is essential for the ecologically sustainable development of South Asia, with a particular focus on water and energy provisioning. Linking the "hard politics" of security to the "soft politics" of the environment and natural resources should be instrumentally used for peace-building. Such a linkage is an underutilized diplomatic and intelligence tool that has much potential for achieving broader international security objectives in the region.

Notes

1 "What Are Expected Impacts of Climate Change in Pakistan?" Clean Development Mechanism–Pakistan (part of the Ministry of Climate Change and initiated under the Kyoto Protocol), www.cdmpakistan.gov.pk/cdm_doc/what%20are%20expected%20impacts%20of%20cliamte%20change%20in%20pakistan.pdf.
2 Planning Commission of Pakistan's Report on Glaciers and Climate Change, www.pc.gov.pk/publications/report%20on%20glaciers%20seminar.pdf.
3 www.nationmaster.com/graph/hea_dri_wat_ava-health-drinking-water-availability.
4 Government of Pakistan, *Federal Budget 2012–2013, Budget in Brief* (Finance Division, Government of Pakistan, Islamabad, 2012), Table 5.
5 Government of Pakistan, *Federal Budget 2012–2013,* Table 16.
6 Government of Pakistan, *Federal Budget 2012–2013,* 34.
7 Saleem Shaikh, "Nuclear Energy Eclipses Climate Change in Pakistan Budget," Sci Dev Net (June 6, 2012), www.scidev.net/en/south-asia/news/nuke-energy-eclipses-climate-change-in-pakistan-s-budget.html.
8 Government of Pakistan, *Federal Budget 2012–2013.*
9 Government of Pakistan, *Federal Budget 2012–2013,* 119–120.
10 Government of Pakistan, *Pakistan Economic Survey 2011–2012* (Ministry of Finance, Government of Pakistan, Islamabad, 2012), 236.
11 World Bank, *Pakistan: Strategic Country Environmental Assessment* (World Bank, Washington, D.C., 2007).
12 R. Khan, "National Climate Change Policy to the Rescue?" Dawn Blog (Feb. 26, 2013), http://dawn.com/2013/02/26/national-climate-change-policy-to-the-rescue/.
13 Vali Nasr, "The Inside Story of How the White House Let Diplomacy Fail in Afghanistan," *Foreign Policy* (March 4, 2013), www.foreignpolicy.com/articles/2013/03/04/the_inside_story_of_how_the_white_house_let_diplomacy_fail_in_afghanistan.
14 Susan B. Epstein and K. Alan Kronstadt, "Pakistan: U.S. Foreign Assistance" (Congressional Research Service, Oct, 4, 2012).
15 www.imf.org/external/np/sec/pn/2012/pn12135.htm.
16 State Bank of Pakistan, "Economic Outlook," *State Bank of Pakistan Annual Report 2010–2011* (State Bank of Pakistan, 2011), www.sbp.org.pk/reports/annual/arFY11/Economic_Outlook.pdf.
17 State Bank of Pakistan, "Economic Outlook," 4.
18 For a detailed review of SAARC's limitations based on these principles see Zahid Shah Ahmed, *Regionalism and Regional Security in South Asia: The Role of SAARC* (Ashgate, Oxford, UK, 2013).
19 In recognition of the importance of development donors and broader strategic interests, SAARC has granted observer status to Australia, China, the European Union, Iran, Japan, Mauritius, Burma, Republic of Korea, and the United States.
20 For a good review of the early days of ECO, refer to Richard Pomfret, "The Economic Cooperation Organization: Current Status and Future Prospects," *Europe-Asia Studies* 49, no. 4 (1997): 657–67. For a broader discussion of regional organizations and their role in peace-building in the region, see Barnett R. Rubin and Ahmed Rashid, "From Great Game to Grand Bargain—Ending Chaos in Afghanistan and Pakistan," *Foreign Affairs* 87 (2008): 30.
21 "Pakistan PM to Take-up Pak-Tajik Road Project," *Daily Times* (Pakistan) (Oct. 10, 2011).

22 Speech by Geoffrey Pyatt, Principal Assistant Secretary, Bureau of South and Central Asia, "Delivering the New Silk Road" (Tokyo, Japan, July, 9, 2012), accessed online from the U.S. Department of State's official website.

23 For a review of SCO in the context of regional environmental cooperation, see Wang Fen, "Grand Strategy in the Great Game—Strategic Interests and Objectives of States of the Shanghai Cooperation Organization" (Institute for Environmental Diplomacy and Security, University of Vermont, Burlington, Vermont, 2011).

24 South Asian University, New Delhi, accessed Sept. 2, 2012.

25 Peoples' SAARC website, accessed Sept. 2, 2012.

26 Indian Prime Minister Manmohan Singh's statement on the NDTV website.

27 The Commission met for the first time in 1983; its second and third meetings took place in 1985 and 1989, respectively. There were no further meetings until the two countries reactivated the mechanism in April 2005 during the visit of Pakistan's then-president Pervez Musharraf, following which the technical groups were increased from four to eight.

28 Jamsheed Marker, *Quiet Diplomacy: Memoirs of an Ambassador of Pakistan* (Oxford University Press, Oxford, UK, 2010).

29 Mission statement from the SARI/Energy website.

10

THE SOUTH CHINA SEA

Murray Hiebert and Gregory Poling

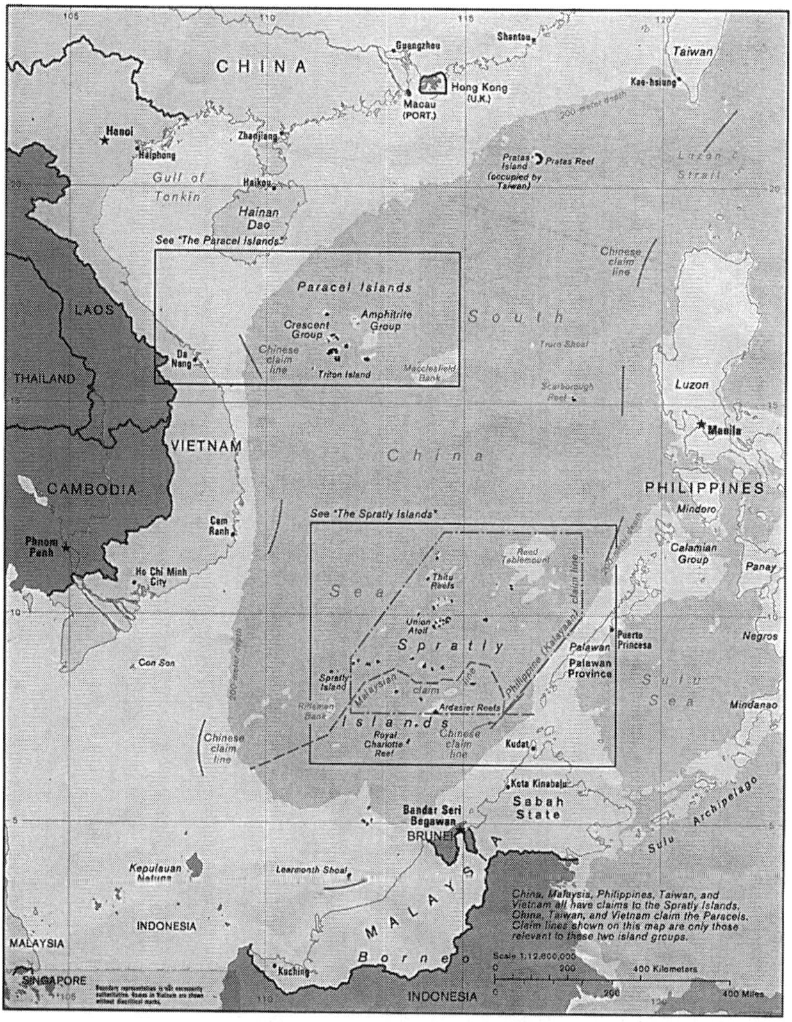

The South China Sea is one of the world's most important waterways and one of the most contested. The semi-enclosed sea is bordered by Brunei, China, Indonesia, Malaysia, the Philippines, Taiwan, and Vietnam. Lying at the heart of Southeast Asia, its economic importance cannot be overstated. It is one of the busiest trading routes on the planet. The western gateway to the sea is the Strait of Malacca, through which 60,000 ships pass each year—four times more than the Panama Canal—carrying one-third of global trade and 15 million barrels of oil a day. That is just 2 million fewer barrels than the world's busiest energy transit route, the Strait of Hormuz.[1]

The importance of the South China Sea as a vital transport route for energy will only grow. China's daily oil imports are projected to increase from less than 5 million barrels a day in 2010 to more than 12 million in 2035.[2] For the nations of Southeast Asia, meanwhile, oil imports will increase from less than 3 million barrels a day in 2010 to nearly 6 million in 2035.[3]

Free and safe transit across the South China Sea is the lifeblood of East Asia, where the South China Sea ties together the region's vital supply chains and provides the most direct route for energy and mineral resources coming from Africa and the Middle East. The South China Sea is also crucial for U.S. trade across the Asia Pacific. In addition to trade, the South China Sea holds vast economic potential.

The level of oil and gas resources lying beneath the South China Sea is a highly contested subject. Official estimates from China have for years hinted at a new Saudi Arabia beneath the waves. Other generally more trusted sources suggest that such estimates are greatly inflated but that the South China Sea's hydrocarbon potential is considerable. The latest estimates from the U.S. Energy Information Agency place proven and probable oil reserves at about 11 billion barrels and gas at 190 trillion cubic feet.[4] This is roughly on par with Mexican reserves and, in the case of gas, more than the proven reserves in China, which helps explain Beijing's increasing interest in the area. In 2012, the U.S. Geological Survey predicted that the South China Sea could hold undiscovered resources amounting to 12 billion barrels of oil and 160 trillion cubic feet of natural gas.[5]

The other major resource at stake in the South China Sea is its rich fisheries. The habitats of the South China Sea's thousands of geological features and archipelagic coastlines have provided rich fishing grounds for millennia. They are the primary food source for communities across Indonesia, Malaysia, the Philippines, and Vietnam. And with the rapidly growing middle class across East Asia, demand for fish protein has soared to unprecedented levels. This has led to more fishing ships than ever plying the waters of the South China Sea and going farther afield in search of profitable catches. Run-ins between fishermen and maritime security forces have spiked as a result, particularly in disputed areas. This dynamic now contributes to more violent confrontations in the region than all other causes combined.

Disputed Waters

In addition to its strategic and economic importance, the South China Sea is arguably the most contested body of water in the world. Six nations—Brunei, China, Malaysia, the Philippines, Taiwan, and Vietnam—maintain overlapping claims to the waters and land features of the South China Sea. This creates a complex tangle of disputes that has so far proven intractable.

The South China Sea contains two major groups of features, called the Paracel Islands and the Spratly Islands, which are home to overlapping sovereignty claims. Both have seen their share of violence, and both seem equally unresolvable in any foreseeable time frame. The Paracels, in the northern half of the sea, are currently under the control of China but are claimed by Taiwan and Vietnam. Chinese forces, which controlled the northern half of the chain, overran Vietnamese forces on the southern features in 1974 and have maintained those positions since. Woody Island, the largest of the Paracels, has been developed by Beijing over the years and now contains barracks, roads, an airport, a bridge, administrative buildings, cell phone service, and other hallmarks of a permanent settlement. In 2012, Beijing announced the establishment of a new prefectural capital city, called Sansha, on Woody Island to administer China's claims in the South China Sea.

The Spratly Islands, in the southern part of the sea, are far smaller, more dispersed, and even more contested. There are thousands of largely submerged features in the chain, along with dozens of above-water rocks. The largest of these, Itu Aba, is barely a third of a square mile. It is also the only feature with freshwater. But despite their size and scarcity, the Spratlys are the focus of overlapping claims by six nations. China, Taiwan, and Vietnam claim them all. The Philippines claims most of them, Malaysia claims a substantial chunk off its coast, and Brunei claims two or three that fall on its claimed continental shelf. Actual control of the features is highly contested, but Vietnam claims by far the most—more than 20—while at the other end of the spectrum, Brunei occupies none, and Taiwan controls only Itu Aba and a nearby shoal.

Two other features in the South China Sea are also subject to dispute. Scarborough Shoal, not far from the Philippine coast, is claimed by China and Taiwan. In 2012, a Philippine attempt to arrest Chinese fishermen poaching at the shoal resulted in a months-long standoff with Chinese maritime patrol vessels. The end result was that China occupied the shoal, roped off its entrance, and has maintained effective control since.

Macclesfield Bank, an entirely submerged feature in the center of the sea, is also in dispute. It is claimed by China, although given that it is an underwater feature, it remains a mystery. This has led others to object to China's claim to the feature, especially Vietnam and the Philippines, on whose continental shelf it could conceivably lie.

The territorial dispute over features in the South China Sea is only half the story. There is also a more expansive and in many ways more troubling dispute about its waters that is affected by but distinct from the territorial disagreements. All parties to the South China Sea disputes are signatories of the United Nations Convention on the Law of the Sea (UNCLOS), which defines the maximum claims and rights that a nation has in its waters. According to UNCLOS, a state is entitled to 12 nautical miles of territorial sea and a 200-nautical-mile exclusive economic zone (EEZ), in which it has sole rights to resource exploitation, including fisheries and ocean and wind power. States are also entitled to a continental shelf, extending at least 200 nautical miles and up to 350 nautical miles depending on geography. There they have the sole right to exploit the seabed and subsoil, including drilling for oil, gas, and minerals.

The vast majority of the South China Sea's waters fall within the 200-nautical-mile claims of the surrounding states, leaving little room for international waters. The situation is made worse by the islands and rocks because UNCLOS allows for islands that meet an ambiguous test of habitability to generate their own EEZs and continental shelves. This means that overlapping claims to the features also create a complicated tangle of overlapping claims to the waters and resources of the South China Sea.

China and Taiwan throw an additional wrench into the works with their so-called nine-dash line claim. This refers to an ambiguous claim to nearly all the waters of the South China Sea, as encompassed by nine dashes placed on a 1914 map, which was officially published by the Chinese government in 1947 and submitted as a note verbale to the United Nations in 2009. Both Beijing and Taipei maintain the nine-dash line claim, but neither has definitively clarified what it means. Some statements have indicated that China claims all the waters within the nine dashes as territorial seas; others have said it is only a claim to the geographic features within the dashes and the waters they would generate; and yet others rely on a vague claim to unspecified historic rights to the waters. Only the second of those options is supportable under UNCLOS.

U.S. Position

The U.S. position regarding the South China Sea disputes has been fairly consistent for decades. Successive administrations have said that, like most territorial disputes around the globe, the United States takes no position regarding ownership of any disputed feature. This does not mean that Washington has no stake in the dispute or position regarding the excessive maritime claims of the disputants. The U.S. government—relevant branches of the Departments of Defense and State, in particular—has issued objections to the various maritime claims it deems unsupportable under UNCLOS, including the nine-dash line. Washington has also objected to attempts to change the status quo on the disputed features by force, as it did in 2012 regarding Scarborough Shoal. But these objections have most often not been accompanied by concrete action. Washington did nothing to prevent or punish China for the invasion of South Vietnamese positions in the Paracels in 1974, the deadly taking of Vietnamese-occupied Johnson South Reef in 1988, the seizing of Mischief Reef from the Philippines in 1996, or the coercion seen at Scarborough Shoal.

The level of attention Washington has given to the South China Sea disputes during the Obama administration has been considerably higher than in the past. This is in large part because of China's 2009 submission of the nine-dash line to the United Nations and the fevered objections from the Southeast Asian claimants. The United States recognizes the threat China's claim poses to international maritime law embodied in UNCLOS, which, despite Washington having never ratified the treaty, still serves as the regime within which the U.S. government, U.S. Navy, U.S. Coast Guard, and private interests operate. President Barack Obama, Secretaries of State Hillary Clinton and John Kerry, and Secretaries of Defense Robert Gates, Leon Panetta, and Chuck Hagel have all made regular remarks supporting peaceful resolution of the South China Sea disputes according to international law, both at home, in bilateral meetings with Asian counterparts, and during significant multilateral forums.

The United States has also stepped up concrete support for the Philippines in an effort to boost the latter's naval capabilities and maritime domain awareness, both of which lag far behind those of Manila's fellow South China Sea claimants. The United States has provided two decommissioned Coast Guard cutters to serve as the flagships of the Philippine navy, stepped up ship visits and joint training, provided radar equipment and other technology for monitoring the Philippines' waters, and is directly patrolling and gathering intelligence in the Philippine claim, according to Philippine Foreign Secretary Albert del Rosario.[6]

Aquatic Resources

The South China Sea is not just a potential cockpit of military conflict; it also has a rich marine environment.

Fisheries

The sea produces fish, coral, sea grass, and other living and nonliving resources for one of the most populous regions in the world. The population of the Asia-Pacific region, much of which borders on the South China Sea, is close to 2 billion people. In Southeast Asia, more than 70 percent of the population lives in coastal areas and depends heavily on the sea for resources and transportation.[7]

The coastal waters of Southeast Asia and China along the South China Sea are remarkably productive and biologically diverse. Southeast Asia, which includes countries not bordering the South China Sea, produced 21 million tons of fish products in 2009, one-quarter of global production.[8] China is the world's largest single producer, harvesting almost 13 million tons in 2009 of a total of nearly 80 million tons, and China has harvested even more since then.[9] Some of this production comes from ponds and rivers outside the South China Sea.

Southeast Asians rely more heavily on fish as a primary source of dietary protein and income generation than any other people in the world. Roughly half the population of Southeast Asia relies on fish for more than 20 percent of their animal protein. That number rises to 56 percent for the average Philippine citizen.[10]

The South China Sea provides up to 10 percent of the global catch of fish.[11] About 70 percent of the fish production in Southeast Asia comes from the vast coastlines, continental shelves, and potential EEZs of regional states, primarily in the South China Sea and the western central Pacific Ocean.[12]

In Southeast Asia, fisheries contribute up to 10 percent of gross domestic product (GDP) and make up a major share of agricultural exports. Fish account for 52 percent of Vietnam's total agricultural exports and up to 38 percent for other countries in the region.[13]

The increasing demand for fish from the expanding, increasingly wealthy population is creating stress on the already depleted coastal fishery resources of the South China Sea region. According to Garces et al.,[14]

> Some researchers estimate that overfishing in South and Southeast Asia has depleted coastal fish stocks by 5 to 30 percent of their unexploited levels. Among the overexploited stocks are coastal demersal and small pelagic species in the Gulf of Thailand and the Java Sea between Indonesia and the Philippines and green mussels and pearl oysters off the coast of Vietnam.

This pressure is pushing more and more fishermen from the countries surrounding the South China Sea to go ever further in search of fish.

Chinese fishermen go to the southern edge of the sea near Vietnam and the Philippines; Vietnamese and Philippine fishermen operate in the northern part of the sea around the Paracels. This prompts the many incidents each year that newspapers report about fishermen being arrested by different governments, naval vessels ramming fishing boats, or maritime policing officials from the rival claimants in the South China Sea firing at and damaging fishing boats from neighboring countries.

Each year since 1999, China has instituted a roughly 10-week fishing ban from mid-May to early August in the South China Sea north of the 12th parallel. During this period, China forbids foreign and domestic boats from fishing in the area, ostensibly to allow maritime resources to replenish.[15] Often, fishing equipment is confiscated from those caught violating the ban. Vietnam's Foreign Ministry dismisses China's unilateral ban on fishing in the South China Sea, saying that it violates Vietnam's sovereignty over the Paracels and jurisdiction over its EEZ and continental shelf under UNCLOS.[16] The Philippines also does not recognize China's fishing ban because portions of the ban encompass its EEZ, although Manila has asserted the right to issue its own fishing ban in some areas, such as Scarborough Shoal.[17]

Over the past 10–15 years, China has strengthened its ability to supervise fishing in disputed waters, including in the South China Sea. The country plans to boost its maritime surveillance forces to 16 aircraft and 350 vessels by 2015.[18] China has been particularly serious about enforcing its claims around the Paracels. In recent years, many more fishermen from Vietnam and other countries have been detained, prompting more confrontations at sea. So far, little attention has been paid to negotiating some kind of fisheries cooperation agreement in the South China Sea. This laissez-faire approach to fisheries in the disputed area results in friction, and the tension could lead to more serious confrontation or accidents in the future.

In 2004, China and Vietnam, recognizing that the lack of a maritime boundary in the Gulf of Tonkin caused disputes and provided an opportunity for illegal activities close to their coasts, ratified a maritime boundary agreement and a fisheries cooperation agreement in the gulf off Vietnam's northeastern coast and China's southwestern coast. The Fishery Agreement establishes a Common Fishery Zone, a buffer zone for small fishing boats. The zone is about 30,000 square kilometers and covers much of the most productive areas of the gulf. This agreement could serve as a model for managing fishing activities in other areas of dispute.[19] Fisheries cooperation could potentially be a relatively low-risk undertaking, and it would probably be easier to achieve than joint oil and gas development in the disputed sea. And fisheries cooperation could potentially build a foundation for other forms of cooperation in the future.

Coral Reefs

The waters around Southeast Asia are recognized as one of the top global focal points for coral reefs in terms of volume and species variety. An estimated one-third of the earth's coral reefs (some 91,700 square kilometers of a total 284,300 square kilometers) are located in the seas off Southeast Asia.[20] The South China Sea is considered to have the greatest diversity of hermatypic corals in the world. More than 70 hermatypic coral genera are recorded from the reefs of the sea, and hotspots of coral species occur at Nha Trang, Vietnam, with 351 species, and Palawan, Philippines, with 305 species. Records of more than 200 species occur in a number of locations off the coasts of Vietnam, Indonesia, and the Philippines.[21]

In addition to their role as a breeding ground for many of the ocean's fish and other species, coral reefs provide communities worldwide with resources and services worth billions of dollars each year. Millions of people and thousands of communities along the South China Sea rely on coral reefs to provide food, protection against storms and floods, and jobs through diving activities and ecotourism.[22]

The coral reefs of Southeast Asia are among the most threatened and damaged reefs in the world, with unprecedented rates of destruction from human activity over the past few decades. The United Nations Regional Working Group on Coral Reefs identifies overfishing, use of destructive fishing techniques, pollution, and sedimentation as the greatest threats to reefs in the South China Sea. It blames "unsustainable practices in the fisheries sector, coastal development, deforestation and unsustainable tourism" as indirect, man-made causes of these threats while noting that coral bleaching is a serious natural threat.[23]

Of coral areas in the South China Sea examined by the United Nations, 16 percent are considered to be under successful management and 37 percent are moderately well managed. In 24 percent of the sites, the management is considered low, and 23 percent have no plans for effective management.[24]

Sea Grass

The South China Sea region has seen a loss of sea grass in recent years. The Philippines has lost 30–50 percent of its sea grass, Indonesia has lost 30–40 percent, and Thailand has lost about 20–30 percent.[25] Sea grass plays critical ecological and environmental roles. It provides food and shelter to many marine animals and serves as a nursery to reef and deep-sea fish. Sea grasses help clean ocean water by absorbing harmful chemicals, protect coastlines by weakening the force of waves, and make it easier for dust and dirt to settle on the seabed. Dead sea grass washed up on the shore brings nutrients to the beach and helps to form dunes.[26]

Coastal Wetlands

The U.S. National Oceanic and Atmospheric Administration describes coastal wetlands as "among the most productive ecosystems on Earth."[27] They are crucial for protection, food, and breeding for fish, waterfowl, and other aquatic life. They also "improve surface water quality by filtering, storing, and detoxifying residential, agricultural, and urban wastes . . . buffer coastal areas against storm and wave damage and help stabilize shorelines."[28]

Overall about 30 percent of coastal wetlands are lost in the Southeast Asian countries along the South China Sea each decade. Coastal wetlands ecosystems are damaged and lost due to population growth, development and urbanization of coastal areas, conversion of land for agriculture, aquaculture, port and harbor development, industry, human settlement, and tourism.[29]

Land-Based Pollution

The United Nations finds that "excessive nutrient loads and suspended solids are among the most common problems in the coastal waters of the countries bordering the South China Sea."[30] Logging, conversion of forests, and other poor land-use practices are to blame for the level of suspended solids, while the discharge of untreated water into rivers and other waterways that empty into the South China Sea is the primary cause of excessive nutrient levels. The level of heavy metals in coastal waters of the South China Sea has also risen.[31]

Growing population density, food production, and industrialization are ultimately responsible for this rise in pollution. Countries in the region have inadequate wastewater treatment, standards, and regulatory capacity.[32] Major planning, development of laws and regulations, and resources for the installation of infrastructure would be required to reverse the causes of land-based pollution in the South China Sea.[33]

Climate Change

Given the biological diversity of the South China Sea, its economic importance, and the heavy reliance of littoral states on its resources, the effects of climate change on the South China Sea will be of great import. The United Nations' Intergovernmental Panel on Climate Change in 2007 forecasted global sea level rise of three to six feet by the end of the century. Annual mean temperatures in Indonesia, the Philippines, Thailand, and Vietnam are projected to rise 4.8 degrees Celsius by 2100 from their 1990 levels, and Vietnam in particular is expected to experience increasingly drier weather over the next two to three decades.[34]

As a result of climate change, much of the low-lying coastal areas surrounding the South China Sea and many of its islands, most of which are between a few inches and a few feet above water, will become submerged. Floods during typhoon season already lead to regular evacuations of coastal regions.

At the same time that this damage occurs, the resources of the sea and seabed, especially oil and gas reserves, minerals, and fisheries, will remain and in many cases increase in importance. Increasing populations and higher levels of development will mean growing demands for energy and food, including fish protein, even as supplies shrink. The region's booming population will also come under water stress, with increased runoff and wastewater management issues and decreasing aquifer quality and groundwater resources.

All in all, Southeast Asia will suffer from climate change disproportionately compared with the rest of the world. The Asian Development Bank estimates that by 2100, annual losses from climate change could reach 6.7 percent of the region's GDP, twice the global average. Damage and absolute losses from climate change will affect all sectors of the economy and society, with particular stress placed on agriculture, forestry, fisheries, health, water resources, and port industries.

Worst-case scenarios are far from certain, and the level of damage to the region is still manageable, given proper commitment. But if they are undertaken, mitigation and adaptation efforts will not be without costs.[35]

Changes in precipitation patterns and rising sea levels will disrupt biodiversity in the region, with up to half of Asia's total biodiversity potentially at risk from climate change.[36] Rising sea temperatures will drive warm-water fish northward, often into the more contested areas of the South China Sea around the Paracels. Agriculture is set to suffer substantial damage because of land loss and salinization from rising sea levels and crop losses from drought and temperature increases.

In addition, tropical forests that are the key to many livelihoods in the region could be replaced by scrublands. And coral bleaching, which is already a threat, will increase. Ocean acidification resulting from higher levels of carbon dioxide in the sea is causing slow coral growth and coral calcification. These issues in turn affect the biodiversity in the South China Sea's reef systems, including approximately 4,000 fish species and a huge variety of other organisms, including sponges, starfish, and sea cucumbers.

Added to these direct environmental and economic costs are a host of health threats from climate change that will place considerable burdens on communities, economic growth, and government services. Thermal stress is likely to increase the prevalence of cardiovascular diseases. Meanwhile, the frequency and severity of outbreaks of vector-borne diseases, such as malaria and dengue fever, will increase. Added to all this will be the variable but doubtlessly high costs of more frequent and severe extreme weather events, including heat waves and storms.[37]

On top of region-wide effects, climate change and efforts to combat it will have specific effects on individual countries in the region, some examples of which follow.

China

Climate change will exacerbate droughts in China, reducing the nation's ability to rely on hydroelectric power and creating increased pressure to boost fossil fuel extraction, including in the South China Sea. In addition, government-supported efforts to increase energy efficiency worldwide will deepen countries' dependency on rare earth metals, the supply of which is dominated by China and sensitive to supply disruptions. Recognizing this dynamic, nations are seeking to diversify their access to rare earth metals and are likely to accelerate attempts to extract them from the seabed, including in the South China Sea.[38]

Indonesia

Indonesia accounts for 59 percent of greenhouse gas emissions in Southeast Asia, mainly because of deforestation.[39] But although it recognizes the problem, the government is having difficulty grappling with it. Pledges to end the felling of rainforests across the vast archipelago are neither easy nor cheap to implement, and while necessary, they add one more point of pressure for a country already facing severe ecological challenges, including rising sea levels and a growing population. As climate change accelerates, it will put added pressure on this already resource-strained country. Drought and water shortages are expected to hit Indonesia particularly hard in the coming decades.

The Philippines

Population increases will exacerbate the decline in Philippine fish stocks, which will suffer as a result of climate change. According to OneOcean, population growth will increase annual Philippine demand for fish from about 2.9 million tons in 2010 to an estimated 4.2 million tons in 2020.[40] Markwith argues that "the average Filipino consumes 98.6 grams of fish every day. Without fish, 89 million citizens would be without half of their proper protein requirement."[41] And fish will not be the only affected food source. The Philippines is expected to experience a 75 percent decline in rice yields.

In addition to added pressure on fisheries, the Philippines is especially vulnerable to the effects of storms and major weather crises, which will only grow more frequent. The country's citizens are the most affected in Southeast Asia by such events, and the archipelago will be disproportionately affected by severe weather events precipitated by climate change.[42] To mitigate damage from this threat, it is critical that the Philippines develops effective early warning systems for natural disasters.[43]

Vietnam

Vietnam's communities are doubly vulnerable to the effects of climate change because of the country's reliance on the South China Sea and the Mekong River. Higher temperatures, increased frequency of storms, flooding, and growing salinity caused by sea level rise may affect fish physiology, ecology, and agriculture in Vietnam. Catfish, a crucial fish for the country, may grow more rapidly but be more vulnerable to disease. Productivity may fall. And the costs of maintaining water quality will rise. Such costs will mostly be borne by private operators.

Reduced arable land from rising sea levels, inundation of crops, and saline intrusion will reduce rice yields. About 590,000 hectares, or 13 percent of rice production, could be lost in the Mekong River Delta in the southern part of the country.[44] Such agricultural costs could disproportionately affect poor farmers. Already, floods of four meters, higher than the one-half to three meters rice needs, are disrupting crops.[45] Half of Vietnam's rice production, 60 percent of its fish and shrimp harvesting, and 80 percent of its fruit crops are found in the vulnerable Mekong Delta.[46]

To mitigate these threats, Vietnam must increase spending on research to develop new crop varieties that are tolerant to drought, salinity, and higher temperatures. It must also increase investment in irrigation infrastructure, especially in the country's central region, where the opportunities are greatest. And the government should increase spending on flood control measures to minimize the effects of inevitable sea inundations.

Natural forests in Vietnam, as in the rest of the region, will be subject to reductions in land area suitable for semi-deciduous forest. Mangrove forests may be damaged or destroyed by rising seas, unless they can migrate inland. Plantation forests may become more variable in terms of productivity. Current and planned port and coastal infrastructure, such as docks and warehouses, are at growing risk from sea level rise and storm surges. Vietnam currently has about 116 ports along its 3,200-kilometer coastline, making the potential costs of damaged facilities substantial.

Recommendations

Policy and Diplomacy

The United States has essentially no clout to resolve the disputes in the South China Sea that are the most immediate threat to the environmental resources of the area. As long as the claimants are committed to confrontation rather than cooperation, efforts to preserve the region's resources and mitigate the natural threats they face will prove elusive. Luckily, resolving the disputes is not necessary to manage them. And in this, the United States can play a role.

The greatest obstacle to collaboration among the claimants is China's commitment to its nine-dash line claim, despite its violation of international maritime law. As long as the other claimants are faced with this all-or-nothing position, they will not be able to muster the goodwill needed to manage their shared interests in the South China Sea. The most critical step, therefore, is to convince Beijing that its interests are better served by promoting its claims within the bounds of international law rather than in defiance of it.

Washington continues to maintain that, while it takes no position on the sovereignty disputes in the South China Sea, it does insist that they be resolved peacefully and according to international law. Unfortunately, as the only major global nation that has not ratified UNCLOS, these calls carry more than a hint of hypocrisy. If the United States wants its position on the South China Sea to be credible, not just to its friends and allies but also to all the claimants, then it must ratify UNCLOS. Failure to do so undermines any efforts by Washington to play the role of mediator or honest broker.

Just as important, ratifying UNCLOS would send a resounding message to Beijing that the United States is committed to defending the legal regime underpinning the current international order. China's insistence on its claims in the South China Sea in violation of a treaty it willingly signed is a threat not only to its neighbors but also to the UNCLOS regime. If Beijing can scoff at its responsibilities under the treaty when it comes to the South China Sea, then any nation can feel free to do so when its interests are better suited by violating than by following international law.

UNCLOS was a landmark treaty when it was signed, and its tenets extend far beyond mere sovereignty claims. It pulls together and clarifies customary law on everything from maritime safety to freedom of navigation and access to resources. It also enumerates the responsibilities of every maritime nation to shepherd the ocean's resources and protect the maritime commons. It is far from a perfect vehicle, but it is preferable to the free-for-all for marine resources that could result from its collapse.

Beyond the ratification and defense of UNCLOS, the United States has a vital interest in ensuring that a violent change to the status quo in the South China Sea is avoided. In this effort, the United States must continue to push the claimants to conclude a binding code of conduct for parties to the dispute. This will be vital for preventing both purposeful and accidental clashes over access to fisheries, oil and gas, and other resources.

Beyond these diplomatic efforts, Washington should ratchet up assistance to the Southeast Asian claimants to help strengthen their maritime domain awareness capacities. The almost back-to-back grounding of a U.S. minesweeper and a Chinese cargo vessel on the Tubbataha Reef—a protected marine sanctuary—off the Philippine coast in the Sulu Sea last year highlighted the dangers of poor awareness, patrol, and interdiction capabilities on the part of regional states. The Philippines faces the most desperate need in this realm, but all the claimants have room to improve.

Effects of Climate Change

Climate change will accelerate and likely intensify resource competition in and around the South China Sea. To help mitigate this competition and limit its geographic scope, the United States should help in efforts to establish credible estimates for the amount of hydrocarbons beneath the sea. The U.S. Geological Survey and the Energy Information Agency have published important estimates, but they could do far more in cooperation with regional partners such as the Philippines and Vietnam, which are already exploring and in some cases exploiting oil and gas resources in the sea.

As Rogers suggests, "the United States can promote civilian science and technology exchanges and military-to-military cooperation that would develop and test second-generation biofuels" to reduce regional demand for hydrocarbons, as well as for use of arable land for energy production.[47] Both these effects could help lower tensions in the South China Sea over the long term.

The United States should also commit to help nations in the region mitigate the risks of food scarcity from climate change. In the case of fisheries, the United

States should support increased cooperation on management, conservation, and sustainable aquaculture among regional states. This might be easier with just the Southeast Asian claimants for the time being, given Chinese intransigence on issues such as its unilateral fishing ban, but it would be a helpful start. One potential starting point for this cooperation is the already established Southeast Asian Fisheries Development Council, which is currently under-resourced and operating with a limited mandate to monitor and report fish exploitation. The council allows participation by outside powers, which so far has only meant Japan. The United States should consider taking part as well.

Changes in rainfall patterns, that is, increased drought in some places and increased precipitation in others, will significantly affect agricultural patterns and undermine food security. The United States should cooperate with Asian nations on the development of climate-resistant seeds and agricultural practices that can withstand changing weather patterns. It should also step up efforts to promote and help develop climate-prediction models and technologies to help regional states prepare for and adapt to significant changes in climate.

The increased frequency of natural disasters that will come with climate change will bring both a need and an opportunity for greater military-to-military collaboration between the United States and states around the South China Sea. Humanitarian assistance and disaster relief exercises are far less sensitive and in higher demand than other types of military cooperation in Asia. They are now a major part of nearly every U.S.-led bilateral and multilateral military exercise in the region. In 2013, such exercises provided the basis for the first joint exercise under the auspices of the Association of Southeast Asian Nations (ASEAN) Defense Ministers' Meeting-Plus. That exercise brought together troops and naval assets from every major Asia-Pacific player, including China and the United States, as well as all 10 members of the ASEAN. Such efforts should be supported and expanded by the United States and its partners.

Notes

1 U.S. Energy Information Agency (EIA), "The South China Sea Is an Important World Energy Trade Route" (April 4, 2013), www.eia.gov/todayinenergy/detail.cfm?id=10671.

2 U.S. Energy Information Agency (EIA), "China" (last updated Sept. 4, 2012), www.eia.gov/countries/cab.cfm?fips=CH.

3 Peter Drysdale, "Securing China's Energy Supplies," *East Asia Forum* (Dec. 5, 2011), www.eastasiaforum.org/2011/12/05/securing-chinas-energy-supplies/.

4 U.S. Energy Information Agency (EIA), "Contested Areas of South China Sea Likely Have Few Conventional Oil and Gas Resources" (April 3, 2013), www.eia.gov/todayinenergy/detail.cfm?id=10651.

5 EIA, "Contested Areas of South China Sea."

6 "DFA Defends U.S. Surveillance Activities," *Manila Bulletin* (Aug. 1, 2013), www.highbeam.com/doc/1G1-338305251.html.

7 Tom Næss, "Environment and Security in the South China Sea Region: The Role of Experts, Non-Governmental Actors and Governments in Regime Building Processes," PhD diss. (University of Oslo, 1999), https://www.duo.uio.no/handle/10852/14400.
8 Robert S. Pomeroy, "Marine Fisheries in Crisis: Improving Fisheries Management in Southeast Asia," in *Managing New Security Challenges in Asia,* edited by R. Hathaway and M. Mills (Woodrow Wilson Center Press, Washington, D.C., 2013).
9 Tabitha Grace Mallory, "China's Distant Water Fishing Industry: Evolving Policies and Implications," *Marine Policy* 38 (March 2013): 99.
10 Pomeroy, "Marine Fisheries in Crisis."
11 Daniel Schearf, "S. China Sea Dispute Blamed Partly on Depleted Fish Stocks," Voice of America (May 16, 2012), www.voanews.com/content/south-china-sea-dispute-blamed-partly-on-depleted-fish-stocks/666766.html.
12 Pomeroy, "Marine Fisheries in Crisis."
13 Pomeroy, "Marine Fisheries in Crisis."
14 Len R. Garces, Michael D. Pido, and Robert S. Pomeroy, "Fisheries in Southeast Asia: Challenges and Opportunities," in *Transnational Trends: Middle Eastern and Asian Views* (Henry L. Stimson Center, Washington, D.C., 2008): 175, www.stimson.org/images/uploads/research-pdfs/Stimson_ch9.pdf.
15 "China Starts Annual South China Sea Fishing Ban," *Xinhua* (May 16, 2013), http://news.xinhuanet.com/english/china/2013–05/16/c_132386383.htm.
16 "Vietnam Dismisses China Fishing Ban in East Sea," *Thanh Nien News* (May 16, 2013), www.thanhniennews.com/index/pages/20130516-vietnam-opposes-china-fishing-ban-on-east-sea.aspx.
17 "Vietnam Dismisses China Fishing Ban," *Thanh Nien News.*
18 Leszek Buszynski, "The South China Sea: Oil, Maritime Claims, and U.S.-China Strategic Rivalry," *Washington Quarterly* 35, no. 2 (2012): 144, http://csis.org/files/publication/twq12springbuszynski.pdf.
19 Zou Keyuan, "The Sino-Vietnamese Agreement on Maritime Boundary Delimitation in the Gulf of Tonkin," *Ocean Development and International Law* 36 (2005): 14–15.
20 United Nations Environment Programme/Global Environment Facility/South China Sea Project (UNEP/GEF/SCS), *Revised Draft Strategic Action Programme (Sixth Draft)* (June 9, 2008): 9, www.unepscs.org/remository/startdown/2086.html.
21 UNEP/GEF/SCS, *Revised Draft Strategic Action Programme,* 9.
22 National Oceanic and Atmospheric Administration (NOAA), "Why Coral Reefs Matter" (revised Dec. 12, 2006), http://celebrating200years.noaa.gov/foundations/coral/side.html.
23 UNEP/GEF/SCS, *Revised Draft Strategic Action Programme,* 9.
24 UNEP/GEF/SCS, *Revised Draft Strategic Action Programme,* 12.
25 UNEP/GEF/SCS, *Revised Draft Strategic Action Programme,* 12.
26 Nature Foundation St. Maarten, "The Importance of Seagrass," www.naturefoundationsxm.org/education/seagrass/importance_of_seagrass.htm.
27 National Oceanic and Atmospheric Administration (NOAA), "Why Are Coastal Wetlands Important?" www.habitat.noaa.gov/protection/wetlands/.
28 NOAA, "Why Are Coastal Wetlands Important?"
29 UNEP/GEF/SCS, *Revised Draft Strategic Action Programme,* 29.
30 UNEP/GEF/SCS, *Revised Draft Strategic Action Programme,* 45.
31 UNEP/GEF/SCS, *Revised Draft Strategic Action Programme,* 45.
32 UNEP/GEF/SCS, *Revised Draft Strategic Action Programme,* 45.

33 UNEP/GEF/SCS, *Revised Draft Strategic Action Programme,* 46.
34 Asian Development Bank (ADB), *The Economics of Climate Change in Southeast Asia: A Regional Review* (Asian Development Bank, Manila, 2009): 62, www.adb.org/publications/economics-climate-change-southeast-asia-regional-review.
35 ADB, *The Economics of Climate Change in Southeast Asia,* 214.
36 ADB, *The Economics of Climate Change in Southeast Asia,* 5.
37 ADB, *The Economics of Climate Change in Southeast Asia,* 51.
38 Will Rogers, "The Role of Natural Resources in the South China Sea," in *Cooperation from Strength: The United States, China and the South China Sea,* edited by Patrick M. Cronin (Center for a New American Security, Washington, D.C., 2012), www.cnas.org/files/documents/publications/CNAS_CooperationFromStrength_Cronin.pdf.
39 Adianto P. Simamora, "RI the Biggest Greenhouse Gas Emitter in SE Asia: ADB," *Jakarta Post* (April 28, 2009), www.thejakartapost.com/news/2009/04/28/ri-biggest-greenhouse-gas-emitter-se-asia-adb.html.
40 OneOcean, "Proposed Philippine Comprehensive National Fisheries Industry Development Plan: Strategic Sectoral Development, Pathway, Scenario and Trajectory," *Overseas* 9, no. 2 (2007), http://oneocean.org/overseas/200710/proposed_philippine_comprehensive_national_fisheries_industry_development_plan.html.
41 Taylor Markwith, "Conflict in the Scarborough Shoal between China and the Philippines: Climate Change's Role" (2013), www1.american.edu/ted/ICE/scarborough.html.
42 ADB, *The Economics of Climate Change in Southeast Asia,* 3.
43 ADB, *The Economics of Climate Change in Southeast Asia,* 90.
44 World Bank, *Economics of Adaptation to Climate Change:Vietnam* (World Bank, Washington, D.C., 2010): xiv, http://climatechange.worldbank.org/sites/default/files/documents/EACC_Vietnam.pdf.
45 Rogers, "The Role of Natural Resources," 92.
46 Rogers, "The Role of Natural Resources," 93.
47 Rogers, "The Role of Natural Resources," 94.

PART III

New Challenges to U.S. Prosperity

11

NEW CHALLENGES TO U.S. PROSPERITY

David Reed

The authors of the country and regional chapters were asked to provide an analysis of ongoing and anticipated environmental changes that are likely to take hold in the country under study. They also reviewed the main contours of past and current U.S. foreign policy toward each country and evaluated the effects and longer-term significance of environmental changes for U.S. economic, security, and social interests. The first part of this chapter summarizes this analysis by looking at the geophysical and socioeconomic effects of environmental change and resource scarcity and the effects on national institutions and relations with neighboring countries. The second part of this chapter highlights the five pathways through which environmental change and resource scarcity affect U.S. prosperity and security interests.

Country and Regional Effects of Resource Scarcity and Environmental Change

The countries and regions covered by the nine case studies represent nations of high priority to the United States. U.S. economic dynamism and national security are deeply intertwined with the economic performance, social well-being, and environmental sustainability of these countries and regions. Chinese and U.S. economies are intimately connected, while the two countries also compete for geostrategic influence at regional and global levels. India, soon to be the world's most populous country, is an emerging economic and political force stabilizing South and Southeast Asia. Brazil represents a major provider of many agricultural commodities on world markets, and the country's agricultural productivity has a major influence on global food security. The Democratic Republic of Congo hosts the world's second-largest tropical rainforest, whose management may be crucial for mitigating the effects of climate change. Congo also is a source of vast minerals, hydrocarbons, and plant and animal genetic wealth. The Russian Arctic is destined to be the home of a massive array of extractive industries and commercial and shipping centers; the area hosts a steadily growing share of Russia's economic activity. Mutually respectful and supportive relations with Mexico, the second-largest U.S. trading partner, remain a key to U.S. prosperity and constructive relations in the hemisphere. Stable relations with Pakistan are central to U.S. geostrategic interests in South Asia, particularly given the country's possession of nuclear weapons and the continuing influence of Islamic radicals. America's prosperity is directly tied to promoting rule-based regimes in the South China Sea, a choke point of global commerce and an area of increasing geostrategic cooperation and competition.

The experiences analyzed in the country and regional chapters illustrate the profound changes unfolding at the national and regional levels that are driven by global environmental change and rising natural resource scarcities, particularly of renewable natural resources, including water, fish, forests, and productive soils. Although these chapters do not present an all-inclusive compendium of the threats the United States will face as a result of environmental change and resource scarcities, the examples help identify the challenges U.S. leaders must address to ensure that U.S. foreign policy guides the country toward a prosperous future. To highlight the dynamics of change brought forward by the country studies, we have summarized the experiences in the following categories: (a) geophysical effects of global environmental change driven principally, but not exclusively, by climate change; (b) socioeconomic effects of environmental change and resource scarcity; (c) effects on national institutions; and (d) effects on relations with neighboring countries.

Geophysical Effects

Global Environmental Change

The studies highlight the effects of global environmental change, notably climate change, increased human population, and a range of policy failures that influence natural resource sectors. No region on earth has been more directly affected by climate change than the Arctic, which is viewed in this publication through the lens of the Russian Arctic. The chapter on the Arctic states that, over the past 10 to 20 years, the region has experienced an unprecedented intensity of climate-related weather events, including "extreme heat waves, floods, fires, and winter snowfall." The tremendous risks of methane production, which is considered 86 times more damaging over 20 years than carbon dioxide (CO_2), arises from the methane clathrates, rotting muskeg, tundra, permafrost, and taiga. Formed by three major rivers, the Russian Arctic delta is two and a half times larger than the Mississippi River basin and has experienced uncontrolled flooding and excessive soil erosion. Coastal retreat through thermal abrasion, wave erosion, storm surge flooding, and sea ice grounding is disrupting coastal communities, wildlife migratory patterns, and species distribution.

Permafrost, which covers 60 percent of Russia, is thawing and shrinking as its southern boundary moves steadily northward. The thawing permafrost releases massive quantities of methane, which further accelerates greenhouse gas–related climate change and the warming of the Arctic. Estimates hold that permafrost thawing may release more CO_2 than current global emissions. The chapter on the Arctic notes that methane released from sub-seafloor permafrost is accelerating the warming of ocean temperatures with "potentially catastrophic consequences within a few decades" on maritime food chains. Ocean acidification is also accelerating, because the absorption of atmospheric CO_2 occurs more rapidly in cold Arctic surface waters.

The Russian Arctic study also highlights the effects of climate change on the toxic legacy of the extensive military and extractive industry activities in the region during the Cold War, noting that the effects will continue to be felt as the region continues to warm. The chapter states that chemical contaminants, "persistent organic pollutants (POPs), solid waste, and radiation contamination" are part of that toxic legacy. These impacts will demand extensive remediation efforts to clean up more than 100 hotspots that pose severe environmental problems.

Brazil's emergence as a major economic power—now the world's eighth-largest economy—is based on its vast natural resources, which include water, mineral deposits, and expansive agricultural lands. In the 1970s, international attention focused on deforestation in the Amazon. Deforestation was driven by multiple economic and geostrategic forces, especially cattle ranching and feed production. To ensure control over its territory in the 1970s, the Brazilian military launched an ambitious trans-Amazon road construction program that established the foundation for decades of construction of roads, rails, and canals. Ranching, commercial agriculture, mining, and construction of hydroelectric dams followed the transportation routes, with each new activity cutting deeper into the Amazon and inviting successive waves of settlers, farmers, and miners to cut down the next swath of forest. Global pressure to halt deforestation, a major contributor to greenhouse gas emissions, went largely unheeded until 2005, when the Brazilian Amazon suffered its worst drought in over a century with devastating effects on the forests, local populations, and economy. Although it was considered a 100-year event, a second equally serious drought hit the region in 2010, affecting 57 percent of the forests in the region. Continuing this disturbing meteorological trend, the years 2011 to 2012 were also drier than usual, which raised domestic concerns that deforestation was directly linked to the increasingly dry and unpredictable weather, especially in southern Brazil's breadbasket.

The South China Sea study underscores the comparatively disproportionate effects of climate change on Indonesia, the Philippines, Thailand, and Vietnam.

Severe weather events will intensify and become more frequent in the Philippines, while Indonesia will experience increased drought and water shortages. Fish stocks are expected to decline in many countries, and mangroves and natural forests will experience widespread disruption from water depletion, fire, and overfishing.

The direct effects of global environmental change on the Democratic Republic of Congo are negligible at present. Congo is one of the world's great storehouses of natural wealth, including minerals. The country has not experienced major scarcities, productivity losses, or social dislocations as a result of a warming climate or disruption of the phosphorus and nitrogen cycles. However, the indirect effects of climate change are increasing because of the need for governments and companies in industrialized societies to offset their greenhouse gas emissions by supporting reforestation efforts in tropical countries. Consequently, industrial country governments and international financial institutions have shifted an important part of their development assistance to reducing deforestation and degradation in Congo to maintain the integrity of the country's immense carbon sink. Moreover, as concerns about ensuring food security intensify globally, foreign governments and private companies have been actively pursuing land-leasing contracts to expand agribusinesses in Congo. These pressures have given rise to a paradoxical situation in which, on the one hand, international development agencies and nongovernmental organizations seek to preserve the intact forests, while, on the other hand, governments and multinational corporations finance the conversion of forested lands to agricultural production.

The country and regional chapters describe the effects of climate change on local resource scarcities. The oft-repeated example is how rising temperatures have increased evaporation rates; decreased the absorptive capacity of fields and lands; dried rivers, lakes, and ponds; and diminished tree cover. Climate change has disrupted hydrological cycles, altering periods of rain, intensifying storm events, and increasing river flows as glaciers melt during some periods of the year while reducing flows during other months. Extensive periods of drought, even over expansive tropical forests, now figure among the major disruptive impacts of climate change. A broad band of additional destabilizing environmental events includes coastal storm surges, rising sea levels, thawing of the permafrost, and ocean acidification. With the international scientific community warning that these changes will accelerate and deepen, national governments and the international community face a growing set of challenges that require basic changes in development policies and international assistance.

Resource Scarcity in the Study Countries

Although the case studies reflect a wide range of causes of environmental scarcities, deficient or outdated policies and regulations are a critical factor in creating resource scarcity. Many countries have not adjusted either management or regulatory systems in response to the new conditions of stress that promise to intensify. A major source of natural resource scarcity lies outside the resource sectors (forests, water, and fisheries). In China, India, Pakistan, and Tanzania, for example, industrial and extractive industry regulations encourage contamination and degradation of natural resources, resulting in diminished availability of clean water for other uses. Energy-sector policies, including gasoline subsidies for pumping water in India, encourage excessive water extraction. Extensive use of charcoal to fuel iron ore furnaces in Northeast Brazil contributes to deforestation.

Another source of increased scarcities is the growth of human populations. The rising demand for basic water, energy, and other natural resources originates as much from rural as from urban areas, and demand continues to rise steadily as population increases.

The economic and social structures of a society also affect increased scarcity of environmental resources. Unequal access to productive lands, forests, and water is prevalent in Pakistan and other countries wherein the wealthy and powerful maintain or acquire greater access to an increasingly scarce resource much to the prejudice of the poor and powerless. Structural inequalities regarding access to natural resources are frequently long-standing and deeply embedded in a country's social and political dynamics.

A further contributing factor to rising scarcity that is underscored in the studies is the lack of enforcement capacity. Foreign actors often acquire scarce resources despite the efforts of a host country to protect its natural resource patrimony. Depletion of fish stocks off East Africa and in the South China Sea are but two examples.

Regardless of the cause of preexisting renewable resource scarcities, climate change is exerting an accelerating or multiplier effect on current resource constraints. China, India, Kenya, Mexico, Mozambique, Pakistan, and Tanzania illustrate those dynamics. This section focuses mainly on water scarcity and marine resources; the country and regional chapters also highlight scarcity of other renewable resources, including land and forests.

India has been a water-stressed country for centuries. Preexisting scarcity has worsened significantly in recent years in large part because of highly inefficient water use and irrigation practices in agriculture, abetted by long-standing market failures in the water and energy sectors. Those failures, including subsidies for water and energy to run water pumps, have accelerated the drawdown of groundwater, often depleting aquifers in the process. Rising temperatures, particularly in northern India, have dried up riverbeds and threatened the livelihoods of tens of millions of rural families at the same time that industrial pollution and inadequate sanitation systems have decreased the availability of clean surface water. Climate change has further intensified and multiplied water-scarcity problems, notably as glaciers are melting and receding by 10 to 15 meters per year, thus creating more flooding during monsoons while diminishing the steady flow into major rivers during other periods of the year. As monsoon rains have become less predictable, more violent, and shorter, water availability has declined, leaving farmers in increasingly precarious conditions.

Water scarcity also threatens India's neighbor, Pakistan. That country must manage not only its rising environmentally induced social problems, such as deepening poverty, internal migration, and rapid population increase, but also internal destabilization pressures from armed insurgencies and external instability tied to the conflict in Afghanistan. Decades-old issues arising from water scarcity are now intimately intertwined with the effects of climate change being transmitted through a significant rise in day and night temperatures (Pakistan is in a heat-surplus zone), longer periods of excessive heat, and a shorter growing season. Long-standing pressures on arable land, complicated by the major structural inequalities of land ownership, are amplified by more-acute water shortages in the winter and increased flooding during the summer caused by glacial retreat.

In China, climate change is intensifying pressures on the country's diverse ecosystems. The warming climate is deepening water scarcity in China's arid regions; decreasing runoff and drainage into major river systems; inducing extreme weather events, such as floods, droughts, and cyclones; and causing greater economic damage to population centers along the coast. Water resources in the North China Plain are already under extreme pressure from agricultural demand. There and in other areas, groundwater is being extracted at unsustainable rates, depleting aquifers that, in turn, are causing land subsidence, salinization, and disruption of environmentally and economically vital ecosystems around dried-up lakes, rivers, and wetlands. Water-intensive industries and rapid urbanization have further stressed water supplies, such that some 100 cities experience frequent water shortages. Extensive water pollution, which has rendered many sources unfit for human consumption, further exacerbates scarcity issues. The government's principal response has been to construct massive water movement infrastructure, mainly to support water-scarce regions in the north. And while water scarcity is intimately tied to agricultural production, it also has adverse effects on the country's energy generation capacity, which is already under severe pressure. Water is a critical input into coal mining operations and in the conversion of hydrocarbons into electricity. Local and provincial policy makers will face hard choices as they will have to distribute water among competing demands for municipal, agricultural, and industrial uses.

Local communities and government offices in northern Mexico and the southwestern United States have worked together to address the shared water scarcity that has shaped lives and livelihoods across the transboundary region over the past century. Decades-long efforts have given rise to a patchwork of cooperative water management systems that have balanced the needs of farmers and others on both sides of the border. Those collaborative management regimes are under increasing strain as rising demand from municipal and agricultural users and diminishing supplies expose the limits of current allocation agreements and efforts to manage water supply and storage. Rising temperatures associated with climate change have diminished the snowpack in the Rockies. The accelerated depletion of aquifers stretching across both countries has been caused by increased evapotranspiration from lakes, reservoirs, and irrigation canals; reduced soil humidity; and diminished river flow in shared waterways. Greater pressures are now being placed on groundwater resources, which are being drawn down at a rate far exceeding potential recharge. The lack of groundwater management agreements is intensifying tensions between communities as drought conditions continue to diminish surface water on both sides of the border.

The extensive marine resources of the South China Sea have experienced steady decline over the past several decades. Coral reefs have suffered from overfishing, use of destructive fishing techniques, pollution, and sedimentation. And about 30 percent of the coastal wetlands are lost in the Southeast Asian countries along the South China Sea each decade. A wide range of factors, including population growth, urbanization of coastal areas, land conversion, port and harbor development, and tourism, contribute to the degradation of natural resources in the region.

Socioeconomic Effects

The economies and social structures of the countries studied are remarkably diverse. Natural resource extraction provides the economic foundation in Congo and the Russian Arctic, while agriculture remains the main economic sector in Kenya, Mozambique, Pakistan, and Tanzania. The economies of Brazil, China, India, and Mexico are diversifying rapidly, albeit with important agricultural sectors, and rapidly becoming major actors at the global level. Authoritarian regimes prevail in China and Russia, while Congo still lacks a central government that could ensure its territorial integrity and control over its natural resource wealth. The other countries host democratically elected governments with varying degrees of public transparency and accountability. Regardless of the economic structures or systems of governance, all the countries are beset by and are attempting to respond to harsher environmental and natural resource constraints. Yet unknown is the success those countries will experience in responding to environmental changes and the degree of social disruption that may occur.

The Russian Arctic region is experiencing the most profound geophysical changes of any region in the world. The Russian government is beginning to address the staggering economic costs while also anticipating extensive economic opportunities that could make Russia a new global economic powerhouse. One major source of cost is the warming and melting of the permafrost, which is causing the sinking of infrastructure as once frozen soils can no longer support the weight of rail and road traffic, pipelines, and industrial plants. The Russian Arctic study states that "20 percent of accidents on oil and gas pipelines in West Siberia are caused by loss of fixity and deformation" of the underlying permafrost and that "the carrying capacity of pipeline pile foundations is expected to decrease by 50 percent," with similar impacts on power transmission lines and land-based infrastructure. Existing infrastructure also will have to be replaced to bear the massive increases in traffic and cargo volume. Arctic thawing will expose decades of prior environmental contamination, which is not yet readily visible because of extreme weather conditions. Another economic cost is associated with the disruption of food chains caused by ocean acidification that is expected to diminish the abundance of fish stocks, which are now the principal source of income and protein for local populations.

The Russian Arctic study notes that as warming continues, however, the economic benefits accruing to Russia from its Arctic region will greatly eclipse the anticipated economic costs mentioned above. The opening of the Northern Sea Route will accelerate both domestic and foreign investment in the extensive mineral and hydrocarbon deposits stretching along the 4,100-mile Russian Arctic coastline. Ports, railroads, airports, pipelines, storage terminals, search-and-rescue capabilities, and entire urban centers are planned for the region, continuing the country's reliance on extractive industries as its economic foundation. Russia's challenge will be to address the current and anticipated environmental changes as it prepares for rapid economic expansion in the region.

Resource scarcity and global environmental change portend little in the way of economic benefit for India. To the contrary, anticipated environmental changes pose many challenges to the Indian economy, which is already beset by structural rigidities, corruption, and inefficiencies. The immediate economic impacts of scarcity and environmental change are stated clearly: "Rising temperatures and drought conditions have driven millions into Indian cities, putting added strain on the infrastructure and the political system." The country's aging and inefficient urban water infrastructure is hard-pressed to respond to the rising municipal demand while diminished water availability is reducing domestic coal production and increasing India's dependence on imported coal and oil. With the country's increased reliance on coal, India's greenhouse gas emissions are projected to rise steadily even past 2050, unless draconian policy changes are implemented. Although the economic costs to India of deepening scarcities are far from being totaled, the national economy is struggling under the worsening environmental constraints. As government leaders slowly recognize, unless environmental challenges are fully integrated into the country's development strategy, major social and economic shocks may accompany India's development trajectory in the near future.

China has recognized and begun to respond to the environmental costs of rapid industrialization. But the chapter on China states that the country's Ministry of Environmental Protection recently reported, "China's environment continues to deteriorate, environmental conflicts are apparent, and pressures on the environment are growing." Examples include the fact that "wages lost by urban residents who die or miss work because of respiratory illnesses linked to air pollution cost the country about 1.1 percent of its GDP every year." Further, "damages from acid rain falling on crops, wastewater being used for irrigation, deserts encroaching on rangelands, and soil nutrients lost due to erosion reduce farm productivity by 1.6 percent of GDP each year." The Chinese government calculates that up to 8 percent of gross domestic product (GDP) is lost through environmental damage. Despite massive infrastructure programs, the agricultural sector will suffer the loss of 15 to 27 million hectares of irrigated land by 2050, which, because of China's impact on global food markets, will strongly influence global commodity prices. Urban air pollution caused more than 470,000 deaths in 2008, with the highest mortality rates in the poorest, most vulnerable sectors of Chinese society.

The projected economic costs of environmental stress in northern Mexico follow a path similar to the ones affecting China and India. Growing water scarcity, rising temperatures, decreased soil humidity, and increased flooding all point to increased economic disruption in the agricultural sector, reduced incomes for smallholder producers, and sharper constraints on opportunities to intensify agricultural production. The impacts go far beyond reduced water for agriculture. Long-lasting heat waves will increase demand for energy at the same time that less water is available to generate hydroelectric power and cool fossil fuel and nuclear generation plants. The World Bank estimates that "48 percent of all land in Mexico is vulnerable to the effects of climate change, especially in the north."[1]

Climate change is expected to dampen economic production in countries on the South China Sea, including the Philippines, where rice yields are expected to decline by 75 percent. The Asian Development Bank estimates that by 2100, "annual losses to the region's gross domestic product from climate change could reach 6.7 percent, twice the global average."[2] The chapter on the South China Sea states that agriculture is "set to suffer substantial damage because of land loss and salinization from rising sea levels and crop losses from drought and temperature increases." The loss of tropical forests and their replacement by scrublands will directly affect livelihoods in many inland communities, while coastal villages will be threatened and displaced by severe weather events. Vietnam anticipates losing as much as 590,000 hectares of arable land because of sea level rise and saltwater intrusion, which will depress growth in national production by some 13 percent. With 116 ports along its 3,200-kilometer coastline, Vietnam also anticipates considerable damage to its many maritime facilities. Perhaps the most significant effects over the coming decades will be on the fishing sector, which will experience intensified exploitation across the South China Sea region. As disputes over access to fishing grounds have sparked a rising number of conflicts among neighbors in recent decades, depleted fish stocks and expanding fishing fleets will likely spawn a growing number of maritime confrontations in the coming years.

The principal economic effects of environmental change in Brazil will be felt through increased temperatures and water scarcity, which have already started to impair the levels of agricultural production. The chapter on Brazil notes that "even moderate temperature increases would cause significant damage to a range of agricultural products in Brazil—including rice, coffee, beans, manioc, maize, and soya—with declines of perhaps 25 percent in soybean production in the short term." As one of the world's major agricultural exporters, any substantial decline in Brazil's production will reduce the world's food supply and lead to rising global commodity prices. If drought also occurs simultaneously in other productive regions, as happened in 2012 in several grain-producing regions of the world, international pressures on the system could contribute to another global food crisis.

The Pakistan study states that "Pakistan's economy is under severe stress" and "its instability will increase over time." The impact of weather-related events, including the devastating floods of 2011 and 2012, deepened the dire economic imbalances besetting the country for years. The government of Pakistan has acknowledged the growing adverse consequences of rising environmental problems. However, among the various budget categories, the government has allocated the smallest share to environmental purposes and has devoted that allocation solely to wastewater management. Expenditures for developing the country's nuclear energy program greatly exceed total commitments to natural resource management. This is reflected, for example, in the massive drop in funds for crop research, despite the fact that Pakistan is a water-scarce country with urgent pressures to ensure food security.

In Kenya, national politics have been shaped over several centuries by tensions between agriculturalists and pastoralists, who have each sought access to productive lands in rural areas. Farmers, often more numerous and politically influential, expand agricultural production into savannah grasslands as pastoralists push back onto agricultural lands, seeking forage and water for cattle. Intense and frequent tribal conflicts over scarce land have injected violence and social disruption into both local and national politics, resulting in the diminished political influence of the seminomadic herders. Conflict and change are certain to intensify as climate-related temperature rise increases demand for land for crop production. Competition over land in Mozambique and Tanzania takes the form of urban and peri-urban expansion into productive lands that had previously been used to provide food for the growing urban centers.

Kenya, Mozambique, and Tanzania share the common challenge of allocating water resources among competing uses for hydropower, industry, agriculture, domestic consumption, and environmental flows, such as maintaining mangroves and offshore fisheries. Climate modeling indicates that reduced rainfall may significantly tighten competition among those users and between different regions of the three countries.

Growing resource scarcities of both renewables and nonrenewables, coupled with the full spectrum of adverse impacts stemming from global environmental change, are drawing more attention to Congo as a potential resource provider.

International pressure to halt forest degradation and deforestation has increased global attention and brought a modicum of financial support to sustainable management of Congo's forest domain. Sustainable forest management is constantly challenged, however, by the government's inability to control criminal syndicates that seek illegal access to high-value timber and other forest resources. The country's inordinate natural resource wealth has undermined the emergence of a more diverse and integrated national economy and supporting governance.

At the international scale, with the exception of the Russian Arctic, the trend seems to be one of increasing difficulties in maintaining production levels in the face of existing scarcities. This is coupled with the probability that further economic declines will follow as resource scarcities intensify. Simple lack of natural resource inputs into production systems, be they agricultural, extractive, or industrial, is the primary constraint registered by the case studies. In addition, the studies on China, India, Pakistan, and the countries of Coastal East Africa project the contraction of agricultural lands, diminished productivity, and increased uncertainty in the agriculture, fisheries, and industrial sectors. What is clear is that the societies examined in the case studies are facing hard choices regarding trade-offs in the benefits and costs of using scarcer natural resources for competing economic options. Providing water for irrigated agriculture diminishes its availability for industrial uses, energy generation, and domestic consumption. Similarly, diverting water to energy-related activities diminishes its availability for agriculture and municipal consumption. While far-reaching decisions are being made by central governments, the trade-offs resulting from pursuing one option or another and the consequences for local communities are seldom fully foreseen by many decision makers. Those decisions often have unintended consequences, such as accelerating rural-to-urban migration that simply displaces the scarcity issues from one area to another without resolving the underlying causes and societal consequences.

The South China Sea study also addresses an oft-overlooked economic cost associated with climate change, namely health impacts:

> Added to these direct environmental and economic costs are a host of health threats from climate change that will place considerable burdens on communities, economic growth, and government services. Thermal stress is likely to increase the prevalence of cardiovascular diseases. Meanwhile, the frequency and severity of outbreaks of vector-borne diseases, such as malaria and dengue fever, will increase.

Given that many factors influence economic productivity and social well-being, we must exercise caution against drawing categorical conclusions that link natural resource scarcities to social instability and economic prosperity. We do, however, take note of the major social dislocations that are unfolding in virtually all the countries we have examined and note that those disruptions are aggravated or accelerated by environmental scarcities. The societal transformation in China, which involves the rural-to-urban migration of some 300 million people, has resulted from fundamental policy changes enacted by the government beginning around 20 years ago. Harsher environmental conditions in the rural areas of China are a significant factor reinforcing that transformational trend today. The same dynamic holds in rural areas of Mexico, Pakistan, and the countries of Coastal East Africa, where adverse environmental conditions in rural areas are accelerating rural-to-urban migration. The social costs of those trade-offs are reflected in China, for example, in the 90,000 incidents of civil unrest per year that are mostly related to environmental degradation and its effects on human health. Should the multiple environmental crises in these countries deepen and expand, it is not unreasonable to anticipate increased challenges to social stability, cohesion, and governance arrangements.

Effects on National Institutions

The projected economic and social development trajectories of the countries covered in this study are already being influenced by unanticipated natural resource constraints and changing environmental conditions. Increased uncertainties about rainfall patterns, temperature variations, fish migration patterns, glacier melt, and dozens of other environmental factors complicate economic planning efforts at all levels of government. Those same uncertainties also induce vulnerable populations to seek greater security through migration to seemingly less precarious localities and livelihoods, thereby increasing pressure on local officials to provide safety networks and social services. These and many other unforeseen environmental dynamics, with their accompanying societal responses, are creating new demands that often challenge the viability of local and national institutions.

The dramatic physical changes in the Russian Arctic have been accompanied by a concomitant increase in government activities to guide the development of the vast mineral, hydrocarbon, and natural resource wealth in the region. Planning ministries have not hesitated to map out and prioritize economic development zones and to plan construction of the infrastructure needed by the rapidly expanding economy in the region. Lacking technological capacity in many areas, the Russian government has opened discussions with foreign companies, particularly those with deep capacity in extractive industries, shipping, and infrastructure construction. Those ties are expected to expand markedly in the coming decades, thereby opening potential cooperation with a wide range of multinational corporations.

Although those opportunities portend increased international cooperation, internally the Putin government has passed a law on noncommercial organizations that requires all civil society organizations receiving foreign funding to register as foreign agents. This measure has already led to the closure of one major organization promoting the interests of indigenous peoples. Further repression of foreign influence in civil society activities and organizations is anticipated.

International treaties, multilateral trade agreements (including the North American Free Trade Agreement), and a broad range of lower-level cooperative agreements have shaped water use across the Mexico-U.S. border for decades. However, the growing pressures on surface water and groundwater are straining the capacities of existing institutions, obliging local communities and state and regional governments to seek new arrangements to manage competition and conflict. Increased activity by local organizations suggests that a broader, more inclusive river basin approach should be the foundation for addressing new problems and creating supportive institutional arrangements. In addition, there are increased pressures for federal involvement to support the creation of higher-level coordination mechanisms. Proponents of this approach favor the development of institutions that take an incremental and procedural approach, for instance, focusing on one aquifer at a time and increasing information exchange on which subsequent joint planning activities could be carried out.

Deepening environmental problems are changing the attitude and engagement of national policy makers in Delhi. The chapter on India notes that "India's environmental issues are increasingly being viewed by policy makers as having a strategic impact, with national security, regional, and international implications." However, recognition of the challenges will not translate easily into the level of response that will be necessary, given the weaknesses in government capacity on many levels. With weak institutional support and fragile resource management capacity accompanied by corruption in rural areas, rising temperatures, drought, and floods are driving tens of millions of rural inhabitants into urban areas. As the study on India states, "Indian cities are not currently equipped to handle the scope of mass urbanization taking place" and

> if this urbanization trend continues, without corresponding investment in city infrastructure . . . Indian cities will face a serious crisis. The crisis will be fueled in part by environmental challenges, and if the crisis is left untended, environmental conditions will be even worse.

As both national and local governments are unable to provide modern energy services to some 293 million people, or 22 percent of the population, the frustrations of the urban immigrants, already among the most vulnerable groups in Indian society, risk metastasizing into broader social discontent and protest.

The Chinese government has moved decisively on many fronts to address the growing environmental challenges associated with scarcity and changing environmental conditions. Successes include significantly slowing deforestation and improving air quality in many cities. But decentralized decision-making processes in China, a de facto federalism, provide ample space for provincial and district officials to undermine national pollution, energy, and water objectives.

By providing financial incentives to local entrepreneurs, failing to enforce local land-use plans, and tolerating, if not abetting, corruption, local authorities can neglect federal goals, policies, and regulations. The country's de facto energy policy, for example, is determined by decisions made at the local level in response to local economic and social pressures. The study on China summarizes the institutional difficulties in the following terms:

> This "fragmented" and "authoritarian" system has led to disjointed policies between sectors, a lack of transparency, rent-seeking behavior, feigned or incomplete compliance, and a relatively high level of individual discretion by bureaucrats at different levels of the political chain of command—all contributing to slow, incremental policy change and weak enforcement of environmental protections that are perceived as detrimental to local industrial growth.

According to the China study, the negative effects of current policies, principally through air and water pollution, most directly affect some "300 million rural-to-urban migrants [who are] at the bottom rungs of urban society," who are "at greater danger from unsafe environmental conditions in the workplace," and who are "forced to cope with poor sanitation." The consequences for social stability are becoming clearer to policy makers, who are now pressured by "approximately 90,000 'illegal mass incidents' (a Chinese epithet for public disturbances or protests) involving nearly 4 million people . . . each year." The minister of environmental protection said in a press conference in 2012, "China has entered a peak period in which environmental risks are becoming clear and pollution accidents are occurring frequently." The official further predicted that "environmental risks may go from being scattered, discrete problems to becoming an all-encompassing problem."

The Pakistan study makes clear that institutional failures and broader social forces, including the influence of the military, have excluded environmental considerations from the national agenda for decades. The "national security state" has given primacy to addressing tensions with its neighbors, notably Afghanistan and India, and to suppressing rising internal insurgencies. Those priorities have contributed to the dire state of Pakistan's national economy, which has been beset by structural problems, including a growing debt burden, declining assistance from the United States, and rising domestic pressures associated with rapid urbanization. In this context, the government has ignored pressing environmental issues, other than in words or proclamations, asserting that such tertiary matters cannot be tended to until national security matters are addressed. This state of affairs ignores pressing environmental issues that are accelerating internal problems and security and causing mass migration to urban areas. Long-standing inequalities in access to land, water, and other natural resources in rural areas have spawned unrest and discontent that have not been addressed. Instead, the landed political elite continue to exert inordinate influence over the national policy dialogue. Despite public promises of reform and begrudging recognition of the impact that environmental change is having on Pakistani society, the study arrives at the following conclusion: "In the final analysis, however, formal government policy and statements [about the environment] can be realized only if the national security apparatus recognizes the connection between environmental scarcity and national stability."

The chapter on Brazil makes clear that the rising environmental problems in the Amazon have not increased domestic political sensitivities to international pressures to alter policies that affect the world's largest tropical forest. Nor have domestic political failures been at the heart of policies undermining the integrity of the Amazon. To the contrary, the political processes that have affected outcomes in the Amazon have been the result of a domestic political process involving powerful agribusinesses, smallholder farmers, local governments, indigenous peoples, and environmental groups. As has been the case for decades, the result of the political process has been the continued dominance of powerful domestic economic interests over other stakeholders, including the interests of foreign governments and international environmental groups that seek to reverse current deforestation trends. Clearly, the losers of the current political alignments are indigenous peoples, whose culture and way of life are being destroyed, and the international community, which is concerned about the negative effects of global environmental changes. However, until water scarcity and climate change further erode the productive capacity of agribusiness in Brazil, changing current policies will prove difficult.

Limited capacity to manage natural resource wealth has weakened economic vitality and social cohesion in Kenya, Mozambique, and Tanzania. Wildlife crimes, such as elephant poaching and ivory smuggling in Kenya and Tanzania, have fueled illegal networks that link local poachers to international criminal syndicates. Those links have eroded public safety, security, and the rule of law in the three countries. Artisanal fishing constitutes 95 percent of the industry along the coasts of the three countries. Foreign fishing vessels, particularly from countries in Asia and the Indian Ocean, regularly violate the 200 nautical miles of the exclusive economic zones of the three countries.

The chapter on Congo offers the most compelling example of the failures of a state apparatus in a country dominated by extractive activities. The chapter states that "a vicious circle is firmly in place. Poor natural resource management handicaps efforts to rebuild the state, and because the state is weak, it cannot regain authority over its natural capital." In an extractive economy with no functioning state reaching across its territory, appropriation of natural resources is the key determinant of power and wealth. In Congo, that wealth begins with bushmeat, forest clearing, and artisanal mining and runs to large-scale mining operations and wildlife crimes. A system of patrimonialism involving mafia-type control over different resources in various parts of the country has replaced government regulatory and management systems, and bribery and corruption are the norms. The establishment of effective, transparent government presence has been rendered virtually impossible by the lack of a national road-river-rail transportation and communication network to link one side of the country to the other. The executive branch of the Congolese government has been eviscerated, and the legislative branch has no capacity to exercise oversight and control over the actions of powerful individuals within government or in the private sector. A sustained reform and investment process led by international financial institutions has fostered the passage of stewardship legislation and regulatory standards but has failed to put in place corresponding enforcement and oversight mechanisms. In the political void, domestic and international nongovernmental organizations have de facto taken on some state functions related to monitoring and managing the natural resource sectors. Despite some modest accomplishments, predatory domestic and external forces remain in control of the country's resource patrimony.

An important point to be drawn from these studies with regard to institutional arrangements is that communities and governments put in place a wide range of institutions and management systems to regulate access to and use of natural resources. In some cases, governments have reached agreements with neighboring countries to accommodate competing national interests and those neighbors have mutually adjusted regulatory and governance mechanisms to meet new conditions over a period of decades. However, the overarching message from the studies is that environmental change and intensifying resource scarcities have eclipsed many domestic and transboundary natural resource management systems. Increased weather variability and extreme weather events associated with climate change have put governance and management systems under such stress that existing agreements are in need of even more fundamental realignment to meet the unanticipated demographic, economic, and climate-related pressures. Further, government offices frequently are not able to respond constructively to citizen demands, be they urban or rural, in regard to the availability of water, productive land, and energy sources. Increased competition involving communities, companies, and government offices for natural resources has given rise to a growing number of social protests that pose direct threats to the stability of local, regional, and national governments. In several countries, such as China and India, the studies indicate a widening loss of confidence in local and national agencies and a corresponding willingness to seek individual and collective solutions outside government systems.

Effects on Relations with Neighboring Countries

Environmental change and resource scarcities do not fall neatly along territorial demarcations. As resource constraints and environmental change extend across large areas, the environmental challenges facing one country are often shared by its neighbors. Shared environmental challenges could provide the basis for collective, cooperative responses. When large imbalances exist in neighboring countries' abilities to project economic, diplomatic, or military power, however, cooperation may be supplanted by coercion.

The opening of the Northern Sea Route will oblige Russia to expand its cooperation not only with its Arctic neighbors but also with many other countries that will seek passage through the previously frozen maritime lanes. The coordination functions of the Arctic Council, which has eight member states and five indigenous observer organizations, will likely expand considerably as commercial and passenger traffic grows in the coming years. A search-and-rescue agreement is already in place, and an agreement on marine oil spill preparedness and response was recently signed. New pressures are likely to arise to support more-direct managerial functions for the council for environmental and commercial activities in the region. In addition, increased transport of European, Asian, and North American vessels through the Bering Strait will require more sophisticated communication systems, icebreakers, and rescue ships. Russia's economic ambitions will require economic and financial arrangements with an ever-broadening range of corporate interests and bilateral and multilateral trade agreements. Russia has the largest geographic reach among the member states of the Arctic Council. If Russia is to fulfill its economic ambitions in its Arctic region, the country will have to play an increasingly active role in this specialized multilateral governance regime, as a progenitor for other regions facing transboundary environmental management challenges.

China's impact on its neighboring countries is enormous not only in creating markets and jobs but also in generating claims of coercion and interference in regional affairs and reinforcing black markets for natural resources. Pressures caused by scarcity of water and energy in China have led to the construction of an ever-growing number of dams on the upper reaches of the Mekong, Irrawaddy, Brahmaputra, Irtysh, and other major rivers. Those projects and other actions have embroiled China in water rights disputes with Burma, Cambodia, India, Kazakhstan, North Korea, Russia, and Vietnam. With more plans moving from the drawing board to construction, tensions promise to intensify, particularly as flooding from glacier melt increases in those regions and as water diversion and drawdown from the Chinese side exacerbate scarcities in neighboring countries.

China's authoritarian mercantilism is driving expansion of that country's extractive industry and infrastructure construction footprint in Africa and Latin America. Lack of transparency, corruption, and unregulated and undisclosed activities with weak host governments pose serious reputational risks to Chinese parastatal companies that have failed to respect internationally accepted social and environmental safeguards. China is the world's largest supplier and user of wood products sourced from illegally harvested timber from Russia, Malaysia, and Indonesia, among other suppliers. China's porous borders with Burma have fueled a thriving black market for timber, gems, and drugs that have sustained insurgent ethnic militia groups in Burma. China has constructed seven dams in Burma that generate hydroelectric power sent to China. With the second-highest subsidies to its fishing industry, trailing only Japan, China has a growing responsibility for depleting the world's capture fishing grounds. Yet China ranks near the bottom on measures to control illegal fishing. China's role as the world's leading manufacturing hub creates considerable liabilities should other countries reach agreement on measures to reduce greenhouse gas emissions that would include tariffs on high-polluting industrial goods produced outside a signatory's borders.

The study points out that China's neighbors to its south and west are highly vulnerable to economic and ecological shocks. The United States and China share a common interest in stabilizing the fragile states to China's south and west, particularly in tamping down the rise of insurgencies and militancy. Although some policy makers in Washington perceive the expansion of China's influence around the world as a direct threat to the United States, the China study proffers an alternate view, stating,

> What the Chinese seek is an equal seat at the table with the United States and other major countries and a greater voice in deciding the rules of the existing international system that has largely been shaped by the United States. If China *does* threaten the United States, it will not be by choice but rather as a consequence of China's environmental decline and its inability to ensure greater sustainability both at home and in its dealings abroad.

China's increasingly aggressive posture vis-à-vis its neighbors, which is often driven by China's pursuit of natural resources, is nowhere more acute than in the South China Sea. This posture has been evident in the expulsion of Vietnam from the Paracel Islands in 1974, the occupation of Scarborough Shoal off the Philippine coast in 2012, more frequent expulsion of fishing vessels and confiscation of their gear in recent years, and the 2009 territorial claims of the nine-dash line, which covers the entire South China Sea. These events have been directly tied to China's efforts to control the extensive hydrocarbon reserves in the region and to ensure access to fish stocks in response to rising domestic demand. As resource abundance declines and domestic demand rises, more confrontations in the region may be anticipated.

Although India is now the world's fourth-largest economy, severe environmental constraints could derail the country from acquiring greater influence in regional and world affairs. Regional tensions around water scarcity have shaped India's relations with its neighbors for decades. The Indus Water Treaty with Pakistan and the Ganges Water Treaty with Bangladesh have served to stabilize relations over the past years. But, according to the chapter on India, "if India's climate change issues continue to worsen, the country may face mass migration within India and from India's neighbors, particularly Bangladesh." Moreover, China's damming of rivers in the Tibetan plateau, whose waters are diverted to China's water-scarce northern provinces, raises fears of hydrological imbalances in northern India and shortages in Bangladesh, which, in turn, could sharpen border tensions between Bangladesh and China. As the chapter on India indicates,

> The bottom line is that an India plagued by internal instabilities would upend the American security framework for South Asia and even East Asia. It would eviscerate the potential for a true strategic partnership; it would require a complete reassessment of policy and possibly significant U.S. assistance, both financial and military, to help ameliorate the impacts of India's severe environmental degradation.

Water disputes, notably those associated with the shared waters of the Indus River, could serve as conflict ignition points with Pakistan's historic rival, India. By the same token, cooperative agreements could serve as a moderating force between the countries' military establishments, as has been the case in recent years. The Pakistan study sets forth proposals for using existing regional agreements, notably the South Asian Association for Regional Cooperation, to strengthen relations and address shared problems relating to the environment, human rights, and education. Several accompanying regional agreements, such as the Economic Cooperation Organization looking westward to Turkey and Iran and the Shanghai Cooperation Organization oriented eastward toward China, provide further institutional means for defusing potentially explosive situations and building practical cooperation. However, the depth of environmental problems besetting Pakistan leads the authors to suggest a fundamental reorientation toward a new security pact with the United States. The aim would be to allow the current transactional relations to give way to broader geostrategic cooperation to address the major environmental and energy issues in Pakistan.

Immigration, trade, and drug-related issues have dominated relations between the United States and Mexico for decades. Meanwhile, water-scarcity issues have remained quietly in the background in the bilateral dialogue. Now that all surface water in the region is fully subscribed, pumping water from aquifers is the major source of clean water in Mexico and parts of the southwestern United States, requiring revised water management arrangements. Unless new cooperative arrangements based on water basin management principles can be reached, tensions between the two countries are bound to rise. Finding solutions to these challenges may offer models to other countries facing similar cross-border water-scarcity challenges.

The chapter on Brazil underscores the country's intention of establishing independent diplomatic positions while building alliances that support its pursuit of status as a great nation in the coming decades. A nationalistic bent has shaped Brazil's engagement in international processes, notably affirming its sovereignty over the Amazon and its right to determine all policies and practices that affect the region's future. Although Brazil's actions in the Amazon, the world's largest tropical forest, fundamentally influence the pace and scale of global climate change, the country's international posture asserts the primacy of national need and interest over international interests and concerns. Signs suggest that only when the effects of the domestic climate on the economy become more severe and internal political dynamics begin to change will the Brazilian government be able to align its domestic policies with the priorities of the international community.

The pressures of domestic scarcities and internal environmental change are not driving better policies in Congo. On the contrary, the long-standing failure of the state to manage natural resources in a transparent, socially beneficial way continues to encourage further depredation by both internal and foreign actors. Patrimonialism, corruption, porous borders, and social relations built on opaque access to natural resource wealth generate economic, political, and social dynamics that reverberate far beyond the country's geographic boundaries. These dynamics fuel illicit trade, insurgencies, and crime among neighboring countries.

The pillaging of Congo's natural resources is a reality documented by a United Nations group of experts.[3] Disputes over oil revenues and offshore oil exploitation blocks continue to embitter relations between Kinshasa and Angola and between Kinshasa and Uganda. There were also disputes over diamond fields in the south of Congo's Bandundu Province and Lunda Norte in Angola. On the eastern front, things could not be worse. Paul Kagame's support of rebel groups in the Kivus is a well-known secret. Congolese timber and minerals are illegally exported to Uganda. Credible sources reveal that Ugandan President Museveni armed rival ethnic groups in the northeast Congo. His strategy was to deliberately perpetuate a situation of conflict to facilitate the illegal export of Congo's natural wealth. The South Sudanese military has joined Uganda in slaughtering elephants in Congo's Garamba National Park, exporting ivory mainly to China.

Congo's failed resource governance creates an opportunity for neighboring governments to derive many short-term economic and political advantages. The lack of governance also provides few incentives for those neighbors to seek mutually beneficial bonds of cooperation with the government in Kinshasa.

The studies underscore how vested interests support maintenance of the status quo in many regions of the world in order to ensure access to natural resource wealth. The studies also highlight the tensions and conflicts that exist under current natural resource management regimes between countries and across regions. The study authors see no predetermined patterns or outcomes regarding the future evolution of those regional tensions. Past and current efforts to resolve domestic resource scarcities by usurping assets held by neighboring countries have not provided long-term solutions for domestic shortages. The evolution of more partnerships and negotiated arrangements will be needed as shortages intensify in the coming years.

Why Global Environmental Change Matters for the United States

In a 2013 assessment of worldwide threats to the security of the United States, National Intelligence Director James Clapper stated in succinct terms many of the basic points analyzed in this publication's country and regional studies:

> Competition and scarcity involving natural resources—food, water, minerals, and energy—are growing security threats. Many countries important to the United States are vulnerable to natural resource shocks that degrade economic development, frustrate attempts to democratize, raise the risk of regime-threatening instability, and aggravate regional tensions. Extreme weather events (floods, droughts, heat waves) will increasingly disrupt food and energy markets, exacerbating state weakness, forcing human migrations and triggering riots, civil disobedience, and vandalism. Social disruptions are magnified in growing urban areas where information technology transmits grievances to larger—often youthful and unemployed—audiences, and relatively "small" events can generate significant effects across regions or the world.[4]

The five points summarized below highlight the ways by which the impacts identified by General Clapper and the studies translate into threats to the U.S. economy and national security.

1. Disrupting Global Supply Chains

The studies in this book highlight how interactions between natural resource scarcities and economic productivity can translate into disturbances of global markets and negative impacts on U.S. businesses, investors, and consumers. Perhaps the most salient of recent experiences is how drought disrupted global food chains, resulting in the global food price spikes of 2008 and 2012. Drought conditions in the Ukraine, Russia, Australia, and the United States and diminished monsoon rains in India quickly translated into a sharp drop in the global supply of agricultural commodities, notably corn, wheat, and soybeans. On a global scale, the price hike of 2012 pushed nearly 130 million poor people into the ranks of the desperately poor, from which status many may never recover.

The demand for agricultural commodities will continue to rise as the world's population continues toward the 9.5 billion mark, living standards rise in many emerging economies, and urbanization continues in many developing countries. To meet the rising global demand for food, greater pressure will be placed on freshwater supplies and arable land, which are already in decline in many parts of the world. As indicated in the China study, the world's most populous country faces the challenge of feeding 20 percent of the world's population while having less than 10 percent of the world's arable land and only 7 percent of the world's potable water.

The more vulnerable countries covered in this publication, including Pakistan and the countries on the coast of East Africa, do not have the economic depth and diversity to absorb such price shocks, and consequently, they will likely experience system-wide downward pressures on incomes and living standards. Often, years are required to recover from such shocks. The emerging economies of Brazil, China, and Mexico will have greater ability to absorb current and future supply chain disruptions, given their diverse economic structures and comparatively more abundant natural resource base. As for the United States, its economic reach, exercised through global production, processing, and marketing networks, will allow U.S. consumers and producers to absorb many of the disruptions in global supply chains, which are likely to affect domestic prices and access. During the half century following World War II, the United States was the ascendant industrial power and U.S. foreign policy was geared to ensuring uninterrupted access to energy supplies and mineral inputs to stoke the manufacturing economy. But the United States is not impervious to the supply disruptions of a broad band of commodities and industrial inputs. This was recently highlighted for the case of rare earth elements, of which China controls approximately 95 percent of global supply.

As during recent global food crises, the international community will call upon the United States in the future to provide relief and food assistance to buffer the economic dislocations experienced by the most vulnerable countries when similar crises take hold. Given the inelasticity of global food demand and the planet's expanding population, supply chain disruptions and the resulting human crises may prove to be a more regular part of future international relations.

2. *Fueling Social Instability*

The 2008 and 2012 global food crises provided powerful reminders of the intimate and complex dynamics between resource scarcity, economic dislocation, and social disruption. Shortly following the onset of those supply chain disruptions, food riots broke out in more than 25 countries, including India and Mozambique. It is important to note that virtually all the countries where food riots took place were water-stressed societies before the onset of the severe global food crisis. Under rising social pressure, governments responded by increasing food subsidies and implementing other unsustainable economic measures that contributed to medium-term economic destabilization. Many Middle East analysts contend that the food shortages and the ensuing social protests were the precipitating events that sparked the Arab Spring, an ongoing process of social uprising that seeks to establish more-democratic forms of governance across the region.

Whether food crises and accompanying riots are to become permanent features of the international policy landscape is widely debated. The case studies in the preceding chapters indicate that, in many cases, the most vulnerable segments of the societies expressed their desperation by moving from rural areas where diminished water supplies and depleted soils no longer provided for their sustenance. Often, the urban destinations of those hundreds of millions of rural refugees have provided equally grim opportunities, because local governments have been overwhelmed by the sheer numbers of new residents. The teeming cities in Pakistan, among other localities, have proven fertile grounds for recruiting new adherents to extremists' views and actions.

As government agencies are unable to provide for the immediate needs of desperate communities, urban dwellers sometimes turn to other organized groups, ranging from social welfare organizations to those driven by radical ideologies, to fill the vacuum. The unanswered needs of growing populations for basic services, resources, and jobs further erode confidence in government and tend to create parallel systems of service provision and local governance. In those circumstances, the ability of the U.S. government to provide effective development assistance and emergency relief dwindles significantly, and the U.S. government is often reduced to the status of observer rather than active participant.

3. *Destabilizing Regional Relations*

Resource scarcities have obliged the governments of the countries explored in this publication to develop bilateral and regional resource management systems to prevent conflicts among neighbors while providing citizens with access to needed resources. Those agreements, such as the Indus Water Treaty, the Ganges Water Treaty, and the many agreements between Mexico and the United States, have provided the foundations of regional stability among nations even when open conflicts have flared between neighbors on other issues. Despite the rising geostrategic struggle in the South China Sea, China and Vietnam reached an accord on shared fishing grounds, through the Southeast Asian Fisheries Development Council, to improve the management of fish stocks. There are many examples of agreements between countries not covered in this publication, such as that between Egypt, Somalia, and countries of the upper Nile River, in which resource management agreements have provided a modest foundation for promoting regional stability.

Resource scarcities have also precipitated bilateral and regional tensions, occasionally breaking out into open hostilities. Domestic needs have led governments to seek resources beyond their internationally recognized borders, such as in the South China Sea. China's sharply rising domestic needs for water, energy, timber, minerals, and other industrial inputs are reflected in its efforts to secure resources from its neighbors. Although China's dam-building activities on the upper Mekong, Irrawaddy, Brahmaputra, Irtysh, and other rivers may not have provoked open conflict, tensions are rising downstream as water flows diminish and become more uncertain. China's acquisition of timber from Russia and timber, semiprecious stones, and hydroelectric power from Burma has spawned widespread illegal resource trade and corruption across the region. Fishing fleets from China challenge the access to and benefits of open-sea fishing areas across the South China Sea. Competition and conflict over the region's resources, ranging from fish to hydrocarbons, pose serious threats to commercial traffic through the Straits of Malacca. Rwanda has encouraged illegal resource trade along its border with Congo, often abetting local insurgencies and corruption, which contribute to regional instability.

Driven by resource scarcities, threats to regional stability will increase, as highlighted in a growing number of studies conducted by the national intelligence and security communities. Sudan has recently tried to restructure the regional water agreements it originally signed with Egypt during the decolonization period. These attempts have significantly escalated tensions not only between those two countries but also between all the nations in the upper Nile watershed. Scarcity issues affecting China, India, Nepal, and Pakistan provide an equally powerful indication of the widespread disruptive potential. The United States, having significant interests in these and other regions affected by resource scarcities, could be drawn into these conflicts if they escalate to the point of threatening U.S. security interests. Once open hostilities erupt, finding solutions and providing support to dissipate those tensions will be more difficult than working to prevent conflict by helping to solve the underlying problems proactively.

4. Undermining Strategic Relationships

Over the past decades, some countries, such as Russia, have been antagonistic to the role of the United States in the world; others, such as Brazil, have opposed specific U.S. initiatives and policies in the international arena. China is, simultaneously, a geostrategic rival, an economic competitor, and a major trading partner of the United States. The remainder of the countries studied in the previous chapters have either built long-term strategic partnerships with the United States or relied on its development, diplomatic engagement and military backing to support their national development objectives.

Regardless of the international positioning of the countries relative to the United States, each has strong, active interests in maintaining the bonds of cooperation on a wide range of economic and security issues with the U.S. government. The studies clearly indicate that when domestic environmental issues impede economic growth and disrupt social order and institutions, they can divert attention from maintaining international relations to addressing internal problems. For example, India serves as a critical ally in balancing influence and power across South Asia and East Asia, particularly relative to China. Should rising environmental and social issues continue to mount in India, the world's largest democracy would be obliged to turn inward, withdrawing from its strategic balancing posture in the region. The national security agenda in Pakistan has held sway over domestic politics for decades, pushing mounting internal environmental and social issues off the political agenda entirely. Now those internal issues are rising to the point that they threaten internal stability and, for lack of attention, are becoming major challenges to national security. Despite its being an economic competitor, the China study underscores the point that China's proactive engagement with the United States could turn sharply contentious if internal environmental decline required the emerging giant to pursue an even more aggressive posture vis-à-vis its neighbors in the Asia-Pacific region. Mexico's economic well-being is intimately tied to a robust, expanding relationship with the United States, and the Mexican government would experience detrimental effects were cross-border tensions over resource sharing allowed to shake relations between the two countries. Constructive cooperation across the rapidly changing Arctic region could be threatened if Russia does not take more responsibility for the environmental challenges accompanying the opening of the Northern Sea Route and the dramatically expanded extractive and commercial activities foreseen for the region.

In each of these and other engagements, partnerships and cooperation with the United States will hinge increasingly on finding ways of addressing the significantly amplified environmental challenges, which only promise to intensify as the effects of climate change accelerate.

5. Spawning Opportunities for International Criminal Activities and Non-state Threats

Illegal trade in natural resources, involving timber, fish, minerals, coral, wildlife, and many other environmental goods, runs in the hundreds of billions of dollars annually. Such illegal resource trade distorts international trade, weakens rules governing international commerce, and causes economic loss to producers and consumers in the United States. The study on the Democratic Republic of Congo provides a casebook example of how illegal natural resource trade creates a governance system cloaked in semisecrecy, managed through long lines of coercive personal and clan control, and geared toward responding to external market demand. The recent slaughter of tens of thousands of elephants in the region was directly linked to generating financial proceeds to expand the military capacity of marauding bands, which, in turn, pose direct threats to state functions in the eastern reaches of the country. Traffic in illegal wildlife, beginning in Central Africa and extending to markets in China and Vietnam, has become but one product line in international syndicates that also traffic in guns, precious metals, drugs, and humans.

Financial returns to illegal natural resource trade, including recent associated wildlife crimes, further fuel the insurrectionist activities of local militias, which are affiliated with neighboring country governments. These non-state actors and syndicates pose direct challenges to U.S. interests in eastern Africa and threaten to destabilize allies and trading partners throughout the region.

Implications for U.S. Policy

We have been careful to avoid suggesting direct lines of causality and outcomes in summarizing the dynamics linking domestic resource scarcity and environmental change with the effects of broader societal and foreign policy. Environmental issues are woven into all facets of human activity and consequently cannot be isolated as independent drivers of societal impacts. Moreover, environmental change and scarcities are woven into other dynamics of social tension and stress that reflect social structures, cultural preferences, and the exercise of power of one group vis-à-vis another.

Nonetheless, the studies indicate that scarcities and environmental change can precipitate social conflict, often starting at the local level but with the capacity to challenge and disrupt prevailing systems of governance at the national and regional levels. Disruption can take the form of local protest and migratory movements involving millions of people seeking refuge from untenable environmental conditions. We have seen how failed government systems, corruption, and predation can undermine national stability and inject lawlessness into regional relations. Some governments have elected to embark on massive infrastructure and economic development initiatives in hopes of attenuating or staving off anticipated resource scarcities. Such large resource-engineering endeavors can have direct effects on relations with neighboring countries, often aggravating existing scarcities among neighbors. We have seen that climate change has significantly accelerated the negative effects of resource scarcities and intensified tensions and conflicts at the local and regional levels. There is every reason to believe that these tensions will intensify in many countries and regions of the world in the coming years.

U.S. policy makers must understand the current impacts and trends relating to resource access and availability in these and other countries and, in keeping with necessary research and analysis, prepare for the intensification of those impacts. Strategic engagements with other countries, whether emerging economies or more-vulnerable developing countries and whether close partners or competitors, must be built on the premise of increasingly acute resource pressures and the need to understand the trade-offs facing other countries, as well as the United States. Understanding the impacts and trade-offs for the United States will require far more sophisticated analysis and tracking of pending environmental changes, which should begin with each country and, at times, specific subnational localities. U.S. policy makers must also systematically integrate these understandings into the full range of foreign policy strategies, ranging from the National Security Strategy and Quadrennial Defense Report to the National Intelligence Council's Global Trends Reports and the Quadrennial Homeland Security Review, which guide U.S. engagements with partners and competitors around the world.

In the concluding chapter, we will offer specific recommendations that provide the foundations for strengthening the U.S. government's leadership role in responding to the new challenges posed by global environmental change and natural resource scarcities.

Notes

1 World Bank, *Mexico Country Note: Climate Change Aspects in Agriculture* (World Bank, Washington, D.C., 2009).
2 Asian Development Bank, *The Economics of Climate Change in Southeast Asia: A Regional Review* (Asian Development Bank, Manila, 2009), www.adb.org/publications/economics-climate-change-southeast-asia-regional-review.
3 United Nations Panel of Inquiry, "Final Report of the Panel of Experts on the Illegal Exploitation of Natural Resources and Other Forms of Wealth of the Democratic Republic of the Congo" (United Nations, New York, 2009).
4 www.intelligence.senate.gov/130312/clapper.pdf.

12

RECOMMENDATIONS

David Reed

Underlying the recommendations offered in this chapter is a vision of the United States playing a powerful leadership role in responding to the new challenges posed by global environmental change and natural resource scarcities. That vision is built on America's economic dynamism, our culture of technological innovation, and several decades of successes in addressing our own domestic environmental problems. Despite the potential severity of the environmental challenges and resulting social disruptions highlighted in the preceding chapters, the United States has unmatched capacities and opportunities to address these challenges domestically and at the global level.

Given current trend lines regarding global demographics, economic growth, and natural resource scarcities, the pace of global environmental change will accelerate considerably in the coming years. As those changes take hold, the need to establish a systemic approach to guide the U.S. government's response will rise in urgency. Admittedly, designing and implementing a comprehensive response system will require years of innovation, testing, and refinement. That said, the recommendations offered below describe specific steps that can be taken immediately to set the firm, flexible foundation that our government will need in the coming years.

Recommendation 1: Institutionalize an Evidence-Based System in which Foreign Policy and International Programs Are Informed by the Latest Research Data on Environmental Change

The purpose of this recommendation is to consolidate the many diverse research activities being financed by federal resources so that a comprehensive, regularly updated analysis of environmental and scarcity threats to U.S. prosperity and security interests directly shapes U.S. engagements with trading and political partners, as well as with competing nations. The intention is to bring the many disparate federal research programs into a coherent analytical platform that is accessible to users who can translate emerging trends into effective responses.

Such an evidence-based system should be composed of four basic elements.

1.1 Strategic data collection and analysis. First, there must be a targeted research agenda for global environmental research and analysis. The agenda should give priority to tracking key trends that may affect the economic vitality and political stability of countries of economic and national security importance.

1.2 Analytical capacity. Second, the data must be subject to policy-relevant analysis that can identify and interpret real or potential threats to America's food, water, health, and energy security. This will require new or redirected human resources.

1.3 Strategic planning. Third, there needs to be a clear process for integrating the findings of such research and analysis into the strategic planning of the federal government. Ensuring that the various departments and agencies are sharing information and coordinating efforts will require a responsible officer in the National Security Council and a directive to address key findings in the National Security Strategy, Quadrennial Defense Review, Quadrennial Diplomacy and Development Review, and Quadrennial Homeland Security Review, as well as other strategic planning documents. Incorporation of research findings into decision making may also require organizational changes that ensure that sufficient numbers of qualified staff at the appropriate levels of seniority are assigned responsibility for global environmental security.

1.4 Early warning and preventive action. Fourth, this systemic approach will require a monitoring and alert response system that will indicate when environmental and resource problems in countries or regions pose potentially disruptive threats to U.S. interests. Strategic plans such as those mentioned above cannot always anticipate the speed or severity of environmental changes around the world or their attendant economic, social, and political impacts. Consequently, the system should monitor and flag environmental problems that have a high probability of triggering human suffering, economic collapse, or social unrest. And the system should ensure interagency collaboration to develop a rapid and coherent policy response.

Several of the fundamentals are already in place. For example, the National Intelligence Council conducts analysis on key global trends and natural resource issues on an intermittent basis while a number of other agencies in the executive branch provide regular analytical updates on climate change, commodities, global market dynamics, demographic trends, and other key issues. In the White House, the Office of Science and Technology Policy (OSTP) coordinates a robust environmental research agenda, including a program involving 13 agencies documenting global environmental change and potential impacts on the United States.[1] There is also a growing recognition, particularly in the intelligence and security communities, of the importance of resource scarcity and global environmental change to U.S. prosperity and security interests. This recognition is reflected in reports to Congress and various policy papers. Moreover, the U.S. Agency for International Development (USAID), the Millennium Challenge Corporation (MCC), and a range of agencies carrying out overseas assistance programs have acquired decades of knowledge and practical experience in supporting partner country efforts to address longer-term environmental and natural resource management problems.

Although those elements provide the foundation for a more comprehensive response to emerging environmental and resource challenges, many shortcomings remain. Chief among these are as follows:

Narrow federal research mandate. The law establishing a federal research program on global change (Pub. L. No. 101-606, the Global Change Research Act of 1990) is limited to global environmental changes that alter the capacity of the earth to sustain life. It does not include research on environmental change in specific countries or ecosystems, which may have important consequences for U.S. prosperity and security without having a direct environmental impact. Moreover, the statute does not require the government to collect, summarize, or disseminate the data and analysis produced under the aegis of the program.

Limited capacity for analysis. Although a considerable amount of research is being done on global environmental trends, often with the support of federal agencies, the U.S. government has a limited capacity to analyze the implications of the data for U.S. foreign policy and economic security. Intelligence analysis of environmental trends is episodic and tends to be focused on countries where there are other security concerns. More research alone would not solve the problem. Missing is a group of dedicated analysts who are able to monitor data and research findings on an ongoing basis, understand the national security implications, translate them into briefing materials for senior decision makers, and recommend directions for future policy-relevant work.

No early warning or prevention system. At present, a structured assessment system is not in place by which potentially destabilizing environmental and resource scarcity conditions in strategic partner countries are tracked and ranked. Consequently, in the absence of an accompanying graduated response mechanism, interagency and public alerts are not released and early responses—similar to the famine early warning system used by USAID's Office of Foreign Disaster Assistance—are not acted on.

Weak management and integration. The lack of a formal coordinating mechanism or a senior advisor on the National Security Staff charged with overseeing international environmental issues means that policy and program response is fragmented and stove-piped. Except for single-issue initiatives, such as wildlife trafficking and energy access in Africa, agencies are not always aware of what the others are doing, which increases the chances of gaps and redundancies.

Recommendation 2: Expand, Deepen, and Accelerate Mechanisms Employed by the U.S. Government to Respond to Emerging Global Environmental Problems

Two strategic concepts arise from the case studies that, in turn, frame our second recommendation. The first of those framing concepts is trade-offs. The case studies underscore the growing constraints that communities, producers, and governments face in accessing the natural resources on which livelihoods and social and economic well-being depend. More frequently than they did in the past, resource constraints are reaching the point where users and decision makers must make difficult choices concerning how best to use the available natural resources. Are water resources to be used for energy generation, smallholder agriculture, consumption by urban populations, or mining companies? Is fertile land around expanding urban areas to be used for food production, environmental buffer zones, or further expansion of the urban footprint? The use of U.S. assistance must be targeted to help stakeholders explore the costs and benefits of various options and to organize public discussion regarding those options.

The second framing concept is resilience. The case studies underscore the increased vulnerability of communities and producers to climate variability and the attendant effects on food, energy, and water security. Although climatologists have considerably improved global climate models that are capable of projecting potential impacts across all regions of the world, impacts at the local level are uncertain and unpredictable. Those uncertainties notwithstanding, a thread shared among the case study recommendations is to focus attention on increasing local and national resilience, that is, to strengthen the ability of affected communities and governments to withstand shocks, rebuild when necessary, and manage longer-term change amid rising uncertainty. While providing additional resources for adapting to changing conditions may be necessary, increasing the resilience of communities and governments depends equally on strengthening governance systems, adjusting policies, and ensuring the robust participation of concerned citizens and stakeholders.

These two strategic concepts—trade-offs and resilience—should serve as signposts for shaping the application of the five approaches and instruments proposed below. The five approaches offered by the authors of the country studies build on technical, financial, and policy mechanisms currently provided by the U.S. government. Benefiting from lessons, successes, and innovations provided by local governments, civil society organizations, and private investors from around the world, the mechanisms referenced by the case study authors have proven their effectiveness and adaptability to the widely varying geographic and social conditions of partner countries. The purpose of Recommendation 2 is to expand the application of those tested instruments, deepen their impact by scaling up the resources provided, and accelerate the delivery of a scaled-up package of environmental support mechanisms. The recommendation addresses the complexity of strengthening resilience, weighing options, and deciding among trade-offs.

An important part of Recommendation 2 is to link the scaled-up, accelerated package of environmental assistance to the monitoring and alert response system proposed in Recommendation 1. The proposed alert system should be designed to trigger responses from key agencies of the U.S. government, ranging from the Departments of State and Defense to Commerce and Energy, before environmental crisis conditions arise in partner countries and precipitate greater social disruption that poses more direct threats to U.S. interests.

Below, we highlight five mechanisms that have a demonstrated history of proven effectiveness when provided under the aegis of the U.S. government:

2.1 Strengthening strategic dialogues. One of the most productive approaches for expanding environmental cooperation with emerging countries is through bilateral strategic dialogue platforms. The U.S.-China Strategic and Economic Dialogue, the India-U.S. Strategic Dialogue, and the U.S.-Brazil Strategic Energy Dialogue have proven to be robust, dynamic platforms readily adaptable to expanding environmental cooperation on many fronts. The dialogues are premised on expediting technical cooperation by creating pragmatic paths for private-sector investment and removing policy and regulatory obstacles that impede bilateral commercial cooperation. Deepening U.S. cooperation with India on infrastructure, water, and energy security and expanding cooperation with Brazil, such as through trilateral partnerships with developing countries, are opportunities awaiting action.

2.2 Using regional platforms to address environmental challenges. Expanding the use of existing regional cooperation agreements to include environmental problems is one of the most promising mechanisms to address emerging tensions and conflict caused by resource scarcities. Most countries have forged cooperation agreements with neighbors to address economic, boundary, transport, and communication matters. The country studies underscore the success of regional cooperation agreements on such economic and border issues in providing the confidence and operational mechanisms by which competition for increasingly scarce natural resources can be managed for mutual benefit. As highlighted by the Russian Arctic, Mexico-U.S., and Pakistan case studies, existing regional cooperation bodies can transition from their original purposes to take on far broader environmental responsibilities. We underscore the important contributions that the Departments of State, Defense, and others can provide in deploying diplomatic, technical, financial, and security support to strengthen regional bodies in areas where resource issues have intensified tensions.

2.3 Using trade and investment instruments for sustainability. Although trade agreements are fairly blunt and limited instruments for imposing environmental obligations on U.S. commercial partners, there is scope for supporting improvements in resource governance through trade and investment. To promote more sustainable practices and reduce the risks of interruptions in international supply chains, the U.S. government can take the following steps:

- Strengthen and broaden the environmental obligations and cooperation component of free trade agreements (FTAs) and bilateral investment treaties (BITs). While recent agreements require that participating governments enforce domestic environmental laws, new agreements should, at a minimum, expand these obligations to include the enforcement and strengthening of domestic rules on sustainable use of renewable resources—including water, forests, land, and fisheries—and prohibit trade in illegally harvested resources and wildlife.
- Facilitate commercial activities that contribute to sustainability. The Overseas Private Investment Corporation (OPIC) and Export-Import Bank (EXIM), key U.S. agencies supporting foreign investment and now up for congressional reauthorization, should significantly expand current levels of environmentally positive commercial activities from just 10 percent (OPIC) and 2 percent (EXIM). In addition, OPIC's greenhouse gas (GHG) cap, which requires a 30 percent GHG reduction across its portfolio over 10 years and 50 percent reduction over 15 years, has resulted in increased renewable energy financing, from $128 million in 2009 to $1 billion in 2012.
- Use FTAs and the U.S. Generalized System of Preferences (GSP) to reward countries that are pursuing sustainability. Going forward, preference for reduction of tariff and nontariff barriers through FTAs, BITs, or the GSP should be based on a country's commitment to pursuing sustainable development practices—including efforts to control illegal logging, mining, and wildlife trade—to promote conservation and land-use planning and to conform to international environmental agreements such as the Convention on International Trade in Endangered Species.

2.4 Focusing foreign assistance. The U.S. government supports a diverse array of assistance programs to help developing countries protect natural resources and engage in sustainable environmental practices. Whether through multilateral institutions, such as the Global Environmental Facility, Climate Investment Funds, and multilateral development banks, or through bilateral partnerships managed by USAID and the MCC, our government has tackled problems ranging from degradation of the global commons to specific issues of energy, food, and water scarcities in partner countries.

Although these assistance programs have been highly successful in many cases, they are not adequately resourced, prioritized, or focused on countries in which environmental challenges are most acute; and they are not flexible enough to respond to emerging needs on the ground. Moreover, there is little interagency collaboration and coordination of programs and policies. Existing programs need to be expanded and accelerated, and new types of programs will need to be developed to build cross-border and regional cooperation, engage the private sector, and mitigate environmental degradation in countries whose governments are not committed to sustainable resource management. These efforts must be part of a whole-of-government effort that builds on the strengths of each agency and ensures accountability for results.

2.5 Addressing the security dimension. The economic and social costs, as well as the security threats, arising from global environmental change and resource scarcities have largely been ignored by the U.S. government over the past decades. With a few notable exceptions, such as the Lacey Act, even the impacts of illegal natural resource trade on the functioning of domestic markets were ignored or considered beyond the influence of the U.S. government. Recently awakened by the slaughter of 35,000 elephants in Africa, the U.S. government has recognized the links between international wildlife trade and international criminal networks trafficking in arms, drugs, humans, and mineral contraband. While outrage against wildlife massacres has captured public attention, illegal natural resource trade of timber, fish, coral, minerals, and other commodities is now understood to threaten the rule of law and undermine basic conditions for the sustainable global commerce on which U.S. prosperity depends. Demands from developing-country partners for U.S. assistance on illegal resource trade have increased significantly. In responding to these new pressures, it is important to set clear objectives and boundaries to guide the U.S. government's engagement. Where possible, a multi-track approach should be pursued, building first on bilateral partnerships that can be complemented by regional agreements and, when possible, international environmental treaties. Priority components of that assistance can include training, institutional capacity building, information and intelligence sharing, communications, and legal support, among others.

Recommendation 3: Pursue a More Ambitious Domestic Policy to Reduce U.S. Greenhouse Gas Emissions

The purpose of our foreign policy is to promote U.S. interests abroad and protect our national security. As the studies and analysis of this publication have shown, the intersection of natural resource scarcities and global environmental change has direct effects on the prosperity and stability of our political and trading partners that, in turn, carry direct, negative consequences for our own prosperity and security. If protection of the longer-term interests associated with our national well-being is to be a policy guidepost, our government, corporate leaders, and civil society organizations must play a visible, sustained leadership role in reducing GHG emissions and increasing resilience to climate change.

The paradox of the third recommendation is that the ability of the United States to provide global leadership on climate change is dependent on domestic U.S. energy policies. To the degree that the federal government acts decisively to reduce the use of fossil fuels and moves with equal deliberateness to promote wide-scale adoption of energy efficiency and renewable energy policies, the United States can exert long-awaited leadership in international climate negotiations and through bilateral and multilateral mechanisms committed to altering climate change trajectories. To the degree that American businesses and political opponents continue to deny the severity of climate change impacts and actively undermine efforts to change domestic and international climate policy, U.S. influence will diminish proportionately.

A further paradox of this recommendation is that the United States appears likely to meet its near-term emissions-reduction goal, which was announced by President Obama at the Copenhagen Climate Change Conference in 2009. That goal commits the United States to reduce GHG emissions in the range of 17 percent below 2005 levels by 2020. The paradox resides in the fact that achieving that goal is likely to occur without having enacted a national climate and energy policy that can ensure steady reduction of U.S. emissions in the coming decades. Although some reductions have been driven by federal and state policies, a large share of emissions reductions from 2005 to 2020 will result from the sharp economic downturn between 2007 and 2009, coupled with the rapid displacement of coal by natural gas in electricity generation that largely is driven by technological innovation. Although the Obama administration estimates that U.S. GHG emissions will be within the range of the 17 percent target by 2020, based on policies outlined in its Climate Action Plan, absent long-term climate and energy policy, U.S. emissions are projected to increase after 2020. Consequently, the United States must develop and pursue a far more ambitious long-term domestic emissions reduction target if the United States is to shoulder its share of the needed global emissions reductions and forestall even sharper climate impacts at home and abroad.

This is the crux of the challenge: only by achieving the domestic political commitment to forge an integrated energy and climate policy can the United States shift our economy away from fossil fuels, take urgently needed measures to mitigate climate impacts, and thereby allow the United States to establish a leadership position in the international community. Eventually, a domestic political agreement must be reached to establish an economy-wide price on carbon, be it through a direct carbon tax, a cap-and-trade regime, or other fiscal measures. Unfortunately, achieving the domestic political consensus necessary to produce major legislation to advance rigorous climate mitigation policies is unlikely in the near term. As unfortunate as it may seem, we may face the political reality that only when the domestic costs of climate impacts caused by drought, forest fires, hurricanes, and other weather extremes become unacceptably high will necessary fiscal policies be enacted. Until that happens, the opportunities for leadership and the center of gravity for driving domestic climate progress will reside in the executive branch of government. As the Obama administration has demonstrated, despite entrenched opposition, a range of regulatory mechanisms and fiscal policies can be employed to nudge our economy in the proper direction.

This push-pull interplay between domestic and international policy will serve as an important tool to promote U.S. domestic and international climate progress. With successive, incremental steps on the domestic policy front, comparable opportunities for strengthening U.S. leadership in international affairs will expand, allowing U.S. foreign policy to serve as a source of motivation for the global community. During this transition period, sustained pressure from domestic corporate leaders and civil society, as well as from foreign heads of state and international thought leaders, will be needed to generate the political momentum required to ensure steady progress toward responsible climate policies.

In Closing

This publication is premised on the conviction that global environmental change and natural resource scarcities will intensify considerably in the coming years. Having already crossed a number of environmental thresholds, there is increased probability that the planet will experience more frequent and intense environmental disruptions, which, in turn, are very likely to bring unanticipated social uncertainty and dislocation. Those unpredictable changes notwithstanding, the World Wildlife Fund firmly believes that the U.S. government can and will assume an irreplaceable leadership role in the community of nations to respond to these new challenges. If adopted promptly, the recommendations offered above can significantly speed up and strengthen the leadership that countries around the world expect of the United States.

Note

1 See the Annex for suggestions on modernizing the U.S. Global Change Research Program of the OSTP.

Annex: Possible Approaches for Implementing Recommendation 1

Diana Ohlbaum

There are several institutional options within the U.S. government for creating an integrated, analytical response system. At present, the system that most closely approximates our recommendation can be found in the OSTP in the White House. The OSTP manages the U.S. Global Change Research Program (USGCRP), which was created by the Global Change Research Act of 1990. The program was intended to fill a glaring research void several decades ago; it would need modernizing to meet the requirements proposed in Recommendation 1. The following list suggests actions to achieve such modernization:

- Amend the definitions of "global change" and "global change research" to include environmental changes and resource scarcities that may alter major ecosystems in ways that could have significant economic, health, political, or security implications for the United States.
- Establish an early warning system that tracks the development of critical environmental and scarcity problems in countries of concern to U.S. interests. Appropriate development, intelligence, and security agencies would be notified when potential destabilization thresholds are reached so that timely responses can be organized.
- Provide hiring authority for a dedicated, full-time, professional staff for the USGCRP, rather than relying on detailees and representatives of other agencies to conduct its work.
- Establish a senior director for the environment position on the National Security Staff to be responsible for ensuring interagency coordination on global change research and informing national security discussions on global environmental matters.
- Add the National Intelligence Council, USAID, and the MCC as permanent members of the committee that oversees the USGCRP.
- Clarify that research may be carried out internationally, and encourage U.S. grantees to enter into partnerships with foreign research institutes to conduct activities under the program.
- Insert a mandate for the USGCRP to function as a clearinghouse for global change research, by collecting, summarizing, and disseminating research and analysis conducted with or resulting from its support. USGCRP-funded research should be posted on the Internet in open and machine-readable data format.
- The Department of State should request that Congress specifically authorize and appropriate funding within the "Diplomatic and Consular Programs"

account for the following purposes: (a) hiring policy analysts to translate global change research into policy-relevant information and (b) issuing research grants in coordination with the USGCRP. The staff and funding could be managed by the Bureau of Oceans and International Environmental and Scientific Affairs, the Bureau of Intelligence and Research, the Bureau of Policy Planning, or some combination thereof.

CONTRIBUTORS

Saleem H. Ali is Professor of Politics and International Studies at the University of Queensland, Australia, where he directs the Centre for Social Responsibility in Mining. Dr. Ali is also a tenured professor at the University of Vermont's Rubenstein School of Environment and Natural Resources. He serves on the board of governors of LEAD-Pakistan, one of the country's largest environmental organizations.

Katrina Brandon is an independent consultant. She has worked as a Senior Technical Advisor to Conservation International and Senior Fellow with both World Wildlife Fund and The Nature Conservancy.

Heather A. Conley is Senior Fellow and Director of the Europe Program at the Center for Strategic and International Studies (CSIS), where she specializes in geopolitical, economic, and security developments in Europe and the Arctic. Conley formerly served as Deputy Assistant Secretary of State in the Bureau for European and Eurasian Affairs at the U.S. State Department.

Ambassador Mark Green is President of the International Republican Institute. A recognized leader in the foreign policy and business communities, Green served as the U.S. ambassador to Tanzania from mid-2007 to early 2009. Prior to serving as U.S. ambassador, Green served four terms in the U.S. House of Representatives.

Murray Hiebert is Deputy Director of the Sumitro Chair for Southeast Asia Studies at the Center for Strategic and International Studies. He previously worked for *The Wall Street Journal* in Washington and Beijing and for the *Far Eastern Economic Review* newsweekly in Thailand, Vietnam, Malaysia, and Singapore.

Admiral Mike Mullen served as the 17th Chairman of the Joint Chiefs of Staff (from 2007–2011) and principal military advisor to Presidents George W. Bush and Barack Obama. He spent 43 years in the U.S. Navy, rising to Chief of Naval Operations. Since his retirement from active duty, Mullen has taught at Princeton University and serves on the Boards of the Bloomberg Philanthropies, General Motors, and Sprint.

Shuja Nawaz is Director of the South Asia Center at the Atlantic Council, a bipartisan think tank in Washington, DC. He is the author of *Crossed Swords: Pakistan, Its Army, and the Wars Within* (Oxford University Press) and numerous papers on Pakistan and the region. He has worked for Pakistan Television, *The New York Times*, the World Health Organization, the IAEA, and the International Monetary Fund and with other think tanks in Washington, D.C., including RAND, Brookings, USIP, and CSIS.

Lev Neretin is a program officer with the United Nations Environment Programme. Neretin previously served as Task Manager for Global Environment Facility projects in the Russian Federation and Iran and has a decade-long career in academia. Neretin specializes in issues of ecosystem management and climate change, transboundary water governance, and global change in polar regions.

Brent Nordstrom is Senior Director Public Sector Finance at WWF-US. He has worked for the past 15 years on issues relating foreign policy and international development to international conservation.

Gregory Poling is a research associate with the Sumitro Chair for Southeast Asia Studies at the Center for Strategic and International Studies. His publications include *The South China Sea in Focus: Clarifying the Limits of Maritime Dispute* (2013). He received an MA in international affairs from American University.

David Reed is Senior Vice President for Policy at WWF-US. He has worked for more than 30 years in social and economic development programs in Latin America, Africa, and Asia at both the grassroots and managerial levels. His areas of expertise include environmental impacts of macroeconomic reforms, poverty-environment nexus, international architecture for climate finance, and environmental dimensions of U.S. foreign policy. He has authored numerous books and publications.

Carter Roberts is President and CEO of World Wildlife Fund–United States (WWF-US). WWF's mission is to advance solutions that conserve the diversity of life on Earth while meeting the needs of people. WWF, the world's largest network of international conservation organizations, works across 100 countries and enjoys the support of 5 million members worldwide, 1.2 million of whom are in the United States.

Christopher Sall is a policy analyst and research affiliate of the Center for International Environment and Resource Policy at the Fletcher School, Tufts University, whose work focuses on the environment, energy, and climate change in China. He recently participated in a joint study by the World Bank and the Development Research Center on "green growth" in China. He is currently writing about green urbanization policies in China for another World Bank flagship study.

Ricardo Ubiraci Sennes is a managing partner at Prospectiva Consulting since its foundation in 2002. He is a specialist in political scenarios in Brazil and Latin America, international geopolitics, innovation policy, strategic planning in internationalization processes, and the design of public policies. He developed an extensive academic work and has published several articles, papers, and books in Brazil and abroad.

Pamela Stedman-Edwards, PhD, is a writer and policy analyst focusing on the intersection of conservation, economic policies, and development. Her work has covered the impacts of trade, agricultural, macroeconomic, and conservation policies, including land tenure, forest, and protected area governance in Mexico.

Theodore Trefon is Senior Researcher at Belgium's Royal Museum for Central Africa, specializing in environmental governance in the DRC. His latest book is *Congo Masquerade: The Political Culture of Aid Inefficiency and Reform Failure* (ZED Books, 2011).

Rich Verma is a former Assistant Secretary of State. He currently serves as senior counselor to the Albright Stonebridge Group and the law firm of Steptoe & Johnson.

INDEX